RELIGION ON CAMPUS

GION ON CAMPUS

CONRAD CHERRY

BETTY A. DE BERG

AMANDA PORTERFIELD

WITH THE ASSISTANCE OF
WILLIAM DURBIN AND
JOHN SCHMALZBAUER

THE UNIVERSITY OF NORTH CAROLINA PRESS
CHAPEL HILL & LONDON

Manufactured in the United States of America
Designed by April Leidig-Higgins
Set in Minion by Keystone Typesetting, Inc.

The paper in this book meets the guidelines for
permanence and durability of the Committee on
Production Guidelines for Book Longevity of the
Council on Library Resources.

Library of Congress Cataloging-in-Publication Data
Cherry, Conrad, 1937–
Religion on campus / by Conrad Cherry, Betty A.
DeBerg, Amanda Porterfield; with the assistance of
William Durbin and John Schmalzbauer.
p. cm. Includes bibliographical references and index.
ISBN 0-8078-2623-5 (cloth: alk. paper)
1. College students—Religious life—United States.
2. Religion—Study and teaching (Higher)—United
States. I. DeBerg, Betty A., 1953– II. Porterfield,
Amanda, 1947– III. Title.
BL625.9.C64 C44 2001   200'.88'375—dc21   00-068311

**The publication of this book was supported by a
generous grant from Lilly Endowment Inc.**

05 04 03 02 01   5 4 3 2 1

CONTENTS

The authors wish to acknowledge, above all, the support of Lilly Endowment Inc. Without the assistance of a generous Lilly grant made to the Center for the Study of Religion and American Culture, the research for this book simply could not have been carried out. Officers in the Religion and Education Divisions of the endowment also showed continuous interest in this project as the research unfolded.

We are deeply indebted to the faculty members, students, and administrators of the four schools in our study, although they and their institutions must remain anonymous. Without their hospitality, interest in our project, participation in numerous interviews, and willingness to let us intrude into their cultures, the study could not have been conducted. Our gracious hosts may not agree with all of our interpretations of their schools, but we trust they know that we have sought to be honest and fair-minded in our observations and conclusions.

Members of an advisory committee for the project met several times to hear and evaluate reports of our research. We are grateful to these committee members for their criticisms and encouragement: Barbara Jackson, Jeanne Knoerle, Ralph Lundgren, Martin E. Marty, E. Theodore Mullen Jr., George Rupp, and Barbara Wheeler.

Conrad Cherry thanks the faculty members of the Department of Religious Studies at Indiana University–Purdue University, Indianapolis, for their critical responses to his chapter on South University. Betty DeBerg expresses gratitude to Tom Romanin for his careful reading of the chapter on West University at various stages and to Martie Reineke and Kim Maphis Early for their helpful comments on an earlier version of that chapter. Amanda Porterfield is thankful to those at East University who commented on a draft of her chapter and refined or corrected her work on several important points.

This caveat is perhaps obvious but nonetheless needs to be stated: none of these helpful persons or institutions can be held responsible for what we have written in the following pages.

RELIGION ON CAMPUS

CHAPTER ONE

INTRODUCTION

This book of case studies originated in a desire on the part of its authors to observe closely the current shape of religion on U.S. college and university campuses. During the last ten or fifteen years, a large number of studies have examined religion in higher education. Historical investigations have depicted religion's changing roles in American colleges and universities. Other, more normative works have recommended ways in which religion's presence on the higher-education scene might be improved or transformed. Still others have surveyed the attitudes of faculty who teach religion on our campuses, argued the relative value of "objectivity" or "advocacy" as a pedagogy in the religious studies classroom, or bemoaned the widespread secularization of the contemporary campus. Largely missing in these studies has been a close, firsthand inspection of religion on campus. In particular, they simply have not supplied answers to basic questions like how, and how widely, do today's American undergraduates practice religion during their college or university years? In what manner do students understand and talk about their religious or nonreligious postures? What opportunities are provided for undergraduates to study religion? What approaches to that study do the teachers of those undergraduates take? These are the fundamental questions this book attempts to answer with respect to four very different campuses in the United States.

The chapters that follow concentrate on the present and chiefly employ the methods of ethnography to determine the present shape of things. All three authors are historians as well as students of the current scene, however, and thus have been sensitive to the ways in which the contemporary situation has exhibited striking continuities as well as arresting discontinuities with the past. Religion has long figured importantly in the history of American higher education, but its role has changed as America and its educational institutions have changed. In the colonial period, a number of major colleges were founded primarily for the purpose of educating clergymen. Thus Harvard College opened its doors in the seventeenth century in order to teach Puritan ministers how to nurture the burgeoning communities of New England with the milk of the Christian gospel. Disputes over the most appropriate preparation for ministers led to the founding of Yale College at the beginning of the eighteenth century and the later founding of William

Tennent's "Log College," which evolved into Princeton. King's College and Philadelphia College, which became Columbia and the University of Pennsylvania, respectively, were founded with broader purposes in mind, but both had ties to the Anglican Church, and religious education was part of both of their missions.

Until the rise of the modern American university in the late nineteenth and early twentieth centuries, when the traditional divisions of scholarly study began to be transformed into academic disciplines presided over by specialized professionals, religious and moral instruction permeated the entire curriculum of many colleges. Educators often assumed that religious principles and biblical knowledge were coextensive with science, history, and languages. And they believed that a thorough grounding in religious principles and biblical knowledge supported advances across the educational spectrum. Those assumptions played a significant role in the early development of advanced education for women as well as the ongoing development of higher education for men. Thus at Mount Holyoke, founded in 1837 as the first publicly endowed institution of higher learning for women in the United States, and other women's colleges that arose in the nineteenth century, higher education for women was justified because it was presumed to be joined seamlessly with piety. Similar arguments accompanied the founding of Catholic and Jewish centers of advanced learning in the nineteenth century. These institutions distinguished themselves from Protestant schools in many ways and, in fact, were established partly to protect Catholics and Jews from assimilation to Protestant culture. But they, too, operated on the premise that religious and moral instruction was fundamental to all other forms of learning.

Largely as a result of the establishment of universities influenced by scholarly approaches to a variety of academic fields, many of these earlier efforts to integrate all forms of learning with basic religious principles began to appear simplistic and grandiose. New advances in research proceeded along diverse lines in the nineteenth and twentieth centuries, making the whole enterprise of academic learning, in colleges as well as universities, more heterogeneous than ever before. At the same time, increased understanding and appreciation of the religions of the world challenged the notion that Christianity could be made the foundation of human knowledge, and religiously diverse faculty and students would call into question the possibility—and the desirability—of making one religious perspective a unifying campus principle.

In the 1990s, several studies of religion in American higher education interpreted these intellectual, religious, and educational developments as parts of a steady and certain process of secularization. George Marsden, for example, has seen in the developments proof across the university curriculum of what he calls "methodological secularization," or the suspension of religious beliefs in order to attain scientific objectivity. He also has detected an "aggressive pluralistic secularism that provides no check at all on the tendencies of the university to fragment into technical specialties," the elimination of a Christian voice in shaping policy, and, "in the name of equality and the rights of women and minorities," the questioning of all beliefs "as mere social constructions." The result for Marsden is that American universities and the colleges that imitate them have radically marginalized religion: "Despite the presence of many religion departments and a few university divinity schools, religion has moved from near the center a century or so ago to the incidental periphery. Apart from voluntary student religious groups, religion in most universities is about as important as the baseball team. Not only has religion become peripheral, but also there is a definite bias against any perceptible religiously informed perspectives getting a hearing in the university classroom." In short, Marsden believes that institutions of higher education have become secular not by abolishing religion but by stripping it of significant influence, confining it to the innocuous realms of voluntary campus groups and religion classrooms where religious convictions are suppressed. As a consequence, "the presence of religion programs in universities is, on balance, not a countervailing force to the secularization of universities."[1]

In a study with a similar slant, Douglas Sloan has argued that the gradual disappearance from colleges and universities of such things as close relations between church and academy, the appointment of clergy to college and university presidencies, required chapel, and mandatory courses in divinity and moral philosophy is a sure sign of a secularization process. Sloan has even suggested that secularized higher education has become an ersatz religion in twentieth-century America: "In important ways the university itself became a major religious phenomenon of American culture. David Levine, in his study of the American college during the first part of the century, has written that as an avenue for social and occupational status (read salvation?), 'education became the secular religion of twentieth-century American society.'"[2]

James Burtchaell has proposed that colleges and universities that have claimed significant connections with Christian denominations have also been secularized. Those schools, Burtchaell believes, have experienced progressive and largely unintentional alienation from their ecclesiastical fellowships. Burtchaell claims that a considerable amount of self-deception can be uncovered in this development: "The estrangement between colleges and churches was effected by men and women who said and apparently believed that they wanted them to be partners in both the life of the spirit and the life of the mind. But they concealed from themselves and from some of their constituencies the process of alienation as it was under way." The chief source of this self-deceiving secularization of Christian colleges was the emergence of pietism, a religious posture that elevates the emotions over the intellect and the personal over the communal: "Religion's move to the academic periphery was not so much the work of godless intellectuals as of pious educators who, since the onset of pietism, had seen religion as embodied so uniquely in the personal profession of faith that it could not be seen to have a stake in social learning."[3]

To a large extent, our study was prompted by a desire to test the adequacy of these secularization theories as measures of the importance of religion on the contemporary campus. Frankly, we were suspicious about their adequacy from the outset for a number of reasons. First, the theories did not conform to our own experiences in higher education. Among the three of us, we have held full-time teaching positions in religion at a total of five state universities, two private universities with distant connections to religious denominations, and one university with a clear affiliation with a Protestant church body. In only one case was the study of religion weakened in its university setting (and that after two decades of strength), and in none of the cases were religious practices among students at all disadvantaged. Religion as taught and practiced has been alive and well in the institutions of higher education that we have occupied.

Second, quite apart from our own experiences, as historians of religion in America, we are convinced that judging the present by the past without due attention to the changing shape of religion can obscure new forms of religious vitality in the present. There is no denying that large numbers of colleges and universities in this century have severed or reduced their ties to denominational bodies and that the training of ministers is no longer the chief purpose of higher education today, as it was at Harvard College in the seventeenth century. Nor is it any longer assumed that advanced learning must be coextensive with piety as a condition for justifying women's admission to college, an assumption that prevailed when Mount Holyoke was founded. College presidents no longer presume to know how the various areas of study in their institutions interrelate, nor do they try to instruct students in the ethical precepts of the Bible and the relationship between those precepts and various areas of human knowledge. Boards of trustees and offices of college presidents are no longer dominated by the clergy, and students usually feel little need to confine their spirituality within denominational boundaries. But these changes seem more clearly to add up to the declericalizing, de-denominationalizing, and, in some cases, de-

Christianizing of campuses than to their secularization or their marginalization of religion.

Third, the changes also may very well reflect the protean flexibility that has characterized American religion as a whole throughout the nation's history. The religion of the American people has demonstrated a large capacity to assume new forms as conditions change and thereby preserve itself as a vital force in American life. This characteristic was apparent, for example, in the nineteenth century as Methodists, Baptists, Mormons, and other frontier groups seized numerical and cultural dominance from "established" Protestants like Congregationalists, Episcopalians, and Unitarians and in the process transformed religious perspectives and practices. It was evident also in the transformations that generations of Catholic immigrants and their heirs brought to their religion as they adjusted to a changing American social order in the twentieth century. Given the overall tendency of American religion to assume new shapes as social and cultural conditions change, it is reasonable to suspect that religion on our college and university campuses has assumed some new appearances as well, appearances that may have gone unrecognized in the secularization theories.

A fourth reason for wondering about the adequacy of secularization theories is that some prominent sociologists have given up on the theories. To some extent, all theories of secularization are based on the assumption that over time science and other forms of modern intelligence will send religion into decline in modern society. This suggests that some previous Age of Faith has been or will be displaced by an Age of Reason (or Science or Technology or Skepticism) that renders religion marginal, obsolete, or, in secularization's most radical form, defunct. Sociologists have been the most avid proponents of secularization, but a number of scholars among their ranks have recently concluded that the assumption governing secularization theories simply does not stand up to empirical fact. Peter Berger, for example, has said: "I think what I and most other sociologists of religion wrote in the 1960s about secularization was a mistake. Our underlying argument was that secularization and modernity go hand in hand. With more modernization comes more secularization. It wasn't a crazy theory. There was some evidence for it. But I think it's basically wrong. Most of the world today is certainly not secular." Berger thinks that the one exception may be a secularized Western Europe, but he insists that the rest of the world, including the United States, is very religious indeed.[4] Sociologist Rodney Stark goes even farther than Berger by claiming that there is no evidence of a decline of religion in Western Europe either. Stark is convinced that the assumption that there was once an Age of Faith does not pass historical muster in Europe, and there is plenty of evidence across the world that individual religiousness is prospering in all kinds of societies. The title of Stark's article pointedly summarizes what he thinks of theories of secularization: "Secularization, R.I.P."[5] If social scientists are so sure of a widespread religiousness in the world, especially in American culture, one has to suspect that the college campus may not be an exception.

In part, therefore, we were motivated to conduct our study by a desire to test the secularization perspective. But we were also motivated by the lack of firsthand, on-site examinations of religion on college campuses. So we set out on campus visits to determine in some crucial cases just how widespread the teaching and practice of religion were among undergraduates and the nature of that teaching and practice.

Fully cognizant that in one study we could not cover the entire range of the nation's colleges and universities, we decided to do an intensive examination of four schools representing diverse points on the educational map. We deliberately chose schools that are quite different in their historical backgrounds, mission statements, regional settings, and perceived relations to religion. (In the interest of obtaining the full and candid cooperation of the representatives of the four schools, we assured them at the outset of the study that we would attempt to preserve their anonymity. Thus, in the book, we have used pseudonyms for persons, places, and the schools themselves, and we have avoided the discussion of historical details except in those cases where some background was necessary for understanding current situations.) We wanted to include a large, public state university to see how a "secular" school, or one making no claims of a religious tradition at its core or at its foundation, formed an ethos supportive of or antipathetic to the study and practice of religion. West University served this purpose. Given the current lamentations about the secularization of Christian denominational schools, we thought it important to look at the shape of religion at a Protestant institution and a Roman Catholic institution. North College, a Lutheran liberal arts college set in a northern region of the country, and East University, a Roman Catholic school in the eastern United States, publicly avow their particular religious heritages as vital parts of their missions and milieus and thus could serve as examples of the connections or disconnections between church and school. The southern university selected for our study represents a different educational universe still. Traditionally committed to the education of African Americans, South University at one time was a denominational institution but now defines itself as a private, nondenominational school with Presbyterian roots.

We know that these four schools do not begin to exhaust the types of colleges and universities in the United States (according to the classification scheme of the Carnegie Foundation, for example). We also know that wide differences may exist among schools of each type. But we are convinced that we have selected schools that are sufficiently diverse to merit comparison and contrast, sufficiently different to yield distinctive perspectives on the state of religion on campus, and sufficiently circumscribed to create a focus for one study.

Conrad Cherry was responsible for examining South University and North College; he visited the former school during the 1996–97 academic year and the latter during 1997–98. Betty DeBerg studied West University during 1996–97, and Amanda Porterfield conducted her study of East University that same academic year. We were greatly assisted in our research by William Durbin and John Schmalzbauer, postdoctoral associates at the Center for the Study of Religion and American Culture at Indiana University–Purdue University, Indianapolis, for the period 1996–98. Durbin and Schmalzbauer developed the instrument for surveying students enrolled in religion courses (see Appendix B) and compiled the results of that survey, wrote focus papers dealing with historical background and issues pertinent to the study, worked on an annotated bibliography of books and articles dealing with religion in American higher education, assisted in the observation of events on two of the campuses, and joined in discussions with the senior researchers respecting our discoveries. Although they cannot be held responsible for the conclusions offered in this book, Durbin and Schmalzbauer were indispensable members of the research team.

We agreed on the basic methods we would employ in our fieldwork, the fundamental questions we would attempt to answer about each of the four schools, the types of events we would observe, the sorts of people we would interview, and the major divisions we would create in our chapters. We also read and critiqued one another's chapters and jointly wrote this introduction and the conclusion to the book. It became apparent to us early in the writing process that the chapters on the individual schools would be the work of individual scholars and that it made no sense to try to hide that fact. Thus we have admitted our distinctive styles, interests, and perspectives by attaching our names to the chapters of the book for which we are responsible.

Our chapters focus on the religious practices of today's undergraduates, student attitudes toward religion, the approaches to the study of religion taken by teachers of undergraduates, and the extent to which the study and the practice of religion are made available to undergraduate students. Although on occasion we examine the historical backgrounds of the schools and use the results of quantitative surveys, the bulk of our study consists of qualitative analysis. Employing the methods of ethnography, we have sought through interviews, observation, key informants, and extensive field notes to get inside the worlds of the schools and understand them in their own terms. (See Appendix A for an elaboration of our research methods.)

When we went looking for religion on campus, we of course considered the obvious places. We observed worship services and meetings of religious groups, interviewed chaplains and campus ministers as well as students who participated in religious activities, listened to the views of administrators on matters pertaining to campus religion, collected syllabi for and sat in on religion courses (especially those that attracted the largest number of students, usually at the introductory level), and interviewed numerous professors responsible for teaching religion to undergraduates. But we also looked at some less obvious persons and places. We listened to dissenting or marginal voices concerning campus religion and tried to assess how widely and significantly religion figured into the undergraduate curriculum outside departments of religion. And in the interest of attempting to determine how, if at all, religion played a role in the ethos or wider culture of each campus, we read student newspapers, paid attention to posters and bulletin board announcements, noted the use of campus space, observed large campus events and rituals, and examined residential affairs policies, student handbooks, and college mission statements.

In the conclusion, we draw out the implications of our study of the four schools by noting the similarities and differences among the institutions in the teaching and practice of religion, by describing how the ethos of each place affects and is affected by the religious presence, by discussing the import of changes that have occurred on the campuses in the late twentieth century, and by making some generalizations about what our study may tell us about the overall status of religion on campus. We also return to the secularization theories and suggest that pluralism of religious opportunity, as well as diversity of religious and curricular choice among undergraduates, is more descriptive of the four scenes than secularization.

NOTES

1. George M. Marsden, "The Soul of the University," in *The Secularization of the Academy*, ed. George M. Marsden and Bradley J. Longfield (New York: Oxford University Press, 1992), 16, 21, 25, 33, 37. See also Marsden's *The Soul of the American University: From Protestant Establishment to Established Nonbelief* (New York: Oxford University Press, 1994), 339, 413–15.

2. Douglas Sloan, *Faith and Knowledge: Mainline Protestantism and American Higher Education* (Louisville, Ky.: Westminster John Knox Press, 1994), 19–22.

3. James Tunstead Burtchaell, *The Dying of the Light: The Disengagement of Colleges and Universities from Their Christian Churches* (Grand Rapids, Mich.: Eerdmans, 1998), xi, 842.

4. "Epistemological Modesty: An Interview with Peter Berger," *Christian Century* 114, no. 30 (1997): 974.

5. Rodney Stark, "Secularization, R.I.P.," *Sociology of Religion* 60, no. 3 (1999): 249–73.

ETHOS

The quiet center of the Old Campus of West University (WU) belies the daily hustle and bustle of a large research university, its 30,000 students enrolled in ten academic colleges in more than 100 buildings on nearly 2,000 acres. The marble steps, landscaped lawns, and ivy-covered brick walls of the Old Campus seem a million miles away from the New Campus across town, where the monumental football stadium and the labyrinthine Medical Center dominate. The liberal arts and central administration buildings reside among the ivy and are surrounded by stately residential neighborhoods, interesting restaurants, student bars and nightclubs, prosperous shops, and steepled downtown churches, all in a small city on neither coast.

The ethos of the campus reflected its geographical location. There was little grunge here. Some students preferred neo-hippie style with its tie-dyed clothing and long hair; some a Marilyn Monroe–Madonna retro-chic; some the flamboyance of urban African American hip-hop culture. But the vast majority of undergraduates carefully cultivated a casual Eddie Bauer/Gap/Levis look. Their haircuts were expensive, their jeans perfectly faded, their backpacks carefully selected, their makeup expertly applied. One of the reasons students chose this university was that it and its city were considered hip, urbane, tolerant, diverse, and liberal, and many students worked hard to achieve such a personal style for themselves.

WU undergrads were very nice—that is, they were polite, respectful of professors and other elders, and unlikely to engage in verbal or physical conflicts. Although some professors wished that students were more intellectually assertive, the public rhetoric of student affairs administrators implied that binge drinking was the most serious student shortcoming. The student bar scene was on everyone's mind. Although WU was not known nationally as a party school, many first-year students knew about the bars before they arrived, as did their parents.

Perhaps the student bars and clubs, along with the classroom buildings and large residence halls, were the places in which the greatest number of students rubbed shoulders over the course of an academic year. Because of the large number of students, there were no opening convocations or special university events that would interest or be able to accommodate even half of them. The largest single-event student gatherings were home football games; about 10,000 student tickets were available for each game. The size of the student body alone dictated that the university at any given time and from any particular perspective might appear fragmented.

The complexity of the university, with its discrete disciplines and professional colleges, diverse student cultures, and competing administrative units, was apparent to many at WU. As one longtime staff member said, "There are really three universities here—the Medical Center, intercollegiate athletics, and everything else." A graduate student commented on the student body: "There's Greeks, athletes, and everyone else."

The university, therefore, relied on lowest-common-denominator kinds of images to provide students with a distinctive identity and alumni with ongoing institutional loyalty. These images were supplied by intercollegiate athletics. "Welcome to West University!," the university president yelled at hundreds of tired and rumpled first-year students gathered in the basketball arena for a rally and dance the night before classes began, an attempt at an opening convocation for entering students. "Are you ready to become Buccaneers?!" This new identity as Buccaneers was frequently reinforced on and off campus. Many students came from families of longtime Buccaneer loyalists, men and women who dressed in university colors and tailgated at every home football game. The regional press covered the major sports obsessively, and the players and coaches were media stars.

Despite the presence everywhere of the team logo and colors and the fact that it was almost always either football or basketball season, intercollegiate athletics did not really unify the campus. Some student subcultures, such as the neo-hippies and the intellectuals, for example, were disdainful of sports. Most students needed other strategies for fitting in, for finding community. Students often spoke to me of loneliness, especially during their first year: "I was very scared. Everyone says college is great; you'll meet all these people. You don't think you'll have to work to meet people, but you do. It's a shock. I've never had that alone feeling before. Your parents drive away, and you're standing there all alone." Said another senior undergraduate, "If you don't find an organization you can belong to, you're in trouble right off the bat."

The university marshaled resources from a variety of administrative units to help undergraduates adjust and find a place for themselves. Students began their university experience at one of about a dozen two-day summer orientation sessions. The director of student orientation, an outgoing young white woman, told one standing-room-only crowd of entering students, many with their parents, that she could remember her own arrival on campus as a first-year student: "My room was three floors up, and my father complained. My mom advised over and over again, 'Stay who you are.' And we kissed each other, and they drove off, and I was alone. But you need to realize you're never really alone. You'll bring your friends, family, history, and values with you." The loud, fast-paced video she showed about life at the university—after a rousing "It's great to be a Buccaneer!"—included cameos by current students urging new students to get involved in student organizations: "It's important to study, but it's important to get involved, too."

There was no shortage of student organizations on this campus. About 350 were officially registered with the Office of Student Affairs. As long as 51 percent of its members were registered WU students, any group with at least five members was welcome to apply for recognition by and funding from the student government out of the money collected as a student activity fee from each student.

RELIGIOUS PRACTICE

Of these 350 organizations, about 30 were explicitly religious. About half of these represented varieties of conservative or evangelical American Protestantism, including Campus Crusade for Christ and InterVarsity Christian

Fellowship. The Protestant-Catholic-Jew religious mainline, identified by sociologist Will Herberg, sponsored the campus ministries of nine Protestant denominations, the Roman Catholic Newman Center, and the Hillel Jewish Student Center. These received support from both congregations and regional or national denominational agencies. Other organizations represented a wide range of religious preferences, such as Islam, Baha'i, Zen Buddhism, Eastern Orthodox Christianity, neopaganism, and Christian Science.

These religious organizations were eligible for official recognition by the student government and the Office of Student Affairs. The advantages of such recognition were many. Probably most important, recognized groups were allowed to use campus facilities and equipment for their meetings at no cost. They also were permitted to use the campus mail system, conduct vending sales and other fund-raisers on campus, keep a desk and mailbox in the Student Activities Center at the Student Union, maintain a university account for their funds and use university money-management services, and receive the generous and expert assistance of the Office of Student Affairs on virtually any matter related to starting and maintaining a student organization.

In the recent past, these student religious groups at wu were not eligible to apply for financial support from the student government's committee charged with distributing student activity fee monies. Changes in wu's policies regarding the eligibility of religious groups for such funding came as a result of recent Supreme Court decisions.

Church and State on Campus

The support for the free-expression clause of the First Amendment at wu has been consistent with recent judicial interpretations of the separation of church and state on state campuses. In 1981, the Supreme Court ruled in *Widmar v. Vincent* that the University of Missouri at Kansas City must make campus facilities available to a Christian student group, Cornerstone, in the same way and to the same extent that it made facilities available to other student groups. The university had denied the use of facilities based on a policy that prohibited the use of university property "for purposes of religious worship or religious teaching." The Court, citing the principles of equal access and of government neutrality toward religion, "rejected the argument that the non-establishment provision requires the state to discriminate against religion." The Supreme Court concurred with the lower court in finding that university policy had violated the free speech clause in that state regulation of speech must be content-neutral.[1]

In 1995, the Supreme Court extended its interpretation of the free speech clause to include the financing of student religious groups on state-supported university campuses in its ruling on *Rosenberger et al. v. Rector and the Visitors of the University of Virginia et al.* The University of Virginia required students to pay an activities fee of $14 per semester. These fees were used to finance "student news, information, opinion, entertainment or academic media groups," so long as they did not sponsor or support "religious activities, philanthropic contributions and activities, political activities or activities that would jeopardize the university's tax-exempt status."

In 1990, a student group founded by Richard Rosenberger had begun to publish *Wide Awake: A Christian Perspective at the University of Virginia*, which, Rosenberger argued, offered a Christian perspective on both personal and community issues and "sought to counter the homosexual-rights and feminist viewpoints heard in other campus publications." Rosenberger's request for a publishing subsidy from the university was denied on the grounds that publishing *Wide Awake* was a religious activity. After unsuccessfully appealing the decision at the university, Rosenberger filed suit, arguing that the university's denial of funding violated freedom of speech and freedom of the press, the free exercise of religion, and the equal protection provisions of the federal and state constitutions. Rosenberger said: "Every viewpoint was out there in the public square, being subsidized by the university, except the Christian viewpoint. There was even a lot out there at times about Christians, but it was always antagonistic or ridiculing us or, we felt, skewed in some way." The university countered by citing its obligation as a public institution to insure the separation of church and state by withholding state funds from explicitly religious activities.

In a controversial 5–4 ruling, the Supreme Court agreed with Rosenberger that the university, by refusing to fund *Wide Awake*, violated the constitutional guarantee of free speech. The majority, applying the principle of government neutrality toward religion, ruled that the university discriminated against the publication on the basis of its content. The principle of neutrality and the right to free speech required a public university to give religious and secular student organizations equal access to state funds.[2]

In response to the Rosenberger case, public universities around the country began to reconsider their policies regarding the funding of student organizations. WU did what many others did—it made religious organizations eligible for funding from student activity fee monies, and it let students know that if any of them disagreed with the university's financial support of religious groups, she or he could get a partial refund of the activity fee, about $3.50.[3]

Campus Ministries

On a sweltering late summer afternoon during the first week of classes, a student activities fair was set up on the Union green. Along three sides of the large field, campus organizations displayed handmade signs, silken banners, and posters full of snapshots. At each table sat one or two representatives of the organization, and most tables were covered with brochures and other printed materials free to new wu students, about fifty at any given time, who braved the heat to wander through the fair.

A dozen religious organizations were at the fair, and they rubbed elbows with fraternities and sororities, athletic teams and recreational clubs, college Democrats and Republicans, special interest and single-issue groups of all kinds. Present were representatives of the Hillel Jewish Student Center, the Newman Center (Roman Catholic), the Lutheran Campus Ministry (Evangelical Lutheran Church in America), the Lutheran University Center (Lutheran Church, Missouri Synod), and the Wesley Foundation (United Methodist). Evangelical Protestantism was represented by InterVarsity, Campus Crusade for Christ, the Baptist Student Union, and the University Bible Fellowship. The Christian Scientists were there, as well as the University Pagan Circle. The only African Americans at a religious organization table were two women from Zion Campus Ministry, sponsored by a local black Protestant church.

Evangelical Protestantism

At the Campus Crusade for Christ table, I met one of two senior full-time staff members, Carla Bohn, a tall, slender, blond woman in her twenties. Over the course of my time at wu, she was generous with her time and trusting enough to invite me to a Campus Crusade staff meeting and students' small prayer and Bible study groups.

Campus Crusade's most visible public event was its large weekly Life Is Real meeting. It was held in a small auditorium in the Union at 7:00 P.M. on Thursdays, and at each of the several meetings I attended, I counted between 120 and 150 people.

On the second Thursday of the new academic year, I was stopped on my way to Life Is Real in the reception area outside the auditorium by an undergraduate student who introduced herself and made a name tag for me. She was a sophomore who, as a high school student, had heard of Campus Crusade on a Christian radio station. At 7:00 no one milling around and visiting with each other in the lobby seemed interested in taking seats inside, but they did so when someone yelled that it was time to start. I was welcomed on my way to a seat in the back of the room by a tall, tan, blond man in his twenties, Terry Lindquist, who informed me that he was a staff member and was willing to talk with me at more length about his work at WU.

Two senior undergraduates, Barbara, who was Asian American, and Brad, who was white, called the meeting to order and explained that Campus Crusade was a Christian group that sponsored men's and women's Bible studies, retreats, conferences, and "outreaches." Brad was very informal: "It's good to see you guys back again."

Brad began by telling a story about a friend of his, Mike, in Campus Crusade who "had a dream, a vision. Who here knows what Juanita's is?" A few people in the audience raised their hands. "It's a Mexican restaurant downtown that serves good food. It is known for its two-pound bean burritos, *el caminos*. Anyway, Mike's dream was for everyone to go out and eat two-pound burritos. So next week, after this meeting, we are all going downtown with Mike, the visionary, to Juanita's. And the week after that we will recognize everyone who managed to eat a two-pound all-bean burrito."

Everyone laughed. Brad continued: "We will also recognize, especially, all the females who do, because girls are esteemed members of this group. And I have an example of what I'm talking about." Brad pulled a paper bag from behind the podium and lifted out of it a bundle wrapped in foil. "Who here would like to demonstrate how to eat a two-pound bean burrito?" A young man in the audience enthusiastically accepted the challenge. As the wrapper was undone, so was his audience, amazed at the sheer size of the burrito within. Brad seated the volunteer in the front row and said that we would get progress reports from time to time as the meeting went on.

Next came the singing. Like other evangelical groups on campus, the Life Is Real audience sang contemporary Christian hymns whose words were projected onto a screen. Three songs were accompanied by two guitars. The tunes were easy to sing, and many in the room seemed very familiar with them.

After the singing, Brad and Barbara got a report from the burrito volunteer, who was almost finished. Brad then introduced another undergraduate, Pete, who operated the overhead projector. Pete removed the hymn lyrics and replaced them with a list of announcements. "Last year," reported Brad, "we had a challenge, and we all went to Juanita's, and there Pete ordered a *quesadilla*! So now we call him Quesadilla Boy."

Terry Lindquist walked to the front of the room to present the announcements. He introduced himself, saying that he'd been at WU three years and was a graduate of a state university in the region. Lindquist encouraged anyone new to Crusade to meet with him at the back of the room after Life Is Real, and he invited new students to his home for an orientation session.

The first announcement was the "game day schedule of events." A home football game was coming up, and Campus Crusade planned to begin its full day of activities with a men's prayer breakfast. After the breakfast, the whole group, including women, were invited to the Campus Crusade "house" near the stadium for an alcohol-free tailgate party.

An undergraduate woman then told the audience about a retreat coming up later in the month: "There's God, there's people, there's food." It would be held at a campground in the state and would be "a chance to hang out, focus on God, get to know each other, and have good fellowship." She asked Bill Shipps, the senior Campus Crusade staff member at WU, to come forward. Shipps, an energetic man in his late thirties or early forties, dashed to the front of the room and promised that if sixty-five people signed up for the retreat, he would shave his head. His audience was having fun and laughed along with him.

Lindquist then announced an e-mail address for "people's concerns and prayers" and a woman's prayer meeting in the Union next week. He concluded: "What we really need right now is to re-energize ourselves with a big scream, and I mean *big*. Ready! Set! Scream!" There was an enormous din.

As the shouting subsided, Barbara and Brad took over the meeting again and announced that it was time for the "mixer." Two couples up front, in the podium or stage area, were to demonstrate. Each man, standing, was to say to the woman, who was seated, that he adored her and wanted her to smile. The women were supposed to reject the male advances and say, "I think the world of you but I will not smile." The first man was to model a "cheap, informal approach." In his final of three pleas, he gave the woman a Kermit doll in a ballet dress. Of course, the woman who was supposed to refuse to smile cracked up every time, and everyone in the audience laughed.

The second man was supposed to take a more formal, elegant approach. His first plea was accompanied by a few roses and his second by a big bouquet; for his third, he got down on one knee, pulled a ring box out of his pocket, and seriously asked the woman, by first name, if she would marry him. The woman was completely surprised by this proposal, then said yes, and they hugged and kissed to big cheers from the crowd. They were apparently a well-known and popular couple in Campus Crusade circles.

After the engagement hubbub died down, Lindquist took the floor again. "This could be you! This could just as well be Campus Crusade for *Couples*! And I guess everyone knows by now that we aren't really doing a mixer, OK? These are two great people, and we worked for some time to come up with this mixer idea. Let's start their engagement off with prayer. Father, I thank you and just ask that you bless this relationship. . . . "

After the prayer, Lindquist delivered the sermon or "message" part of the gathering. "For those who are new, we actually do talk about God here. I want to welcome you guys. If you're thinking you're the only one here who doesn't know anyone, you're wrong.

"I grew up in a single-parent home. My father was an abusive alcoholic. My mom kicked him out of the house. Finally, his liver, heart, and lungs all gave out at the same time, and my father died when I was eleven. The minister of my church was a foster parent, and he realized I had no father figure, and he became that for me. He took me fishing and to baseball games, and he told me about Christ, that he died for our sins. My life didn't get any easier, being without a father and very poor.

"I did sports and the academic thing in high school and then went off to college. Only thing I knew when I got there was that I had to find a Christian group, and I tried out a lot. Eventually God led me to Campus Crusade. God gave me Christian friends, accountability, activities.

"But they didn't keep me out of trouble. I'm a person who has a tendency to make bad decisions. Now, I say stupid things. But I don't mean those kinds of minor mistakes. I mean subtle bad decisions that are gradual, and we don't realize how they shape our lives. Decisions about what we give significance to.

"Many of us get our feeling of significance from the approval of others. You think you have to meet certain standards to be someone, especially good grades. 'If I fail, I'm not significant.' This is a lie. The world is trying to feed this to you. Significance comes from Christ himself.

"I'm going to read a Bible story about the wisest man who ever lived, King Solomon, David's son. David gave Solomon his kingdom, and Solomon said, 'Cool! I'm diggin' that.' Yet in God's eyes, Solomon failed. He looked elsewhere for significance. He looked to wealth and power. He threw himself into his work, into alcohol and sex. The Bible says he had 300 concubines or something like that.

"Solomon wrote a little book called Ecclesiastes. It's like a little diary that he kept. Out of all that jazz, all the stuff he had, he came up with two things: One, it's all meaningless. From Ecclesiastes: 'All is vanity.' And two, it is all God. Again from Ecclesiastes: 'Fear God and keep his commandments, for this is the full duty of man.' Therefore, Solomon concluded that everything is meaningless without God, and this is from a man who had it all. Solomon knew the right thing, but he chose not to do it.

"This makes me think of Howard Hughes in our own time. He had it all but became a recluse. He just sat in his bedroom and watched movies, sometimes hundreds of times over again. When he died he weighed just a hundred pounds and had hair and a beard down below his waist. This man was worth 2.3 billion. He was lost. Why? Without God everything is meaningless.

"Our desire here at Campus Crusade is for you to walk with God. How? Number one, spend time in his word reading the Bible; and two, spend time in prayer. Just like any other relationship, you need to spend time talking, getting to know each other. If there are those here who think I'm way out in left field, who don't know what I'm talking about, please come and talk to me after the meeting."

After Lindquist closed, the student presiders announced a social on Friday night and gave a door prize to one of the people who signed a visitor's card as they came in at the beginning of the meeting. Brad then asked that we bow our heads in prayer. "O Lord, we want to thank you for this meeting and for Terry's message. Help us remember that as we go to classes, worry about the future and about getting jobs, that you are the most important. . . . "

These weekly Campus Crusade Life Is Real meetings were the largest regular religious gatherings on the wu campus. Only the attendance at some of the Newman Center's masses was larger. With a typical weekly attendance of well over 100, Campus Crusade's Life Is Real was the envy of other campus ministries. And the students present, in both the leadership and the general audience, were an attractive lot—no gathering of losers here.

It would be hard to overestimate the importance of contemporary Christian songs to the worship experience of Christian students. The evangelical Protestant student ministries used no other kind of music, and the mainline Protestant ministries and the Roman Catholic Newman Center incorporated them regularly, although not exclusively, into their worship.

One of the students I got to know best, Phil McGarey, was a very bright first-year student who came to wu from a nearby state to major in biomedical engineering. He grew up attending his parents' mainline Presbyterian church and during his first month at wu conducted a rather thorough and earnest search for a Christian group with whom he could worship and pursue other religious and social activities. He attended weekly gatherings conducted by the ecumenical mainline Protestant Campus Ministry Center (cmc), Campus Crusade, and InterVarsity, another nondenominational evangelical Protestant campus ministry. In late October, he described his first weeks at the university and his questions about campus life: "I thought about this before I came. Freedom! Accountability! Freedom to do what you want. I'm a Christian, but would I drink? Be sexually active? Party?

"When I got here I saw signs go up about religious groups and that helped a lot. And at June orientation there were booths and I talked to cmc. They had an early dinner for new students. cmc is what I'm used to. They get together, eat, talk, make applications to your life. Then Wednesday came, and that's InterVarsity. InterVarsity had a big cookout at the beginning of the year, and I went for five minutes (I had something else I had to go to that night), and they said, 'Come Wednesday night to the regular meeting in the Union.' InterVarsity is very liberal." I was surprised by this comment because I knew that InterVarsity was theologically quite conservative.

McGarey explained why he considered InterVarsity liberal: "Well, they sing songs, not hymns, just songs for thirty minutes or so. And that scared me at first; everyone was raising their arms. [Some students at InterVarsity meetings gently waved one or both of their arms over their heads as they sang contemporary hymns.] So, I'm like, what am I doing here? I didn't want to go back to InterVarsity, but the people there were so nice to me. I went a second time and everyone was so responsive. Everyone talked to me. I really liked the talks. I've learned a lot. So I kept going to both CMC and InterVarsity."

McGarey described the CMC as "conservative" based, too, on the music used in worship: "CMC is very conservative. We sing hymns and stuff. Inter-Varsity is more liberal because we sing contemporary Christian songs instead of hymns. People are completely different at these two groups. Inter-Varsity looks at the Bible. I know five to ten people in InterVarsity, and they all read the Bible every day and pray, and they look at the literal translation of the Bible. At CMC we were talking about how we make decisions. And I said that I pray to God and ask him to tell me what to do. And four or five people looked at me and said, 'No, we look inside for what's best for us.' InterVarsity asks God; in CMC it's all inside. We just have to search. Whoa! I'm completely different from CMC. I go directly to God. I tried not to look at CMC as below me. I look at their relationship with God as not as concrete, outspoken, or obvious. I pray to Jesus every day; he is a friend. I know CMC believes in Jesus, but I can't understand their relationship with him. I know God controls everything, so I wonder why God doesn't lead CMC closer. This confuses me. So I've stopped going to CMC. There's something superficial there. We talk but, it's like, about the weather. The topics and conversation were pedestrian. I saw applications, but I'd heard it all before. Now, [Lowell] York [the director of the CMC and an ordained Presbyterian minister], he's a great guy, but when I looked at the student leaders, I didn't see any leadership there. When it's time to sing a hymn, they just looked at each other. Weak student leadership. One leader in specific has a boyfriend who spends nights in her dorm room (they're on my floor). I know they drink, but I don't want to be judgmental, but everything's just adding up. I can go to CMC, but why would I go?"

Campus Crusade for Christ and InterVarsity were the two most successful evangelical ministries at wu, that is, they attracted more student participants than any of the others. Both were large international nondenominational organizations primarily devoted to Christian outreach to college and university students. InterVarsity's "Basis of Faith," printed in the organization's 1994–95 annual report, listed five beliefs:

1. The unique divine inspiration, entire trustworthiness and authority of the Bible.
2. The deity of our Lord Jesus Christ.
3. The necessity and efficacy of the substitutionary death of Jesus Christ for the redemption of the world, and the historic fact of his bodily resurrection.
4. The presence and power of the Holy Spirit in the work of regeneration.
5. The expectation of the personal return of our Lord Jesus Christ.

Both of these ministries at wu held large weekly meetings; InterVarsity called these "seeker meetings." In addition, staff members trained juniors and seniors to conduct small Bible study groups with other students, plan social events, and organize groups of students to go on retreats and attend regional or national conferences. Both staffers and student leaders from these two organizations spent some of their outreach time in residence halls. An important strategy for reinvigorating InterVarsity at wu in the two years or so prior to this study had been motivating student leaders to move back into the residence halls so they could be models of Christian life and organize small study and prayer groups there.

Students fully involved in InterVarsity or Campus Crusade had busy schedules and were part of a close-knit community. McGarey described his weekly InterVarsity activities: "At 7:30 A.M. Monday through Friday there's prayer in the dorm. I go Fridays; I have class at 7:30 Monday through Thursday. Nights Monday through Thursday is inductive Bible study. Then there's Wednesday night worship. Weekends are great. There are two groups—Dana's and Mary's room, and the one on the other side of campus in Douglas Hall. We have two rooms right together. We watch movies there. There's always about fifteen people. We also go bowling. We had a campfire at some guy's grandparents' place—marshmallows, guitar, praise songs. Every day I go to someone's room and hang out, sometimes until 2:00 A.M."

Small groups in the evangelical orbit typically met for Bible study, but these meetings also devoted a significant amount of time to sharing personal troubles and concerns, often about dating. Jane Hunter, a full-time InterVarsity minister only four or five years out of college herself, invited me to an "inductive Bible study" group she led for students who were preparing to become leaders of Bible study groups for first-year, or otherwise uninitiated, students. The session was to meet from 7:00 to 9:30 P.M. on Halloween in the basement of a nearby Baptist church. Seven students, including two men, two juniors, five sophomores, and one religious studies major, came well prepared with notebooks, loose-leaf double-spaced texts of the Gospel of Mark, handfuls of colored pens, and short rulers. An observer would never have known it was Halloween—there were no costumes, no bat earrings, no orange or black anywhere until Hunter served cookies with orange frosting at 8:30.

Hunter began the meeting with "sharing time," during which students spoke with one another in pairs, mostly about their days: "I'm half done with bio"; "I've been really tired all day." After each partner offered a short quiet prayer for the other, Hunter called them to order and asked them to begin work on the text, a three-page portion near the end of the gospel. The students began to read the text, underlining in red, perhaps, circling words in blue, connecting words and phrases with orange lines.

After forty-five minutes or so, Hunter asked them questions about the structure of the text. "First, let's do paragraph breaks." Students discussed earnestly whether the first paragraph ends more appropriately at the thirteenth or fourteenth line, and so forth.

"Now let's go to interpretation." Students contributed observations about frequently mentioned words or phrases and their connotations. They also noted that the passage contained imagery, such as references to the vineyard, that is used in the Old Testament. In these ways and others, Hunter and her students, in dialogue with one another, deciphered the "parable of the wicked tenants." InterVarsity was proud of its inductive method of Bible study. A how-to article on inductive Bible study on the InterVarsity website explained that "because you are looking together to God's Word for answers, your friends will not feel 'preached at' and much of the pressure for clearly presenting Jesus is taken off of the leader and put right on the Word of God."

Not until 9:40 or so did Hunter get to "application," applying this text to students' lives. Students wondered what group on campus the vineyard might represent and how they could be better tenants, better servants of the landowner. One student defined a servant as "anyone who points out sin in my life, not necessarily InterVarsity leaders." Hunter reminded them that "the question is how you respond to them. What are the issues in your life that people are pressing and how are you dealing with that? Listening or shutting them out? What have you been shown or taught that you don't want to obey?"

By this time, the meeting had gone way past 9:30. After a significant pause in the conversation, Hunter asked, "Anything you all want to share?" Almost immediately, a woman blurted out, "Sex has such a hold on me!," and she tearfully told us of her struggle over having sex with her boyfriend. "I am physically, emotionally, and spiritually drained." She spoke quite openly about sexual activity, tensions with her boyfriend on the issue, and her failure to live up to standards that she believed were unbending.

Other group members immediately offered visible signs of support. As soon as the speaker began to weep, the woman next to her took her hand and held it while she spoke. A woman across the table made her way over chairs and around the crowded room to give the speaker a big hug and sat behind her with her hands on the speaker's shoulders. Hunter said a long prayer in which she expressed understanding and concern but also asked God to give the despairing student strength to wait until marriage for God's gift of sexual intimacy.

Campus Crusade's Carla Bohn invited women who were being trained as student leaders to her apartment one evening a week for instruction in theology, Bible study, and evangelistic outreach. Each of the two sessions I observed also began with programmed intellectual work, a discussion of study questions based on Neil T. Anderson's book, *Victory over the Darkness: Realizing the Power of Your Identity in Christ*, and then progressed to intensely personal sharing, which often left members in tears. Both Campus Crusade and InterVarsity had stable memberships over time, and it was obvious that the members knew each other quite well and trusted one another.

Bohn and Hunter wielded their authority as full-time staff members lightly. They, too, shared personal revelations about their religious and private lives in these small group meetings. In language, dress, hairstyle, humor, and taste in movies, they were part of the popular culture in which their students dwelled. At the same time, they were professional, hardworking, dedicated, specially trained, and intent on carrying out the duties of their positions in the campus ministries.

Several smaller evangelical ministries were active at wu. They were more radically fundamentalist than Campus Crusade and InterVarsity, and their presence made the two large nondenominational groups look theologically and socially moderate. One of these smaller groups, University Bible Fellowship, was directed by Mark Tyler, a man in his early forties. He had a Bible college education and had worked in a University Bible Fellowship chapter directed by his father for several years before directing his own chapter at wu. I met Tyler on my first day on campus at a table in one of the mall areas of the Union. These table locations may be reserved by any officially recognized student organization, and Tyler was there every day during the first week of classes and once a week or so during the rest of the semester. A young woman and recent graduate of a Baptist Bible college worked full-time with Tyler on this campus and another one nearby. Two women worked part-time—Tyler's wife, who "does the music," and a woman in her forties who devised special outreach programs for international students and their families. Each of them ran their operations out of their own homes or apartments, although Tyler's home was close enough to campus to be the site of occasional social events for the fellowship.

Tyler was one of the best-known campus ministers at WU because he preached on a busy street corner in a part of the city full of student bars and because every semester he prepared a flier for students in Professor Joseph Falk's popular general education course on Judaism. I attended Falk's class on a day that Tyler and several students stood outside the classroom building distributing fliers to students as they entered the building for class. The flier, entitled "A Response to Joseph Falk," began: "I know that it's gutsy to dis-agree with Professor Falk. After all, Dr. Falk is one of [WU's] favorite pro-fessors, and it is no wonder. His lucid articulation skills are as impressive as Michael Jordan's basketball skills. Yet herein lies my caution: Don't get so caught up with Falk's communication skills and charm that you end up believing the bites of heresy he teaches. Beware of his presuppositions, inferences and blasphemies. They are like sprinkles of poison mixed into a luscious plate of food." After quoting three excerpts from a book on Judaism authored by Falk, the flier continued:

> I hope the three quotes from Falk's book, as listed above, will help you understand why I, as a Christian who believes "everything that is written by the Prophets" (Lk 24), feel compelled to write this response. And maybe this response is justifiable when we keep in mind that the people that Jesus chastised the strongest were the heretical Jewish religious teach-ers. . . . Moreover, I believe that this response is legitimate because college students, who are supposed to think critically, should have the oppor-tunity to hear the other side.

Although about half of the students in the auditorium were reading the flier before class began, Falk made no mention of it. In an interview, one of Falk's teaching assistants for the course laughingly called Tyler's flier "a tradition" and seemed absolutely unconcerned about it. She said that to her knowledge students in the course had never mentioned the flier to Falk or the teaching assistants. A staff member at the Hillel Jewish Student Center reported that one or two Jewish students, however, were upset by it and came to Hillel to discuss it with the center's staff.

A second small evangelical ministry I got to know was Campus Christian Fellowship, the campus ministry of the Churches of Christ denomination. Dave Stone, the director, had moved to the city that summer in order to start a new chapter at WU. He had come directly from a very large established chapter at another public university in the region and was surprised at how difficult it was to get things going at WU. He didn't realize until he arrived how many religious organizations existed at WU. I never saw more than twenty students at his weekly worship gatherings, and a well-publicized lecturer he brought to campus to speak on the dangers of New Age religion drew about twenty students. Stone had expected 200 or 300.

Zion Campus Ministry was directed by Corrine Thompson, a lay member of a local African American church, Zion Apostolic Church. Thompson held meetings about twice a month in the Student Union. Six students, four of them African American, attended a meeting in early September. What was striking about the Zion Campus Ministry was its focus on concrete problems and practical solutions. Thompson said the group's goals were "to be a support system for students, to be a family away from home to them, to help them solve whatever problems they may have. Students have a lot of things going on: relationships, money problems. During my first two years here I really needed help; I was clinically depressed. This city is a real shock for a lot of students who come here from major metropolitan areas." At the student activities fair at the beginning of the school year, Zion Campus Ministry was the only group to have a handout that contained advice about getting settled and getting around in the city. It was entitled "Community Resource List," and it included places of business, as well as social, legal, health, and crisis intervention services in town. Thompson emphasized her desire to be of practical assistance to students and said that one student came to her for help with a class registration mix-up.

The evangelical and fundamentalist campus ministries were relatively apolitical. I was on campus during the 1996 elections, but I never heard mention of electoral politics at evangelical functions. Nor did I hear preaching against abortion. Mark Tyler was the only evangelical minister I heard speak publicly about homosexuality as a sin. Jane Hunter of InterVarsity told her inductive Bible study group that she was troubled by the presence of an openly homosexual minister in the Campus Ministers Association, of which she was a member, but she had not yet spoken to the homosexual minister or the association about it.

According to the Campus Crusade minister in charge of outreach to international students, conservative Christian groups were afraid to speak out on issues such as homosexuality on this liberal campus. "The Christian community here is a scared, fearful community. They are afraid of the reaction they'll get. The gay group gets the university president to attend their meetings and talk to them. The university is for the underdog, and it sees gays that way. But in a sense we're the underdog. Gays won't be attacked here—maybe elsewhere, but not here—but here Christians are likely to be rejected. I doubt the president would come to one of our meetings. Christians are perceived as being intolerant. And as soon as they say that *they're* intolerant."

Were *all* Christians perceived in this way? "In the university community you have a spectrum. A lot of Christians try to ride the fence. People in the middle only play up God's love. But people who are searching for God want a true God, not a wishy-washy one. They want a God who's holy and whatnot. There's a part of the Christian community willing to ride the fence that gets no trouble here, and they aren't growing. Any stand on right and wrong automatically puts you at the extreme. We may take stands in small groups but nothing campus-wide. We are very open and welcoming—trying to reach out and bridge to the university. We have to love even more to break down the notion that Christians are intolerant. We have such a huge thing to prove God is love on this campus."

Athletics

Evangelical Protestantism at WU wore its most public face in intercollegiate athletics. A local newspaper, on the Sunday after the first home football game, ran on the front page a color photograph of members of both teams kneeling and "giving thanks" after the game before they hit the showers. Inside, one of WU's star players, when asked how he dealt with the recent death of a parent, explained that he relied on his religious faith: "It's tough. You have to rely on the man in the sky and your family and friends." A few weeks later, another local paper ran a large color photograph of the same football field assembly on the front page of the sports section. The headline read, "Buccaneers Mix God and Goalposts." The article began: "Contrary to popular opinion, Head Coach [Gordy] does *not* have ultimate authority on the [WU] football team. Let defensive end [Ned Simon] explain. 'I am a Christian who plays football, not a football player who's a Christian. Because I know when I'm on the field, who I'm playing for and why I'm here. What helps a lot is when you have other guys on the team who feel the same way.' " Two other players, both African Americans as well, were quoted in the article. The first told the reporter that he attended a Baptist church every Sunday morning and team chapel service during the week. "The Lord has been in my life before football and he will be in it afterwards. Jesus gave his all for me so how can I give less?"

The second, also a Baptist, said his spiritual faith had always been his first priority. "I can't remember a time when I wasn't believing in God and accepting Jesus as my savior. He's brought me a long way. I've done some things that I didn't even think I was capable of. He chose me, I didn't choose him."

The head football coach attributed the "very strong Christian thread throughout our football team" to the influence of African American players who came to the university with strong Christian family backgrounds. "Those kids in particular, they're used to going to church once or twice a week and prayer sessions. Usually, grandma put a Bible in their hand when they were just little-bitty toddlers and they believe very strongly in the good Lord."

What the coach did not say was that the prayer gathering between the two football teams that got so much publicity was the result of a call from the director of the Athletes in Action program at the opposing school to the director of Athletes in Action at WU, Luke Carson. Carson was doubtful that such a meeting at the fifty-yard line would work because "the head WU coach wants the team to get together and hold hands after every game." (In fact, the head coach says the Lord's Prayer with his team before and after every game.) But Carson told "three Christian players" about the call, "and they just passed the word around the field." Some of Carson's friends asked him if he wasn't mad that the coach did not credit him with helping organize the prayer meeting, but Carson believed that the coach wanted to give credit to the players.

Through Athletes in Action, one of the five major divisions of Campus Crusade for Christ, conservative Protestant evangelicalism has achieved establishment status at WU. Although virtually everyone I spoke to was unaware of it, Carson was named by the head coaches the chaplain of the big-three sports teams—the football team and the men's and women's basketball teams. "The process by which I got to be chaplain was different for all three sports," explained Carson. His first try with the football team was a series of "optional chapels" in a dorm lounge. Few attended, but one player who did went with Carson to see the head coach to "ask about chapel services." The head coach agreed. "Everyone who suited up and all the coaches had to go—about 80 to 100 people," Carson said. "The head coach never said it was mandatory, but it was unspoken mandatory. Players could stand outside the door if it bothered them. Now I do chapel on the Thursday before every game during team meetings. I just give a talk for ten or fifteen minutes. About half the team comes. The head coach himself doesn't come anymore because his local TV show is on Thursdays. A couple of the coaches come, though. And I lead a coaches' prayer meeting every week in one of their offices. It's just for the football staff. Sometimes for it I'll use something from the Promise Keepers magazine, *New Man*."

The tragic death of a player led to his appointment with the men's basketball team. Carson had been meeting regularly with this player, who was "beginning to witness to the rest of the team" before his death. "When he died, the coaches welcomed me. Everyone wanted to come to regular chapel service scheduled for the next day. Now two coaches come all the time; one was an atheist before the player died, and now he comes to the church I attend. They looked to me and another person on the university staff to do grief counseling. I am good friends with the trainer. Every year, through him, players get an itinerary that includes chapel on it, but students have to request chapel."

He and his wife became chaplains of the women's basketball team after the arrival of a new head coach. A former WU player was traveling across the country with the Athletes in Action team, which plays exhibition games with university teams as publicity and witness for Athletes in Action. During the head coach's first year, the Athletes in Action team played the WU team, which provided an opening for Carson. "I meet with the coach personally every two weeks to go through Scripture. My wife and I have a weekly Bible study for the team. Five or six students come. My wife and I trade off doing home game chapel services."

Athletes in Action publicity materials carried endorsements by both men's coaches. The football coach wrote: "All of the players and coaches join me in expressing our sincere appreciation to Athletes in Action for the wonderful ministry provided each year. We have grown as a family through the Christian environment established by their leadership. We will always be grateful." The basketball coach stated: "Athletes in Action . . . have been an important part of the Athletic Department and we appreciate their support very much."

In recent years, the Athletic Department hosted a Fellowship of Christian Athletes/Athletes in Action Recognition Day. Members of these organizations and their families received discounted tickets to the football game and an antidrug rally, a sack lunch, a soft drink, and a Buccaneer souvenir.

According to Scott Peters, a starter for the football team, the football players who were "neutral, not negative toward religion," sometimes wished other players would leave their religious views out of the newspapers. "They think the public will think all the players are religious like this. They feel misrepresented. They want personal credit, or team credit, not credit to go to God."

Carson was especially sensitive to the pressures under which student athletes live. "They try to please too many people—professors, parents, coaches. And high-profile teams face unbelievable temptations—sex and alcohol. Girls just throw themselves at them. And they live in a fish bowl. Everyone knows who they date, if they fail an exam." From Peters's perspective as a student athlete, "the student athlete and the regular student are nothing alike—two different animals really. The reasons first of all are time management. We have to fit everything in. Second, we have so many commitments to keep. Third, our reasons for being in college are entirely different. We're more well-rounded, more ambitious. We can handle competitive situations. I mean, everything I do is toward football: Can I do it before practice or after practice? Everything I eat I eat in order to maintain my weight. I have to do so much lifting each week."

At a meeting of Athletes in Action held in a lounge in one of the residence halls one winter evening, twelve students were present, five of them women. Carson led a discussion of Romans 8, which contains passages that Christians have found of great comfort over the centuries, such as "If God is for us, who is against us?" and "We know that God causes all things to work together for good to those who love God." When the students were asked to apply God's promises to athletic performance, one man said: "It gives me security. Especially from injuries. It means a higher power is looking out for you." Another commented: "Sometimes you get so nervous out there. I say a little prayer, and it eases my fears." One woman said: "It puts my sports in perspective. I have a higher purpose. If we lose it's not the end of the world."

The Mainline

The more liberal, or mainline, Christian and Jewish campus ministers at WU, identified explicitly with denominations, have been organized for years into the Campus Ministers Association (CMA). The CMA's statement of purpose was very different from Campus Crusade's, for example, which was to "tell every student about God's love and forgiveness" and to "help lost students become Christ-Centered Laborers." CMA members, instead, commit themselves to providing "comprehensive programming in order to widen vision, explore and deepen faith, strengthen character, stimulate creativity, enhance personal capacity for leadership and service, and equip students to think rationally, act responsibly, and work productively as persons of faith in a complex society."

InterVarsity was the only nondenominational or parachurch ministry affiliated with the CMA. And it was only after what one CMA member described as "a long discussion" that the CMA admitted local InterVarsity staff to its membership. CMA members expect truth in advertising. A founding member expressed displeasure that some groups on campus that were connected officially and financially with denominations did not make this connection known to students. "A group may be from a particular church and give themselves another name for campus work. We think you should be open, up-front. If you're Lutheran, say you're Lutheran."

CMA members represented the Hillel Jewish Student Center, the InterVarsity Christian Fellowship, the Greek Orthodox Church, the Roman Catholic Newman Center, and Protestant denominational ministries including Christian Reformed, Episcopal, Society of Friends, United Methodist, Evangelical Lutheran Church in America, Missouri Synod Lutheran, Southern Baptist, and the combined American Baptist, Church of the Brethren, Disciples of Christ, Presbyterian, and United Church of Christ ecumenical CMC. The CMA functioned as an informal religious establishment of its own on the Old Campus, and members had numerous contacts and professional relationships with university personnel, mostly in student services.

Academic personnel knew of the CMA from the letter and calendar it sent in the fall to academic department heads. The letter, signed by Frank Hirsch, director of the Hillel Jewish Student Center and president of the CMA, informed its readers that the enclosed calendar contained the dates of Christian, Jewish, and Muslim holy days and festivals "for the purpose of informing them about times when students might be involved in religious observance. It is hoped that this information will be taken into account when University events and class assignments and examinations were scheduled."

Student Services

WU held over a dozen two-day summer orientation sessions for new students and their parents. Students and parents had different orientation schedules and programs, each carefully planned by the university. The program for the first session for parents, entitled "Change Is in the Air," stated: "Growth and change occur in individuals throughout their lives. How can you remain a responsible and loving parent despite some of the changes that are bound to occur as your sons and daughters experience college?" This session was moderated by James Milligan, a Roman Catholic priest and director of the Newman Center. He wore a clerical black suit. He was one of four experts who gave presentations on the intellectual, interpersonal, moral, and career changes many undergraduates experience during their university years. The other speakers were the director of academic advising, the director of career development, and a counselor from the Student Counseling Center.

Milligan conducted the segment on moral development during young adulthood. He told the parents that moral development is predictable. Young adults go "from simple to complex reasoning about what's right and wrong. They struggle with differing value systems they find at the university."

ien the orientation staff acted out a vignette in which a new student, on
hone with her father, expressed concern about other students' conduct.
ryone in high school was a lot more like me. You should see what people
ere—cheat on exams and papers, drunk every weekend. Like they
haven't heard about AIDS. I think they should be punished. They're breaking
the law." Her father responded: "Honey, just make sure you make decisions
that you are comfortable with. And instead of coming home this weekend,
why don't you stay there and meet some of your roommate's friends?"

After the vignette, a parent who worked with the orientation staff and
acted in the skits told the audience: "As parents we don't know 1 percent of
the moral computations that go on inside our students' heads. It's better that
way [laughter]. These things deeply distress all of us, but a thread of moral
fiber prevails on this campus. I encourage students to continue in their
religious or denominational paths, and this is also a good time for them to
try on other denominations. There's a lot of help and opportunities here."

Then Milligan took the podium again. "I represent the Campus Ministers
Association, and we make all kinds of resources available to you and to
students." He commented on the vignette: "Students here encounter other
students who view the world very differently. The student in the vignette is
still making decisions on the basis solely of her parents and her hometown.
Everything else is wrong. That's dualistic thinking. Here, new ideas in the
classroom and encountering those from many different cultures move most
students from dualistic to the relativistic stage—'You do your thing; I'll do
mine.' All is up for grabs; everyone makes their own decisions. This stage is
liberating and exhilarating but dangerous.

"The third stage is commitment in a diverse world. Students learn to
make decisions based on principles they've adopted on their own. They are,
and know they are, their own person. It's hard to wait to see how your
student will turn out. The best way to anticipate it is to look in the mirror.
It's scary [laughter], but research shows it's true.

"Your students here will be liberated and exhilarated, but they will also
feel alone and experience a sense of loss. How should you parent during this
time? First, nurture your student's self-worth. Give them comfort and security without smothering them. Second, give them the benefit of your own
thoughtful reasons and carefully challenge their own thinking. Reveal your
own moral doubts without repeating platitudes. You can count on all of us
at the university to help."

The director of academic advising talked about intellectual development.
"Intellectual development is not learning facts, but consists of challenges on
a more personal level: What is truth? Professors will play a major role. We
know that people usually leave high school thinking everything is either

right or wrong. Professors will often use the Socratic method—getting students to think for themselves. If your student seems uncertain about what he or she believes, remember that college is usually a time for intellectual confusion. They may be resistant, confused, afraid. It's a normal step on the road to establishing their own beliefs and values. They will even question *your* beliefs and values, ones you thought were securely held. But it's normal that they do that.

"They question authorities such as parents and professors as they learn to think more independently. Yet they will often seek your guidance. Listen, offer support, tell them it's normal to be confused. Encourage them to talk with professors, their adviser, and older students. The most important thing is that a student develop confidence in his or her own beliefs and values."

The next orientation program for students consisted of a wide array of special events held during the first week of classes. The schedule of this "Welcome Week," which each new student received, included (along with tours of the library, movies, CLEP testing, and special lectures) worship services, open houses, and meals provided by the Mennonite, Episcopal, Lutheran, and ecumenical Protestant campus ministries, all affiliated with the CMA.

University officials most often turned to this professional association in situations involving religion. In fact, membership in the CMA seemed to validate a religious leader's or campus minister's professional standing and competence. The Student Counseling Center referred students to CMA members for counseling when they expressed "spiritually based concerns." The director of the Student Counseling Center had a master of divinity degree from Princeton Theological Seminary, where he had studied pastoral counseling on his way to a Ph.D. and licensure as a clinical psychologist. He described the kinds of religious issues students brought to the Counseling Center, such as "a profound sense of guilt and shame, especially about sex. Can I ever be forgiven? Am I shut off from God now? Reconciliation is, in my judgment, a pastoral function. I prefer to see it that way than to reduce this to a psychological function." He explained that some of the counselors on his staff "might do more with religion and spirituality than others. For me, I collaborate with the student about what kind of follow-up after the assessment interview makes most sense. For example, if a lesbian student comes in with religious concerns, I know that there is a member of the CMA who works with gay and lesbian students about religious concerns, and I might suggest to the student that she speak to this minister. For non-Christian, non-Jewish students, referrals are made to the spiritual director of the nearby mosque for Muslims, for example."

The CMA had an exclusive arrangement with the Admissions Office. Each year, CMA ministers received two sets of mailing labels from Admissions. In the spring, Admissions sent a set of labels that included prospective students who had applied to the university for admission and who had indicated their religious preference on their SAT or ACT exams. If a student noted on the ACT or SAT personal profile section that he or she was Roman Catholic, for example, the Newman Center received his or her name and address. In the middle of the summer, Admissions sent a second set of labels that included all students who planned to enroll at WU and who had listed a religious preference. The Admissions Office made the labels available to any CMA minister who agreed, in exchange, to send each student on the first list a letter letting the applicant know a bit about the campus ministry program and to send each student on the second list a notice of campus ministry events during the first week or two of classes.

Morrie Redlinger, the director of admissions, explained that nearly ten years earlier, the CMA had asked university officials in charge of admissions and student orientation whether there were more effective ways to get and pass along information about students' religious affiliation. The CMA had been depending on a form that new students voluntarily completed as they filled out a stack of other forms during orientation. Redlinger said: "I felt that we were overlooking a source of information that students had voluntarily provided and far more frequently—the SAT and ACT student profile information. Specifically, two factors—first, the *voluntary* completion of these items on the profile; second, the test company's sending of such data to the university for its use when such use could be beneficial to students and the university—made me think this was a good idea.

"Although this state isn't exactly the Bible Belt, we take note of the conservative nature of families in this part of the country and the liberal reputation of the university itself. I thought it could help recruiting if we gave authorized religious groups belonging to CMA information prior to their enrolling. We supply the mailing labels and many members of CMA, if not all, send an information letter: congratulations on your admission to WU; we note that you have indicated a religious preference; we hope you'll visit our center when you're on campus, etc., etc. Please share this letter with your parents.

"I think it's a good idea to exploit a marketing edge, and I don't care to measure the success of this effort. If it offended some—and by the way, I've never heard that it does—then I'd rethink, but it costs so little, and as long as CMA plays by the rules, I think it's a good idea."

Redlinger was on the board of directors of the Wesley Foundation, where he advised Cal Huff, the senior minister and director of the foundation's campus ministry, and Gail Wicker, the associate campus minister of the foundation. Huff, about sixty years old, was the most senior member of a mainline Protestant triumvirate that had been at WU since the late 1960s and also included Lowell York of the ecumenical CMC and Hal Rausch of the Lutheran Campus Ministry (ELCA). Huff had been a member of the staff of the large United Methodist church near the university before he left to direct the Wesley Foundation, housed in a building next door to the church. He had gotten to know university faculty in the congregation. "There were over two hundred M.D.'s and Ph.D.'s in the congregation, and I realized that I could run with this crowd, so I began to consider something in higher education.

"I started in 1969. Of course, that was a year of horrible unrest—antiwar protest and whatnot. I came in with an empty building and no student community. Students back then were anti-institutional. So I decided I had to be the church without looking like the church. And I had to get the building used. So we started a youth hostel and shelter in 1971. Until 1977 it was the only shelter for poor and homeless people in town. We housed 3,000 a year. We brought in a free clinic, which is still operating a floor below us.

"Anyway, I kept on taking courses at the university, and took comps [comprehensive exams] in religion and personality, student personnel, counseling, and psychology. My program was out of the College of Education, which was very flexible. All the while I worked full-time. Well, I did my dissertation and got a divorce at about the same time."

Huff defined his ministry in this way: "To be faithful to Matthew 25. To make disciples, be of service to the world. This can be translated into all different kinds of ways. This Wesley Foundation is unique in its community service programs. We are giving students a chance to see the gospel made real. With continuing reflection and community building behind it. And all kinds of people are involved. We have lesbian atheists working in the free clinic, and a bunch of straitlaced dentists who work in the dental clinic. We have a bunch of elderly Methodist and Roman Catholic women working in the soup kitchen.

"A lot of things have started here. We had the first and only men's center on campus. We had a radical women's therapy group meeting here. During my first years here, the SDS [Students for a Democratic Society] met here. In the early 1970s, the gay community couldn't meet on campus so they met here for five years—the Gay Liberation Front. All kinds of twelve-step programs have met here. Korean, Chinese, and black churches have used our space; so have Buddhists and Muslims.

"So all these years we had to do a student program on top of all this. That's the only way to get denominational support. Many [Wesley] Foundations went entirely out of existence because they just did social action. It's always a tightrope between prophetic and traditional pastoral ministries to students.

I've always been able to pull it off because I've been very active in the Annual Conference [the United Methodist administrative body that oversees regional churches and church organizations]. They get to know me and say, 'Give Cal money; he's not so bad.' Three-quarters of a million dollars go from the Annual Conference to the four Wesley Foundations and the four denominational colleges in the conference.

"People came to know and trust me at the university, too. For fifteen years I was a member of the committee that reviews human subjects research. I have a special contact in the medical school and have lectured there regularly on ethics. Early on, I lectured in counselor education and social work classes, but not lately. Also, I have big input into the new student orientation program. In the 1970s, the university didn't do much student orientation, so the campus ministers did an alternative orientation, 'Orientation II.' Students were invited to stay an extra day for it. I knew from my student personnel work that this was important for new students. I wrote a program for their parents that the university is still using. I am on a first-name basis with deans, especially in student services, student counseling, and student health.

"We raise more of our own money than most other Wesley Foundations. We get only 65 percent of our budget from the United Methodist Church. Most of our own income comes from rent on building space.

"The building is both a problem and a blessing. It's old now. I've changed every light switch in the building. An alum does what he calls a 'plumbing ministry'—teaches plumbing to others by redoing ours. We rent rooms in the other wing to thirteen students, most of them our peer ministers. The rooms are very popular. The president of the student body lives here now.

"And my salary is high because I've been here so long. I noticed that once I reached fifty I was not invited back for interviews for other jobs. I guess people worry about energy level, familiarity with pop culture, having anything in common with students. So since 1978, we've used peer ministers.

"This is how peer ministers work: The first stage is recruitment. Every year we try to decide which students to invite to apply. We interview all applicants. (It's good experience for them.) Usually we have fifteen to eighteen applicants. We are never sure how many we'll hire until we see the mix of gender, race, majors, etc. We always need to recruit early; the university is looking for them, too, to be RAS [resident assistants in the dorms]. We have a meeting each spring for the new crop and ask them to come back three days before classes start in the fall for intensive training in community building, theological and pastoral concerns. This all works because of the supervision process, which I modeled after CPE [Clinical Pastoral Education]. Each peer minister meets with her or his supervisor, Gail [Wicker] or me, one-on-one biweekly and alternate weeks in a small group. They turn in a log to the supervisor for the one-on-one session, so accountability is built in. They get housing for $50 a month, or if they live in the dorm, we pay half of the dorm expenses. The job is worth $1,300–1,400 to them. We expect ten to twelve hours of work a week.

"There have been 125 peer ministers over the years. Maybe 20 of them are now ordained ministers; most of the others are active laypeople. Half of the value of the peer ministry program is developing these leaders." The Wesley Foundation was not alone in using undergraduate peer ministers to plan and implement its programs. So, too, did the CMC and the Lutheran Campus Ministry. In Hillel, a set of student officers advised the director on programming, and the Newman Center recruited and trained student leaders for retreats.

How have university students changed over the years since 1969, and what is this crop like? Huff said: "I try to learn about them by observing and reading. I can say some things: They have been highly stimulated all their lives by visual and sound images. So ministry that's comfortable for them uses Christian rock, etc. But I don't think that's healthy, so I run a counterrevolutionary ministry that encourages quiet reflection and isn't so superficial.

"They don't plan ahead at all. I heard a group of them discuss on Sunday evening whether they would go into the city the next day for a big concert. I couldn't believe they hadn't made advance plans for this big night out, but they weren't even sure by the night before that they were going. Well, it turns out that they went. They all got tickets when they got there, and they had a great time.

"The e-mail thing. They are used to instant communication. We got e-mail here this fall to be there with them.

"They are really scared about the future. I saw a recent survey that indicated that current college students think they're more likely to see an alien than social security! Many of them know that their generation is going to be less educated than their parents. They can't be sure of getting jobs. A lot think unemployment can't happen to them, but it's a shadow over all of them, and they know that just the best and brightest get good jobs. There's less purpose to be in college than in earlier times.

"It takes them four or five years longer to mature, accept responsibility, marry. They are still idealistic and want to make a difference. They are more likely to do it with hands-on stuff locally than peace or environmental stuff, say, like Amnesty International. There are a lot of student volunteers in the free clinic.

"Students in campus ministry go to church now. They are more accepting of mainline stuff that looks like church. I can look more like the church again. In the early 1980s was the first time a student-led Bible study was requested, and they'd kill me now if we didn't have one. But they don't want ministers at these meetings. It's their thing. My small groups discuss relationships, marriage, sex, the environment. This year we have a group going based on the book, *Meeting Jesus Again for the First Time*. Each year we run small-group ideas past the peer ministers, and they tell us what will fly."

Each Wednesday, an evening worship service was conducted jointly by the ecumenical Protestant CMC and the Wesley Foundation. The service was held in the Wesley Foundation building, a few blocks from the Old Campus, at 9:00 P.M. During the second week of classes, about twenty people gathered for this service in a large lounge, furnished in well-worn couches and armchairs arranged in a circle around a round coffee table. Some sat on the floor since there were not enough chairs. The room was not air-conditioned and the evening was hot, so two electric fans were circulating the air noisily. Before the service began, a couple of students distributed United Methodist hymnals, from which we sang the first hymn accompanied by three guitars. Gail Wicker, remaining in her seat, asked us to "come present to this moment by becoming aware of our body and breath," to relax our muscles and focus our attention on breathing. She told us to get comfortable in our chairs, straighten our backs, and take deep breaths. "Breathe into our stomachs; let our stomachs hang out." Then she asked us to introduce ourselves and tell the group one thing about ourselves that was unique. I used this opportunity to tell them my name, that I was studying campus religious groups, and that I hoped to be able to sit in on their meetings. The three campus ministers present welcomed me.

Wicker did not give a homily but instead posed questions. She asked, "How can we keep God's song going? How can we encourage another to sense the gift of God's indwelling spirit?" She paused after each question long enough for perhaps three or four members of the group to respond. She asked us to focus on the burning spirit of God inside us. "How can we keep the spark of God burning inside us this week?"

Then Wicker stood at the coffee table, on which rested four ceramic chalices and a plate holding two homemade flat loaves of bread. She seemed to extemporize as she picked up the plate, telling us that the bread was the New Testament of Christ. She picked up a chalice and told us that the wine was the blood of our salvation. "This is an open table. These two [chalices] hold grape juice, and the two taller ones hold wine." (Some Protestants use wine in the Holy Communion ritual; some use grape juice.) She tore a small piece of bread from a loaf and handed it to a woman in the circle, who ate it. That woman then tore another piece from the loaf, said something quietly to the man next to her, and handed him the piece of bread. Wicker started the second loaf in the same way at the opposite point of the circle. At each point of the circle, she then passed the two chalices, one filled with wine and one with grape juice.

As the loaves and chalices were being passed, someone started singing the folk song "Kum Ba Yah," which everyone seemed to know. The student next to me, an enthusiastic singer, performed the hand motions to this song of church camps and campfires.

Most of the service after communion consisted of a reading, or litany, from the book *Song of the Seed*, which contains imagery of "God sitting beside you" in the other people present, "each of us a little spark from the great light." God was called the "great light of the universe."

After the litany was an informal period for announcements. The campus ministers distributed a one-page flier, "Mid Week at a Glance," which listed upcoming events. York mentioned that student volunteers were needed to run the "Household Pantry," a garage and basement containing donated furniture and household items for international students. Huff then announced that it would soon be the Wesley Foundation's turn to serve free hot lunches at a soup kitchen called the City Table, housed in the foundation's basement.

Then Wicker led the group into a more meditative state, asking, "How can we keep the spark of God burning inside us this week?" The responses from the students were varied: "Be kind to people." "I'm a vegetarian, and that's religious to me." "Smile." "Take time to be quiet and alone." "Volunteer at City Table." After this, we sang another song, the last of four hymns sung that evening. Two of them, including this one, were hymns for evening or the end of the day in the Methodist hymnal.

After the hymn, students asked for a "concerns circle," a form of closure they apparently had come to expect. Everyone pushed back their chairs and stood close together in a circle, holding hands or clasping their arms behind those on both sides. About half of those present mentioned things that were on their minds: a pregnant sister due to give birth, a boyfriend's crisis, a father's big job promotion, the visit of Huff's grandchildren.

Fay Warner was a recognized student leader at the Wesley Foundation and an art history major working on a senior project on photographer Andres Serrano, of *Piss Christ* fame, concerning alienation in twentieth-century visual art. As a peer minister, she directed the foundation's volunteers who cooked and served free lunches at the City Table. She was also a member of a small spirituality group run by Wicker. Warner had just made the decision to attend seminary instead of law school, and campus ministers who knew her, especially Wicker, were very proud of her.

Warner, reared a Roman Catholic, assumed that she "had a larger spirituality than most do in high school. I actually thought about God and prayed from time to time. I was moved by thoughts of God and knowing there was a God."

When she arrived at the university, she "went to the Newman Center and really liked it. Everyone's friendly, and the priests are really liberal. It's a really nice Newman Center, and I did a lot of stuff there. A woman in my dorm suggested that because I talk about spirituality issues that I talk to Lowell [York]. She was Presbyterian and knew Lowell. Lowell suggested that I do peer ministry in his program. Meeting Lowell was the first contact I ever had with Protestantism. So I was a peer minister with Lowell. Those peer ministers meet weekly in group and each work on their own ministry project. I liked it, and as I learned about Protestants I had this complete breakdown in belief in the Catholic Church and Catholic theology."

She enumerated things about Catholicism she questioned, such as "papal infallibility, celibate clergy, salvation through the sacraments. For me all the issues, outside the sacraments, stem from the pope. There is no democracy. Celibacy doesn't *have* to be. It's the pope's decision. And the worship is vacuous compared to Protestants', and it's all ritual. I went to Lutheran, Baptist, and UCC [United Church of Christ] worship once each during my first year. I liked the way Protestants spoke about the Bible. I didn't see much spirituality at the Newman Center. It's all about fellowship. I never felt attached to the clergy even though my uncle is a priest and my aunt a nun. My sophomore year, I looked for a church, and I chose Disciples of Christ, and I'll be ordained in that. I was baptized a Disciple during my sophomore year, and I go to the Disciples church near campus. My mom's upset, but it's her issue, not mine. My dad's ecstatic because at least I'm a spiritual person.

"Back then I wanted to be a lawyer. I thought about seminary on and off, but I was afraid of the idea because it's a lot bigger deal to go to seminary than into law. It's a whole different life. Clergy can hide, I guess, but it's harder." For Warner, "hiding" meant "self-deception." "Law school doesn't demand that you open yourself up to core issues. This year in Spiritual Growth Group, Gail [Wicker] has been real important. She's not much for details—Cal [Huff] is—but she's into growth, honesty, the continuing process of going forward. I used to be repelled by New Age stuff, and Gail is New Agey. So we did a meditation on television, and I was reading Paul Tillich for my honors thesis. I almost heard a voice that said, 'Don't go to law school; do what you really want to do.' In peer ministry group, I said, 'This is a big week; I realized I don't have to go to law school.' I felt really free.

"Life has changed so much for me now that I've let God be in control." What does that mean? "It means being open to God's voice. That your life is given to you by God, and the best life and happiness is a life in which I'm a tool of God and not reaching out in self-will to try to change and manipulate things. God's in control. I can go to seminary, and it will work out.

"I was meditating on TV vegging. It came to me, 'Why do I want to invest in a fallen economy, a consumer culture?' I was worried in law I'd help people file for bankruptcy and get divorces so that I can buy things from Crate & Barrel. I'll live eighty to ninety years. Why spend that time full of fear, accumulating stuff, and drafting wills?"

Warner was one of the majority of students I talked to about religion who used the term "spirituality" to describe their religious beliefs, experiences, and activities. Her take on what spirituality is and how it is made manifest in people's lives was influenced greatly by her conversations with Wicker and her participation in Wicker's Spiritual Growth Group. For Warner, spirituality is a "relationship with God in all things. In relationships, in what you do to yourself, how honest you are with yourself. What kind of self-talk you do. What you do to the environment."

Warner expressed appreciation for the programs offered by the Wesley Foundation. "Wednesday night worship is number one. A lot don't go to church on Sunday. I love it because there's a wonderful sense of community. It's informal with communion every week. I'm used to that. I like the messages from Cal, Gail, Emma [York's associate campus minister], and Lowell a lot. And there's a lot of sharing.

"Second, is getting to live at Wesley. Peer ministry is really a good intense community, with responsibility. It's learning how to deal with people, learning to share and be giving both materially and spiritually. The big thing is learning to have respect for people, even if they're not as smart or grew up on a farm.

"Also, having the resources of Cal and Gail. The United Methodist Church spends a lot of money on us. That's two full-time salaries, and I can just stop by and chat with them.

"And then all the people I've met who share liberal Christianity. Some try it here, and realize they need to get to Campus Crusade. I've learned that radically different interpretations of the Bible just don't mix. I've never once seen it work at Wesley that someone who believes the Bible is the unerring word of God stays."

Warner has been on the staffs of various popular off-campus retreats held for students by Protestant campus ministries, and she described the retreat experience in this way: "I like it. It's focused on issues that most students deal with. One theme over and over again is finding your own instead of your parents' religion. We always hear about the transition from high school to college: thinking on your own, developing a mature sense of God, making a *choice* to be a religious person instead of just going along with your parents. We develop a true sense of community. We're all stuck at the state park.

"My number one experience in campus ministry here has been community. I've found my best friends here. The Greeks [fraternities and sororities] are big here for community. I was really lonely until I found a religious community."

Warner resembled many of the other undergraduates I got to know at WU in that her denominational identity was fluid; she went from Roman Catholicism and the Newman Center to the ecumenical mainline Protestant and then the Wesley Foundation peer ministry staffs, and she joined the Christian Church (Disciples of Christ) denomination. Another student was a member of an Esoteric church in her home city but attended Wicker's Spiritual Growth Group at the Wesley Foundation every week. Another student who was quite heavily involved in Campus Crusade attended a Newman Center retreat; she had made a deal with her roommate that she would go to a Newman Center retreat if her roommate would go on a Campus Crusade trip. A peer minister at the Lutheran Campus Ministry was also active in InterVarsity, another was Presbyterian, another was Disciples of Christ. A peer minister at the CMC was Roman Catholic. A staff member of InterVarsity worked part-time as the secretary at the Hillel Jewish Student Center.

Lowell York, a Presbyterian minister and director of the ecumenical CMC, disagreed with campus ministers who "have denominational identity as a controlling priority. Students don't think that way. Denomination doesn't seem to matter to them at all. I can't believe campus ministers who know this don't put more pressure on their denominations to be more involved ecumenically. Well, I know why: The money comes from the top down in denominations. It's top-down decisions that hold ministers and ministries loyal. At the grass roots, we all know it's an ecumenical situation."

Two realities of campus ministry at WU stood out. The first was how few undergraduates participate in campus ministry activities of any kind offered by any organization. Warner, as a peer minister responsible for planning programs and recruiting students for them, had opinions on this topic: "I wish I knew why more students aren't involved. This is the first time people can choose to go to church, and they're working with their old expectations of church that it's boring, dry, and prudish. And now they're ready to cut loose and wouldn't even check a place like Wesley out. Also, most eighteen- and nineteen-year-olds have not had a huge crisis yet. There's not so much reason to find God. They don't have kids or are married yet. Religion's just not considered cool. You're taught you're going to college to drink, have sex, set your own schedule—no one to tell you what to do. And there's a huge bar culture here."

Professor Katherine Franson, in an academic skills class with about seventy diverse students, presented the "wellness model" that student life officers use to develop and enrich dormitory policies and programs. One of the twelve aspects or dimensions of wellness, along with the "social" and "sexual" aspects, was the "spiritual" dimension. It was included as the outside of twelve concentric circles in a diagram Franson handed out. "Why," she asked students, "do you think it's last, in the outer circle?" Students' responses to this question addressed their lack of interest in religious activities: "We're not willing or able to articulate our life's purpose yet." "The word 'spiritual' makes us think of church, and we had to go to Catholic church all the time, and when I got here I don't want to go anymore." "It takes until you're older. It may take losing someone or tragedies to make us interested in church." "We're so caught up in everything we need to do—see our adviser, go to class, go out, hang out with friends. We know we can always think about religion when we want to." When Franson asked the group how many "do religious groups or activities regularly," about ten raised their hands.

The second obvious characteristic of virtually all religious activities on campus was that they drew many more women than men. "We always notice that here," said Warner. " 'It's all chicks!,' we say. Throughout life women are more thoughtful; they're better students. Women think more abstractly than men. A mature spirituality requires abstract thinking. Also, women are socialized to be nice and therefore drawn to the church. Also, women are into community more than men. These religious organizations are community- and feelings-based. They revolve around real relationships, and relationships are so important to women."

Ian Stimpson, an engineering major and an experienced peer minister at the Wesley Foundation, had this take on gender dynamics in campus ministries: "I think part of it is that most friendships between men don't go very deep. With women relationships tend to go deeper. A guy will come to open house with all these friendly people, and he'll look out of place. Men just don't know how to react to the atmosphere. Men just aren't used to in-depth relationships. I had one [in-depth relationship] in high school, certainly not with my parents. I just called him (after more than a year), and one of the first things he asked me was 'Any personal insight?' Guys come from high school and don't know how to achieve those in-depth relationships. A lot of guys come here with a woman, and they can fit in because women bring them out of their shells. We try more active, low-interaction stuff, and it's still hard. In-depth relationships are key. That's what brings people back. That's why they come."

Jerry Rasmussen, a lay minister on the Newman Center staff, explained why the center's programming attracted more women than men. "The retreats and the semester-break service trip to Mexico had a majority of women participating. A lot of men are OK with just weekly liturgy level of involvement. Women have more freedom to be relational, and in peer culture, women have more freedom to take emotional risks. I reflect a lot on the question, What in our institutional church appeals to the masculine? It's all very feminine. Our Rite of Christian Initiation training group [for adults interested in joining the church] was experiencing one of these rites and reflecting on it. It was touchy-feely. I thought about the men in my family, and I couldn't imagine them sitting through this. I'm into experiential education, but this was feminine. Maybe this is a pejorative way to talk about it, but it just won't attract men. One man there pushed us for more content—not so much sharing. I had a good discussion about this with a priest recently. He thinks what really attracts male students is the structure, and 'you'd better not mess with it!' Maybe more focus on mission would attract men. What are we *doing*? Maybe working together on a project. So I think the Newman Center, with its weekly liturgies, has a kind of inroad to male students that the Protestant ministries don't."

Despite Fay Warner's take on the Roman Catholic Church, more undergraduates participated in the Newman Center's worship services and programs than in those of any other CMA organization. Approximately 1,200 undergraduates attended a week's worth of masses at the center. University demographics were in the Newman Center's favor: 30 percent of the fall 1996 freshmen for whom SAT/ACT religious profiles were available indicated that they were Roman Catholic (35 percent indicated affiliation with mainline Protestant denominations; 5 percent noted affiliation with what I consider conservative Protestant denominations; and 2 percent were Jewish).

The center, located in a spacious contemporary building near the Old Campus, had a large staff and a busy schedule of programs. There were six full-time staff members: three ministers, two of them priests, a music director, a secretary, and a building coordinator/janitor. In addition, three professionals worked at the center part-time: a marriage-preparation lay minister, a pastoral counselor, and a public relations and development officer.

The priests conducted a eucharistic liturgy every evening in the main chapel, two on Saturday evenings, and two on Sunday mornings. A more informal Eucharist held in the main lounge at 10:00 on Thursday evenings was popular with students. At the Thursday evening service, the congregation of about forty, half of them men, sat in armchairs or on the floor, with the presiding priest robing and then taking a seat in the middle of the room behind a small table on which rested bread and wine in glass dishes and chalices. Some present looked exhausted, but others looked lively.

The congregation was full of good singers who seemed to like the contemporary hymns that were chosen. The sermon was usually a short presentation designed to elicit student comments. George Leister, a priest on the center staff, began one sermon with reflection on a parable in Luke about a traveler who is persistent in asking for hospitality. Leister asked those present to reflect on prayer, on their asking God for things and God never refusing. "When people come to us and say they don't know how to pray, that they feel lost, that they are thinking of ending it all—and that's no one in this room, right? [nervous laughter]—I don't tell them, 'Oh, God loves you.' Instead I tell them to go to a place that's sacred to them and to ponder God's presence. I know you know these places. Where do you go when you need to find God? To feel good? To pray? To get rid of the down, the blues? My place is walking around the university. This is an amazing place. I've lived in a small town, and there a cultural event happened about every three months. Here there are five or six a day. Think of all the ideas generated here, of all that's gone on in these blocks. So where are your sacred places?" About fifteen students spoke, naming places that were special to them: "the forest," "by the river," "under my piano," "my car," "an outdoor basketball court late at night," "a church," "my grandparents' farm," "my backyard."

After this part of the service, Leister turned immediately to intercessory prayer, and about fifteen students offered petitions for grandparents, families in difficult times, a roommate facing five exams, student leaders of the upcoming retreat, a cousin who was getting married, the football team, a brother going on his first date, a friend who'd been in a car accident, a little brother who was doing badly in school, "not letting the Cards [the St. Louis Cardinals baseball team] suck again this year," the pope's health, and safe travel. The full eucharistic liturgy from a contemporary service book was used, and those present passed the bread and wine around the room, serving one another.

Like most other campus ministries at wu, the Newman Center organized or sponsored several types of small groups. The Justice and Peace Group, the Relationships and Sexuality Group, and the Ethics Discussion Group met every other week. The latter was intended to stimulate an interdisciplinary dialogue on current controversial issues. One of the first meetings of the fall semester was on abortion.

The most popular small groups at the center, however, were faith-sharing groups. The first faith-sharing group had started several years earlier when a group of students met to talk about converting to Catholicism and decided to continue meeting. According to James Milligan, director of the center, students used faith-sharing groups to talk about "whatever is going on with them: relationships, school problems, family concerns. They don't have to commit themselves to addressing a particular set of concerns and to attending a public program that addresses them—a group on relationships, for example."

One faith-sharing group composed of undergraduate students met without a center staff member at 9:00 on Thursday evenings in a basement room furnished with comfortable old couches and overstuffed chairs. This group of four men and two women had worked together the previous year as the leadership team for a Newman Center retreat. They had decided to keep meeting even after the retreat was over.

At one meeting in November, everyone sat with their coats on their laps because it was chilly. These students, like most of the others I approached at WU, listened carefully to my explanation of the research project and then welcomed me to observe their meeting. They began by reading short commentaries and discussion questions from a study guide based on the week's lectionary readings. The first text was a passage from Proverbs about the good wife. The commentary noted that women in the text are praised for things other than their appearance, and discussion questions asked the group to think about how our culture glorifies youth and beauty. No one present eagerly engaged this topic.

The second pericope was the parable of the talents. The commentary asked the students to think about what their talents were. This initiated a discussion of their career plans. One of the women had just changed her major from speech pathology to education and was doing a practicum in a first-grade class. She was struck by the children she saw who came from difficult situations. They came to school dirty, with torn clothing. One of these children often laid his head on his desk. She had approached him recently and asked if he'd like to read with her, and he had brightened up. He asked her if she'd be back. She admitted being overwhelmed by these children. She wondered if she was simply afraid to get involved in their lives.

One of the men confided that he wanted to be a writer. "But what if I fail?" His friends in the group immediately began to suggest other career options. Another man, a chemical engineering major, reported that he had done an internship the previous summer working with kids and had really liked it. "What if I hate engineering? I need to work with people and make a difference in the world." The group launched into a long discussion of how it might be possible to make a difference in a number of different jobs or careers but how easy it is to overestimate the difference we make if we choose certain kinds of jobs—"cushy," selfish jobs. The time passed quickly, but the group broke up after an hour. Most of the students wanted to be in the main lounge by 10:00 for the informal Thursday night mass.

The woman in this group who was doing the elementary education practicum, Carey Spoonheim, was "raised Catholic and went to church every weekend at a very conservative parish." For her, the Newman Center was a breath of fresh air. "I thought when I came here I would never go to church. The first weekend here my roommate and I were trying to decide what to do, so we went to the Newman Center on Sunday morning and we thought, 'Let's stay for all the masses!' Then we went to an ice cream social where we registered our names."

She now attended mass on Sunday after a period of attending only on Thursday nights. "I've gotten away from Thursday night mass now. There's a different crowd there now, and I've been busy doing my own stuff. I liked Thursday night mass because it was my crowd, a good community, a home away from home. On Thursday night it's more personal because during the homily people can speak if they want to. Sunday is still a performance thing, and I'm sure a lot of people are there because they think they have to be. The priests on Thursday come down more. If I could have the Thursday liturgy on Sunday it would be perfect."

Spoonheim went on a Newman Center Antioch retreat during her first semester at the university. "It was what I needed at the time, a good community-building event. My roommate went, and we had a great time." She described the issues and concerns that people on the retreat shared with one another: "The change between home and college life. At the time, I didn't realize how big it was because I was with a bunch going through the same thing. Also anxieties, fears. The big one is being lonely. That's what I was afraid of. We had been prepared for being lonely at college, but it was an ending to who I was as a person. We also did a lot of silly things not at all deep and spiritual. Played a lot of games, a lot of singing and warm-ups.

"Then I got back from Antioch and was a spiritual junky. I got attached to the Newman Center and to looking at life in a different way. I was addicted to that whole feeling, the spiritual high you get from Antioch. My entire freshman year my roommate, my boyfriend, and I would talk a lot, go to the parks. The Indigo Girls were a big part of that. We drove together to their concerts. They are the most amazing musicians I've ever heard. A friend I met last week says he cries when he listens to the Indigo Girls." Which songs? " 'Strange Fire,' 'The Wood Song,' 'Closer to Fine.' Also the *Rites of Passage* album. We spent one night in the dark in our room listening to the Indigo Girls."

The Newman Center was a central part of Spoonheim's life at the university. She planned to teach elementary school for a while after graduation and then "look for service opportunities, like Newman Center work. I'd really like to do what Jerry [Rasmussen] does for a living. You'd get to work with a whole bunch of different people. He's big on service and justice, which I've never done and don't know much about. Jerry gets to do all the retreats, and that would be my number one thing, along with the service work. I want to be doing good things with my life. I'm capable of this, and I don't want to be doing stupid things like just earning money."

The mainline campus ministries represented in the CMA took public stands on two controversial social and political issues during my stay at WU. The CMA contributed to a fund to bring to campus a speaker against the death penalty, and it organized a memorial for a professor who was shot to death that included a presentation in favor of gun control. The Hillel Jewish Student Center was the only campus ministry organization that seemed interested in electoral politics. Hillel hosted "Meet the Candidates" events featuring candidates for state and federal offices.

Jon Stuba was the mastermind and organizer of these evenings with the candidates. Stuba was an officer of Hillel; student officers and an advisory group worked with the full-time director of the center to plan and carry out policies and programs. He was a political science major and religious studies minor. Like most Jewish undergraduates at WU, he had grown up in a predominantly Jewish neighborhood and attended a predominantly Jewish high school. He appreciated having a Jewish community more now since there was such a relatively small one at the university. Trying to cope with the "extreme culture shock" he experienced during his first weeks as a university student, he went to Hillel to "be with other Jews. I went to Hillel to meet people and to eat good food away from the dorms, and it kind of grew on me. My first year was the greatest college year I've had. But if you don't find an organization you can belong to, you're in trouble right off the bat."

He also got involved during his first semester in the American Israel Public Affairs Committee, a pro-Israel lobby, and at Thanksgiving time, he went to Israel with a group of U.S. college students. "Israel was never a big deal to me before that first Thanksgiving break." The Hillel Center encouraged student travel to Israel.

Stuba and his family went to a Conservative synagogue, and he was bar mitzvahed. Now his parents let him make his own decisions. "They told us that at home you will do as we ask, but here I'm on my own." After he discovered Hillel and his interest in politics, including U.S. policy regarding Israel, he decided that he would marry only a Jew. In his mind, the maintenance of Judaism over time and generations was Hillel's primary mission. "In college, a lot of kids go away from what their parents say. If connections aren't made in college, they're gone—through assimilation, intermarriage—and pretty soon there's no Jewish community. Hillel is an extended family. You have to be able to walk in and feel comfortable. You can come and talk with someone, hang out, study, with always someone there to count on.

"A lot of students might know we're here, but really not know we're here. They know they can come to services, and that it's here if they need it. Our mailing does that. And that's a big part of it. I put on a pool tournament at a bar downtown for Jewish students and got lots of people who didn't show at Hillel. And we didn't see most again, but it sparked something in them. It's important to do events outside the building. I know Jews who don't feel comfortable at Hillel."

Stuba taught religious education classes as a volunteer at a nearby synagogue. Many of the student leaders in campus ministries provided valuable volunteer support for local congregations. During the semester that I observed the Newman Center, twenty to thirty students from the center were teaching religious education classes in local parishes. Staff and student leaders of Campus Crusade taught at a large evangelical church in town that included Campus Crusade in its budget.

Frank Hirsch, director of the Hillel Center, cast his net widely. Hillel brochures indicated that a Jewish student at WU was "automatically a Hillel member." He tried to appeal to "two different kinds of Jewish students: those interested in a social group, with some sense of Jewish cultural tradition such as meals and high holiday gatherings, and those who are serious about being Jewish." For the first group, he announced Rosh Hashanah events at the center in this way: "On the eve of Rosh Hashanah and the eve of Yom Kippur, our chef will serve up one of her special meals—close to what you would get in your own home on the holidays—and pleasant company. When you want a feeling of Jewish community, these holiday dinners are the place."

For the second kind of student, he held Friday evening Shabbat services twice a month and met every Saturday afternoon with a small Torah study group that read passages from the Torah in English and then discussed them. "It's a very nice thing, sit around a table on the Sabbath. We are, all of us, at CMA, fighting mainstream American culture.

"Hillel especially is fighting Jewish assimilation. And it's also a time for students to establish independence from parents, and often the cost of that is their Jewish identity. If we're not here, what's around that's Jewish? What's around that looks like home, that's theirs? They see Hillel as their place; some go to synagogue, but they don't see it as theirs. This place is student-owned. Otherwise, between the age of thirteen—bar mitzvah, bat mitzvah—and thirty, without Hillel, there would be no involvement in a Jewish community. And at thirty, they'll be making decisions and have responsibilities for relationships, families, spouses."

Most campus ministries did not "compete" with local congregations but rather supplemented them. But there were exceptions. Besides Hillel's Shabbat dinners and services, the Newman Center, the two Lutheran campus ministries, and the bilingual Chinese church, pastored by a Christian Reformed campus minister, held worship services on Sunday mornings at the same time that local congregations were holding services. Sunday services at the campus ministries tended to include university faculty and staff as well as students.

On the Margins

The Chinese church, which met in the Wesley Foundation building, had more graduate than undergraduate student members. This was not surprising since the vast majority of international students at WU were enrolled in graduate or professional schools. International students had access to a variety of organizations on campus and various kinds of religious groups in the city. There were student clubs based on country of origin, such as the Japanese Club and the Chinese Club. There was a Muslim Student Association, but it did not sponsor religious events on campus. Muslim students attended a mosque near the campus. The Muslim Student Association made a public complaint in the student newspaper that the university did not offer enough courses in Islam, the history and politics of Islamic nations, and Arabic languages.

Campus Crusade had a person on staff dedicated to evangelizing international students, Joyce Holsten. She had "two premises" about ministering to international students. First, "a lot of students here are from countries closed to missionaries, who have never heard about Christ. This time may be their only chance to hear a rational, sensible presentation of Christ. It takes a lot of apologetics. The reason for rejecting Christ for U.S. students is emotional; for internationals it's rational." Second, "I want to talk with only those who want to talk about God. Out of the thousands of internationals, how do I find the ones who are interested? I joined all the international clubs. One woman in the Japanese Club got to know me, and the two of us hosted a film meeting, and she had Japanese materials. They are so grateful. They get to practice English and learn about Christianity. This Japanese group is still going. A guy in the Chinese church said I could join the Chinese Club. Hey, I'll get the mailing list."

There was also a Zen Center and a Baha'i organization close by. The Baha'i group worked with Wesley Foundation students one day to prepare and serve the City Table meal. About a dozen students from Baha'i wanted to mark the birthday of their founder by performing some service to others, so they called Cal Huff at the Wesley Foundation and asked him what they could participate in. He sent them to the City Table.

Another of the smaller religious groups on campus was the University Pagan Circle (UPC). Many members of this organization were not registered students, and its leaders were concerned that student membership might fall below the prescribed university guidelines for official recognition. The UPC posted lots of fliers inviting people to attend meetings involving "goddess worship, Wicca, Santeria, magick, Daoism, Native American traditions, neopaganism, shamanism, druidry, Yoruba, Shinto, discordianism, asatru." Many of the fliers posted on campus and around the city were torn down right away by unknown persons.

Kate Jones was a sophomore with long straight hair, and when I interviewed her, she was dressed in jeans and a gauze shirt, clothes that could be characterized as typical or not unusual. She said she "started out Roman Catholic, in my early years, then when my parents got a divorce my mom started taking me to Methodist Sunday school. My mom is not at all religious, but she wanted me to be exposed." Jones saw one of the UPC's fliers on campus: "They're everywhere!—and I figure, why not? This stuff interests me. I was nervous at first because religious groups can be pushy and overbearing. I was also worried about being flaky, and there are a lot of pagans out there lost in the clouds. This group is serious. It's an outreach group. Its goal is to educate the public about paganism. I mean, you hear the word 'pagan' and think you're sacrificing cows or something.

"I hoped there were people out there who share my values and whom I could learn from. I hadn't found anybody I could talk to about my pagan ideas: The need to respect nature and respect your place in it. The idea that there are forces and energies not recognized in the scientific community that need to be explored." Where did she get these ideas? "My mother made it clear to me one day that she didn't believe in God. I was surprised. 'Mother, you go to church and now you say you don't believe in God?' She said that God's a convenient fairy tale, but it's really about power. When religions started, there was probably someone who decided to make God up and claim authority.

"I am active in the Pagan Circle because of the people and activities. I've made friends there who share the same ideas I do and that I can learn from. Tom [one of the leaders of the UPC] is a Wiccan priest who's studied for some time and is very knowledgeable in magick [Jones asked me to be certain to spell *magick* this way], runes, divination, and whatnot. And he makes a point to be available to anyone, and Peg [another leader] is very active in feminism. I don't always agree with her, and she gets me angry, but she's someone I can learn from and talk to. And they're not snobs or cliques. They are all my friends now. They are always asking others, 'Why don't you come over for dinner?,' and we just talk. It's fulfilling. Lots better than sitting in your room with a book trying to learn. It's better to have other people.

"I'm not Wiccan; I study it. I don't know enough about it to call myself Wiccan. I don't want to be part of any religion until I know a lot about it. 'Witch' is a bad word, but it's a lot of stuff that I do. Wiccans practice magick, worship the goddess. I don't do that; I'm not into mythology. I want to take care of the earth. I prefer to call myself neopagan."

Was it difficult for Jones to be a neopagan at wu? "I live in a dorm. It's a pretty liberal campus so most people don't really mind. I've never really gotten any grief. You have to watch out for the fundamentalist Christians. They will try their damnest to convert you.

"In classes, people here automatically assume you're Christian. It's not intentional, but it's an assumption because Christians are a majority here. I took one class about religion. It was about the Greeks from classics. It was cool.

"In experimental psych, we saw a film about a famous debunker of everything paranormal, which is ok, but psychic phenomena are a vital part of pagan religion. I was trying not to be offended by his statements that his research suggests all paranormal stuff is false. I wasn't too irked, but it makes me mad that there are guys like this out there who think science can explain everything. My prof seems open. He probably hadn't even considered a situation like mine."

Did she agree with those who characterized wu undergraduates as uninterested in religion? "They might be partially right. The majority of people in the U.S. are Christian, and Christianity is dying. It's no longer a benefit to our society, and a lot of undergrads feel the same way, and they don't have a spiritual side to keep them balanced. Religion to most undergrads is dressing up and going to church, listening to boring sermons. Most are not exposed to the side of Christianity that's more than going to church and listening to sermons. I think everyone should have some sort of spiritual side to them. It's a comfort when something bad happens, like the death of a loved one or you don't get into med school. My father died recently, and I take comfort in the fact that he's returned to nature. Or he's gone to God or to heaven. Students need a balance. There's a hole in you, a big empty space if you don't explore your beliefs and morals. You're stuck with just the physical mundane part of life, and you're out of balance. The fact that every culture's created a religion should say something."

TEACHING RELIGION

Religious Studies and the Courts

In 1963, the Supreme Court, in its decision in *Abington v. Schemmp*, ruled that Bible reading in public schools constituted an establishment, or state support, of religion and therefore violated the First Amendment. But the majority opinion in this case opened the way for the academic study of religion and for the founding and growth of religious studies departments in public universities across the country. In his majority opinion, Justice Thomas C. Clark reiterated previous Court opinion about the importance of religion in history, especially in the United States: "Nothing we have said here indicates that such study of the Bible or of religion, when presented objectively as part of a secular program of education, may not be effected consistently with the First Amendment." Justice William J. Brennan Jr. added that the ruling "does not foreclose teaching *about* Holy Scriptures or the differences between religious sects in classes in literature or history." Justice Arthur J. Goldberg recognized a difference between "teaching *about* religion" and "teaching *of* religion in the public schools."[4]

The Academic Study of Religion

On the first day of class on a beautiful late summer day, about 300 students took seats in a large, high-tech lecture hall. A big section of seats in the back was taped off, and the students sat in the front rather than remove the tape. Professor John Hanson, head of the religious studies department, went through the syllabus for the course, which was entitled Living Religions of Asia, concluding that "this course will be fun. What's the fun in learning about people who are just like you?"

During an interview in his office, Hanson reiterated that the heart of religious studies is the study of "the other." "If you're a Lutheran, you should study others than Lutherans." Since he was raised "right of center"—he has a degree from a large evangelical seminary—he made a special effort to study the liberal Protestant tradition in graduate school before he turned his attention to South Asian religions, his current specialty. One of the senior members of the department, Hanson articulated best and most consistently an ideal of complete objectivity in the classroom.

The topic of Hanson's first lecture in this large class was "the academic study of religion," which he said was "different than being religious. There is a fine line between empathy and detachment. Sometimes the academic study of religion is opposed by people who mean well. First of all, it may be opposed by those who believe religion is something an educated and cultured person should outgrow. They press detachment to the extent of ignoring the object of study. Many state universities don't even have a department of religious studies. They wouldn't consider not having a department of history! They are ignoring a dominant force in human history. How can we understand the Mideast, Northern Ireland, or Kashmir without knowing about their religion?

"The second group is opposed to the academic study of religion on the basis of their religious piety. These people cannot entertain approaching religion with detachment. 'Religion is to be practiced! Don't subject God or sacred books to detached study! It's blasphemous.' But don't despise these people. They are the objects of our study. To them I say, 'If your religion is all you say, certainly it's worth intellectual study and analysis.'

"In this class, we do something less than religion. What is religion?" Hanson, like many other religion scholars, gave a definition of religion formulated by twentieth-century Christian theologian Paul Tillich. Tillich defined religion as a person's ultimate concern, primary value, or final source of meaning. It is a functional definition of religion in that primary loyalty to *any* thing, cause, or value—be it Jesus or making money—*functions* as religion in that it is the guiding value, principle, or commitment around which a person orients her or his life. "In this class, religion is 'ultimate concern.' And religion is something in which people, by definition, must be engaged. But the academic study of it—of religion—falls short of ultimate concern. It falls short of praying although it may ask the meaning of prayer for a given believer or religious community. This definition implies that we are dealing not so much with God or ultimate reality but with people's ideas about ultimate reality. Religion is a dimension of human existence—a value some person places on an aspect of that person's world.

"I don't aim to make students religious or irreligious. We're not trying to mess you up, convert you, or give you the truth. Instead, we are going to study what has been of ultimate importance to people in other times and cultures."

One issue debated in the past by those who practice the academic study of religion is whether it is better to study a given religious tradition as a believer or as an outsider. Hanson took up this issue: "You cannot believe everything at once. At some time in this semester you will encounter a religion with which you do not agree. Can you really understand a religion you don't espouse? Can a Protestant understand an Orthodox Jew? You say you're not religious? But everyone has ultimate concerns! And the ultimate concerns of others may be different from yours. What about the possibility of understanding other people?

"There have been two responses most often heard: First, wouldn't it be better to be uncommitted to any religion in order to best study religion academically? Is the agnostic the best student of religion? Not necessarily. Faith doesn't make it impossible to understand another person of faith. We believe such understanding is possible.

"Second, isn't it necessary to be a member to understand a community's customs and beliefs? Membership is not an adequate criterion of understanding. Many members don't understand their own rituals. We'll never understand a person's religion exactly as that person understands it, but understanding depends, first of all, on the degree of sensitivity on the part of the investigator. Some people who study religion are simply too parochial. They are only interested in their church, or in American culture, or in the Western tradition. Yet, here in the U.S., you see Hindu temples in Chicago. Second, understanding another person's religion depends on what you mean by 'understanding.' Learning about another takes place by working through concentric circles to the inner core. How close to the center of a person can a learner get? An accurate and clear understanding is more difficult the closer you get to the center. The center of a person is profoundly psychological and mysterious. Even I don't understand all of myself!"

Because one of the criticisms of the academic study of religion is that it treats all religions as if they were equally valid, Hanson made one last argument. It concerned relativism. "Religious beliefs and practices are relative to time and space and, in that context, are equally valid. Your religion is true for you and mine for me. Psychologically this is a comforting position: it eliminates the struggle for truth and the need to make hard decisions. Dealing with all these religions side by side in a class like this gives the illusion that they are all commensurate or true. But I included all these religions on the syllabus not because they are true or valid but because so many people out there believe them. I will not try to determine if their faiths are valid or true."

Erika Miller, a student in Hanson's class, appreciated his objective approach. She was a member of an Esoteric church in her home city and part of Gail Wicker's small Spiritual Growth Group at the Wesley Foundation. "I loved that [Hanson's] class! It gave a very objective view of three different religions and really didn't place a judgment on their activities."

But how did Miller know that Hanson was objective? "When Hanson explained the academic study of religion and what was involved. Before I'd always been involved, just kind of dove in, and never really stood on the outside. I think this was a chance for me to look at things from the outside before I dove in. I knew some of the material already because of its use in the Esoteric Church and my own reading. In the course, I grew to appreciate Taoism more and dislike Zen more. I found every time we started a new section, I was attracted to that religion, and he told us we would be."

Objectivity in the Classroom

Thirty-two students, slightly more of whom were men, gathered in a science lab lecture room in an old building for the first class of an intermediate religious studies course, Theology of the Old Testament. Roland James, an easygoing, self-deprecating man in his sixties with top-pedigree degrees from Yale Divinity School and Union Theological Seminary in New York, explained his three purposes. The first was to examine dominant categories and major ideas of Old Testament thought. "Anyone who studies the Old Testament, with or without personal faith, will have to confront the theological meaning of the text in order to comprehend the text."

At this point, he clarified the nomenclature he would use in the course: "To say 'Old Testament,' for many people it implies that there's something beyond that's new and improved. So I think it's better to call it the Hebrew Bible or Jewish Scriptures.

"The Bible can be studied in synagogue and church, but also more neutrally as a cultural document or product. Think of the diversity in English literature over a thousand years! From Beowulf to Virginia Wolfe. Same with the Hebrew Bible. Most often the Hebrew Bible statements don't sound like a coherent theological system. But it has the raw material for that. Ideas of God in the Jewish Bible develop and change chronologically. But the Hebrew Bible rarely argues its position on theological issues. Look at Psalm 14:1: 'Fools say in their hearts there is no God.' This is a statement—a poem—not an argument. The Hebrew Bible is a profoundly religious book that testifies to God actively at work in the world. It is a story of a supreme sovereignty who created the world and enters into the lives of humans. This course need not screw you up on Sunday morning. You will get to know the material and perhaps become more passionate about it. For example, many Christians hear Isaiah 40 read in church on the first Sunday of Advent. I can listen to it, and I don't have to think of the research [in academic biblical studies] indicating that a new writer begins here."

James's second purpose was "to experience the Old Testament itself," and the third, "to encounter representative Old Testament theologians. You are participating in an intellectual quest that went before and will go after you. You'll meet a few leaders of it."

He explained his rationale for choosing required textbooks. The major text was Walter Zimmerli's *Old Testament Theology in Outline*, around which most lecture-discussion classes were organized. James said he only recommended rather than required Brevard S. Childs's book, *Old Testament Theology in a Canonical Context*, because it was "written by a liberal scholar at Yale Divinity School; it has intonations I don't think appropriate for a state university. I learn from Childs but I don't require his book." Some class sessions were devoted to discussion of controversial issues in Old Testament interpretation. Students were assigned chapters in Gerhard Hasel's *Old Testament Theology: Basic Issues in the Current Debate* or scholarly journal articles. Topics for discussion ranged from "the question of methodology," "story and history in biblical theology," and "creation and ecology" to "Is Old Testament theology an essentially Christian theological discipline?" and "How does the Bible present women?"

James had passed up a chance to move to the faculty at a United Methodist seminary because he was comfortable at WU. He liked "not having to feel constrained or monitored by a church and its expectations." His training in the bastions of liberal Protestantism at Yale and Union gave him a perspective on biblical studies that seemed completely appropriate at a public university. He taught Old Testament theology "the way I saw it done at Union and Yale," and his prophets course "is taught the way it might be done at a private church-related college. I don't ask how does Amos want us to behave but *describe* what social-justice issues Amos was interested in."

What sort of pedagogy might be inappropriate at a state university? "Conspicuous Christianizing of the Old Testament—saying that 'obviously Isaiah was anticipating Jesus.' I don't mind indicating parallels between Isaiah and the New Testament. I'll say the church can look at it the way it wants, but Isaiah wasn't predicting eight centuries into the future."

James described a second kind of inappropriate professorial behavior as "getting too personal." "I try to keep away from the personal faith of students. I'm not confrontational with students, though, to destroy their faith. I dissect the text but like to think I put it together again at the end. 'What does the text in its final form say to us?' " As he spoke of his course on the Old Testament prophets, he emphasized the power and relevance of these ancient texts. "I tell my students that we are not a department of antiquities. These [prophetic] themes are timeless. As [Phyllis] Trible said, 'The Bible is engaged with continuing human experience.' " It was in a course on women and the Bible that James believed he most emphasized the contemporary relevance of biblical texts. "I deal with contemporary and personal issues, especially translation issues, and I venture there more of my own opinions. I deal more with what it means to be male or female than with what the church or the Christian should think. I've been freer since my first ten years or so to let students know that I'm a mainline Protestant, an ordained Methodist minister who goes to a Presbyterian church because it's around the corner."

Objectivity? "There's a fine line between enthusiasm and advocacy. If a Shakespeare scholar is truly enthused about Shakespeare, no one questions his objectivity."

Professor Joseph Falk taught courses on Judaism and the Hebrew Bible. His introductory course met university general education requirements and always attracted as many students as the large auditorium in an old science building would hold, about 700. Thousands of students over the years had become acquainted with the academic study of religion and with the religious studies department in this and another equally popular general education course he taught, Human Identity and Religious Meaning.

On the second day of his course on Judaism, screeching microphone feedback announced the beginning of class. Falk immediately began his lecture, outlining the "simple point" he had made the first time the class met. His simple point was actually four generalizations about the Hebrew Bible and the religion of the people who produced it. The first was "Jewish diversity and freedom." His example of a difference of belief and practice among Jews was circumcision. "Is it central to Judaism? No. Only morons claim that getting the end of your dingdong snipped off is central." Second, the only dogmatic part of Judaism was the Ten Commandments. "They are a masterpiece. There is no escape from them. If Jesus, the gentle Jew, affirmed the Ten, then Christianity and Judaism have much in common at their very core." Third, there is one central character in the Hebrew Bible—Moses. "He is the same (three in one) as Elijah and Elisha. God actually took up residence in these three, and all three have amazing deaths." The fourth generalization involved "death and mortality. An unthinkable fact. Judaism (like Christianity) would of course offer interpretations of what death means. What does death mean? We have a limited amount of time to get it right. Every choice is pregnant with consequences. A real urgency to life. The number one sin is to waste time. Don't be bored! (This says volumes about university life.) Rebel! No wonder the three major characters in the Hebrew Bible are defined by their deaths." After describing scenes in two movies (*Casualties of War* and *Blade Runner*), which according to Falk defined the nature of death, he concluded: "The meaning of life is to learn how to die. Learn how to live with death."

The notion that the Hebrew Bible contained valuable resources for his students came across loud and clear in Falk's courses. In a lecture in which he related the story of the giving of the Ten Commandments to the story of the banishing of Adam and Eve from the Garden of Eden, he explained that the Ten Commandments "are a stand-in for the Tree of Life. They in some way function as an antidote to the Tree of the Knowledge of the Good and the Bad. Outside of the Garden it *is* possible to have both trees. Whereas the Tree of Life in the Garden kept you from decline and death, the Tree of Life outside the Garden heals not the body but the spirit. Everyone born will die, but a kind of salvation is possible outside the Garden. Anyone who takes the Ten seriously can be comforted by the following: When life has run its course and it's time to die, if you have lived in accord with the Ten you won't be ashamed of yourself. This is no small thing!" In his previous lecture on the Ten Commandments, he suddenly interrupted himself in mid-sentence to exclaim, "Who can explain these texts? I ain't good enough! I ain't good enough!"

Falk testified again to the literary and existential genius of the Hebrew Bible in a lecture in which he discussed the commandment against adultery. He answered the arguments of some feminist biblical scholars that the Hebrew Bible both depicts and reinforces the devaluation of women—arguments that his undergraduates had probably never heard. He outlined carefully the procedure described in Numbers 5 for judging a wife whose husband suspects her, without evidence, of adultery. "You can always trust the Bible to be right, even if it at first seems wrong," he declared, and then he interpreted the ritual in such a way that it actually protects wives from their husbands' rages and abuse.

I suspect that Falk's popularity with students wasn't merely the result of his profane and irreverent demeanor or his rather light reading and writing assignments. Students I interviewed told me that they often stayed up late at night in the residence halls talking about Falk's classes. Many students had parents or high school teachers who had been Falk's students and recommended his courses.

Nicole Huber, a first-year student, regretted taking the course on Judaism because she got a bad grade. "I loved going to his lectures, but I couldn't get everything over my head down in my notes. I loved Falk. He's so powerful in what he says. He really feels it, yet he can step back and loosen up. I thought he was hilarious. Some of the things he said hit you in the inside, and you could tell he believed it too. I think he's Jewish. I think he's more religious, too. I'm Catholic, but only go at Christmas and Easter. I think he grew up with it. I think he lived his whole life around the Jewish experience."

In an interview, Falk, like James, compared teaching the Bible to teaching literature in the English department. "I think the Bible has to be taught as literature. It stands beside the great creations of the human spirit and deserves a hearing outside the church and seminary. It deserves the same hearing Shakespeare gets. It needs a hearing and a strong advocate because the culture so abuses the Bible in both sacred and profane ways so that its literary power is lost. These kids, many of them, are brought up pious and don't even know they don't know the Bible. The way the Bible is taught in a religious atmosphere below the seminary level is a joke. They're taught that this is what God wants you to do, and in a very one-dimensional way at that. And all these emphases on miracles! The way Jonah is taught, for example, as if the whole deal is about being swallowed by a fish and coughed back up. But what's the relationship between faith and miracles? In our culture, old is out and new is in, so the Bible is viewed as not relevant. I try to raise this question in all my courses: Is this an intelligible book? Written by artists of the first rank? So I do careful readings and analysis of texts for students who don't read Hebrew."

Objectivity? Despite his enthusiastic profession of the existential wisdom and truth contained in biblical texts, Falk's teaching met his own criteria for objectivity because he was not advocating Judaism, his own religious tradition. "I make an attempt to present Judaism in a dispassionate way passionately. And the number of people I've had come to me wanting to convert to Judaism over the years is in the hundreds. So first I mock them, asking them how well they know their own tradition, and then I tell them that if I had been raised a Christian I'd still be one. So I do no missionizing. The only thing that matters to me is that they understand the text. No religion should be taught as the truth. It should be subject to the same criteria as any other subject matter. I felt as uncomfortable teaching any other great literature— Hemingway, say—as I do the Bible. I feel unqualified to teach this kind of genius. I don't try to push Judaism."

Daniel Madison, a senior member of the department, taught a general education class on the New Testament. Madison was worried that students too easily applied New Testament texts to contemporary situations, and he designed a course to take them back, as fully as possible, to the world of first-century Palestine and the larger Roman Empire. On the first day of class in a well-appointed lecture room holding eighty-five students, he explained: "My focus is on the New Testament texts themselves in a critical and appreciative kind of way. They need light shed on them, however, because their world is so foreign. So, we'll look at other first-century texts, primarily Jewish, and slides of sites and artifacts, topography, landscape, cities, etc. I'll also ask you to draw maps.

"I want you to read the New Testament in historical context. They were composed by real people living at a certain time and place dealing with particular situations. We'll see people in Corinth fighting about this or that and the writer trying to respond to that. So think about people, events, predicaments, and happy situations when you read. You'll find people much like ourselves dealing with problems both like and different than ours. The tricky thing is finding how your humanity can groove with and understand theirs and at the same time recognize the gap between their world and yours with its computers, cars, and electricity.

"How we express the truth is always conditioned by the world in which we live. These books of the New Testament are classics not because they spoke in such general language and of such general things, but because they are so ad hoc. Because Paul is addressing specific people. That's why they're classics. They become classics because they lend themselves to reinterpretation over centuries.

"The Christian use of the Bible has created a tradition for reading the Bible that's put a patina over the text. Christians will approach New Testament texts from this traditional viewpoint. How many wise men? [Everyone in the class answers, "three."] What does the New Testament say? It says they brought gold, frankincense, and myrrh. What if two men brought three gifts? All we know are the gifts. Where was Jesus born? [Students respond, "stable."] Well, Luke says stable, but Matthew says house.

"Of course, these texts are sacred to a community of faith, and these faithful want to know what the text means for them. No preacher worth salt is interested in simply giving a historical lecture about Paul in Corinth but also in what the text means for the preacher and his or her neighbors. The art of theology is trying to explicate what ancient texts mean for the faithful today. But we don't want to get to step two too quickly because then anything goes. If we want to be a serious theologian we need to know what the text meant in the first place. If you just want to use the text to justify your own ideas, fine, but serious wrestling with the text dictates historical study. The best analogy I have is concern with the authors' intent on the part of the Supreme Court regarding the Constitution.

"I'm not knocking piety, but how do we make decisions or judgments among them? First, ask what it meant before asking what it means. Of course, in this department we are not in the business of preaching. Our job is descriptive. What did these texts mean in the ancient world? And this semester we will do both a critical and appreciative reading of them."

Because this course met general education requirements, the students enrolled were mostly freshmen and sophomores and from a wide range of fields of study. Of the forty-four who completed a survey at the end of the semester, over a quarter were business students. The rest studied about twenty other fields, from Asian studies to athletic training. Most indicated that they were either Roman Catholic or Protestant. Over half said they went to church at least once a month; nearly a quarter reported weekly attendance. About a quarter of them reported, even at the end of the semester, that "the teachings of Scripture" were their "most reliable sources in matters of truth." It is fair to say that this course contained a significant number of relatively conservative Christian students.

Was the academic study of the Bible a traumatic experience for them? The survey asked them if the course strengthened their faith, weakened it, or did neither. About half of the students said the course neither strengthened nor weakened their faith. Another group almost as large said the course strengthened their faith. Only two indicated that the course had weakened their faith. Ninety percent chose neither "conservative" nor "liberal" when given a chance to describe Madison; most chose "knowledgeable." Two students active in Campus Crusade responded briefly to open-ended questions on the survey. Both credited Campus Crusade with strengthening their faith since they came to the university. In response to the question, "How has your experience in this course changed your view of the New Testament?," one responded: "I have gained an in-depth verse by verse understanding as well as the skills to do it in the future. Interpretation is key." The other replied: "The course allowed me to see the New Testament through the context in which it was written."

Student Spirituality in the Classroom

Lewis Benton, a recently tenured member of the religious studies faculty, offered for the first time a course in Western mysticism. Forty students, nine of them men, packed into a small, stuffy classroom on the first day. More students than expected had enrolled in the course, and there were not enough seats or course syllabi to go around. Benton was formal but congenial as he called the roll, and he asked those who "want to drop after the first hour" to turn in their syllabi as they left so he could give them to others.

He then took up issues of definition. Does "mysticism" include "spirituality"? "The relation between the two is problematic and highly debated. There are strong arguments for there being only one tradition, and equally strong for recognizing them as separate enterprises. Mysticism is private, elite, unique—uniquely powerful, unique experience. It's intense. It's your contact with God after all the cultural baggage is stripped away. It's immediate. So there are these two paths to experiencing the holy, and they are mutually exclusive. These are arguments for saying there are two traditions. On the other hand, if you think experience rather than thought, then the two form one genre."

He noted that students' research papers "should not be about your experience with crystals or the spirituality section of your local bookstore. This course will use the norms of objectivity and academic rigor and apply them all the more seriously in this kind of course. I warn you that the subject of this course can easily lend itself to the subjective. But the paper will not be a personal chronicle but a study that will exemplify the methods and the manner in which we've discussed the material all along."

Most of the required reading for the course consisted of the writings of several Jewish, Christian, and Muslim mystics. A major issue in the course was the use of proper methods of interpretation. "The texts of theologians are more accessible because we are trained in logic and systematic analysis. They are writing about ideas, and we read ideas critically.

"Now mysticism is different and harder because the subject matter is not ideas, and we don't share what the author is writing about. When someone writes about the experience of God, which is outside the realm of ideas, logic, and arguments—something very personal—the text is not immediate for the reader. The text is about something not rational: feeling God. We're here to see how such a text works, to analyze an artifact, and we have to have more distance and exercise more rigor. Say you're studying poetry, which is affective, about the heart of the poet, which expressed feelings too powerful for ordinary explanation. But go study poetry in the English department, and they have criteria for validity even though poetry is intense, emotional, personal, evocative. In a poetry class you're not there to groove on the poetry, to fall in love with nature. You may fall in love with nature, but that comment is outside the bounds of the academic study of poetry. Now, reading mysticism may make you love God more, but that comment is outside the academic study of this material. We need to bypass personal, private, touchy-feely 'Oh, I just love Brigitt.' We have to find criteria for mystical texts beyond subjective response. Maybe coherence is one: the text needs to hold together. How does the fire metaphor work in the text? Does the text exhaust the metaphor? If erotic metaphors are present, is the love of God simply a sublimation of erotic urges, or is eroticism a convenient image used because it's such a powerful experience? Must a text be consistent in its use of imagery? There are other concepts we'll develop, and there are ones we won't use, such as a text's adequacy to human experience, its evocative power, and its spiritual efficacy. I don't want to see the candles in your dorm rooms for Teresa! We can't have this in this class. Maybe in another setting, OK, but not at this university. We can't seek either objective or subjective truth in this course. We have to find some other way."

Benton was not alone in expressing concern that students might focus too much on their own religious experience or reactions to the subject of study.

Along with Hanson, Matthew Schyller, a senior religious studies faculty member, stressed objectivity. He characterized himself as a "lapsed Presbyterian" from an evangelical background who was trained as a historian. For Schyller, keeping students' personal religious views out of the classroom was important. "This is a land grant institution operating under the First Amendment. We have to learn to operate in a certain way here. And I could be called on it if I didn't. I try to deal nonjudgmentally with all material and encourage students to do the same. I ask them to 'bracket' their own convictions and try to figure out what's going on with others and to understand these others on their own terms. This ought to apply to other departments, but I fear that some use the lectern for a pulpit—left-wing deconstruction, anything that may be a metaphysical point of view. I guess I believe this not so much for the First Amendment but for the sake of fairness or objectivity. And I do believe in a kind of chastened, soft objectivity as a historian. There is a place for trying to restrain your own prejudices. I'm very conscious of operating in a situation in which my salary is paid by a wide range of citizens of this state. They are Christians, Muslims, etc. Students have commended me on course evaluations for my fairness. They can't tell that I favor any particular group or perspective."

But, of course, the study of religion evokes passionate and personal responses from many students. How is a professor to handle such situations? "I don't slap undergraduates down who produce personal statements, but I try to help them distinguish between confessional and intellectual judgments so far as possible. I want to better enable them to produce a scholarly product that can pass muster in the secular academy because that's where they are. I may say on a paper, 'I'm seeing in your paper a lot of judgments from your, say, own Lutheran confessional background. Can you try a thought experiment to try to see how a Calvinist, or anyone else, would see it? Can you downplay your own emotions?'"

Schyller taught a course on American religion into which he invited practitioners of several religious groups. These religious groups—Jehovah's Witnesses, Christian Science, and the Church of Jesus Christ of Latter-day Saints—are considered exotic or misguided by many more traditional Protestants and Roman Catholics. Schyller gave religious leaders from these communities a chance to present their religious beliefs and practices in their own way, and he gave students a chance to encounter these religious "others" and ask them questions.

These presentations over the years have been controversial. Evangelical Protestant students have, for example, come with Bibles in their hands to argue about the interpretation of certain passages with Jehovah's Witnesses. Schyller did not let that kind of discussion go on very long. "This way of spending time isn't most profitable for the class as a whole." After a series of general questions from students and answers from the visitors, Schyller adjourned the class and invited students with more specific remarks to talk to the visitors after class. "The guests have always been happy to do so—you can imagine—and many students do so, but I don't stay for it." Schyller expressed discomfort at the idea of a professor asking students, for example, to discuss in small groups during class their responses to various religious movements and perspectives. "It would be objectionable to me if the activity were required because some course would be set up and state facilities used for the purposes of a 'religious discussion group.' "

Peter Martin, too, ran out of syllabi on the first day of his course on Buddhist philosophy. Martin, a quiet, unassuming man in his fifties, was a member of the philosophy faculty. Before him sat thirty students, the vast majority of them men. Seated at a desk at the front of the room, Martin said simply and quietly, "I am Professor Martin. This is Buddhist Philosophy. Now I'll go through the roll."

He told the students what he hoped to accomplish in the course: "I want you to be able to study Buddhist texts on your own. This course is a foundation for your further work. By the end of this semester you'll have terms, tenets, major works, and commentaries. Next year in my Eastern philosophy course I'll be doing another Indian Buddhist text. So this will be a kind of catechism class at first. We have to know the basics of Buddhism in order to go on to a difficult text by a Buddhist philosopher.

"I'm going to approach these materials in the same way I learned them from Buddhist monks, with emphasis on practice. To practice Buddhism one has to first realize one is suffering. So there is a lot of meditation on suffering. When we fully realize we suffer in cyclic existence, we have to realize our ignorance, so we meditate on ignorance. We don't know our true nature. In order to rid ourselves of suffering we must meditate on its cessation—nirvana, noncyclic existence. At this point, Buddhism most becomes a religion. You have to have faith that you can get rid of suffering and that some have done it in the past. We have to take refuge in the Buddha, his teachings, and his spiritual community."

Martin explicitly doubted academic objectivity. "We'll go through the Book of Tenets, and look at it as much as possible from the inside. We will not simply do a listing of characteristics. That kind of objectivity is false. The best way to know it is the way the monks know it. I want you to internalize and understand it fully. If you don't like it, toss it in the garbage. Maybe you'll find a nugget here and there you'll be able to use."

Martin also invited visitors to his class who were experts in their religious traditions. The students were to perform the spiritual exercises the visitors described. He told the class: "I've arranged to have the director of the Buddhist Center meet us at the center and show us six preparatory exercises. Later, a Buddhist nun will be there to teach and, after that, a highly educated Tibetan monk.

"If you want to get the most out of this course, aim at wisdom. You may in the end think Buddhists don't have it right, but if you aim at wisdom, you can't go wrong. If religion and philosophy tell us anything, it's not to waste our time, particularly at this juncture in your life. This is time for a lot of self-examination and thinking about what's really important. Don't go on automatic! Read and study this material, pulling out of it what can be most useful in your life. Unless you're a cold fish, you will not be unaffected by what you study in this course. I know you all have your own value system and on many levels know what you're doing. But take yet another semester to think through things. I'm not trying to convert you, but the goal of liberal education is wisdom. Instead of worrying about grades and money, think, 'What kind of life is the most meaningful?' I plead with you, don't read these texts as you would a newspaper! Don't waste your time in this class with trivialities!

"In every course I teach, I try to find the very best in material and share it with you. So much of academia is concerned with finding everything wrong, finding errors. That approach isn't too helpful to me. Eastern and Western philosophical traditions are both full of wisdom. If you go into it anally, worried only about good notes, for example, you won't get anything out of it. Many of us are unaware of the path we're on. Here we'll get some of the best thinking of the East to help us think through our lives, become better persons, have more meaningful lives. The university should aim at giving you more meaningful lives, not just ways of making a living or getting graduate degrees in philosophy. Take a look inside and stop looking at all the externals. What, deep within you, will make you really happy? Stop repeating the mantras of parents and TV commercials! This is the most important part of your life. All is before you. Don't waste it!"

Although Martin's approach was suspect to some in the religious studies department, others endorsed a focus on religious practice and experience in the classroom. Paul Wagner was perhaps at the farthest extreme in the religious studies department from the "objectivist" or "distanced" approach. For Wagner, religious studies was an important discipline for undergraduates precisely because it brought to the fore very personal issues. "Religion deals with matters that are so familial. It's associated in students' minds with their family upbringing, their past. It's these reasons that make it valuable. It does get at fundamental structures in a way that other studies don't accomplish."

His most popular course was about ritual. Over the course of the semester, he met with students once a week at his home, and they put together their own ritual and performed it at the end of the semester. Wagner described the last ritual they designed as "a kind of rite of passage" and believed that the seniors, who were at the end of their undergraduate careers and facing their own set of complex passages, found the performance of the ritual especially meaningful. "It really resonated with their experience and concerns."

Wagner tried to balance lecturing with other more active, student-centered pedagogical methods. "I'll talk maybe half an hour or so, but mostly my pedagogical style is to push people into thinking about the material. I want to push them, push them, push them. I want to teach them how to think. Learn how to develop their ideas. Come out of the closet with their creativity. I want them to think and write things they wouldn't do in other classes. Every week I require a two-page paper on how their life relates to the assigned reading. I want them to move their heads and hearts around. The heart aspect is a unique role that religion plays in the academy. We're trying to effect change for the better in students' lives. Not trying to evangelize them, but try to get them to open up their minds and hearts. We are too rigid in the academy about that.

"Where do you draw the line between enthusiasm and evangelizing? You have to have your intentions straight. We do have to show our students enthusiasm. It's a delicate issue with no definitive answer. I've been involved in religious practice most of my life, thus I have some kind of faith that religious practice is good for a person. I'm not doctrinaire. I think a person should consciously cultivate and have dedication to what you think is right at every level—personal, philosophical, academic—and if you're sincere about it, and if you don't mix what you think is right with the most destructive part of your ego, it's good."

Debra Shannon had recently been the first woman granted tenure in the department. She was an active member of a local mainline Protestant church. Her course on sexual ethics, an intermediate religious studies course, enrolled as many students, about thirty-five, as the assigned room would hold. After introducing more general Christian, Jewish, and secular philosophical approaches to human sexual behavior, she had students look closely at two issues: homosexuality and abortion.

During the final meeting of the class, she revealed to her students her intentions regarding their learning. "I wanted to pursue three goals this semester, encourage three things. First, that we all listen to others' perspectives on these issues. Second, that we learn to listen to what's behind the voices—how these perspectives make sense given a particular worldview, even if the perspective may be abhorrent to you. And to cultivate a generosity of spirit that would give another perspective the benefit of the doubt that, within its worldview, it may even be virtuous. Third, develop our own critical-thinking skills, so that we begin to assess what others think."

In a conversation with me in her office, she spoke about her vocation as an ethicist at a public university. "My main role is to educate people about people—what human beings are, why they do what they do, how they construct worlds of meaning that allow them to survive with dignity—their need for order to give them solid ground on which to live their lives. And to help students understand what is done around the world. I hope they will better understand that others live under different canopies of meaning, and until they understand others at this level, they won't work through conflict. There are ethical reasons for me to cultivate tolerance. Not tolerance of anything—I'm not a relativist; I believe in evil—but tolerance as a presumption in favor of discovering something good and workable in another person's worldview. And this makes you reflect on your own worldview at the same time. It's never just criticizing another's worldview to strengthen your own. I think public institutions in particular have a responsibility to prepare students for responsible citizenship. The kinds of questions we ask make people more self-reflective, better critical thinkers. Maybe more imaginative about constructing good community. All this is good citizenship."

Students were required to write position papers on homosexuality and abortion and, after the papers were completed, to participate in a large group debate on these controversial issues. Throughout her own lectures in the course and as she moderated and directed student discussion during the debate session, it was virtually impossible to detect Shannon's own views. She presented the ideas of liberal Protestant ethicist James B. Nelson with the same enthusiasm and attention to detail that she devoted to the very conservative ideas of Joseph Cardinal Ratzinger. She did, however, on the last day of class, reveal more of herself to her students. "In regard to my own perspective on these issues, I've tried to stay out of it, but I do confess to trying to steer you between the extremes of rigid absolutism on one hand, and ethical relativism on the other. To the extent that my values have entered into the course, it's been at this point."

Shannon believed that "preaching"—advocating particular religious or political viewpoints—was inappropriate in wu classrooms. She had been criticized by women's studies students who enrolled in her course on sexual ethics and discovered that she was "not on the feminist soapbox." She tried to explain to them that, although she was a feminist, she believed the soapbox was inappropriate. "I assign texts and explore positions that I personally find disgusting. I try to imagine a best possible world in which even these positions can be seen as loving and constructive. It's hard for me sometimes, but I try to shed the best possible light on all positions. I don't want to convert people but shake up their habits of thought. To take responsibility for their own thinking and feeling. To be a responsible moral agent. To have *reasons*."

Shannon wanted students to voice their own opinions. "A wide variety of them participate in discussion. When students voice their opinion, I've been grateful. They get to hear themselves in public, and I can restate it so they hear another say it. And I do raise critical questions about comments. If someone says, 'I find this perspective totally disgusting,' I say, 'Well, say more about that. What is it that you find disgusting? I appreciate your passion but. . . .' I also think it's out of bounds in classes when everyone says whatever they want with no critical reflection. This happens in women's studies classes—generalizations about men. But this self-expression does them no good. It's better to help them find their voice in a more critical way. I explicitly ask students to be respectful of others. There's a difference between disagreeing and treating them like a jerk. There are rules here. You can't say anything you want. I do this to generate a safe learning environment for everyone. I tell them this at the beginning of class and at the beginning of the homosexuality and abortion units. I tell them that they have to be aware that there are people in class who have had abortions and those who have pick-eted abortion clinics."

How did her feminism affect her teaching? Shannon believed that a course constructed around the "normative statements of a tradition" with no crit-ical assessment of the tradition would also be out of bounds in a university setting. Her history of Christian ethics course "goes right along from Paul to Aquinas to Luther. I present these figures as strongly as I can, and then I critique them. Students then have a basis on which to judge that traditional thought. They know it from primary texts and have a chance to see criticism at work. I use other scholars to critique the canon, not so much my own voice. I could—I'm a member of the academy—but in class the power dy-namics are such that they could perceive me as pressuring them."

Twenty-nine students in the sexual ethics course completed a survey on the last day of class. There were slightly more women than men, all between the ages of nineteen and twenty-four. Four identified themselves as Roman Catholic, four Lutheran, two Methodist, and one each Congregationalist, Mennonite, United Church of Christ, Protestant, Jewish, Conservative Bap-tist, Muslim, and nondenominational. Seven had no religious preference; four were agnostic or atheist. None chose the term "conservative" as a self-descriptor; ten chose "liberal." Two chose "born again," and two chose "evangelical." Ten chose "spiritual." Five never attended religious gatherings or worship; five did so every week. Seven participated in a campus ministry program, mostly evangelical parachurch groups. About half said they enrolled in the course because "it was an interesting topic."

How did the course fit into the students' own religious lives and perspectives? None claimed that it weakened their religious faith. All said it either strengthened or neither strengthened nor weakened their faith. All but two reported that the course was very or somewhat helpful in making them think "about the meaning of life"; twenty said the course helped them "grow spiritually" either somewhat or a great deal. All reported that the course was either very or somewhat helpful in enabling them to understand their own religious traditions as well as religious traditions not their own. Half believed the course gave them a more positive view of the traditions of others. All but two concluded that the course helped them to "be more tolerant of other religious traditions." One wrote that the course "made me think about what I agree with and disagree with in my religious perspective. I have to face issues with which I disagree with my tradition and wrestle with them. It has given me insight into other religious perspectives. It has made me grow as a person both spiritually and ethically." Another said, "It has forced me to look at both the philosophical and intellectual reasons why I believe the things I believe *and* the experience I have in my faith personally. But how it has changed my perception is to force me to try to understand the differences in other people's experiences and understandings of the world. I guess I have changed by trying to learn to balance holding what I hold—my theology, experience, etc.—with respect for others' experience and understandings."

An ethic of inclusion operated in the classrooms of other religious studies faculty members. For Joseph Falk, the ethic was so strong that he even included in his Holocaust course consideration of those who deny that the Holocaust actually happened. "In my Holocaust class my students are interested in the arguments some make that the Holocaust never happened. I could laugh that position out of the room, but doing so is inappropriate. Do I instead let these ideas speak? My students are interested in this. Why do some, even Jews, argue this? So I look up their writing, and let students research it if they want to. In a class of 300 there may be 20 or 30 who believe the Holocaust never happened."

To Martha Turner, a junior member of the religious studies department who taught East Asian religion, it would be inappropriate at a state university "to teach in such a way as to not allow the students to think of other approaches. In religion, this is especially tricky because religion is so personal.

"Also inappropriate would be a faculty member who is part of a religious community trying to persuade students to join and trying to pull down other religious groups—blatantly proselytizing. Not that professors don't have preferences that students don't get the drift of. I think it's OK to tell students what religion professors are, but no proselytizing. I'm in a position of authority. What I say could be taken as a sanction. If I'd wanted to do that I'd have gone into the ministry.

"On the other hand, also inappropriate would be a professor who would preach the point of view that there is no such thing as religion, or that religion could be reduced to material or sociological conditions—a kind of militant secularism. I guess it has more to do with *degree* rather than with the content of the professor's beliefs. It's the exclusion of alternative views, religious or secular, that's out of bounds."

Religion across the Curriculum

In a quick survey of the university catalog, I noticed that a number of academic programs offered courses that gave attention to religion, including aging studies, African studies, African American studies, American studies, anthropology, art, Asian languages and literatures, classics, film studies, English, geography, history, humanities, music, social work, sociology, and women's studies.

Students I interviewed reported that religion was a topic in a wide range of courses in many departments. One student concluded that her organic chemistry professor was Christian. "It comes up all the time. He'll say, 'the good lord' or 'You can't change the laws of nature unless of course you're God' or 'This is an argument for evolution, if you believe that.' I don't think he believes in evolution. My Spanish TA [teaching assistant] is Christian. He teaches our class in Spanish about half the time, and a lot of people can't follow, and he'll be talking about God and how to be saved. When he discussed conjunctions he used this example, 'You will know the truth, and the truth will make you free.' He uses biblical quotations in teaching grammar all the time. As a biology major we get evolution on a daily basis, and to me that's an alternative religion. I've never seen a discussion of evolution and religion by students in a class. I just think there's a distinction between understanding the theory and believing it. You have to know the theory to have an intelligent discussion about it. This class is definitely hostile toward religion. The professor said that 'anyone with a brain can see evolution is true.' I've wanted to forget this. I know I've got a brain, and it bothers me that he would influence others this way."

Several students noted that religion was a subject in the required general education course in critical thinking and writing, Language and Logic. Because instructors and students were always looking for topics about which students felt strongly, religion was often the subject of student essays. Students also mentioned that courses in literature, history, classics, psychology, political science, art history, theater, sociology, anthropology, music, and education dealt with religion.

Nicholas Cole, a theoretical physicist on the physics faculty, said that since his undergraduate years he had "been on a religious and intellectual quest. In the Tillichian sense of everyone being religious. Here because of the religious studies and philosophy departments, there's been a cadre of scholars, even atheists among them, who are perplexed together about these things. Since the 1960s, I've done courses with the people in religious studies. There's an interdisciplinary program in science and the humanities that I teach in. For me, the issues are science and theology. One course I've taught takes up the central question, 'What does it mean to be human in a technological society?' I've taught with an English lit. prof. a course dealing with issues of the social construction of reality. The ultimate resolution to these issues is theological.

"Now I teach with John Gilbert [a theologian in the religious studies department]. We'll offer a course next semester that will begin with doing philosophy of science. How is it you can make cognitive statements in science? I've also taught with someone in philosophy. We dealt with, 'How can you make religious statements that are testable?' We had students do a project to find any religious community that makes testable claims and to discover how they test them. Last year, I taught a course with a philosopher, a Jewish atheist, who is concerned with these questions. *The Physics of Immortality* was the main text. We looked at eschatological cults—cargo cults, etc.—then at eschatology in the Old and New Testaments, and then at this book."

The Religious Studies Major

The religious studies department counted about 100 religious studies majors. In order to receive the major, a student was required to take a set of introductory courses in Western and Eastern religious traditions and in theoretical approaches to religion. Then each student was to choose an area of concentration in which to pursue more advanced study. Some of these areas of specialization were biblical studies, theology and ethics, method, religion and the arts, and religion in ancient, medieval, or modern societies.

The department described the rationale for the religious studies major in the following way:

Religion is a major factor in human culture, with the power to unify and divide it. Given the diversity of cultures in a shrinking global context, an understanding of religion and its personal and social roles is a significant element in a liberal education appropriate to the 1990s. The department of religious studies helps students acquire an appreciative and critical understanding of the history and literature of major religions in the East and West, and insight into the meaning of the religious dimensions of human culture.

Why, at a time of employment uncertainty and amid an undergraduate ethos of careerism, would undergraduates choose to major in religious studies? Students in the department's senior seminar wrote short essays about why they chose the major. Their responses were illuminating. One wrote:

First of all, I must confess that religious studies is an unusual choice. There are not very many of us, and we are subject to misunderstanding— every time I tell someone what my major is, the next question they ask is if I am planning on being a minister (which I am not).

I came to the university with aspirations to go to medical school. I had success in my academics on that path, but along the way I took a few courses as electives in the religious studies department and became so interested that I decided to shelve medical school and major in religion. I love all the intangible, abstract thought involved in studying religions of the world. I also see great value in the study of religion because few forces have had such profound effects upon the course of history.

The biggest drawback is that the major does not seem to be of much value when it comes to trying to establish oneself in the "real world." It is not like a chemistry or engineering major, which allows one to step into the job market fairly easily. This makes many religious studies majors, myself included, nervous. I am taking steps to diversify myself to protect myself; I will probably end up with English, philosophy, and religious studies majors and a German minor. This provides more options in graduate or professional schooling and could lead me to publishing, editing, and/or writing.

Despite the uncertainty and anxiety associated with the major, I continue on with it because I am fascinated by it, and I think it is enormously important. The material and ideas I study in my religion classes are some of the most intriguing that I have encountered in my studies thus far, and I find it difficult to imagine myself not majoring in religious studies now that I know what it involves.

Similar themes were present in many of the other responses, especially the compelling nature of the subject matter of religious studies courses. One student commented: "To be honest, I have no idea why I am a religious studies major. I basically stumbled into the major. During my sophomore year, I took several religion classes, and I was hooked. My area of concentration is Eastern religions, specifically the religions of India. One of the reasons I decided to become a major is to learn more about myself and my heritage (I am East Indian)."

In an interview, Jeni Geraud, a sophomore religious studies major, described her journey to the major:

> I was a music major but didn't like the music program here. Then was an open major, and then took a Falk course. I was already turned on by the subject anyway. I was thinking about philosophy, anthropology, different kinds of people studies, then about different kinds of cultures. I even looked at history. I'm interested in why we believe what we believe, and where we came from, and I think religion is a big part of that. For me, religious studies is the best way to study the historical and the present. So when I took Falk's course, he made it so exciting and didn't tell me what everyone's telling me my entire life. I spent days and days trying to decide what I believed, and I cried and cried. It was the first time I ever studied something that I was so passionate about. My husband is a philosophy major, and we talk for hours. I like having something I feel passionate about and there's not necessarily a right answer. I don't like having someone tell me what's right. I won't go into a religious field. This major is for me, my education, and my spiritual education, too. I'm so used to being career oriented, and this didn't have anything to do with a career but with my *life*.

Two other religious studies majors who wrote essays were conservative Christians. One wrote that he or she wanted "to share my faith to everyone. I also want to be sensitive to other religious traditions and be able to show them Christ's love. I don't want to be antagonistic or pushy to those who don't believe in Christ, but at the same time if I did not tell them I would not really be loving them."

Values at the University

The president and the provost of the university, one would imagine, would be pleased to hear what I heard from these intelligent and reflective religious studies majors. The provost, in his short address to incoming students and parents at summer orientation, quoted Francis Bacon: "If a man will begin with certainties, he will end with doubts; but if he will begin with doubts, he will end in certainties."

The president insisted that the university's strategic plan begin with an articulation of the institution's central values—values that seem religion-friendly. In this document, the university declares that it "vigilantly protects free expression of thought, respects differences, and fosters opportunities for all members of the community to generate and discuss ideas." The plan affirms that the university "measures itself by exacting standards, honors high aspiration and achievement, and expects all persons associated with [it] to strive for excellence." It recognizes the importance of community—the responsibility to provide a "safe, supportive, and humane environment" in which people encounter each other "in a spirit of cooperation, openness, and mutual respect."

Top university officials expressed no fear or loathing of religion. The dean of students, Raymond Harris, addressed many of the most important themes of this study in an interview. He believed that this generation of undergraduates was more interested in "spirituality" than student cohorts of the recent past: "There seems to be a bigger desire on the part of students to have an anchoring—religion, values, grounding, a base, whatever. So I went to a Campus Ministers Association meeting. I've noticed more students talking about values in direct or indirect ways, clearly indicative of a need for guidance. They are interested in what's right and want to do it. There's also a lot of hedonism, and wanting a mooring may be a reaction to that. Freedom ain't free! Camus said, 'Man is condemned to be free.' The extent to which people can exercise freedom depends on what they believe."

What kind of religious activities or organizations on campus did Harris, as chief student affairs officer, think might be inappropriate at the university? "Well, preaching so loudly on Old Main Square that it disturbs classes. Once a preacher was only about ten feet from open classroom windows, and he was asked to move. Once we had Hare Krishnas accosting people and putting up a display in people's way, and we asked them to move. They can't disturb classes, but otherwise we have to live with cults. They can't go door-to-door in dorms but can stand outside them. Asking for money, even on the sidewalk, may have to do with civil ordinance. We only allow solicitation of money in the Union if the group is recognized by Student Activities."

But Harris recognized the overwhelmingly Christian culture and assumptions of the place. "There needs to be more attention on our part to expanding religious options. More students now are Islamic, for example; more are aware now of Ramadan, for example." I told him about a student I had interviewed the day before who said that there was an assumption at the university that everyone was Christian. "Yes, that's what I'm talking about.

We know everyone isn't Christian, but we don't sound as if we know all the time."

Since I am sensitive to critics of universities who argue that Christianity is somehow discouraged there and that Christians are excluded from the center of university life, I asked a member of the InterVarsity staff if she believed WU was hostile to religion. I told her that some believed it was. "Really?," she blurted. "I'd say they don't know what hostile is. This is a big enough place, and the administration is open. It's hard at a state school to take down religion because it's such a big place."

CONCLUSIONS

The state of religion at WU may be summed up in economic terms as healthy supply and weak demand. Undergraduate students found no shortage of well-designed and well-publicized religious groups and activities from which to choose should they be so inclined. University officials, especially those in the student services departments, offered assistance to these organizations and encouraged them, not in the least part because student services personnel believed that religious organizations and their leaders were allies in the war on binge drinking. The WU administration was dedicated to the free-expression emphasis of recent Supreme Court decisions and seemed unconcerned by the "most-favored" status given to evangelical Protestantism by the athletics department and to the mainline CMA by Admissions and some student services departments.

The religious organization field at WU was dominated by Christian groups, just as the university's ethos was dominated by Christianity. This became apparent as I interviewed students in marginal religious organizations who spoke of the assumption at the university that "everyone was Christian." The strongest non-Christian player was Hillel, organized around a model in many ways like the campus ministries of the mainline Christian denominations. The other major camp of Christian groups, some associated with denominations, was evangelical. The largest evangelical groups were the nondenominational parachurch groups, Campus Crusade for Christ and InterVarsity.

Differences between the mainline and parachurch ministries were striking, especially differences in the training and institutional expectations of campus ministers. Parachurch groups did not require formal graduate or professional education for their ministers. Undergraduate student leaders interested in becoming parachurch campus ministers moved into staff ministry positions, where they continued to be taught and mentored by senior staff. The Campus Crusade staff meeting I attended, for example, was devoted to both program planning and strategy and theological education. On that day, one staff member took his turn telling the story of his religious life, then the others responded and asked questions. This was followed by a study session on the meaning of grace led by Carla Bohn, whose primary responsibility as a senior staff member was the "personal ministry training" of students and junior staffers. Those on the staffs of parachurch groups were required to raise their own salaries. Luke Carson, who directed Athletes in Action, reported that finances were always on his mind. He had to raise all of his salary and expenses, plus 12 percent off the top that went to the Campus Crusade headquarters in Orlando, Florida. Like other parachurch ministers, he raised money from individuals and churches, soliciting pledges made to him personally.

In the mainline denominations, those in full-time positions were most often ordained ministers who had received extensive professional training in seminaries or divinity schools before they were hired. Some had graduate educations. They were salaried employees of either the church bodies themselves or the local campus ministry organization. It is now more likely than it was in the past that campus ministers in the mainline would be expected to do fund-raising and institutional development work, but the mainline ministries at WU were not dependent on such efforts. Ministry to university students was considered a church-wide responsibility and was financially subsidized by local, regional, and national church organizational structures and budgets.

The parachurch ministers I observed were all young and wholesomely attractive. It was impossible to know most of the time how to reach them because they did not have "offices." Their primary responsibility was student contact, so they were usually somewhere on campus. University facilities, especially dormitories and the Student Union, pizza restaurants and coffee shops, and their own apartments and homes housed their work and worship. Their success was measured by their ability to raise their own salaries, to initiate and sustain contact with a large number of students, and to recruit and mentor potential new ministers.

The mainline ministers I observed were mostly men over forty years old. They were easy to contact because they had secretaries and offices in campus ministry centers or buildings that were owned and maintained by a church body or the ministry itself. Their primary responsibilities were the planning and implementing of programs for students, the managing of building use and maintenance, denominational relations, long-range planning, and fund-raising. They worked with boards of directors and denominational oversight committees. They worried about gaining moral and financial support for constructing new buildings or making expensive repairs to old, crumbling buildings, lobbying the denomination for continued or improved financial support. Not often on campus, they nevertheless understood that outreach to faculty, staff, and graduate students was also part of their mission.

Professional excellence for mainline ministers consisted of having a degree from a good theological school and a position at a well-established and relatively prosperous campus ministry organization within their denomination or an ecumenical campus ministry supported by several denominations. Successful mainline ministers also had good relations with influential people at the university and in the churches. They were responsible for making financial and program reports to the denominations that included a record of student attendance at these programs.

Although radically different models separated the parachurch and mainline ministries, they were united in one primary goal. Both wanted to, and believed they in fact did, offer undergraduates an alternative life-style or culture. Parachurch ministers were worried about an undergraduate culture marked by the use of alcohol and drugs and sexual relations outside of monogamous heterosexual marriage. They were afraid that pressures on students' time and pressures to conform from students' peers would make it impossible or unlikely that students would take time for prayer, Bible reading, and worship and find their primary community among other Christian students. In response, parachurch ministers planned alcohol-free social events; organized small groups of students for study, prayer, and sharing; and encouraged students to set aside time each day or the entire Sabbath for religious reflection, study, and conversation. They warned students not to take too much pride in good grades or physical beauty. They celebrated when parachurch men and women dated and married each other.

Mainline campus ministers were very critical of an undergraduate culture they described as careerist, materialistic, fast paced, and shallow. Blaming society at large and the students' "boomer" parents, mainline professionals worried that students would fold under enormous pressures to make good grades, get good jobs, and maintain comfortable life-styles—or worse yet, perhaps, that they would *not* fold, unreflectively stepping into lucrative but meaningless careers, unconcerned about their own spiritual health and the plight of those who were less fortunate. These ministers organized trips to poor communities in Mexico, volunteer work at settlement houses and soup kitchens, and "busy-person retreats." Lutheran, Catholic, and Methodist campus ministers manned a booth at the huge career fair each year, talking to the handful of students who approached them about denominational Peace Corps–type volunteer programs, various kinds of church ministries and careers, and other sorts of social justice work. They celebrated when a top-notch prelaw student decided instead to go to seminary to become a minister.

The evangelical parachurch groups and mainline Protestant, Catholic, and Jewish campus ministries attracted the vast majority of undergraduates active in any way in the on-campus practice of religion. The other religious organizations, as interesting and diverse as they were, drew but a handful. In fact, it is perhaps misleading to refer to the "success" of the largest groups because very few undergraduates at WU were involved in any religious organization at all. Attendance at Campus Crusade and Newman Center activities and worship stood out only in relation to attendance at the programs sponsored by other organizations. Probably fewer than 10 percent of WU undergraduates participated in the programs of the thirty religious organizations registered with the university during the months I was on campus.

The students I met who chose to be involved in religious activities on campus did so for both religious and social reasons. Generally uninterested in "church" or "religion" as they knew or believed it to be, they nevertheless expressed keen interest in "spirituality." They wanted to know and listen to God, pray, read biblical and other religious texts, sing, worship, serve others, selectively receive the counsel of ministers, and reflect on the meaning and purpose of their lives. Despite their weak sense of denominational identity, I often thought of how lucky any parish, congregation, or synagogue would be to count these students as members, especially those who had leadership and peer ministry training.

Many students joined religious groups for social reasons. Perhaps feeling lost and alone on such a large campus, some found in religious groups just what they sought: close friends with generally similar values, dependable and attentive adults, a variety of social events and programs, and a pool of good potential mates. It was rare to find members of sororities and fraternities also active in religious organizations. Students generally did not seek both types of primary social groups.

A WU student was more likely to take a religious studies course than to participate in an extracurricular religious organization. Seventeen courses offered by the Department of Religious Studies could fulfill general education requirements. Professor Falk's courses, in fact, were the most popular and largest general education courses in the humanities, with long waiting lists each semester. The religious studies major was healthy, with about 100 undergraduate students taking a wide variety of courses.

The religious studies department has benefited over the years from Supreme Court decisions permitting, even advocating, the objective study of religion at state educational institutions. The meaning of "objective" and its implications for the classroom varied from instructor to instructor. Religious studies faculty disagreed with one another about classroom methods and approaches. Some lectured most of the time; others seldom lectured. Some believed that the religious studies classroom at a state university was the wrong place for discussions of students' personal religious lives; others insisted that personal religious questions and quests were what made the field most important for and attractive to students.

Yet religious studies faculty members approached their teaching with an ethic of inclusion. At one level, this ethic ruled out one-sided or extremely biased presentations of their subject matter. Conscious of the power a professor has in the classroom, WU religious studies faculty members examined a variety of points of view so that students could see the complexity of the subject matter and be better able to make up their own minds. Hence, they considered the "feminist soapbox" inappropriate, as well as proselytizing for a particular religious or secular persuasion.

An ethic of inclusion also prompted the faculty to teach about a wide range of religious traditions, great and small, and to do so with some detachment and objectivity. Although WU and the state that supported it were overwhelmingly Christian, the religious studies faculty were very sensitive to religious pluralism and committed to fair representations of it in their classrooms and curriculum.

Interest in the academic study of religion was not confined to the religious studies department. Interdisciplinary courses combining humanities and scientific disciplines frequently included religious and philosophical texts and perspectives, and a considerable number of departments offered courses that gave attention to religion. Concerning the study of religion, too, the supply side seemed healthy, with a wide range of options available to students.

In all, WU seemed to provide a rather friendly environment for the practice and academic study of religion. From the perspective of the vast majority of undergraduate students, the university's academic and extracurricular programs must have seemed far more interested in religion than they were.

NOTES

1. See Data Research, *U.S. Supreme Court Education Cases*, 2d ed. (Rosemont, Minn.: Data Research, 1991), 89; and Terry Eastland, ed., *Religious Liberty in the Supreme Court: The Cases That Define the Debate over Church and State* (Washington, D.C.: Ethics and Public Policy Center, 1993), 267–69.

2. See Winifred Fallers Sullivan, "The Difference Religion Makes: Reflections on Rosenberger," *The Christian Century* 113, no. 9 (1996): 292–96; Jennifer Ferranti,

"Time to Strip the 'Lemon' Pledge?," *Christianity Today* 39, no. 1 (1995): 47–48; and Scott Jaschik, "Religious-Activities Decision May Force Colleges to Alter Rules," *Chronicle of Higher Education* 41, no. 44 (1995): A22–23.

3. As I prepared this chapter for publication, the Supreme Court in its ruling on *Scott H. Southworth, Amy Schoepke, Keith Bannach, et al. v. Michael W. Grebe, Sheldon B. Lubar, Jonathan B. Barry, et al.* found that the University of Wisconsin at Madison was not required to devise a student activity fee system that paid refunds to students who disagreed with the religious or political positions of student organizations funded by student activity fee monies. This decision will set off a new round of policy changes at state universities.

4. See Eastland, *Religious Liberty in the Supreme Court*, 149, 152, 162.

SOUTH UNIVERSITY

ETHOS

South University (SU) is a historically African American university with some 1,300 students and 80 full-time faculty. The campus consists of 100 acres of land and 50 buildings and sits on the outer periphery of the downtown area of a southern city that numbers over 1 million inhabitants in its greater metropolitan area. The school is surrounded by a neighborhood that was once solidly African American middle class. Since a flight to the suburbs beginning in the 1960s, however, the neighborhood has deteriorated into a high-crime area composed mostly of poorly maintained houses, convenience and fast-food stores, a few gas stations, and a number of churches.

The physical plant of the university represents a mixture of architectural styles that reflect various phases of construction. Although located at one edge of the campus near the main entrance, Stephens Hall, the imposing dark orange brick administration building constructed in the late nineteenth century, dominates the scene by occupying the highest ground and rising over the other buildings with its four stories and tall clock tower. Red brick residence halls dating from the late nineteenth and early twentieth centuries are sprinkled among the Student Union, the library, the gymnasium, and some classroom buildings that sprang up in the 1960s and 1970s and are modern-functional in design. A couple of very new structures of Georgian-colonial architecture sit toward the rear of the campus. A Carnegie Library building, now used for administrative offices, is just a few steps from Stephens Hall. Dedicated in 1911, it has the typical Carnegie appearance of a small neoclassic temple. About fifty yards down the road from Stephens Hall stands Bellamy Memorial Church. Erected in 1929 and named after su's chief benefactor at the time, the church is an attractive colonial brick and limestone structure with a porch roof supported by four massive stone columns. At one time the location of a duly constituted Presbyterian congregation, the church now functions as a nondenominational university chapel. A large multistoried science and technology building is under construction immediately behind Bellamy Memorial and threatens to overshadow the church.

The functional center of the campus is Stephens Hall, the Student Union, and what is known as the "Square," an expansive concrete patio extending from the front of the Union to the rear of Stephens Hall. In addition to housing the major administrative offices, Stephens Hall contains a large auditorium where student assemblies, university convocations, and other plenary university events are held. The student cafeteria and some meeting rooms and lounges occupy the first floor of the Union. The basement of the building contains a snack bar, game rooms, student government and student activities offices, student bulletin boards, a lounge, and the bookstore. The top floor is a banquet room where large receptions are held. The Square is the favorite place for congregating, holding pep rallies, and serving refreshments during Parents Day, Orientation Week, and homecoming.

The university's 1995–96 *Fact Book* indicated that 56 percent of the faculty members were African American and 31 percent were white; the few others were Indian, Asian, and Hispanic. Comparable figures on the students were not available. I remember seeing two young white people on campus during my year there, but it was not clear whether they were students or visitors, and I saw no white students in the several classes I visited. One professor told me that he had taught a few Asians during his ten years on the faculty. In any case, there is no doubt that su is a university composed overwhelmingly of African American students. The 1996–97 university catalog revealed that 48 percent of the students hailed from su's home state and the adjacent state, and 44 percent came from the northeastern region of the United States.

According to an officer at the university's Information Center, SU alumni are important sources of enrollment at the university.

SU was founded by white Presbyterian missionaries shortly after the Civil War chiefly for the purpose of "training a Calvinistic ministry for the Colored Race," and it included a high school division and a seminary as well as a college division. In 1929 the high school division was eliminated, in 1932 the college became coeducational, and in 1969 the seminary moved to a different area of the South—about a year after the Presbyterian Church renounced control of its colleges. Today SU describes itself in its official publications as an "independent, private, coeducational institution" with "Christian roots." The chaplain of the university while I was there was Presbyterian and SU receives some small gifts from Presbyterian churches, but this is the extent of the Presbyterian connection. The Presbyterian Church is not represented on the board of trustees, there are no religious tests for students or faculty, and a mere fraction of the students identify themselves as Presbyterians. In 1995 2 percent of the freshmen and in 1996 5 percent of the seniors were Presbyterian, whereas 54 percent and 51 percent, respectively, identified themselves as Baptists. This is not to say that *religion* is an unimportant factor at SU, but that the *Presbyterian* factor is relatively unimportant. As we shall see, religion, particularly the Christian religion, is a pervasive force on the SU campus, but the school is not defined by a significant Presbyterian presence.

In the sections that follow, the persons described and interviewed are African American unless otherwise noted.

Graduate!

"You are the class of . . . "—slight pause, few responses. "You are the class of . . . ," then a loud and full response came from the audience: "2000!" Betty Sweeney, vice president of student affairs at SU, was addressing a standing-room-only audience composed mostly of freshmen and other new students and their parents who had gathered on this late August morning in the auditorium of Stephens Hall. "There are over forty student organizations on campus," Sweeney explained to the new students, "and we hope that you will find a way to get involved in some of these organizations. We are especially looking for help with the yearbook and the student newspaper. And we hope that some of you will get involved in student government. But your major goal here at SU is to graduate. That is your dream, and that is the dream of your parents and grandparents." During the rest of her fifteen-minute presentation, Sweeney alluded twice more to the dreams and hopes of the students' parents and grandparents. She also urged the students to take responsibility for the success of their classmates as well as their own success.

"If you are good at math, help that student who is having trouble with math. Help others as well as yourself to graduate."

Sweeney's remarks opened a three-day orientation for new students that included sessions on such nuts-and-bolts matters as placement tests, assignment of faculty advisers, and the taking of class pictures, as well as parties, a reception at the president's house, and speeches by faculty, administrators, athletic coaches, dignitaries, and student leaders. Woven through many of the speeches were the same themes addressed by Sweeney: graduate, help others graduate, and thereby fulfill the dreams of your parents and grandparents. This was the message of the varsity basketball coach who also served as athletic director and of a local successful African American businessman and inspirational speaker who delivered the concluding plenary address at orientation. It was also the advice of James Brand, president of the Student Government Association and an ordained Baptist minister, when he greeted his fellow students two weeks later at the opening convocation for the school year. "You have come to su to raise yourselves to excellence. You have come to lay to rest the rumors that members of our race are lazy slackers. And you have come here to succeed. These are your challenges." Brand's five-minute welcoming speech, delivered extemporaneously and with passion, had the rolling cadence of an African American preacher and held the students in rapt attention. He concluded by saying: "There is an attitude that cannot prevail here, and that is the attitude that I can make it alone. We must help each other. We must do it together. And you must keep before you your one true goal: graduation!"

The administration at su has been concerned about the low retention and graduation rates at the school (a problem that has afflicted many other schools across the country), so an office was established to track students' progress through their college years and funding was obtained to investigate remedies for the low rates. Of the 382 freshmen who entered su in the fall of 1991, 19 percent graduated in four years or less and 30 percent graduated in five years. Of that class, 77 percent returned for their second year, 58 percent for their third year, and 44 percent for their fourth year. The message at orientation—graduate and help others graduate—clearly was connected to this statistical profile.

The exhortation to graduate and the message that was often linked to it—graduation leads to success, particularly financial success—also took the students' backgrounds into consideration. The local businessman told the class of 2000 in the concluding address at orientation: "You should make as much money as you can [after graduation because] only with money can you pay the light bill and make a difference in the world. God gave you the same abilities he gave the white man, so there is no reason you shouldn't have as much money as he does." Approximately 35 percent of the freshmen entering SU in 1995 were the first members of their families to go to college, 24 percent had fathers who held college degrees, 13 percent came from families that earned less than $10,000 a year and 38 percent from families that earned less than $30,000 a year, and 58 percent were reared by a single parent. It is understandable, therefore, that a large percentage of SU students hold paying jobs while attending school. Over 46 percent of the seniors in the academic year 1996 reported working at least 20 hours a week. And it is not surprising that the most popular major (over 30%) among those seniors was business and that 94 percent of the seniors said that "being very well off financially" was an "essential" or "very important" life goal for them. (It is noteworthy, however, that 86% of the seniors also said that "helping others in difficulty" was essential or very important, a viewpoint that will be taken up later.) The official doctrine, urgent message, and pervasive tenet of the school to graduate and succeed that were apparent at orientation matched the profile and expectations of the students. But other messages and hopes emerged as well.

"Zero Tolerance": Codes of Conduct

James Gray, chief of campus security, gave a straightforward, no-nonsense talk during freshman orientation shortly after Vice President Sweeney's remarks. If Sweeney meant to inspire the students to keep their eye on the future goal of graduation, Chief Gray seemed determined to direct their attention to the present, a present he insisted was fraught with danger and should be closely confined by a code of conduct. Gray warned that there was "significant serious crime" in the vicinity of the campus, including occasional shootings, and cautioned that students "should not frequent the area late at night." It was legal in the state to bear firearms even in automobiles, he said, so students should be careful about their associations off campus. "This is no hick town, like some of you students from New York or D.C. may think; it is a world-class city with, unfortunately, world-class crime." Students should make sure their rooms were locked when they left them. Most thefts on campus were committed by students against students. Freshmen were not permitted to bring automobiles on campus, except with special permission (for example, for those who worked off campus), and unauthorized vehicles would be towed. Chief Gray noted that it was important for students to carry their ID cards with them at all times. Because security personnel did not know new students, they would sometimes ask for identification to make sure students were not intruders on campus. The chief handed out a flyer that indicated that during the academic year 1995–96, crime on campus resulted in 1 case of aggravated assault, 5 arrests for weapon possession, 39 cases of theft, 10 judicial hearings for drugs, and 14 judicial hearings for alcohol violations. Gray fired a last warning shot: "There is zero tolerance at su for drugs, alcohol, and bearing any kind of arms. You are responsible for your visitors' observing these rules."

Approximately a quarter of the 126-page student handbook, referred to by Sweeney and other administrators as "the student's Bible," was devoted to codes of conduct and sanctions for unacceptable behavior. Using the same language as Chief Gray, the handbook stated that there was "zero tolerance" for alcohol, drugs, drug paraphernalia, and firearms on campus. Loud music and other disturbances in the dorms were strictly forbidden, as were overnight visitors of the opposite sex, gambling, hazing, verbal abuse, and obscene language on clothing. An elaborate series of hearings and appeals proceedings, involving both student and faculty judicial committees, was outlined, along with levels of disciplinary action from fines and community service to expulsion from the university. The handbook also emphasized that good taste and self-respect should govern student behavior. "What is frequently remembered is how well students comport themselves on campus and in the larger community. It is, therefore, immensely important that all students display respect for themselves and others, that they maintain impeccable personal and professional integrity." The dress code stipulated that it was mandatory for men to wear a suit or pants and a dark jacket, a dress shirt, dress shoes, socks, and a tie and for women to wear a dress or dressy skirt and blouse, dress shoes, and hose at "all formal university events including, but not limited to, formal dining events, pageants, and those which, when announced, indicate that the dress code is enforced."

Messages of danger, prohibition, code, and sanction swirled throughout the su campus during my visits there, but they by no means exhausted the spirit of the place.

"How *Don't* We Have Fun?"

Margie Haskins, a recent graduate of a large public university in the state, had been director of student activities at su for about a year and half when I interviewed her in the fall of 1996. She expressed some frustration with her job because she believed that students tended to find most of their fun off campus. "They go to clubs [where alcohol is served]—that's their major social outlet. Parties on campus just don't work because the campus is dry." On reflection, she revised her claim somewhat: back-to-school parties early in the fall semester were well attended, but later parties were lucky to draw 30 people and she was somewhat disheartened at trying to organize on-campus parties. In her opinion, on-campus life was fairly boring since students preferred to congregate before television sets in the dorms. Many students worked, and that cut down on their social lives. Basketball games were well attended, as were football games lately because of a winning team. But other varsity sports did not draw large crowds, and intramural sports did not attract many participants. Talent shows on campus could be successful, and regional pool and ping-pong tournaments sometimes did well. Still, the real partying was alcohol-related and occurred off the university premises. This was quite a contrast to Haskins's experience at the state university. "At State people came to parties after they had done their drinking somewhere else. Here they just drink somewhere and usually don't bother with the dry parties."

James Brand, the student government president who during the convocation urged fellow students to keep graduation before them as their primary goal, did not disagree with Haskins's assessment of students' tendency to gravitate to bars and alcohol-related parties, but his view of the overall campus recreation scene was more upbeat. To my question during an interview in the Square, "How do SU students have fun?," Brand responded, "How *don't* we have fun?" He alluded to the partying at the downtown clubs and the attraction of the basketball games, "although we haven't had a winning basketball team in a long time," but he also mentioned informal types of entertainment like ping-pong and pool in the Union, pickup football games on the green spaces scattered throughout the campus, and the camaraderie and joke telling that were common in the Square. Indeed, those activities were apparent during my visits to the campus. The students were friendly and outgoing, and as Brand suggested, they seemed to find plenty of informal ways to relax. The strict behavior code, the warnings about city dangers, and the large number of hours devoted to work for pay certainly did not add up to a dour environment.

Also, the drinking off campus by no means decimated club life on campus. There were eight Greek fraternities and sororities at SU, which required high grade-point averages of their members. Although only 8 percent of the students belonged to the Greek organizations, both Sweeney and Brand indicated that student leaders tended to join fraternities and sororities, and the Pan-Hellenic Council was an important presence in campus politics and the promotion of community service activities. Furthermore, 32 student organizations were officially registered on campus in addition to the Greeks—all of them referred to as "clubs" at SU—including the Science Club, the Student Christian Association, the Shaki Modeling Troupe, and the SU chapter of the National Association for the Advancement of Colored People (NAACP). One of the most popular organizations, both in terms of the number of students wanting to join and the response of other students to their performances, was the su gospel choir.

Fun, Pageantry, and Religion

Homecoming is a major event at su every year that reveals the manner in which elements such as clubs, campus fun, and dress codes coalesce in the ethos of the school. In the ceremonies occurring throughout the event, the school's sense of place in the community comes alive, and the importance of religion to su's identity springs clearly to light.

The su homecoming is a coming home for the African American community in the city as well as for the alumni of the school. In October 1996, this was apparent in the high attendance at the homecoming football game (which su won 14 to 6) played at a center-city stadium, as well as the parade that preceded the game. On that Saturday, one of the streets leading to the stadium was blocked off between 9:30 A.M. and noon, permitting over thirty floats and about thirty marching bands to make their way along a route lined with African American students, older adults, and young parents and their children.

The usual types of floats made their appearance: those representing sororities and fraternities, their queens and kings aboard, and those for other campus organizations and dormitories. The su marching band was there, clad in striking green and white uniforms and white headpieces. There were also numerous marching bands and drum groups with majorettes and pom-pom girls from local high schools, a strut band representing the city's Police Association, Boy Scout troops with official backpacks, and a Brownie group. Three local churches had constructed floats with their names and the names of their pastors written on the sides, each with a waving pastor aboard. A large float from a wedding consultant business carried people clad in formal wedding garb, followed by a car advertising a hair care business. Three floats representing day care centers took their places in the parade, along with a car with the name of a local disc jockey prominently displayed on the doors, a local swing band with a drum major attired in a tuxedo, and floats for the city alumni association as well as the alumni chapter of New York, New Jersey, and Philadelphia. An attractive blue and white float occupied by the su homecoming queen was the last vehicle in line, followed by an African American cowboy dressed in a black leather outfit and black hat and mounted on a high-stepping stallion.

The pomp of the parade was matched by the theatrical pageantry of another homecoming ceremony, the coronation of the queen, which was laced with religious solemnity. An invitation to the coronation in the student newspaper indicated that it would be held at 6:00 P.M. in the Affleck Gymnasium on the Thursday evening prior to the parade and that "attire is semiformal." That evening, male and female ushers in formal dress (the men in tuxedos) handed out printed programs at the gym's main entrance. Most of the men who filed into the gym were dressed in slacks and nice sports shirts and the women in sweaters and skirts, but a number of men wore dark suits and some women wore fancy dresses.

The basketball court had been covered with a dark red plastic drop cloth, and a stage had been constructed at the end of the court opposite the entrance. Three red, spotlighted thrones occupied center stage. The largest throne was in the middle and was draped with pink gauze thrown over two Doric columns; the other two sported white backdrops and a Doric column on one side of each throne. Directly behind the stage and on one side of the scoreboard hung banners for the basketball team's championship years, and on the other side hung a large sign reading "Welcome to su Madness." At 6:00, people continued to drift in—students, senior citizens, parents with small children. On the gym floor, a row of folding chairs in front of one set of bleachers was occupied by thirty young men dressed in tuxedos. These were the kings who would rise to escort the student queens in the ceremony. Across the basketball court sat one of the university's religious choirs, and directly across from the choir, several rows of chairs had been reserved for special guests of the university. The ceremony began at 6:15, at which time about two-thirds of the seats in the gym were filled. People continued to arrive, however, and by 6:50, about three-quarters of the seats were taken. The audience numbered about 400 by the time the ceremony was in full swing.

As an amplified piano played some tunes, the mistress of ceremonies took the microphone in front of the chairs for special guests and issued a welcome; a greeting followed from the president of the student government. Thus began a ceremony that would last two hours and fifteen minutes. There were some departures from the printed program, but by and large, the ceremony proceeded according to plan.

The choir sang the hymn "Holy Spirit," a soft and rolling melody, which was followed by polite applause. A group of fifteen women student dancers, attired in top wraps and skirts, appeared on the court and performed an African dance to the accompaniment of drums. They were soon joined in the dance by fifteen men, shirtless and clad in short wraps around their waists. Women students in the audience laughed, issued catcalls, and whistled at the male dancers. The men were smiling and seemed self-conscious in their performance of the dance. Loud applause followed the dancers as they exited the floor. A recitation of James Weldon Johnson's "Creation," accompanied by a dance interpretation by a lithe young woman in a white dress, followed, and there was loud applause for the dancer's spellbinding performance. Then the choir sang a selection of gospel songs, with different soloists for each piece, and the audience swayed and clapped in time with the choir. The thirty dancers returned, this time with the women dressed in white skirts and yellow shirts and headdresses. The men still were without shirts and again were greeted with hoots and whistles from women in the audience. The dance this time was modern and performed to the accompaniment of recorded music, after several false starts of the tape recorder.

A moment of seriousness interrupted the gaiety. A male student took the microphone to memorialize eight students and staff members who had died over the course of the year. He asked the audience to hold hands and said: "Their deaths have created holes in our lives. Let us close those holes as we hold hands together and remember each one of them." He slowly called out each name, announced a period of silent prayer—about three or four minutes in length—and then resumed his seat in the reserved section.

The MC announced that the "Grand Procession of Fulfilling the Promise" (the theme of the ceremony) would commence. There was a long pause, someone whispered to the MC, and she informed the audience that "makeup is still being put on." There was a delay of fifteen minutes, during which the pianist played a few tunes. The audience grew restless.

The Grand Procession finally began with the appearance of about thirty queens elected by their organizations—Greeks, the NAACP, the Student Christian Association, dorms, and choirs. Each queen, wearing a ballroom gown and high heels, walked through the gym entrance doors toward the stage, where she was met by one of the kings (who were also elected representatives of organizations), and then turned with her escort to stand in a line on one side of the gym floor. As the MC read the names of the queens and the organizations they represented, family members and friends in the audience applauded and cheered. Romantic music played on the piano provided the background for the reading of the names and credits. This part of the ceremony lasted about thirty minutes.

The lights were dimmed, and a student in a tuxedo rolled out two white runners from the stage to the entrance doors. Her Majesty's Court, two runners-up in the homecoming queen contest, strolled down the white runners with their escorts as their accomplishments were acknowledged by the MC and then stood before their respective thrones. Now it was time for the arrival of Miss SU, the homecoming queen, Carla Smiley, and her escort.

The pianist played more romantic music as Smiley entered and strolled slowly with her escort toward the stage. She wore a white sequined dress with a train and carried a bouquet of white flowers—she could have been mistaken for a bride. She had a bit of difficulty walking in high heels, but she carried herself with an air of royalty. The MC read a long list of her accomplishments as she approached her throne, including being a member of the university choir, the gospel choir, and the judiciary board; a volunteer for the Upward Bound mentorship program, the American Red Cross, and the Black Community Crusade for Children; and chaplain of her sorority. After she reached the throne and turned to face the audience, smoke was released on the stage to loud and long applause. While she and her attendants remained standing, the MC announced that the choir would "sing a Scripture," a slow gospel hymn, "Total Praise," with the refrain "Lord, you are the strength of my life." The crown was then bestowed by the homecoming queen of the previous year, and the royal scepter was passed to the new queen by "Little Miss Green and White," a four-year-old girl from the community who had been chosen as the mascot for the event. The audience gave loud cheers for the mascot. With the piano playing softly in the background, university chaplain Peter Adams offered a brief prayer to "God, our Blessed Parent"; praised God for all that was beautiful, good, and strong in Smiley; and requested her protection as she wore the crown for all members of the SU community. With the royalty still standing, a "special tribute" was offered by a female student dancer who moved swiftly across the floor to a recording of "Didn't My Lord Deliver Daniel?," her arms and hands continuously shooting to the heavens in praise. Following loud applause for her performance, the choir sang a romantic song "Carla, You're Our Queen." The queen and her attendants then took their seats on the thrones.

The MC asked if anyone in the audience wished to offer tributes to Smiley. Brand took the microphone to say that he had a small gift he wanted to deliver on behalf of the student body, then he knelt before the throne and handed Smiley a small gift-wrapped package. A young woman walked to the microphone and declared, "Carla, I want you to know that you look beautiful tonight, and I love you. You are my best friend." Another young woman, a member of Smiley's sorority, told the queen how proud all of her sisters were of her and delivered a gift. The vice president for academic affairs congratulated the queen on behalf of the university president, who could not attend the festivities, and concluded by remarking that the coronation ceremony "has captured so much of SU: both pageantry and spirituality."

The MC announced that the new queen would like to join the choir in singing the final selection, "Holy One," as "her gift to you." Smiley then served as soloist for a gospel/blues piece that employed the language of the Book of Isaiah (and of Handel's *Messiah*). Her voice was full, powerful, and emotional. She sang: "When I am down, / you are my protection. / When I am low, / you are my direction, / O Holy One . . . / Holy, Wonderful,

Counselor.... / I'll never forget you, / Holy One." The standing ovation was deafening. Smiley's gift was clearly the high point of the ceremonies.

Chaplain Adams offered the benediction: "God who created everything out of nothing . . . you have brought us up out of the ashes of pain and struggle.... Promises have been made here to you tonight that we will build a community out of the ashes.... You have given us a queen, a royal queen, a spiritual queen, a strong queen." And then to the audience, Adams said: "Be encouraged, then, no matter what you are going through." Accompanied by piano music, the queen and her court and the other queens and their escorts exited in a procession.

Public Religious Ritual

su events such as the coronation of the homecoming queen, Founders Day, convocation, freshman investiture, and commencement were at their core worship services. Besides the obligatory invocation and benediction uttered by a preacher, they included processionals and recessionals, choir performances, the singing of hymns by the congregation, and the development of religious themes by the key speakers. Many of the events took place in Memorial Church. Strictly religious services were offered on campus on Sundays and other days, but religious ritual also pervaded public occasions in which su celebrated its identity and honored its members. The school's celebration of its founding is a case in point.

The rain was pouring at 2:00 P.M. on a Sunday in April as the Founders Day celebration began, but attendance was excellent. Every pew in Memorial Church was occupied, and some people stood in the back. (Seniors, who were required to attend, submitted their names on cards when entering the church.) Faculty and administrators attired in academic regalia had taken seats in the front rows to the left, along with other dignitaries. The senior class, wearing caps and gowns, occupied the front rows to the right. Members of the university choir, dressed in green and white robes, filled the chancel. The procession consisted only of those who would take the platform. The university president later explained that because of the bad weather, faculty and seniors could not line up outside for a long procession.

In a departure from the printed program, university president Janine Bowker was the first to speak following the processional. She greeted the audience and then gave a five-minute summary of the history of the university, mentioning the founding presidents, the Presbyterian missionary heritage, the seminary that was once part of the campus, the importance of the support of su's major white benefactor in the early twentieth century, and the establishment of Memorial Church and its congregation. She then introduced the guests on the platform and noted that the director of the university choir was sick, so a student conductor would stand in. Marking a return to the order of the printed program, Chaplain Adams offered the invocation, in which he praised God for "having brought us from yesterday until today" and expressed confidence that God would lead the school into a strong future. A "Hallelujah" piece composed by the choir director and performed by the university choir followed. The choir sounded professional, singing in clear, well-trained voices. The audience responded with light, hesitant applause. Later in the program, the choir sang a spiritual, "Witness for My Lord," with a male student soloist. That performance brought down the house.

Five guests greeted the assembly. The city's mayor pro tem thanked the university for its many contributions to the city over 130 years and for creating a place where young people could prepare themselves for life. The white chair of the County Commission congratulated the school for having gone far beyond the original purpose of training preachers and teachers to teaching "the worth and dignity of all people through very difficult and painful times and experiences" of racism and racial hatred and equipping African Americans with the knowledge that "we are all children of God." He then read a proclamation from the commission honoring the school's 130th birthday. The president of the student government told the audience that the "founders did not grow weary, nor should we as we grow bigger and better every year." The chair of the board of trustees recalled that 130 years earlier eight students had formed the first class, slaves and the children of slaves; they had "opened up the best of times because they had been through the worst of times" and "brought us hope that the days of darkness are now behind us." The president of the su Alumni Association announced that the association would be contributing 300 new Bibles and hymnals to Memorial Church and informed the seniors that they would soon join a distinguished group of alumni. Like their predecessors, they should never consider themselves average because "average is only halfway from the bottom."

Following the greetings, President Bowker assumed her place at the pulpit to announce that a descendent of the first university president (a white Presbyterian minister) was in attendance. He stood and the audience applauded, then Bowker invited the audience to an unveiling of a portrait of the first president at a reception to be held in the Union banquet room following the ceremony. Bowker then introduced the main speaker for the occasion, a minister of a large Presbyterian congregation in Washington, D.C., and an alumnus of the university and its seminary. She also pointed out that she and the speaker were fellow students at su in the 1960s.

In his address, which quickly became a sermon, the speaker declared that he had spent the best years of his life at SU. At the university, he had been privileged to hear speeches by Martin Luther King Jr. and Malcolm X. He said he unfortunately also recalled the food in the SU cafeteria (the students laughed), and he remembered required chapel, bonfires, and his participation in protest marches and sit-ins at segregated downtown lunch counters. These had become his most cherished memories. He then invoked the motto of the university included on SU's official seal, "Sit Lux," or "Let There Be Light," and this became the theme of his remarks. The white ministers who had founded the school knew that something had to be done, that light had to be shed for African Americans so that they might be set free. This founding light was nothing less than "divine inspiration." The light still shone 130 years later so that "we can keep a focus." He told a story about trying to take a photograph of smoke as it rose from the guns of his friends on a hunting trip when they shot at game but losing his focus and missing the moment. "Whatever you do, keep focused. . . . That is the way to use our light." He warned the seniors that they would enter a world characterized by cutthroat competition and that they should go into that world not cocky but confident because "the light still shines." Above all, he told them, "be a part of something significant in your lives." His voice cracked occasionally, and he shed some quiet tears toward the end of his address. He obviously was speaking from the heart and was moved by the occasion and his memories. He received a long, loud standing ovation. Bowker thanked the speaker and said the audience should know now why she had invited him. The singing of the alma mater, the benediction, and the recessional brought the ceremony to 3:15, after 1 hour and 15 minutes.

A heritage had been celebrated, including the religious dimensions of that heritage, and the celebration had been cast within the framework of a Christian worship service complete with prayers, hymns, and a sermon. It was a framework typical of SU's official public events.

"We Still Take Many of Our Marching Orders from the Church": Community Service

Religion also framed—and inspired—much of the university's service to the surrounding community. All SU students were required to perform at least ten hours of community service per year for no academic credit; students enrolled in the honors program had to complete thirty hours of service each year. Workshops conducted by the Office of Service and Service Learning helped students select their venues of service and instructed them in the nature of their tasks. Students made informal oral reports about their service to their academic advisers at the end of the year. In addition, campus bulletin board notices and announcements in the student newspaper indicated that sororities and fraternities and other campus clubs performed volunteer work in the community, ranging from voter registration drives to Big Brother and Big Sister programs to the collection of canned goods for the poor at Christmas.

In 1994, with the partial funding of a grant from the Ford Foundation and the United Negro College Fund, su created a service-learning program designed "to help students develop a greater sense of self through service learning and community service" and structured in such a way that students might "venture out into the [city's] community and bring all their experiences back to the classroom for reflection." Students could earn academic credit for service learning by taking established courses in the curriculum. During the first year of the program, sixty students were engaged in service learning, and at the beginning of the 1996–97 academic year, seventy-five had enrolled and the same number were waiting for courses with a service-learning component to open. Courses that could be used for service-learning credit included the liberal studies course Identity: Citizen and Self, a course in adapted physical education, Introduction to Social Work, a course in childhood psychology, and a course in community health.

Laura Kennedy and Gretchen Wise talked animatedly about su's community service programs when I interviewed them in Wise's office. Kennedy, a professor of English, was the first director of the Office of Service and Service Learning and was instrumental in securing the Ford–United Negro College Fund grant. Wise was the current director and had been hired by Kennedy. Wise explained that the university cooperated with "fourteen community partners, and the list grows longer each year." She elaborated on a few of the partners. An African Methodist Episcopal Zion church in the neighborhood of the university sponsored a "Kids at Risk" program for 350 students in kindergarten through sixth grade. The goal of the program was to "stop the violence," and it was part of a larger campaign promoted by the National Association of Social Workers. su students who participated in the program used as their guide the association's brochure "100 Ways to Stop Violence"; they rode school buses with the children, brought them snacks and soft drinks, and served as role models. Another community partner was the downtown Arts and Education Center, which in 1996 had brought to the city an exhibition focused on the reconstructed slave ship the *Henrietta Marie*. su students served as docents for the exhibition after receiving extensive training from the museum staff, and they worked with two su history professors on the interpretation of slavery and their responses to the slave experience. "This," Kennedy volunteered, "is education at its best: students learning by learning from and teaching the community." Another example was the "Save the Seed" program begun by a former mayor of the city, which was devoted to helping young African American males develop self-esteem, strengthen family relationships, and avoid drugs and alcohol. In this case, the youth came to campus to link up with role model college students and observe some of the college rites of passage into responsible adulthood.

Kennedy and Wise agreed that service to the community had long been part of the stated mission of the university, but they noted that until a few years earlier, a split had existed between town and gown. Kennedy thought the turning point had come in 1994 when students in a sociology class conducted a door-to-door survey to determine what people in the neighborhood of the university felt was the most pressing community need. The most frequently mentioned need was for a community recreation center, which was recently established in the basement of a nearby building. The survey and the plans for the recreation center became, in Kennedy's judgment, a stimulus for the community service and service-learning emphases at SU. But she also believed that the university finally came to see that the real initiative in community service was being taken by churches in the neighborhood, like the African Methodist Episcopal Zion church, and that such initiative was worthy of imitation and affiliation. Kennedy said that such church initiatives were an extension of the community activities of the African American churches during the civil rights movement. "Yes," Wise added, "and we [at the university] still take many of our marching orders from the church."

There is no evidence that community service at SU is driven altogether, or even primarily, by the engine of religion. After all, community service is required of all students, and not all of the courses that include a service-learning component are centered on religion. Yet the connections that the university has forged with programs offered by neighborhood churches and the way in which African American Christianity has become a model for the university's own service activities signify that the university has taken some of its "marching orders" from the churches. And although it is impossible to say whether the high percentage (86%) of seniors who view "helping others in difficulty" as a major goal in life is a cause or an effect of SU's emphasis on service, the high percentage is noteworthy and correlates with the school's service emphasis. Community service, much of it connected to African American religion, constitutes the message and ethos of SU as much as admonitions to graduate, enforcement of codes of behavior, the need to earn money, or the pleasures of entertainment and pageantry.

Attendance at chapel services had not been required of su students since the late 1960s, but services on Sundays and occasionally on weekdays were conducted by Presbyterian minister and chaplain Peter Adams, and they were a conspicuous and central part of the practice of religion among many su undergraduates.

In Memoriam

An announcement and a printed program were available from the ushers in the vestibule of Memorial Church at a memorial service held on a Thursday at 10:00 A.M. The announcement was in the form of a memorandum from Chaplain Adams to students, faculty, and staff and carried Wednesday's date. It read, "The University Community has experienced a lot of grief since the start of 1996. A number of students, faculty, staff, alumni, and friends of South University have endured death and have gone home to be with their God. Their departures have left a void in the lives of those who knew and loved them. So that we might honor them, a Memorial Service will be held in the Memorial Church on Thursday, October 10, 1996, at 10:00 A.M. The South University Community is invited to attend the service." Five members of the university community were being honored: a female student killed in a drive-by shooting at her parents' home the previous summer, a male student killed in an automobile accident a week earlier, a sophomore who hanged himself in his hometown the previous summer, a retired professor and vice president who died during the previous academic year, and a staff member/recruiter who died of a heart attack during registration week the previous month. Adams was dressed in his U.S. Air Force Reserves uniform, worn, he explained to me later, in honor of the student killed in an automobile accident, who was in the military prior to enrolling at su.

About seventy-five people had taken seats in the church when a soft piano prelude began the service. People continued to drift in during the early parts of the service, and by 10:15, approximately 200 people made up the congregation. Quite a few faculty and administrators were present, but the majority of those in attendance were students. A dozen members of the university choir occupied the front right pews, and they, as well as most of the students in attendance, were informally attired in clothes suitable for this cool, sunny fall day: mostly sweaters or sweatshirts or light jackets and jeans or slacks. Chaplain Adams, President Bowker, and student government president Brand were on the stage.

Adams walked to the central pulpit and uttered a loud "Good morning!" and then again, when most in the audience repeated the greeting. Adams said that the purpose of the service was to praise God for those "who walked among us at su" and to celebrate their lives. A responsive call to worship followed, and Adams introduced the first hymn, "A Mighty Fortress Is Our God," as one of his favorites that "I grew up with in my church." He invited the audience to "sing along the hymn with the choir." It was apparent from the weak singing and the large number of people who did not try to sing that most in attendance were unfamiliar with the Battle Hymn of the Reformation. After the first verse, Adams said, "ok, now that you know the hymn, let's sing the second verse." The singing was only slightly better. Adams introduced Brand, who offered a brief, extemporaneous invocation in rapid rising and falling cadence that called on "our Gracious Father who has given us this great day, a day we will never see again," to guide us through these troubled times. "You are the author of our faith and lives, who can give us peace and joy." His "Amen" elicited "Amens" from most of the congregation. Bowker led a litany of thanksgiving in a loud, clear voice, and the congregational responses were strong:

Leader: Give thanks to the Lord, for He is good.

People: His love is everlasting.

Leader: Come, let us praise God joyfully.

People: Let us come to Him with thanksgivings.

Leader: For the good world; for things great and small, beautiful and awesome; for seen and unseen splendors.

People: Thank you, God.

Leader: For human life, for talking and moving and thinking together; for common hopes and hardships shared from birth until our dying.

People: Thank you, God.

Leader: For work to do and strength to work; for the friendship of labor; for exchanges of good humor and encouragement.

People: Thank you, God.

Leader: For the young; for their high hopes; for their irreverence toward worn-out values; their search for freedom; their solemn vows.

People: Thank you, God.

Leader: For growing up and growing old; for wisdom deepened by experience; for rest in leisure; and for time made precious by its passing.

People: Thank you, God.

Leader: For the lives of those who were once among us but are no longer here. For their spirits that will live on with us each day.

People: Thank you, God.

Leader: For your help God, in times of sorrow and trouble; for healing us when we hurt; for preserving us in temptation and danger.

People: We thank and praise you, God our protector, for all of your goodness to us.

Leader: Give thanks to the Lord, for He is good.

People: His love is everlasting.

Adams said that the two scriptural passages he would read should be familiar to the congregation. He read the 23rd Psalm quietly but with great feeling, then recited the passage from Luke 24, the story of the risen Jesus' appearance on the road to Emmaus, more loudly and enthusiastically, closing with: "This is the Word of the Lord. May it find a place not only in our heads and hearts but also in our lives as we walk with our brothers and sisters." Adams then introduced the university choir and the soloist for the musical selection "The Battle Is Not Yours."

Sung a cappella, the selection was a gospel hymn, with the refrain carried by the soloist and the response by the choir: "The battle is not yours; it is the Lord's." The soloist was a petite student who could barely be seen as she sang from behind the massive pulpit, but her voice was strong, full, with great range, and loaded with emotion. There was applause at the conclusion of the piece and quiet weeping among some members of the congregation. Adams wiped his eyes with his handkerchief as he approached the pulpit and said: "After that, I will make no comment. I do not have to. It is comment enough. It is sermon enough."

Adams requested that those who had attended the funerals of the five people being memorialized stand, and as he called each of the five names, many stood, the largest group being those who had attended the service for the staff member struck down by a heart attack at the beginning of the semester. Adams indicated that he would "offer a brief word of encouragement" and take as his text verse 17 of Luke 24: "And he said to them, 'What is this conversation which you are holding with each other as you walk?' And they stood still, looking sad." With soft piano accompaniment, Adams offered a brief prayer, asking for God's help in moving from "the depths of sadness to where you are, so that we may open our lives to your service and strengthen this community." He prayed that everyone acknowledge that "though we are from different backgrounds and cultures, you have created all in your image. In the name of God who loves us, Amen." The congregation responded, "Amen."

For about fifteen minutes, Adams preached a sermon on friendship, sadness, and recovery. His voice was soft at the beginning, but it increased in volume and intensity as he built up to the final three points he wanted to leave with the congregation. He used notes, but he seldom lost eye contact with the congregation and his words were pitched toward his auditors; he held the congregation spellbound. He prolonged his vowels, changed his pitch, and repeated key words, and his remarks received an occasional "Amen" and "That's so" from the congregation.

"Friendship is a special commodity; there's nothing like it," he said. A friend is someone to whom we can tell anything, someone who can deal with our bad breath, our snoring, even those things we don't like about ourselves. Adams remarked that he knew almost everyone would be familiar with the song "Lean on Me." He cited some verses, and the audience supplied the missing words: "Lean on me, I am [audience, 'your friend']. . . . We all need someone [audience, 'to lean on']." Each time, the congregation grew louder in supplying the missing words.

Then Adams recalled the story of Jesus' encounter on the road to Emmaus with two friends who did not recognize him. A week before, there had been parties, palm waving, good times. Now the friends said of Jesus, " 'We were with him just last week, had no chance to say goodbye, if only we had treated him differently.' That's the way we feel when we lose a friend to death. There must have been lots of talking on that walk between Jerusalem and Emmaus, time to get some things straight, to deal with the sadness of a missed friend." Adams suggested three ways to gain solace after the death of a friend, three ways of "dealing with all that stuff that has been happening to us at this university." First, "don't become so distraught that you have only regrets." Instead, celebrate the bonds of friendship, and "talk about all that stuff; don't hold it in and be overcome by grief." Second, "don't take people for granted. Do you hear me? Don't take people for granted [some loud 'Amens']. Use your time at SU to build lifelong relationships. Some of you will work together later. Some of you will marry. Some of you will hire one another. Say it today; don't wait until tomorrow. Talk to people today, not tomorrow. Love people the way you want to be loved." Third, "our lives are not ours; they are God's. My life doesn't belong to me; it belongs to God." Adams recalled the funeral of the student recently killed in the automobile accident. A friend of the deceased had struggled to the pulpit to say a few words, crying out in agony, at first unable to talk. Then he said: " 'I never thought this day would come. I wasn't ready for it. But I'm selfish. I want my friend back,' and then he began to address his friend, 'I want you here now. But that's selfish. You wouldn't come back even if you could.' " Adams insisted that the healing can begin once we recognize that ultimately our lives are not in our hands or in the hands of our friends but in the hands of God. "Your lives belong to someone higher, one who can do everything, but may not." Adams concluded with a brief prayer, "We praise you God for those you have given us for lives of service," and he mentioned the names of the five people being memorialized. "We praise you Jehovah, great enough to create us and to dry our weeping eyes. . . . Give us new hope, brave hope, for we know we will see our friends again."

After weak singing of the third verse of "A Mighty Fortress," Adams called attention to a memorial fund that had been established for the student most recently killed and explained that numerous boxes would be scattered around campus for those who wanted to contribute. He then offered a simple benediction: "Be encouraged, no matter what you are going through. May the God who can do all things bless you, keep you, and give you courage." Members of the congregation filed out quietly to a piano postlude. Some hugged and comforted each other in the vestibule and on the front steps, but most hurried off to their 11:00 classes.

Sunday Worship Services

The following Sunday, Chaplain Adams again conducted services in Memorial Church. The Sunday services had some similarities with the memorial service, but they had some different features as well, features more typical of the practice of religion on the SU campus.

Although the university choir is the most elite of the four choirs at SU, the gospel choir is the most popular among the students. Its performances tend to draw large numbers of students, whatever the occasion. The gospel choir was singing on the Sunday following the memorial service.

Adams, attired in a dark gold and black African-motif robe, greeted people inside the outer doors of the church as they entered. Members of the congregation and the eighteen members of the gospel choir (seated in the front left pews) were dressed in suits, sports jackets, and nice dresses. An audio tape of gospel music was playing as the congregation took their seats, and the choir swayed to the beat of the music. The choir leader was seated at the piano to the left at the front of the room and would serve as pianist as well as director. At 11:00, about 60 people were seated; by the time the service was in full swing ten minutes later, 150 were in attendance, two-thirds of them female. Some adults were in the congregation, including a couple with a two-year-old child, but most of those present were students.

Adams and the four students who assisted him with the order of worship took their chairs behind the pulpit. The choir stood and with their backs to the congregation performed a gospel hymn, "Lord Let Me Be Your Lover," sung loudly in parts and with hand clapping by the choir and the congregation. The choir grew louder with each verse before ending the song abruptly. There was light applause. Thus began a Sunday service that, although it included some of the formalities of typical Presbyterian ritual—such as responsive reading, prayer of confession, assurance of pardon, and doxology—was not formal in any sense. Its high points, those eliciting strong responses from the congregation, were the singing of the gospel choir, the sermon by Adams, and informal moments that occurred throughout the one-hour-and-forty-five-minute service.

Early in the order of worship, the students on the platform took the pulpit to make announcements, report on the work of the Student Christian Association, and plea for help during Alcohol Awareness Week. They read their remarks in soft voices, and the congregation chattered restlessly. Just prior to the offering, Adams assumed full charge of the service and descended from the podium, proceeded a short way down the center aisle, and pronounced a loud "Good morning!," to which the congregation responded with its own loud greeting. "God is good," Adams announced, and the congregation responded, "All the time." The chaplain used this greeting in all of his worship services.

Adams then introduced the two sponsors of the day's service. He asked representatives of the first sponsor, a dormitory, to stand; twelve students stood as the congregation applauded. He asked the second sponsoring group, the peer counselors in several dorms, to stand; three stood and were applauded. He requested that all freshmen stand, and about half of the congregation rose. Adams cajoled the freshmen good-humoredly. They were supposed to have invited five other freshmen apiece, and he gave them the same charge for next week, adding: "Write a note to that young man you have been eyeing all week, and ask him to the service [laughter]. Go up to that good-looking sister and invite her to come with you to church [laughter and 'yes']." He asked the sophomores to stand, and ten got up from their pews. Adams urged each of them to invite five other sophomores. Next, a dozen juniors were prompted to stand. "How many should they ask? Let's say two apiece. They shouldn't have to beg like freshmen and sophomores." Ten seniors were asked to rise. "How many should these seniors invite?" Suggestions and laughter emerged from the congregation. "Let's say two," declared Adams.

Then Adams moved farther down the center aisle and introduced his sister. "This is my big sister. She used to beat up the bullies for me. She took good care of me." Adams explained that she, like himself, was an su graduate. He asked her if she had anything to say. Standing and turning toward the congregation behind her, she said: "Keep the faith in the Lord while you are at su, and he will take care of you." The congregation applauded warmly. Then Adams introduced his brother-in-law, who was married to another of his sisters, a few rows back. Adams explained that this sister could not be there because she had just given birth to a baby girl. The congregation applauded. Adams inquired if any alumni were present. None stood. Parents of su students? A man directly in front of me stood, as did the couple with the two-year-old, and the audience applauded. "We have another guest in the back. Brother Conrad, would you stand and introduce yourself?" I rose, disclosed that I teach religion at Indiana University–Purdue University in Indianapolis, indicated that I was studying religion on the su campus, and thanked the members of the su community for their warm hospitality. The congregation applauded.

After Adams returned to the pulpit, he announced that the offering would be taken in two plates at the front of the sanctuary, one plate for the general work of the church and the other for the memorial fund for the recently deceased student. Adams said he hoped emphasis would be placed on the memorial contributions. All members of the congregation moved to the front by the side aisles, filed by the plates and dropped in money, and returned to their seats by the middle aisle. During the offering, the choir sang a gospel piece, "Praise Him, Praise the Lord," clapping as they sang. Following the congregational singing of the doxology and readings from the Old and New Testaments by students, the choir rose and turned to face the congregation. With piano accompaniment, they began clapping and then sang loudly "Jehovah is God forever, evermore. . . . He holds us in his hands." Most in the congregation clapped in time with the choir. The woman at the piano stood periodically to vigorously direct the choir and then returned to her playing. There was loud applause following the hymn.

Adams then went to the pulpit to begin his sermon. "I almost wanted them to keep on singing," he admitted, "but they will sing for us again a little later." He mentioned the fact that the su football team had lost its game the day before. "That's the way life is. Win a few . . . ," Adams paused, and the congregation finished, "Lose a few." Adams announced that he wanted to take as his text Acts 1:1–12, previously read by a student, and he read a few of the verses again before starting his sermon. "[Jesus] said to them, 'It is not for you to know times or seasons which the Father has fixed by his own authority. But you shall receive power when the Holy Spirit has come upon you; and you shall be my witnesses in Jerusalem and in all Judea and Samaria and to the end of the earth.'" The title of his sermon, he indicated, was slightly different from the one printed in the bulletin. Instead of "What Happens When the Power Goes Out," the title should be "What to Do When the Power Goes Out."

Adams then preached a forty-minute sermon on the loss of spiritual power. He alluded to the necessity of physical power: electricity to watch TV by and to power lights, gasoline to fuel cars. He then took up the importance of spiritual power and observed that many in the su community seemed to be devoid of it. He concluded by pointing to three things the congregation could do to restore their power: improve their prayer life, examine their worship and fellowship life, and be patient and wait for the Spirit. Adams's voice alternated between a barely audible whisper and a loud shout, and he employed repetition and pauses to drive his points home. "We need the power . . . to lift that stone. We need the power . . . to light our lights. When the power is out of our lives . . . we dry up and die. When the power is out . . . we cannot go on." He often moved from behind the pulpit, wiped his brow with his handkerchief, drew out his vowels, and occasionally read with energy from his notes. His remarks prompted "Uh huh," "That's right," "Oh yes," applause, and chatter from the congregation. His humor was contagious and frequently produced laughter, such as when he imitated the sound of trying to start a car that is out of gas or when he described the joy of driving a powerful car. Grasping an imaginary steering wheel and leaning to one side of the pulpit, Adams declared: "Brother, you can leeeeean in a Lexus."

When he had finished his sermon, he walked from behind the pulpit and stood at the front, level with the congregation. "Is the power out of your lives?," he inquired. "I now want to give you the opportunity to plug into Jesus. Those desiring special prayer should come forward." None came. He offered a different invitation: "Those who desire to make prayers of thanksgiving and to pray for others should come forward." About half of the members of the congregation stood, and Adams instructed them to line the side walls if there was not enough room for everyone at the front. With the piano playing softly, those who stood made their way to the front and the side aisles near the front. Adams asked for prayer requests, several people named others to be prayed for, and there was a moment of silent prayer. Then a student near the front began to pray rapidly: "Every day we need you, God. . . . God, step in and heal. . . . We just love you, God, and just praise you, God." When the student had finished, Adams offered a brief prayer invoking the presence of the Holy Spirit in everyday life. He invited the people who had come forward to hug their neighbors and say, "God love you," which they did. The choir softly sang "He will give you rest" repeatedly as Adams went to the rear of the church and the others returned to their pews. The choir then faced the congregation and sang a gospel hymn with the refrain "Jesus Christ is kyrie" as the choir and the congregation clapped and swayed. The singing grew louder and more intense with each refrain. With a quick wave of the hand from the pianist/director, the singing stopped abruptly, and the congregation offered loud applause. From the rear of the church,

Adams asked each person to face a neighbor and repeat the words of benediction: "God bless you and love you." The congregation filed out as the
choir resumed the singing of the kyrie.

Diverse Views of the Purpose of Worship

Janine Bowker, an alumnus of SU with a doctorate in history, became university president in 1994, after having served for several years on the university's
board of trustees. She hired Adams as university chaplain shortly after she
became president, at a time when a recruiter for the school devoted just a
few hours a week to the duties of the chaplaincy.

A practicing Episcopalian, Bowker believed that organized religion needed
to have a strong presence on the SU campus. She indicated in a conversation
with me that although she thought it was important that SU honor the beliefs
of non-Christians on campus and thereby broaden the religious perspectives
of Christians, "Christianity is our base." She quickly added, however, that the
university was "in the Bible Belt, where there is a lot of intolerance of
religious diversity," and she had no use for the "religious prejudices of the
born-againers." In her judgment, the university should be a place where
Christians were encouraged to be tolerant and not to debunk or demean
other religious traditions. She expressed serious reservations about the tone
and style of the worship services on campus, not because they were intolerant but because they failed to lift the worshipers, especially the student
"born-againers," to a dignified level. "I myself will not attend any more
Sunday services unless they change. Imagine, services that last one and a half
hours! And I don't want to stand up when my name is called. I will not file
down to the front to drop in my offering. I don't like the swaying and
shouting and amening. All this is stressful, and I have enough stress in my life
without this." She drew a contrast between Adams's services and those during her undergraduate days at SU. To be sure, she admitted, many of her
fellow students "cheated and skipped" required chapel in the early 1960s, but
the services were formal and dignified and included beautiful anthems and a
perfectly played organ. "All of this was done within a well-thought-out time
frame. We were out by 12:00 noon on the dot." Above all, "there was none of
this testifying and shouting."

Clearly, Bowker was critical of the way Adams conducted Sunday services
at Memorial Church and the religious proclivities of students in the 1990s.
She objected to the evangelistic fervor and informality of the services out of
a conviction that the "born-againers' " religious tastes and practices should
be elevated and cultivated, not indulged and intensified. And although she

refrained from insisting that Adams always do things her way, she refused to participate in a form of worship she found distasteful. Adams, of course, had a quite different view of "born-again" religious expression.

Peter Adams became university chaplain in January 1996 and had been in office less than a year when he conducted the Sunday worship service I attended. A 1977 graduate of SU, he went on to acquire his ministerial degree from a Presbyterian seminary in the South, served several rural parishes, and, during the seven years prior to returning to SU, worked in a Presbyterian synod headquarters in charge of collaboration among parishes. Adams is a friendly, easygoing person who can become intense and emphatic when talking about the religious needs of the campus.

His intensity was apparent when in an interview he spoke of the criticisms that the president and other administrators had expressed about his style of conducting services. Some of the criticisms had seeped down to him indirectly, but others had reached him directly. He mentioned that the administration had originally wanted to plan and control the memorial service for the five deceased members of the university community, but he had insisted on being in charge of the service, with the president assuming responsibility for the litany of thanksgiving. "They fear emotion. I don't yell and rant and rave, but I'm not afraid to let my emotions show." The administration knew from his Sunday services that he did not avoid emotion. "Some people around here want this to be a white university. They want to impress funding sources and others that we are just a good university like white schools. They have no use for what makes us a black school, all those religious traditions that make us what we are." Adams explained that he hoped to appeal to the informal, evangelical traditions of African American Christianity and at the same time educate students in the larger Christian traditions. This, he said, entailed employing "both traditional and contemporary styles of worship," and he cited as an example the use of traditional hymns like "A Mighty Fortress Is Our God" and contemporary gospel music.

Adams said that much of his time had been devoted to building up the Student Christian Association, which had declined when the school had no full-time chaplain, as well as organizing informal student gatherings and getting to know faculty during his first year on the job. He also had been giving much attention to the counseling of students as crises arose in their lives. On the day of the interview, a student who had attended the memorial service had come to his office to talk about the recent death of his older brother. The previous week, a freshman shot two nonstudent acquaintances in town, killing one and paralyzing the other. The police put out an all-points bulletin warning that the student was armed and dangerous. "For a black person," Adams insisted, "that is a death sentence. Shoot first and ask questions later." Adams talked with many students who were disturbed by the shooting and the bulletin and encouraged them to contact the student and tell him to turn himself in, which he did later in his hometown. Adams felt that more counseling than he had time to perform was needed on campus. He found the dormitory counselors to be caring but lacking in the skills required to help students with severe crises. "For many of our students, the safest place they have ever lived is the dorm. It is the closest thing they have had to a family, and the administration needs to find counselors to cultivate their community." Adams was encouraged that the administration was bringing in a professional counselor from town twice a week to conduct sessions on "bereavement, grief, death, and dying."

Adams taught two sections of an introductory course in religion each semester, but first and foremost he considered himself a minister. "I am still learning to be an academic, but I know how to be a preacher and chaplain. I have lots of experience in that." In addition to expressing confidence in his ability to carry out his diverse duties and to find ways to merge traditional and contemporary styles of worship, Adams's remark was an obvious response to the criticisms of his mode of religious practice.

The disagreement between Bowker and Adams reflects more than simply a difference in personal taste in religious matters, more than a divergence between university worship practices in the 1960s and those in the 1990s, and certainly more than any mere personality conflict between two admittedly strong-willed people. Their disagreement points to a tension that has appeared in the culture of black middle-class churches. As many of those churches have supplemented their decorous and ordered worship services with the enthusiastic and emotional practices of the evangelical and charismatic movements, they have widened their appeal and increased their memberships. By doing so, they have created avid defenders and severe critics. The supporters argue that the combination of "the letter and the spirit," "the intellect and the emotions," has revitalized the middle-class churches, which were in danger of losing touch with their emotional heritage, and has attracted a larger proportion of African American Christians. The critics insist that the importing of enthusiastic practices destroys the decorum appropriate to the dignified worship of God and breeds a "spiritual chauvinism," an attitude that only those touched emotionally by the Spirit of God represent the right way of being a Christian.[1]

Adams's insistence on "letting his emotions show," his emphasis on "all those religious traditions that make us what we are" as an African American school, and his mixing of what he called "traditional and contemporary styles of worship" place him squarely in the camp of those who would broaden the appeal of black middle-class Christianity by combining letter and spirit, intellect and emotions. Bowker's criticism of long worship services characterized by the informality of "swaying and shouting" and her suspicions of the religious intolerance of the "born-againers" put her on the other side of the larger cultural schism—with those who insist that formality, dignity, and decorum are appropriate to the worship of God among middle-class blacks.

"No, but Most of Them Are Very *Spiritual*"

Student government president James Brand was convinced that the infusion of traditional orders of worship with evangelical religious styles was absolutely crucial if the appeal to the current student generation was to be effective. When asked in an interview if he thought su students were very religious, he said after some reflection, "No, but most of them are very *spiritual*." The word "religion" connoted for him the institutional churches, above all, the received traditions and customs of the denominations. "Spiritual" meant the students' developing "concepts of God and values that are directly related to their lives, rather than church-centered." He believed that it was probably easier for students to be spiritual at su than back home because "in a free university setting we are free to break down the denominational barriers, and we can pray and express ourselves the way we want to." He thought there might be a trend among college students away from the church, "but I would emphasize *trend*." He was convinced that things were changing as the churches took the spirituality of youth more seriously and realized that "spirituality may be the way a young person responds to a piece of rock music." Brand said that he had been greatly influenced in his thinking about churches and spirituality by a course he was taking that semester from Reverend Gary Robertson on "African American spirituality and liberation." In the course, students were required to interpret for the class the spiritual meaning of a piece of music, a drama, a photograph, or an event associated with the "hip-hop generation." In any case, it was clear that Brand approved of the chaplain's efforts to combine the traditional and the contemporary in campus worship services. It was evident as well that despite his defense of students' breaking down of denominational barriers, he himself was committed to imbuing organized religion with contemporary spirituality rather than breaking with the institutional church. He was active in a Baptist church downtown but also attended chapel services on campus, and he was planning to attend seminary at the Yale, Harvard, or Vanderbilt divinity school.

The preference for using the words "spiritual" and "spirituality" to describe student perspectives and the attraction of contemporary forms of religious expression were by no means limited to preseminary types like Brand. They were evident also in the views of students like Jane Kemp, a junior pre-med student from Philadelphia, and Alice Hawkins, a freshman political science major from Virginia. Kemp became interested in medicine because she was a cancer survivor. She told me over lunch one day that her experience with cancer also led her to become "more spiritual, to find a personal relation to God. I found my faith at su, found a Christianity that makes me feel good about myself." She credited the religious programs offered by Adams, especially his counseling and the music in his worship services, for sustaining and enhancing her spirituality and her sense of self-worth. Hawkins, who sang in the gospel choir and came from a Pentecostal background, told me that she liked the expressive and emotional elements the chaplain included in his services and believed that "witness to God is best [accomplished] through music."

Another student, Jeffrey Jackson—a junior history major from North Carolina who was vice president of the Student Government Association, a representative on the university board of trustees, and parliamentarian for the Student Christian Association—placed the current religious scene at su in recent historical context. When he was a freshman, there was no campus chaplain and campus worship services were led by student Pentecostals. "There was lots of shouting, and attendance was high," he said. Then an "old-fashioned Presbyterian minister" filled in as chaplain one year, "and all he wanted to do was sing some old-fashioned hymns that nobody knew. The students boycotted the chapel services." After a year of a part-time chaplain who did not give much attention to the job, Adams came on the scene and began to build the attendance at worship back up by combining orderly services with the religious interests and styles of the students.

Those interests and styles—and the overall spirituality of su students—sprang in great part from the religious backgrounds and orientations of the students. Although the university environment might, in Brand's words, create the freedom to "break down the denominational barriers," in a sense freedom from the strict orders of worship associated with mainstream Protestant denominations was already established by the time most students arrived on campus. The majority of the students came from one of the many varieties of black Baptist churches in the United States that emphasize evangelical preaching, gospel music, altar calls, vocal responses to preaching by the congregation, and, in some cases, Pentecostal praying, shouting, swaying, and dancing under the spell of the Holy Spirit.[2] Students' penchant for what Peter Adams called the "contemporary" style of worship, with its unapologetic emotionalism and responsive informality, was thus bred in the students by their own religious tradition. Also, the "spirituality" that the students preferred over "religion"—that is, a deeply personal experience of God that was connected to the expressions, especially the music, of their own generation—was closely connected to their backgrounds. An SU survey revealed that 43.5 percent of the 1995 freshman class identified themselves as "born-again Christians." Born-again Christians understand personal conversion to and salvation by Jesus to be a life-transforming event that constitutes the heart of authentic religion. Born-again Christianity thus may be construed as a species of that deeply personal spirituality that SU students preferred.

Furthermore, there is evidence that the preference for "spirituality" over "religion" did not entail for most of the students, any more than for Brand, a complete dissociation from organized religion. A university survey of seniors in 1996 indicated that 64 percent attended church services and meetings (on and off campus) one to two hours per week and over 10 percent attended at least six hours per week—a striking percentage given the large number of hours the students worked for pay. Women students (12%) were much more likely to spend at least six hours per week at religious services or meetings than men (7%). Only 17.5 percent of the seniors said they never attended services, but male students (30%) were much more likely never to attend than female students (11%). The predominance of women SU students at religious services and meetings matches the profile of people attending black churches in general.[3]

Athletic coaches at SU were keenly aware of the religious backgrounds of the students, and they sought to foster student spirituality for the sake of the sports teams and the religious growth of the athletes. Athletic director and basketball coach Luke Simon told me that most of the varsity athletes at SU came from Christian homes, but when they arrived on campus, they asked: "What do I do now? Should I go to church?" Simon and other coaches encouraged their team members to attend local churches by selecting a different church for the whole team to attend one Sunday a month. "We don't want to favor one religion, so we select different churches." Simon said he urged the athletes to attend Sunday and weekly services at Memorial Church, but he thought it was also important "that our players attend local churches. We want them to be in touch with the community so they don't withdraw on campus." Simon also wanted the students to draw on religion as sports contestants. Both the basketball and the football team said a short silent prayer, then recited the Lord's Prayer aloud, before each game. And the previous (part-time) chaplain would visit the teams, usually before practice once a week, to read from Scripture and lead a meditation for about ten minutes on topics like team work, friendship, and self-respect. Simon said he would like to see this practice resumed by the new chaplain. He was convinced that "religion contributes to getting along with each other, coming together as a team of human beings, and helping us learn how to be better." And that, he insisted, "is also exactly the way I view athletics."

The head football coach, Bill Nelson, shared Simon's view of religion and its function among varsity athletes. Like Simon, he took his team to different local churches once a month, and he encouraged the football players to attend chapel services. He said in an interview that he was especially pleased that he saw many football players at the recent memorial service. One of those being memorialized, the young man killed in the automobile accident, had been a football player. "He wasn't a starter. He was a 'Rudy' [a Notre Dame player commemorated by a film of that name], a tough little guy, a former marine, who was a blocking dummy in practice who would get up and just take more punishment. He would paint his face with war stripes before every game, even though he didn't get to play much. We all loved him very much. He gave us spirit." The death of this young man "hit the team hard," and the players approached Nelson about what to do besides attending the memorial service. The coach came up with the idea that after every practice players who felt moved to pray would offer prayers that would honor their teammate's "spirit and memory and would give the players strength." Religion "helps it all come together," Nelson observed; it contributes to "bonding and developing young lives." He admitted: "I want to win, sure, that's why I was hired—not to lose. But we can't let winning become so important that we forget the really important thing: honoring Him."

Opportunities for the enhancement of the spirituality of su undergraduates were not restricted to worship services at Memorial Church and the downtown churches, the chaplain's counseling activities, the performances of religious music, or the promotion of piety by the varsity sports coaches. They were available as well in the undergraduate curriculum, mid-week prayer meetings, and programs sponsored by the Office of Student Affairs. Some courses in religion were explicitly designed to promote as well as study African American spirituality, and courses in other parts of the curriculum embraced the same goals. The honors program, an interdisciplinary curriculum open to students with superior academic skills, included a course in "wellness" that promoted "practical skills with regard to the spiritual or religious practices and interpretation concerning wellness." The liberal arts core curriculum required that all freshmen take the three-credit course Identity: Citizen and Self, which sought to "enable students to examine themselves as individuals and citizens" and entailed an analysis of factors "which may have formed their individual identities: family, religious, political, and sociocultural systems." Adams began a new program, the "Hour of Power" services, informal meditation and prayer sessions held at Memorial

Church at noon each Wednesday. And during the period of this study, Adams was a speaker in the Student Affairs Development Series—evening meetings covering such topics as "accepting differences," "health and wellness," and "cultural awareness," all of which were designed "to promote holistic growth and the development of each student."

The cultivation of undergraduate spirituality at SU thus had an educational as well as an experiential component, one found both inside and outside the formal classroom. The extracurricular educational effort to promote spirituality was particularly evident in the school's Religious Emphasis Week during the 1997 spring semester.

The Real Tie That Binds

Religious Emphasis Week was a popular event on denominational college campuses in the 1940s and 1950s. A combination of worship and education, it was an occasion when campus religious leaders could direct the attention of the college community to vital religious issues of the day and bring in prominent religious leaders from outside the community to speak on those issues. The event largely disappeared in the 1960s, although it has resurfaced periodically since that time, sometimes under a different name. SU restored the occasion in 1994, under the leadership of a member of the English department who was disappointed with the attendance at the different sessions during the week. Adams decided to reinstate the event in January 1997 and chose as the title, "Merging Rivers of Faith: The Ties That Bind." Concentrating on Christianity, Judaism, and Islam, the week was devoted to examining how the three historic faiths are bound together around common values.

The 1997 SU Religious Emphasis Week opened on 26 January with a Sunday worship service in Memorial Church. Although no faculty or administrators were in attendance, the students in the congregation numbered over 150, most of them female. Ten members of the freshman choir, a branch of the gospel choir, were the musical performers that day. The order of worship was typical of the Sunday services in Memorial Church. Adams greeted the student congregation with "God is good" from behind the pulpit, and the congregation responded, "All the time." This service was sponsored by the student Shaki Modeling Troupe, which, one of the members explained during the service, was "more than a fashion group. Shaki means grace, poise, sophistication." The club was open to all students who wanted to improve themselves along those lines. Four other students assisted Adams: a male who read the selection from the Old Testament, a female member of the troupe who offered the call to worship and led the prayer of confession, another female member of the troupe who made announcements and read the New Testament selection, and James Brand, who gave the prayer of thanksgiving and the prayer of dedication. The hymn of praise, "To God Be the Glory," was unfamiliar to the congregation, and few people other than the choir members tried to sing it. The remainder of the music was contemporary gospel led by the freshman choir, with clapping and swaying by members of the congregation and the choir and each piece of music drawing loud applause at its conclusion. Although most of the members of the congregation were somewhat formally attired, the entire service was informal, with frequent laughter and shouts from the congregation. The assurance of pardon, for example, consisted of Adams inviting each member of the congregation to turn to someone and say, "I am forgiven, God bless you," hugging himself or herself in self-acceptance and then hugging those nearby—all of this done with much laughter and commotion.

In his thirty-minute sermon, Adams remarked several times that he would not keep the congregation long because he knew their thoughts were on the Super Bowl, which would be played later in the day. He asked the congregation to pray with him and for him as he attempted to bring the Scriptures to bear on their daily lives. Drawing on the texts of the day—the story of Jonah and a passage from Mark 1 ("The Kingdom of God is at hand; repent, and believe in the gospel"), Adams preached a sermon entitled "Repenting Is Good for the Soul." As usual, Adams's preaching was a mixture of following a prepared text, sharing off-the-cuff stories, moving from behind the pulpit, and speaking in a soft crisp voice that rose in the same sentence to a loud exclamation. He called attention to how the unexpected can invade our lives. "Some of us start the semester with no money to buy books with. We didn't do too well last semester. We were getting dressed and our nice shoes split down the side [laughter and 'Amens' from women in the congregation]. We try to put on that dress, and it's just too tight and the zipper splits [laughter and 'Amens']." We choose one thing, but God may choose another. This was true of Jonah, he said, a minor prophet who resisted God's call to witness. But God overcame his resistance and even rescued him from the belly of a fish. Jonah repented. Repenting, Adams explained, means turning around, finding a completely new direction that is a response to God's calling. "It is time for you to make up your mind to change. God can accomplish anything through you." Adams left his hearers with three suggestions. First, there is no place where we can run away from God, even in the pleasures we take. Second, we will never have peace in our souls until we repent and turn to God. This means more than saying we are sorry; it means turning in a new direction. Third, when we repent, it creates a chain reaction. Others will repent because of us, just as Nineveh did in response to

Jonah, and we can even change the heart of God by our repentance. "You must decide whether to repent and follow Jesus or continue to tolerate those bizarre, unexpected situations."

Following his sermon, Adams strolled about a third of the way down the center aisle and to the accompaniment of soft singing by the choir issued an altar call. "This could be the day for you to make the decision to turn your life in a new direction and find the peace of soul that God can give you." He asked those who felt the need for repentance to come forward. All but a few males jammed into the center aisle, and Adams offered a prayer of thanks for God's patience and care in seeking our repentance. Adams then walked to the back of the church, where he gave a formal benediction. The choir sang a gospel tune, and the congregation applauded and then filed out noisily. The service had lasted an hour and thirty-five minutes.

During the course of the service, Adams referred several times to events scheduled to take place during the remainder of Religious Emphasis Week. He called special attention to a session on Tuesday that would feature a speaker on Islam. "There will be something for everyone" during the week, he promised. He did not address, however, the ways in which religions could bind together. The first session was a worship service typical of other worship services on campus, one with a mainline Protestant order of worship infused with informality and emotion. The sermon, complete with an altar call, had focused on repentance. The session had not made clear how this powerful religious presence on campus could or would merge with other religious traditions.

Only four of us attended the Monday noon meditation in Memorial Church, the second event of Religious Emphasis Week. Betty Sweeney, vice president of student affairs, was there, as well as another middle-aged woman and a female student. We sat on a front-row pew. Standing before us at pew level, Adams led the thirty-minute meditation.

Adams seemed unperturbed by the low attendance and remarked at the beginning of the session that Memorial Church was used for different purposes, from well-attended Sunday services to private meditation by individuals who came at all hours of the day. "I sometimes see students kneeling here in front," he said. He explained that this session was an occasion for quiet meditation, and he was quieter and more subdued than at Sunday services. The session of meditation, he informed us, had two purposes: it allowed us to get away from the world we inhabit for a while and to begin to look at God beyond the confines of our denominations. He then read from three sources: the New Testament beatitudes, a passage from Exodus "representing the Jewish faith" that details the slaughtering and sharing of the lamb and God's ire passing over the faithful, and a prayer from Islam that celebrates God's power to do what he wills. Adams invited us to meditate silently for a few minutes. "I challenge you to pray for unity among religions. The mission of a university is to educate the minds of students. The mission of a corporation is to produce goods. But the mission of religion is different: religion is a moral and ethical culture that brings people together in God." Three or four minutes of silent meditation followed. In a period of "guided prayer," Adams asked us to respond with "O Lord, deliver us" to the various dangers he invoked: "Evil . . . hatred . . . killing and war . . . pride . . . national vanity that poses as patriotism . . . self-righteousness . . . love of money and power . . . trusting in weapons of war to solve social ills . . . suspicion and fear that divide us from each other and God." In the benediction, Adams declared that the more he thought he knew about God, the less he really knew. God changes, or at least his views of God kept changing. He asked that we remain open to a God who manifests himself to different people in different ways, the theme, he said, of Religious Emphasis Week.

On Tuesday from 10:00 to 11:00 A.M., a session on Islam was held in the large auditorium in Stephens Hall. About twenty people attended; all but Betty Sweeney and the wife of the guest speaker were students. In welcoming the audience, Adams elaborated on the theme of the week: "All religions which seek to worship God in spirit and truth should be helping the world to be a better place." He said this session would be devoted to one of those religions. Adams introduced the speaker, Ali Syed, a man born in Washington, D.C., whose father converted to Islam when Syed was five years old. Syed became a devout Muslim and studied the Koran in Pakistan; he earned his living locally as an electrician.

An African American in his mid-thirties, Syed approached the lectern in the large auditorium. He began his fifteen-minute presentation by offering one of the daily prayers of Islam, first in Arabic and then in English. He touched on some of the central doctrines of his religion: Islam means peace found through obedience to Allah; there is no God but Allah, and Mohammad is his last messenger; other messengers have testified to Allah's oneness (Abraham, Jacob, Moses, Jesus); Allah has many names and attributes (he is merciful, forgiving, holy); Mohammad's coming was foretold in the Hebrew Bible; Mohammad brought forth the Holy Koran, a book of "law and spirituality." After providing a brief historical account of the spread of Islam, Syed observed that Islam is the most practical of religions, with the Koran covering all aspects of existence—economics, government, human relationships—and it is an ecumenical religion since it honors other messengers and treats Mary, the mother of Jesus, as a virgin. He concluded by averring: "Christians, Jews, and Muslims are commanded to find the ties that bind— in the laws that they believe in common."

After thanking Syed for his presentation, Adams divided the small audience into groups of five to discuss the question, "Can people of different religions come together to solve the problems of the world? I am a Christian, but can I come together with others?" Each group was to designate a spokesperson to report to the audience as a whole. In the discussion group nearest me, the participants agreed that Christians should not lay their beliefs aside when cooperating with others because that would simply hide conflicts in any joint endeavor with other religions. No spokesperson was designated for this group, and the point was not brought before the session as a whole.

During the reporting period, one male student rose to say, "We have trouble getting it on with other religions because different religions are fighting [with each other] around the world." Syed replied that such disputes were not really religious wars but conflicts based on land and politics. Christians, Jews, and Muslims have a faith that can bring them together beyond those conflicts. A female student gave a minisermon in which she claimed that people should concentrate on identifying problems and then reach consensus beyond "religion and race" about how to solve those problems. "We are all humans, all created by God, regardless of race and religion," she concluded. Syed indicated that he agreed and that "the age-old struggle of man since Adam" has been to root out the evil within ourselves; we must start social reform with the reform of ourselves. Adams asked Syed to elaborate on the differences among Muslims. Syed answered that there are Shiites, Sunni, Black Muslims, and others, but "we must go back behind these divisions to the roots, to Allah and Mohammad, to the ties that bind us together." Anyone who does not go back to these roots is not a Muslim. "There cannot be Black Muslims because the Koran doesn't say Muslims are black." Another student proclaimed that in his view people seemed to be going about the affairs of the world separately, and he wondered if they could ever come together. Syed replied that the observation was accurate, but the goal needed to be "global unity. Some people don't want that, but I do."

Adams then took the lectern to suggest that "we must put a comma, not a period," after this discussion since it should be the beginning of an ongoing dialogue. He offered a concluding observation: "If the mission of General Motors is to build the best automobile, if the mission of the Green Bay Packers is to produce the best football team in the nation, if the educational mission of su is to offer to African American students the best possible education, then the mission of the religions of the world is to bind people together in unity, so we can achieve peace and can care for one another. Each of us must work for this in our own little world."

The fourth event in Religious Emphasis Week, the Wednesday prayer luncheon at the banquet hall in the Student Union, was by invitation only and featured a lecture on Judaism by a local rabbi. About forty people attended, half of them student representatives of various campus clubs, ten or so administrators and faculty, and ten guests from the community (including four local ministers). After lunch, James Brand introduced the speaker, Rabbi Richard Stein, a 1978 graduate of Indiana University and a 1984 graduate of Hebrew Union Seminary who had served as rabbi of a Reform congregation in the community since 1993.

Rabbi Stein opened his remarks by reporting that he had come to know and appreciate the important educational vision of SU, although this was his first visit to the campus. He said he believed his presence there would send a crucial message to his congregation regarding cross-religious cooperation. "I want to tell my story as a Jew," he stated. "It is not better than your story, but it is my story. And perhaps there is a joint story for all of us as God's people."

He picked up the theme of the week—the ties that bind religions on behalf of service to the world—by telling a Hasidic tale. A wealthy owner of a soap factory complains to his rabbi that religion doesn't really work because it hasn't been able to prevent all the evil, war, and hunger in the world. The rabbi points to the dirty, unwashed children in the street and says, "Your soap must not be working." "Of course," replies the wealthy Jew, "the soap must be used to do any good." "So with religion," replies the rabbi. Religion must be put to work to solve social problems. How has Judaism been put to work? Moses is a model in that he called his people to "go forth into the future." The Midrash says they crossed the Reed Sea when a man named Courage plunged headlong into the sea and it divided. We must have the courage to have a vision of a world devoid of war, poverty, and injustice. In the Middle Ages, the Jewish mystics said creation entailed the scattering of sparks of the Divine across the world. It is the task of the Jew to regather the divine sparks and thereby "repair a world that is broken." Judaism is more a religion of deed than a religion of creed, Stein said, the deed of repairing a broken world and tying people together in unity. The celebration of Passover is more than a remembrance of a past event. It celebrates the idea that Jews who once were slaves should never let slavery happen again—to them or anyone else. One of the great rabbis of Judaism, Rabbi Hillel, once proclaimed that the whole Jewish tradition could be summarized while standing on one foot: "What is hateful to you, do not to others." Stein urged the audience to find sparks of divinity in everyone. He was a forceful speaker who lectured without notes, and he had no trouble holding the audience's attention for thirty minutes.

Adams indicated that Stein would answer questions after the conclusion of the program, and the chaplain repeated the analogy he used at the previous event. The mission of GM is to produce good automobiles, the mission of SU is to produce good students, and the mission of all religions is, in Rodney King's language, to help diverse people "get along," he said. Rabbi Stein then offered the benediction.

The concluding convocation of Religious Emphasis Week was a religious service held at 10:00 A.M. on Thursday in Memorial Church. Most of the 175 people present were students, informally attired, but a few administrators, faculty, and visitors from the city also attended, dressed in suits or nice dresses. The large university choir, clad in red and gold gowns, filled the chancel. On the platform with Adams were three male students, who would assist him with the prayers and Scripture readings for the service, and a female professor of social work, who would introduce the speaker for the day. One of the student assistants was a football player known on campus as "the Reverend" because he served as a preacher in the local Holiness/Pentecostal Church of God in Jesus Christ. Another of the student assistants was also a football player, a runningback, and a Pentecostal. After offering the invocation, Adams announced that the minister who had been scheduled to preach that day, who was also an attorney, had to appear in court for an important case, so Lawrence Abbott, a Presbyterian minister from a neighboring town, would preach instead.

The congregation began the opening hymn, "Joyful, Joyful, We Adore Thee," with something less than gusto but warmed to it gradually. The closing hymn, "The Battle Hymn of the Republic," was well sung. The university choir was in fine form in its performance of the spiritual "Good News" and its rendition of a soft gospel piece, "Let Your Light Shine." The choir members sang with clear, accomplished voices and picked up their parts flawlessly.

Reverend Abbott was a tall, thin man in his early thirties with a powerful voice and palpable charisma. He often read from a prepared text, but with ardor and the engaging presence of an extemporaneous preacher. He regularly turned to speak to the choir and other people on the platform, stepped from behind the pulpit, and used the rising-falling rhythm and refrains that characterized the preaching in Memorial Church. His refrains produced frequent "Amens," "Yes sirs," applause, hand waving, and shouts from most of the students in the audience. When he began, he asked for the congregation's help in preaching God's word and then read a few verses from 1 Peter 2: "You are a chosen race, a royal priesthood, a holy nation, God's own people. . . . Once you were no people but now you are God's people."

Abbott's twenty-minute message was a combination of revivalist sermon and motivational lecture. The subject was "I am somebody." "Turn now to someone near you," Abbott demanded, "and say, 'Neighbor, I am somebody. Thank God for you and me because I am somebody.'" The congregation loudly obliged. "By being created in God's image, you are strong and beautiful and caring. In God's image, we are light and dark, kinky haired and straight haired, thin and pleasingly plump. We are from Philadelphia and Stone Throw, high-rises and little houses . . . but we are all somebody." Abbott said we should praise God for creating this diversity. "God doesn't have time to make junk." Because we are somebody, "there is no way a brother can beat a woman if he loves himself." Today's news indicates that seven times more blacks are in jail than whites, that heart attacks among blacks are on the rise, that black music is corrupt and evil. "But you are Generation X, and you should be proud of it! That means you are ex-users, ex-cons, ex-debtors. And your music is great. Want to hear me rap?" He did a rap piece to loud applause. "You should be proud to be students at South University. And I am proud of you. We have come this far by faith, and we shall go forward on the shoulders of our mothers and grandmothers. We got here by the grace of Almighty God. Never forget to go back to church and the old-time religion. That's our power. Put God first, and all things will be added. You are special, you are a blessed people . . . so praise God. Amen." A long standing ovation followed.

Before pronouncing the benediction, Adams thanked everyone who had participated in Religious Emphasis Week and observed that having Abbott as the substitute speaker was an act of the grace of God. He appealed to his analogy for the week: "If the mission of GM is to make good cars, if the mission of SU is to produce good students, then the mission of religion is to create people who are up to the task of making the world better than it is. Your task is not to change the world but to change your piece of the world because you are somebody."

The note that Adams had sounded throughout the events of Religious Emphasis Week was the need for collaboration among different religions for the improvement of the social order. That collaboration, he had insisted, is the tie that binds the religions together or the point at which the rivers of faith converge. But another, more persistent note had been sounded by the events of the week: Christianity, African American Christian spirituality in particular, was the water of life that nourished the souls of the members of the SU community. To be sure, the integrity of other religious traditions had been honored in the sessions on Islam and Judaism, and the speakers on those occasions had picked up the theme that the religions of the world should unify in their concern for the good of humankind. But those sessions were sparsely attended and were overshadowed by the well-attended, dynamic worship services at the beginning and end of the week, services to which the students were most responsive. In these services, the theme of unity among diverse religions was muted by the gospel music, the evangelical preaching, the call for repentance, and the celebration of being "somebody" that derived from African American spirituality. The teaching about other religions that had occurred was important since university surveys revealed that only six students identified themselves as Muslim and one as Jewish in the freshman class of 1995 and one as Muslim and none as Jewish among seniors in 1996. The university community, especially some of the students, had been exposed to the prayers, ideas, and practices of other religions, but the community participated more intensely in the music, ideas, and practices of African American Christianity. The real binding religious tie on the su campus during Religious Emphasis Week was the spirituality that prevailed there during other weeks of the academic year.

TEACHING RELIGION

There was no religion major at su and no religion department. Until the seminary left the campus in 1969, most of the undergraduate courses in religion were taught by seminary professors, and most of the undergraduate papers were graded by seminary students. After the departure of the seminary, a much-reduced religion department and a major remained in place until they were eliminated in 1975. A handful of students picketed the administration in protest of the elimination of the program (including Peter Adams, who was a religion major at the time), but to no avail. In 1973, only 1 graduating student out of a class of 225 majored in religion, and in 1975, only 1.3 percent of freshmen planned to major in religion. Since the 1970s, religion courses have been offered within periodically restructured curricula, however. Religion 131, Survey of the Great Living Religions, was taught in two sections per semester by Chaplain Adams, and the course satisfied a liberal studies requirement. Several professors in the English department also offered courses in religion, and religion was featured as a central component of a number of courses throughout the undergraduate curriculum. The formal teaching of religion occupied a place, if not a pivotal place, at su.

"They Hired a Reverend to Do That"

Nancy Baines was a white professor of English and humanities who had been teaching at su for six years. "I used to teach Religion 131," she indicated in an interview early in the fall semester of 1996, "but then the university changed things. They hired a reverend to do that." When she was responsible for the course, she taught "the religions of the world phenomenologically [or objectively]." She was unsure how Adams would teach the course, but when he sought her advice, she said she "warned him not to preach. That will get him into trouble. Students here don't want to be preached to unless it's their own religion that's being preached!" su students, she continued, "tend to be myopic about their religious views," and teachers of religion "have to be very careful about how they teach the subject. They have to be careful that one point of view doesn't take over the class and that no student is offended."

Previously, the basic religion course at su had been a Bible course, but several years ago, Baines had taken it over and turned it into a course in world religions. Very quickly word of mouth among the students made it a popular course, every section filling during the first day of registration. She was convinced that it became popular because of her approach. She allowed the students to teach each other and make the religions "their own" in class. She gave a lecture on each religion being studied and divided the class into five research groups, each group responsible for reporting on a given religion. "The students really got involved. They would make their presentations dressed like Hindus, use films. . . . They literally drowned themselves in that religious tradition." They also occasionally brought in outside speakers, did library research, and actively participated in class discussions. "They took charge of the course." Baines deeply regretted having been relieved of teaching the course. "I absolutely loved it and gave my all to it."

Although forced to surrender the course when the new chaplain was hired, Baines found ways to teach religion in other courses. A course in world cultures that was part of the liberal studies requirement for all undergraduates and for which she served as team leader of the various sections included a large component on Africa that gave her an opportunity to lecture on African religions. And she managed to teach occasionally in her specialty, religious existentialism, in the unit of the world cultures course that dealt with "twentieth-century thought." In the fall of 1996, she also taught a course called Religious Autobiography in the wellness branch of the honors program. Using an approach similar to the one she used in her course in world religions, she tied autobiographies to religious traditions, and each of her eleven students was responsible for reporting on one autobiography within one religion.

Chaplain Adams's Teaching of World Religions

Both Chaplain Adams and President Bowker were aware that the national trend in colleges and universities over the past several decades has been to establish a clear division between the chapel and the classroom, between the study of religion and the practice of religion, between the role of the campus religious leader and that of the professor of religion. Both were convinced, however, that at SU it was altogether appropriate, perhaps even necessary, for the university chaplain to teach in the classroom. Bowker felt the chaplain's dual role was desirable "because that has always been the tradition at SU" but also because "the chaplain should be an intellectual leader on this campus" and teaching was one way of establishing intellectual leadership. Although admitting to being a novice as a teacher of undergraduates, Adams saw his two roles as complementary. He claimed that in his Great Living Religions course, he sought to introduce the students to the religions of the world and stimulate their concern for social justice, but he also wanted "to transform the students themselves in their own lives and make them more caring individuals. I hope as a teacher to help make the students rounded individuals. I want to nurture them. That ['nurture'] is a good Presbyterian word. I want my classroom to be a nurturing community."

Surveys of the students in one section of Adams's Great Living Religions course indicated that to some extent his teaching did foster a nurturing environment. Seventy-two percent of the twenty-seven students believed they were "very free" to bring their own religious convictions into classroom discussions, 80 percent found the course either "very helpful" or "somewhat helpful" for thinking about the meaning of life, and 75 percent thought the class helped them grow spiritually either "a great deal" or "somewhat." It is noteworthy, however, that only 36 percent of Adams's students found their own religious faith strengthened by the course, and over 92 percent said the course focused on the objective study of religion. It would seem that from the students' perspective, therefore, whatever spiritual nurturing was encouraged in the course was tied principally to the disinterested study of the religions of the world and did not much enhance the faith they brought with them to the class.

The student perceptions matched Adams's design of the course and his approach as a teacher. After dealing in introductory units with theories and types of religion and some of the basic human questions asked by religion, Adams's course took up the study of religion in South and Southeast Asia, East Asia, the Middle East, Africa, and the contemporary scene (the so-called "new religions"). Perhaps as a result of Baines's advice, classroom sessions included lectures by the instructor, visits by guest lecturers, and presentations by students who had been divided into groups, each of which studied a different religious tradition. The course description in the syllabus set the tone: "This course is a study of the living religions of the world, including the religions of Africa, in the light of their historical developments, beliefs, practices, and contemporary importance." The rationale in the syllabus broadened the intent of the course: "The purpose of the course is to enable the student to deal with the fundamental questions, such as: What is the meaning of religion in human history? How do we explain and interpret the similarities and differences between and among religious traditions? What and how do people in various traditions worship? What are the major religious practices, and how may they be compared and contrasted?"

On 12 September 1996, Chaplain Adams met his hour-and-a-half class for the fourth session in the semester. He arrived a few minutes before the starting time of 11:00 A.M. and greeted the students with "Good morning." Most of the 21 students who would attend this class (14 females and 7 males) had taken their seats in a classroom that held 40. They sat facing a large desk for the instructor in front with a wall-sized blackboard behind the desk. The students' attire was typical student garb for a warm September day: jeans and T-shirts. A few students wore shorts. Adams wore a suit and a shirt with a clerical collar, and he removed his jacket before printing in bold on the blackboard: "Human transformation in response to perceived ultimacy." Adams walked over to two male students in the front row and chatted with them about baseball; one of the students apparently played on the school team. Adams then moved behind his desk, on which he had placed some papers. He remarked to the class that the local newspaper had carried a brief article on Buddhism the previous day, and he passed around a copy of the article. He reminded the students that they should be working on their group reports on religious traditions and that their presentations would be coming up before they knew it. He indicated the reading assignment for the next class session, a chapter in the textbook for the course, *The World's Religions* by William A. Young.

Students had been assigned reading in the textbook for the class and had been asked to write a paragraph on "What does religion mean to you?" The class session was the second of three devoted to "setting the stage" or preparing for the study of religions of the world. Adams told the students to sit with members of their group, share their written views of religion, come up with a "consensus definition," and choose a member of the group to report the definition to the class. The groups were given ten minutes to complete their task, and then the five elected representatives went in turn to the front of the class and read the consensus definitions. The definitions varied. "Religion is the beliefs and values of a specific culture as they worship a supernatural power." "Religion is a spiritual belief that tries to define natural and/or supernatural events. . . . Individuals and groups sacrifice for the belief." "Religion is love and loyalty to the creator of life and existence, and it is the expression of belief by individuals and groups." "Religion is believing in a higher power and knowing where you came from." "There is no way to pinpoint religion; it has a wide variety. For example it can be belief, trust in the strength of the force of the Father, the Son, and the Holy Spirit." The members of each group applauded their representative after each presentation. Adams wrote on the blackboard words that the definitions had in common: "belief," "supernatural," "worship," "spiritual," "faith."

Adams consulted the notes on his desk, then looked up and said: "Let's reason together for a while about how important it is to define things." He informed the students that the way we define religion can make a difference in how we respond to people who are different from us religiously. We need definitions that allow us to be open to the views of others on this "most important topic of religion." He then went to the board and pointed to the statement he had written earlier: "Human transformation in response to perceived ultimacy." This definition of religion, he explained, was from the textbook. "What is your response?" One student asserted that the definition was too specific. Adams did not respond. Another said it meant "changing in order to achieve perfection." Adams said OK to that and asked for other responses. Another student said it meant "striving to be as perfect as God." Adams referred to his notes again, observed that the responses had focused on the word "transformation," and underlined that word on the board as well as "human," "perceived," and "ultimacy."

Adams then delivered a lecture on the textbook definition. Occasionally referring to his notes, walking in front of the desk, and frequently asking for student responses, he explored the meaning of the underlined words. He suggested that one thing involved in the definition is that religion is something humans do—not ducks, not leaves on a tree, but humans. And it is a response to what humans perceive as the ultimate, something higher than we are. Different names for the ultimate include "God," "Allah," and "Jehovah." One purpose of religion is to help us be more human. And religion transforms us. Adams asked how many students had seen the movie *Malcolm*. Most had. He pointed out that when Malcolm converted to Islam, he had a "strut to his step"; he had put "being a thug" behind him, and now he had a promising new future. A male student near the front sporting red dreadlocks offered the view that Malcolm was also transformed when he discovered on his trip to Mecca that people of many races and colors shared the same faith. Adams responded: "That's a believable interpretation of religious transformation." Adams pointed out that the author of the text believed that religion is innate, that we are born to be religious, and he asked the students if they agreed. One student said that meant to her that people must change their lives. Another said that we all must feel that we are part of something higher than ourselves. Another volunteered that "humans are not perfect but must strive to be the ultimate." Adams stipulated that the definition is a functional, working definition: it moves us forward in the study of religion, even though it may be imperfect.

He introduced another idea from the text, "secular religion," explaining that the Marxist concept of the classless society and the capitalist accumulation of wealth have their ultimates. He inquired of the class: "Why are people religious? What is the answer in the text?" Several students mentioned the ways in which psychological and social needs are met by religion as it deals with threatening situations and interactions with other people. Adams indicated that the author of the text also believed that we are compelled to be religious, that we don't really have any choice in the matter, and asked if the students agreed. The student in dreadlocks disagreed, saying that religion has been used to oppress people, which is a choice, not a necessity. Adams averred that this was one of Marx's points about religion. Adams glanced at his notes, obviously wanting to move on to another point, but some of the students persisted. A student commented that slaves were oppressed by the white man's religion, and another said she did not think any religion "should be put down. They might think oppression is right." The student with dreadlocks disagreed: "Right is right; wrong is wrong. You can't justify religion that way." Adams was eager to end this debate, so he asked another question: "Why are there so many religions?" One student suggested that the existence of many religious leaders results in many followers. Another said, "To justify our different actions." Adams nodded at both responses but was seeking another answer: perception. He contended that different languages, cultures, and societies lead to many different types of religion. Such things shape the way we see the world religiously. Adams turned to another question, "Why is religion so important to us?," and quickly asked another: "Who is the fellow so much in the news today?" "Saddam," several answered. "Yes," replied Adams, "and religion is present in his politics." He then called attention to how debates over abortion, economics, and the arts also reveal religious influences. "Religion will not leave us alone," he concluded. "It shows up in what most concerns us."

Near the end of the hour-and-a-half session, Adams noted that the next day's assignment in the textbook would include a number of terms—such as "symbol," "myth," "polytheism," and "monotheism"—that probably would be unfamiliar to the students. He asked that each student make a list of the words and define them. The students filed out of the room quietly, a few stopping to talk with the instructor.

Nancy Baines need not have worried about the chaplain preaching to his class. Adams the teacher was a different kind of performer from Adams the preacher. His object as a teacher was to get students to appreciate both the diversity and the unity of religious traditions. Although he seemed to be uncomfortable with debate among the students on such sensitive topics as the relation between slavery and religion (and perhaps my presence as the only white person in the class had something to do with his discomfort), he did encourage the expression of diverse opinions and interpretations. And although he broached such existential issues as personal transformation and the innate quality of the ultimate, he pulled the students back to the textbook's analysis of religion and the social sources of religious diversity. It is understandable that the great majority of Adams's students perceived his course as focused on the objective study of religion. This was not the overwhelming student perception of a course taught by another minister.

Reverend Robertson's Course on African American Spirituality

Gary Robertson was the minister of a Baptist church near the SU campus. A soft-spoken man in his early thirties, Robertson was completing a doctor of ministry degree at a southern seminary. The title of his doctoral dissertation was "Communicating African American Spirituality to the Hip Hop Generation." He served as a part-time instructor at SU, where he taught a section of the course on identity and, for the first time in the fall of 1996, a course entitled African American Spirituality and Liberation. In the latter course, he did very little lecturing, preferring to prompt student discussion with assigned readings, class visits to churches and other institutions in the city, student presentations of examples of Generation X spirituality, and guest lecturers. Robertson indicated on the course syllabus that "learning is an active/interactive process. In this inquiry course, you and your professor will be colearners." On the afternoon of 25 October, the topic for colearning was a comparison of Jewish and African American spirituality. The guest speaker was Professor Isaac Polotov, an Israeli philosopher who was giving a series of lectures on campus.

Robertson arrived a few minutes before the start of the class dressed in a dark red turtleneck and black trousers and talked to two students in the front row while other students straggled in. The students (thirteen females and four males) wore informal clothes: jeans, sweat suits, and sport shirts. Attired in a blazer, dress shirt, tie, and slacks, Polotov arrived, spoke briefly with Robertson, and took a chair in the front of the room facing the students. An older man entered, introduced himself to Robertson, and got his permission to sit in on the class. Robertson asked the students to arrange their chairs in a large circle. At five minutes after the designated start of the class, Robertson greeted his students with "Good afternoon," and they responded in kind. Robertson added, "Homecoming seems to have taken its toll on us," referring to the large number of absences—eleven of the twenty-eight students enrolled in the course. Sitting next to Professor Polotov, Robertson introduced him and asked if he would give a bit of historical background on the Jewish religion and make some connections with the topic of the course, spirituality.

In a twenty-minute presentation, without benefit of notes and with a thick accent, Polotov informed the students that at least since the Middle Ages, two strands have existed in Judaism side by side without connecting—one emphasizing learning, logic, and philosophy, the other stressing the spiritual parts of our lives. He mentioned the philosophy of Maimonides as an example of the first and the popular texts of the Middle Ages that dealt with spirits and angels as examples of the second. Then he shifted to the eighteenth century and spoke of the rise of Hasidism, in which learning was stressed as well as music, singing, dancing, and other forms of spiritual ecstasy. This movement gained many adherents because of the ghettoized nature of Jews in Eastern Europe at the time. He gave Cabalism as another example of Jewish spiritualism and remarked that even nonreligious people have been attracted to Cabalistic books and ideas that deal with the mysteries of heaven. To some extent, he claimed, the division between knowledge and spirit still exists in Israel today. His delivery was a bit stilted and he did not write names like Maimonides and Hasidism on the board (and from the looks on their faces, the students had trouble spelling them), but during the following discussion, Polotov became animated and held the students' attention.

A male student wanted to know whether in the future all religions might agree on what is good spiritualism for all people. Polotov responded that some religions are syncretistic, borrowing from other religions, whereas others are not. Examples of the latter are Christians who say Jesus is the Messiah and Muslims who say Allah is the prophet. Furthermore, congregations of religious people often are divided internally over seemingly minor issues. There were many nods of agreement from the students on the last point. The older visitor pressed several questions. He wanted to know if logic and spirituality always must be divided and observed that the terms needed to be defined. Polotov replied that the two things do not have to be divided, although that has been the historical pattern. For definition, he suggested that logic could be correlated with "physics" and spirituality with "metaphysics," the former dealing with what we can see and touch, the latter with what we can't see or touch "but we know exists." The visitor kept pushing: "What does it mean to know? not know?" Several students rolled their eyes, and one guffawed loudly. They were growing impatient with this intruder in their class. Robertson intervened, saying that he wanted to give the students a chance to get into the discussion. There were noticeable sighs of relief around the circle.

Robertson asked the lecturer if he would say a bit more about music in Jewish spirituality since music figured prominently in the course's work on African American spirituality. Polotov gave a vivid description of a Hasidic wedding—dancing while holding a handkerchief, working up to frenzied movements, and so on. He mentioned the role of the cantor and chanting in Judaism and suggested parallels with African chants. "Often it is only the music that is remembered by a Jew about a service thirty years later." Many students nodded in agreement.

A female student inquired about the divisions between men and women in Judaism. Polotov answered that radical divisions among men and women are not adhered to by many Jews today. In Hasidic communities, there is a clear division of labor: for example, the father educates the sons, the mother the daughters, and women keep the budgets and are in charge of the house. "There may be some advantages bought by the price of subordination to the males," Polotov added. There were no responses to that remark. Another female student asked: "What happens in Judaism if you are only raised by your Mom because of divorce?" Polotov replied that in strict Judaism there is no such thing as divorce; marriages are arranged and are not based on love since love is construed as a "passing thing," and Jewish women marry at about the age of eighteen. The student who raised the question remarked: "I had a friend whose marriage was arranged, and she committed suicide." "Hmmm," said the guest lecturer.

Robertson then asked Polotov to elaborate on the role of the rabbi in Judaism. Is he a spiritual guide? Polotov responded that according to Judaism, you should look around, find a rabbi to your liking, and then follow his advice. There are basically three types of rabbis: the expert on the law and regulations governing all aspects of your life; the spiritual counselor who does not know the law and regulations but is a good spiritual adviser; and the leader of the community, the wise man, a leader by nature, "the chief elder of the tribe."

When a female student asked if Polotov resented being known "as a Jewish man rather than as a person," he answered that Judaism is not only a religion but also a nation. Members of this nation can live in many places but are still members of one nation. Jews can have many types of religious beliefs, but what unites them, what gives them their identity, is the national ingredient. Polotov insisted that he had no problem with being known as a Jew "since that's who I am—a member of a nation." Another female student wondered what happens to national Jewish identity when Jews convert to Christianity. After considerable reflection, Polotov replied, "That is a tricky question for which I do not have a good answer." The same student pushed further. Christians view themselves as "brothers and sisters in Christ, while Jews are nationalists and don't seem to be able to move beyond their nationalism," she proclaimed. With a slight sigh, Polotov declared quietly that the land of Israel has become a home to people with many cultural and linguistic differences, and there is a kind of unity in that. Robertson announced that he thought everyone had probably reached the limits of their attention spans, and he ended the hour-and-a-half class a few minutes early. There was strong applause for the guest speaker.

Later in the academic year in an interview outside of class, Reverend Robertson made clear that he had no interest in conducting a disinterested study of religion in his course. He explained that as a teacher he tried to get the students to recognize the spirituality in their own lives and in the world around them, he attempted to enhance the students' own spirituality, and he sought to connect spirituality with issues of social justice. He admitted that the last aim had been a difficult undertaking despite his use of readings from Howard Thurman and James Cone, who reveal connections between African American spirituality and social practice. "I don't know if it's because of the ages of the students or because of the university and the culture," he said, but the students responded more readily to the personal spirituality in their lives than to the ways in which that spirituality can lead to social liberation.

By the word "spirituality," Robertson said he meant "interest in God and basic human questions rather than the way such things may be packaged by the mainline churches." The "packaging" was for him "religion," and that, he insisted, "is also what Generation X means by religion." The visiting lecturers, the student presentations in class, the daily journals that students were required to keep, and the field trips the class made all were occasions for unpacking, detecting, or celebrating the spirituality that was appropriate to this generation of students. Robertson gave as an example the trip he and his class made to the exhibition of the reconstructed slave ship, the *Henrietta Marie*, in a downtown museum. They toured the exhibit during class time, met briefly at the museum following the tour, and then discussed the exhibit at the next class session. Students' reactions to the exhibition during the discussion at the museum ranged from stunned silence to expressions of shock and anger at the slave system to admissions that they did not know what to make of it. Most of them, however, were struck by the shackles, especially the small shackles for children, and the gloomy ship's hold where the slaves were held during the ocean passage. During the class discussions, the students were able to apply spirituality to the exhibit as

Robertson directed their attention to the notion of suffering as a dimension of the spiritual life, drawing on their reading of Thurman's works. A few students said they were "awakened to the need to succeed by this heritage and be better students."

Several of Robertson's students who were interviewed attested to the appeal of the course to their own sense of spirituality. In one of the exercises in the course, students brought to class recordings of music they found to be spiritual. One student said he wrote in his journal after hearing a jazz piece that such music "is a sanctuary." Another student said she appreciated that a popular musician included an ultrasound of his unborn child in a song, adding that she would never have considered that an expression of spirituality before listening carefully to the song in class. Another said that he did not bring in the music he found to be spiritual because it contained some "dirty words." If the criterion for inclusion in the class was whether a given piece of music could be "played in church," he said, his selection would not fit. Yet he had found spiritual sustenance in it because it addressed the "struggles I have gone through in life," especially men's treatment of women, sexuality, drugs, and community life. A female student cited Joan Osborne's song "What If God Was One of Us?" as an example of a spiritual pop song.

Although Peter Adams used the word "nurture" to describe one of his purposes as a teacher, the word was even more appropriate to the teaching of Gary Robertson. Robertson's course aimed to enhance the spirituality of his students by stripping away the husks of traditional religions to reveal the spiritual kernel within and by discovering in the culture of Generation X hitherto unrecognized spiritual elements. It is no wonder, therefore, that in surveys of the students in Robertson's course, all of the students found the course to be focused on personal spirituality, and only 33 percent believed it focused to any degree on the objective study of religion. Over 90 percent of the students thought the course was "very helpful" (66.7%) or "somewhat helpful" (23.8%) for thinking about the meaning of life, and over 66 percent said the class strengthened their own religious faith. There is no question that Robertson's distaste for the disinterested study of religion and his predilection for the promotion of student spirituality shaped both the character of his course and the student responses to his teaching.

Keeping Hands Off Religion and Holding Religion at Arm's Length

Despite the pervasiveness of religious practice at SU and the availability of courses that nurture student spirituality—perhaps even because of those features of campus life—some teachers at the university were leery of dealing with religious issues in courses where such issues could arise. One such teacher was physics professor Subir Chaktari.

A native of India who joined the SU faculty in 1968, Chaktari explained during a lunch conversation that he regularly taught a section of the basic physical science course in the required liberal studies curriculum. He said that he always refused to let religious questions come up in this class although religious views of such physical matters as the origin of the universe and the origin of life exist. "I make clear when I introduce the course that science is not a matter for religion, nor religion for science, that they are two different ways of approaching truth. . . . I explain that science can offer no proofs for religious beliefs and that religion has no proofs to offer the scientist." Sometimes, he admitted, later in the course students would try to argue for biblical perspectives on God's involvement in the origin of things, but when that happened, he repeated what he said in his introductory comments, "and that ends the matter." He added that he had little use for traditional religions. "They only create religious wars. I have my own religious beliefs, which I would define as 'the religion of man,' that may or may not borrow beliefs from traditional religions. Anyway, no religious belief is relevant to what I do as a scientist."

Avoidance of religious perspectives and issues also characterized the teaching of Andrew Tompkins, a white professor of philosophy in his fifties who began teaching at SU in 1987. Tompkins offered a wide variety of courses, including Ethics, Political Science and International Affairs, Logic, Introduction to Philosophy, and a Studies in Society section in the liberal studies core curriculum. Religion, he told me in his office, "doesn't really come up in my courses. Or if it does, I reject it." In his ethics course, for example, he would tell his students early in the semester that "there is a difference between the religious question of sin and the ethical question of right and wrong. The latter, not the former, requires critical reflection" and was the concern of their study. Even when dealing with the philosophy of Immanuel Kant, who had quite a lot to say about religion and ethics, Tompkins said he refused to deal with religious issues. "When the students try to bring [religion] up, I cut it off." He said that he has told students that religion should find a way to justify itself rationally, that "blind faith won't do," but he did not consider it a part of his teaching task to help them achieve a rational justification of their faith. "Students here are too emotional about religion, and that stymies what I want to do in the rational exploration of values." Furthermore, he believed that far too much instruction at SU "speaks more to the psyches and self-esteem of the students instead of to their minds," and his taking up of religious questions, which are so emotional for the students, would only exacerbate a pedagogical situation already marked by widespread anti-intellectualism.

Unlike Chaktari and Tompkins, Matthew Lord indicated in an interview that he occasionally broached the subject of religion in his teaching, but cautiously and minimally. A white professor of chemistry and physics in his mid-thirties, Lord joined the SU faculty in 1988 and was a lecturer and team coordinator in the multisection course Science, Technology, and Ethics in the liberal studies core curriculum. In the spring of 1997, he also taught a new honors course, Research Ethics, which was based on case studies and designed to raise questions about the morality of scientific and technological research. The class dealt with the morality of such matters as copyright infringement, proper crediting of others' work, and the use of human and animal subjects. Religion did not enter into the ethical deliberations at all.

Lord said that in his teaching of the Science, Technology, and Ethics course, however, he did give some attention to religion. The overall aims of the course, he explained, were "to promote scientific literacy among non-science majors, to overcome the attitude 'I am not good at science,' and to connect science with the everyday world of the student." The emphasis of the course was on scientific methods, what they are and how they have changed, and on the social sources of scientific explanation. After exploring such topics as astronomy, energy, and molecular structure, Lord concluded the class by taking up contemporary issues like global warming and acid rain. Religion figured into the picture as the students looked at the ways in which religious worldviews have shaped earlier views of science. "I give Christianity a pretty hard time as a religion that has resisted scientific change," Lord avowed, "especially its resistance to Copernicus." He also tied religion to science when he dealt with Newtonian theory and informed the students that theologians of the time believed, like Newton, that God was a great clock winder who set the mechanical world order in motion and then left it alone. When he came to contemporary ethical issues like environmental pollution and global warming, he posed dilemmas and required the students to develop their own answers to them: for example, "An automobile generates its own weight in carbons, so what is your answer to that problem?" Lord said that he defined ethics as "moral decision making" and that religion did not arise in the ethical section of the course because he was "interested in the decision-making system rather than how a system comes about."

Religion for Professor Lord was apparently confined to dealing with the origin of things, and its significance was limited to its shaping of earlier scientific worldviews. Although he by no means kept his hands off religion, Lord handled it only occasionally and at arm's length.

Much study of religion across the SU curriculum was not characterized by the promotion of African American spirituality, the avoidance of religion, or the minimalist treatment of religious subject matter. Approaches similar to those of Gary Robertson and Andrew Tompkins did appear in other course offerings. Robertson's advocacy of African American spirituality, for example, was much like the stated aims of the required freshman course on identity, and in his ducking of religious questions, philosopher Tompkins found a comrade in physicist Chaktari. But neither extreme captured the approach to religion that I found turning up widely in the SU humanities and social sciences that combined an empathetic appreciation with an objective analysis of religion.

This combination was encountered in Nancy Baines's teaching of the world religions and religious autobiography courses, in which she encouraged her students to make an unfamiliar religious tradition "their own" for a while and at the same time gain an understanding of the diversity of world religions. It was the approach of Peter Adams in his Great Living Religions course, in which he analyzed the beliefs and practices of several religions in historical and cultural context and invited his students in their group work to get inside at least one religious tradition that was not their own. Understanding of religion attained through both critical distance (analysis) and personal participation (empathy) showed up as an aim in other SU courses as well.

The purpose was detectable in sociology professor Mary Reagan's introductory course, Principles of Sociology, which included discussion of the origins of religion, examination of the function and appeal of diverse religious institutions, and reading selections from great theorists of religion such as Ernst Troeltsch, Max Weber, and Emile Durkheim. It was a purpose apparent as well in English professor Beverly Davis's advanced course, Afro-American Literature. Davis devoted much of her course to an analysis of "literary climates, movements within literature, aspects of culture which the literature reflects, and—when appropriate—writers' religious themes" as she guided her advanced students through the study of the works of selected African American writers. She also explored "the evolution of opportunities, including opportunities for the students themselves, for creative African American expressions." And she instructed her students in the ways in which "the church has created such opportunities for them and their predecessors." The marriage of analysis and empathy also characterized the teaching methods of Professors Charles Lindsey and John Little.

Lindsey, a mild-mannered white man in his early fifties, came to the SU history faculty in 1973 and was known around campus as a demanding, respected teacher with high academic standards. "He works you to death," student leader Jeffrey Jackson said. Much of his teaching each year was done in the world cultures courses in the liberal studies core curriculum, but his favorite course, one he taught frequently, was an elective open to students of all levels, Introduction to Africa. The course typically enrolled about twenty-five students and entailed considerable study of religion. Lindsey and the textbook for the course covered traditional African religions, the impact of Christianity and Islam on developments in African culture, and the roles played by different religious figures (diviners, shamans, priests). In addition, as his syllabus revealed, he assigned contemporary novels and autobiographies that dealt with individuals' lives in Africa, many of which (for example, Peter Abraham's *Tell Freedom*) portrayed the importance of religion in the lives of the protagonists.

Contrary to the view of his colleague Tompkins, Lindsey told me in a conversation about his teaching that he found the class discussions of religion to be "very professional, with toleration of diverse points of view. There is never any emotional haranguing." Lindsey doubtless was able to avoid emotional student outbursts in part because of his own professional, dispassionate analysis of religion and other potentially explosive issues. He said that one of the controlling aims of his course was "the appreciation of the complexity and sophistication of African life." He sought to offset through analysis a widespread perception, perhaps created by the media, that African culture is simple. But Lindsey also pursued an aim that was by no means dispassionate or disinterested analysis; he hoped to inspire empathy and perhaps even a kind of advocacy. "By understanding Africa in its complexity," he explained, "the students can see that its level of achievement is on a par with other cultures. I don't put it this way to [the students] exactly, but I want to give them some ammunition for dealing with the white man's prejudices about the superiority of white cultures."

Provision of such ammunition was not a purpose of Lindsey's world cultures courses, but in those classes, he attempted to direct his students toward both an analytical and an appreciative awareness of religion's diverse roles in human cultures. Religion—the religion of hunters and gatherers, Christianity, Islam, Buddhism—was treated when the values of different cultures were explored. Religion also appeared as a social stimulus and response in Lindsey's interpretation of the industrial and scientific revolutions, as a vital ingredient in his discussion of European expansion, and as an issue worthy of consideration when he addressed contemporary concerns respecting gender and politics. "Somewhat to my surprise," he remarked, "the students do not get agitated when their own religious values are being challenged—for example, by Darwinian evolution." As in his course on

Africa, his world cultures students seemed to be quite open to diverse religious and cultural perspectives. Such openness to religious and cultural differences was not the experience of Professor John Little, although he shared many of Lindsey's teaching aims.

Little, another white faculty member in his early fifties, started teaching sociology and anthropology at su in 1983. A course he taught with some regularity was Sociology 133, Cultural Anthropology. In a class of twenty-five to thirty students, about three-quarters of whom were sociology majors, he devoted a few weeks to different types of religious practitioners and leaders, authority structures used by religious groups, and the distinction between church and sect that has become standard for sociologists. In his interpretation of his course outline, Little said that "the church-sect business is especially interesting to su students because they see how their own religious institutions might classify either way and how in some cases their sects have evolved into churches." The overall theme of the course was cultural evolution. Little sometimes attempted to show students how the emergence of the different ways in which people earned their living as hunters, farmers, and industrial workers was tied to religion and religious expectations. On occasion, some of his students "can get pretty upset when I refer to the notion of physical evolution, as background to the discussion of cultural evolution." He attributed their emotionalism to the fact that so many su students "come from Baptist, Pentecostal, and Four Square Gospel backgrounds that are antiscience." Yet he said that on the whole his students seemed dispassionately interested in the religious facets of cultures and appreciated the overall aim of the course of "tasting societies and cultures other than their own." He did not discourage the students' pursuit of interests in which they seemed to have a personal stake, however. In addition to the church-sect distinction that especially interested them, they could get caught up in "anything that is at all mystical and involves a spiritual quest. They are particularly intrigued by ecstatic visions worked up when people do strange things to their bodies." Little was not certain why such things appealed to the students, but he suspected it was because many of them had used drugs that prompted similar experiences.

The Limitations and Opportunities of the Study of Religion

Although he was an enthusiastic booster of su and its overall educational program, student government president James Brand did have some complaints about the availability of religion courses at the school. He felt that Survey of the Great Living Religions, African American Spirituality and Liberation, and several history courses, especially those offered by Charles Lindsey, had provided "a good, broad introduction to religion" and had given him "a sense of tolerance and respect for other religions, although I may not agree with them." But Brand believed he would have received better preparation for his future role as a seminary student if more religion courses had been made available to him at SU, especially courses in the New Testament, Christian thought, and relations among Christians, Jews, and Muslims.

Brand's commentary on the opportunities and limitations of the study of religion at SU applies to the school irrespective of his own plans and preparations for professional training. A number of opportunities existed within the SU curriculum to study religion, especially at the introductory level, but no courses allowed for the study of religious phenomena in depth. A place was made for the teaching of religion in the liberal studies core curriculum, but that place was restricted by the absence of a departmental faculty highly trained in religious studies. The orientation of many of the courses dealing with religion toward diversity contributed to respect for religious difference, but undergraduates had few opportunities to explore the distinctive character and context of different religious traditions.

The limitations placed on the study of religion at SU derived from the history of the school as well as its recent programmatic emphases. As we have seen, until the late 1960s, the theological seminary on the campus provided the manpower and the motivation for teaching religion to undergraduates. Although a major and a faculty in religion were retained until the mid-1970s, student demand for courses and a major in religion radically declined. The 1970s were also a time of severe financial hardship for the university—and thus a time when unpopular majors were eliminated—and they marked the beginning of increased student interest in majors like business, computer science, and psychology that seemed to promise secure postgraduation careers.

To some extent, SU was heir to the emphases of the 1970s during the academic year 1996–97. Although no longer operating under a crushing debt, the school continued to face financial hurdles and student interests still ran to majors with perceived career payoffs. Over 30 percent of the seniors in 1996 chose business as a major, 28 percent opted for the social sciences, and 8 percent chose education. Although the liberal arts made up the required core of study for all SU undergraduates, options for the study of religion in that core were severely constricted in comparison to options in the other humanities and social sciences and in the natural sciences. When I pressed President Bowker about the possibility of the expansion of the religion curriculum in the future, she replied that she was uncertain about whether the religion major would be restored or whether offerings in religion would be increased but she believed that any such changes would have to be market driven. Restoration of a large religion program was, in her words, "certainly possible if demand justifies it. Social work used to be one course at SU but has become a strong, popular program now. And look at how computer science has expanded here and elsewhere." She maintained that for the foreseeable, however, religion must be taught at SU without a separate departmental faculty or undergraduate major.

Given such limitations, the different contexts in which religion was taught at the school in 1996–97 as well as the range of approaches in the teaching of religion are noteworthy. In addition to courses devoted entirely to religious subject matter, courses in different parts of the SU curriculum gave considerable attention to religion and its roles in human cultures. Classes dealing with the major religious traditions of the world, African American spirituality, and religious autobiography existed alongside units on religion in classes in science, sociology and anthropology, English, African American identity, history, and world cultures. And if professors like Subir Chaktari and Andrew Tompkins betokened some faculty aversion to the discussion of religion in the classroom, other professors in several disciplines eagerly took up the consideration of religion as a topic vitally related to the understanding of history, society, and culture.

For the most part, during my visits to the school, I found the teaching of religion at SU to be a combination of dispassionate analysis of diverse religious phenomena and empathetic consideration of those phenomena. In his role as a religious practitioner, Chaplain Peter Adams was an unapologetic advocate and revivalist for the Christian faith, but in his role as a teacher, he was an open-minded student of diverse religious traditions. Historian Charles Lindsey and his colleagues in sociology, English, and chemistry wanted their students to understand the role of religion in the formation of worldviews, societies, and literatures—and they were not at all interested in whether their students subscribed to a particular religion. Even Gary Robertson, who could not be described in any sense as disinterested, objective, or dispassionate about religion, did not proselytize in the classroom. Surveys of Robertson's students in the African American spirituality course indicated that the large majority found their professor to be tolerant of other points of view and appreciative of different student perspectives. Nonetheless, many of his students believed that Robertson was an advocate of Christianity, and an advocate he was. If Robertson's course did not aim for conversion, along with the identity and wellness courses, it did attempt to enhance the spirituality of SU students. And if in his teaching Adams was chiefly concerned with broadening the students' understanding of religion and religious diversity, it is well to remember that he also hoped to nurture the lives of his students. Furthermore, even a professor as scrupulously academic in his approach to religion as Lindsey aspired in his Introduction to Africa course to give black students a sense of pride in their heritage. Sometimes the line separating objectivity and advocacy was very thin.

CONCLUSIONS

The Presbyterian heritage of SU was barely detectable during the course of this study, but the presence of religion on campus was unmistakable. The chaplain was a Presbyterian minister, the order of worship in the Sunday services was Protestant mainline, a Presbyterian minister had assumed responsibility for the basic course in world religions, and the university honored its Presbyterian roots on Founders Day. Those instances of Presbyterianism were mere tokens of a past identity, however, in comparison to the pervasive religious atmosphere on campus. The large majority of students hailed from Baptist and Pentecostal backgrounds, and they responded most readily to the preaching style, the music, and the congregational informality characteristic of their backgrounds and made available by the university chaplain. The term undergraduates preferred to use to describe themselves and their campus was "spiritual" rather than "religious," by which they meant the deeply personal nature of an experience that transcends denominational boundaries. The courses that treated religion were focused not on Presbyterianism but on world religions, religious factors in society and literature, and African American spirituality. And the nurturing that was attempted in some of those courses was not an effort to cultivate good Presbyterians but an effort to expand the more general spiritual horizons and experiences of undergraduates.

The practice of religion at SU was almost exclusively centered on the university chaplain and the activities and meetings he arranged. There was little student-led religious practice and not much discernible private devotion. Jane Kemp and Jeffrey Jackson, both student resident counselors in SU dormitories, were unaware of any student-led prayer or Bible study groups in the dormitories. And Alice Hawkins revealed that she and her friends sometimes said their prayers together before going to bed, but to her knowledge, such practices were the extent of religious devotions in the dorms. Kemp and Jackson believed that more student-initiated religion existed on campus before the arrival of Peter Adams as chaplain, but he now provided adequate and appealing outlets for the religious expression of SU students. To be sure, the basketball and football coaches assumed some responsibility for getting their players to attend church services and engage in devotions and prayers, but the athletic director expressed the hope that the new chaplain would soon get involved in the religious practices of the athletes. As the person who provided the focus of religious practice on campus, Adams attempted to embrace the more sedate and formal features of mainline Protestant worship as well as the more expressive and informal components of African American Christian worship—the former because he wanted to expand the religious perspectives of the students, the latter because he knew the students needed and demanded it. Clearly, however, it was the style of African American evangelicalism that dominated the religious scene at su. This style was evident in the Sunday worship services at Memorial Church, the popularity of gospel music among the students, and the latent and manifest messages of Religious Emphasis Week.

Religious practice at su was by no means confined to occasions specifically designated as religious. One of the most remarkable features of religion on this campus was the manner in which virtually every public event became a worship service. Founders Day, freshman investiture, commencement, convocation, and the coronation of the homecoming queen were framed as orders of worship, included the presence of the chaplain, were saturated with religious music, and focused on religious messages. The ethos of the school was constructed of many elements: exhortations to graduate, strict codes of conduct, a penchant for pageantry, fun-loving students who also worked many hours for pay and performed a substantial number of hours of volunteer work. But the ethos was also decidedly shaped by public religious ritual.

The teaching of religion at su was not nearly as pervasive or prevalent as the practice of religion. Because of the absence of a department and a major in religion, only a few courses dedicated strictly to the study of religion appeared in the curriculum, and the chaplain was responsible for teaching the multiple sections of the basic course in world religions. In light of the fact that contemporary colleges and universities tend to fashion themselves and their educational missions according to the specialties of faculties organized into departments or programs, the undergraduate study of religion at su occupied a comparatively disadvantaged position. Nevertheless, religion was taught in units of courses across the curriculum, several courses did take up the study of religion exclusively and found their places in the liberal studies core and the honors program, and some teaching of religion was included in extracurricular activities like Religious Emphasis Week. Furthermore, a range of approaches had been adopted by the teachers of religion, and undergraduates were exposed to the origins and manifestations of their own African American spirituality as well as to the diverse religions of the world. As student leader James Brand noted, although the opportunity for the study of religion in depth was missing at su, a broad introduction to the subject was available.

Taken together, the practice and the teaching of religion created an environment at su that is perhaps best described with the preferred student word—"spiritual." The practice sprang from a heritage of African American Christianity that does not respect clear denominational boundaries and is oriented to the expressive worship of evangelical Protestantism. The teaching sought to cultivate that spirituality or broaden the students' awareness of and appreciation for the different religious views and practices of humankind. It would stretch the limits of plausibility to the breaking point to conclude that the defining identity of su was Presbyterianism. But it would stretch the limits even farther to conclude that the school was secular.

NOTES

1. For an elaboration of this conflict, see C. Eric Lincoln and Lawrence H. Mamiya, *The Black Church in the African American Experience* (Durham: Duke University Press, 1990), 385–88.

2. Surveys of students conducted by SU did not include Pentecostalism or Pentecostal churches as categories of religious identification, but word of mouth on campus indicated that a sizable number of students came from Pentecostal backgrounds.

3. See Lincoln and Mamiya, *The Black Church*, 304–6.

CHAPTER FOUR

AMANDA PORTERFIELD

EAST UNIVERSITY

ETHOS

On a cool, drizzly morning in the late summer of 1996, I drove through the stone gateway of East University (EU) and down the curved drive to the Gothic building whose central tower dominated this part of campus. Having overestimated the time it would take to drive to campus from my hotel, I had time to wander around before my first appointment with the dean of arts and sciences. Since it was raining, I walked inside the building with the central tower, which housed the dean's office, and eventually found myself in the rotunda. Huge murals depicting the historic endeavors of the Society of Jesus, including one of missionaries in a canoe piloted by noble Native Americans, stretched high above the stone floor. But the main attractions of the rotunda were the four life-size alabaster statues of Jesuit priests, including at least one representing Ignatius of Loyola, the founder of the Society of Jesus in 1540. The stone priests were androgynous figures, small in stature, almost translucently white, with sensitive-looking fingers, soft skirts, and lace hems. They encircled a statue of the virile archangel Michael situated at the center of the rotunda. Michael wore a plumed helmet and was touching down onto the bowed and gristly back of Lucifer.

Although Michael and Lucifer occupied the center of the room, I found the four figures around them more compelling, partly because they were so exquisite and partly because I was surprised to see Jesuits represented so sweetly. My preconception of Jesuit culture as militaristic and sternly patriarchal had prepared me to feel uncomfortable here. I found myself unexpectedly disarmed. It crossed my mind that the young women who were students here must feel safe. Although my understanding of women's roles in the university would become more complicated over time, I never lost that visceral, female sense of safety.

Entering the dean's suite, I got the impression that Don Marsh was as much an object of respect and appreciation, in his own human way, as the lovely statues of Jesuits in the rotunda. His secretary was protective and obviously fond of her boss. "Father will be in right away," she said. After a pause, she explained: "Father had a busy day yesterday and might be a minute late."

Not a minute late, Dean Marsh appeared, full of good cheer and compliments. A slender, balding, and energetic man with a relish for conversation, he ushered me into his office with great ado. This large wood-paneled room was a strikingly pleasant place with great long windows and a big red oriental rug. It was as much a living room as an office, with a coffee table, couch, and armchairs as well as interesting art, a lot of books, and a big easel with a display of informal photographs. We talked on into lunchtime in a meandering, friendly way about the church, the university, the arts, and various forms of academic theory. At the end of our meeting, as we shook hands in his secretary's room, he leaned over and, with a hint of conspiracy, said: "If you call me Don, I'll call you Amanda."

The Contested Role of Religion on Campus

I found religious life at EU to be complex and multifaceted. The students, faculty, and administrators held diverse opinions about the nature and meaning of religion and the role religion should play in shaping the work of the institution. Some thought the school was moving too slowly in affirming religious diversity on campus; others thought it was moving too fast in this direction and endangering its Catholic identity. Some pressed the university for greater commitment to social activism and liberal interpretations of Catholic teachings; others pressed for firmer allegiance to the church and strict interpretations of and obedience to Catholic teachings. Some focused on the importance of nondenominational moral and spiritual values and hoped the university would commit itself further to these; a few were uncomfortable with any kind of religion and uneasy about mixing even nondenominational religious values with the open-ended inquiry of academic life. This articulate minority hoped the university would not strengthen its commitment to religion any more than it already had.

Despite the conflict associated with this variety of attitudes toward religion, several forces worked to unite people on campus as participants in a common academic and religious culture. One of these forces was the consensus that existed with respect to academic substance. Whereas considerable discussion occurred over the question of how academic excellence should be defined in relation to the school's religious identity, no one thought the university should water down its academic rigor. The university's program of undergraduate education was among the highest ranked in the country and its commitment to academic substance firmly established. As one administrator pointed out, "Catholic" was the adjective and "university" was the noun.

At the same time, no one visiting the university could fail to sense the Catholic ethos that permeated many aspects of campus life and worked to bring people together as participants in a common culture. Advertisements for Catholic-sponsored programs printed on sheet-sized banners were strung from trees on the main campus, crucifixes were hung prominently in dining halls, and the seasons of the year were marked by the big Christmas tree the Jesuits lit in their garden in December and the colorful pageant and solemn ritual of the annual baccalaureate mass each spring, in which the university's ties to the Roman Catholic Church were splendidly displayed. In addition to the visibility of Catholic traditions and programs on campus, the majority of people on campus were Catholic. Although the institution had become much more diverse in recent years, its legacy as a school for Irish American Catholics was readily apparent in the names of rooms and buildings and in the names, faces, and to a lesser extent, speech inflections of many students, faculty, and staff. As one student commented, "Half the world's Irish Catholic here and it's definitely the cool thing to be." The extraordinary sociability of people on campus and the school's ties to many prominent political figures also reflected something of its Irish Catholic heritage.

A significant degree of religious diversity existed on campus, with numerous non-Catholics representing a wide spectrum of religious belief coexisting with a Catholic majority representing various forms of Catholic belief. Nevertheless, a definite religious ethos distinguished this university from other types of Catholic higher education as well as from many non-Catholic institutions of higher learning. This religious ethos was more humanistic than that of more conservative Catholic schools whose mission was more clearly centered on upholding the sacred authority of the church in the midst of a perceived onslaught of religious declension. And it was more adventurous than that of schools whose Catholic identity was more taken for granted and whose faculty and administration were less focused on leading the way in the ongoing intellectual development of Catholic teachings and their implications for the world.

The religious ethos of this school was not something that had existence or meaning apart from the people who created, maintained, and developed it. In large part, it was comprised of personalities and the patterned interactions that took place among people and shaped their ideas, concerns, attitudes, and actions. It was also shaped by the physical plant of the campus, with its combination of Gothic and modern architecture, libraries and laboratories, and Division 1 athletic facilities. The religious ethos of the school was nurtured by its healthy endowment and strong connections to Wall Street and political leaders at both state and national levels. All this was held in fine balance by a complex network of relationships to ecclesiastical authority and especially by a delicate relationship between the university and the conservative bishop within whose jurisdiction the university was situated.

Faculty members were free to express their opinions in the classroom, and many pursued their work without feeling constrained to defend or even define its value in religious or ethical terms. Especially in the sciences and social sciences, a number of faculty members had been hired solely on the basis of their academic skills and without inquiry into their religious preferences. In fact, quite a few of the committed Catholics associated with the school worried that too many of these faculty members had been hired and that in the process of becoming a prestigious American university, the school was rapidly becoming indistinguishable from its secular counterparts. As Father Andrew Tofanelli, one of the chaplains, put it, "Catholicism is inclusive, but do you hire someone who's an atheist to teach here?" Like others who were troubled by what they perceived as indifference or antagonism to religion on the part of some faculty members, this priest hoped that the problem of irreligious faculty would be addressed by the new president of the school. "I would be opposed to the idea of firing anyone or coercing people to go along," Tofanelli emphasized. "But maybe now with the new president, we can start fresh and hire faculty who affirm the religious identity of the school."

I did meet some faculty members who wanted nothing to do with the

Catholic mission of the university, although they seemed to be much fewer in number than Father Tofanelli suspected. One of the most charming and articulate of these dissenters was Professor Arthur Stone, who agreed to be interviewed in his office, a room with a lot of afternoon light and a bicycle. After being assured that I would not use his real name or departmental affiliation, he launched into a fast-paced monologue on Catholicism and its role at EU. "Catholicism is a repressive religion," he stated as a matter of fact. "I was shocked and horrified to read the other day that it is the largest religion in the world. I would have thought that Hinduism or Buddhism, religions I'm more comfortable with, would have been larger than they are, but it's the repressive religions, like Catholicism and Islam, that are dominating." From Stone's perspective, secularization is a "wholesome process." Moreover, "there's a conflict between dogmatic theology and open-ended inquiry," he asserted. "And there's also a conflict between diversity and openness to different positions and identities on the one hand and authority and hierarchy on the other. This institution has been dragged toward diversity and openness kicking and screaming."

"Of course, everything's in transition, but it's really obvious here," Stone went on. "Before 1940 or 1930, people knew what the institution was—a commuter school for lower-middle-class Catholics. Now being here is like being a secular Jew in Jerusalem—surrounded by wailing and various other intense forms of public religious expression." Along with rampant anxiety about change, Stone reported, the school has experienced a series of deliberate efforts to refurbish its religious ethos. But these efforts seemed forced to Stone. He explained: "When you have an identity, you don't have to go on and on about what it is or should be. It's like Kwanza, a manufactured holiday. There's an attempt to create an identity and shove it down people's throats. But you can't control culture without being a lot more repressive."

The Sacred World of the Past

From his conservative perspective, Father Michael Salatino would have agreed with Stone's assessment that the religious situation at the university was confused and artificial. But he could not have taken a more opposite stance with regard to secularization. A slender, forthright man with a gift for fluid and colorful talk (and, in these respects, much like Professor Stone), Father Salatino was one of the few priests I saw wearing a clerical collar on campus. When I first met him, he was also wearing a black beret, which gave him a sort of rakish appearance. Loved by some but despised by others for his tirades against religious liberalism, he identified himself as "a lightning rod for hostility." In a borrowed office in the philosophy department one morning, he admitted to me that he and his fellow traditionalists on campus were "a bit tough, a bit harsh" in their complaints against the infestation of liberalism. But that, he claimed, "is because we're under siege." He and his fellow conservatives were uncompromising because they feared being compromised. And this fear went beyond the personal. "On the one side are the traditional Catholics, on the other, the skeptics who substitute themselves and their personalities for the authority of the Church," he explained. "*We* defend the church. *They* situate themselves in opposition to it."

Personally, he confessed, "I've been stung by all the negative things said about me, but I don't want to give in to the ill will. I've got a clear conscience—well, not completely clear—but on many of these things I do, so I have to keep living my life and being me. I've got to save my soul, so I don't want to be filled with hate." After listening to my comment that for all the debate about the true nature of Catholic piety on campus, there seemed to be an extraordinary degree of civility, Salatino grimaced dramatically at the thought that life was even more terrible elsewhere. "Things may be worse at secular universities where the distance separating people is immense and people are shooting at each other," he agreed. But he wanted me to know that some of the things published about him in the editorial pages of the student newspaper had been "very vitriolic."

With regard to students at the university and their relationship to Catholicism, "we are living in the pluperfect tense," he asserted. Catholicism throughout the United States was watered down with liberal interpretation, he told me, and only small minorities preserved the true faith. The students here, he complained, were "dim, fourth-carbon copies of religious people. Certain things remind them of religion—crosses and statues. But theology is in desperate straits here. It would die without Buddhism and other religions to discuss." On one hand, he said, "traditional theology strikes students as extremely dogmatic." On the other hand, he explained, "nontraditional theology does not offer students the certainties they are looking for. The leftist, subjectivist theology taught by many of the faculty confirms student rebelliousness against their parents and what their parents—or more probably their grandparents—might have had."

As these comments demonstrated, controversy over the question of whether the university was too preoccupied with religion or not serious enough about it was quite heated. But there was little disagreement that the religious atmosphere of the institution had undergone significant change and was still in the midst of that process. There was also widespread agreement that a coherent and more isolated world of sacred meaning once existed in the past. According to a retired professor of philosophy who was an undergraduate at the school in 1940s, "Being Catholic then was like being

Amish is today—sealed off from the larger culture." As a youngster, his habits "were formed by the devotionalism of the Catholic Church," and he was "guarded from outside influences" by his parents in ways that television and other media now make it impossible for parents to guard their children. As Philip Lazlo, a professor in the theology department, explained about growing up in the 1950s and 1960s, "Many Catholics grew up in a world that was all-Catholic. When I grew up, I knew one or two Protestant boys, but that's it. Protestants were strangers." Although EU still draws a high percentage of Catholic students, two things have changed, according to Lazlo: "Many of the Catholic kids come to us without any religious education. We never had that twenty to twenty-five years ago. The other thing is that we're getting diverse types of Catholics—from Asia, Hong Kong or Taiwan, Vietnam, Cambodia, and Thailand. I used to go down the roster and see all Irish names—not any more."

A professor in the nursing school recalled her experience as an undergraduate at the university thirty years earlier: "It was a commuter school for working-class kids. It was a school for people who were working hard to pull themselves up by their bootstraps." And it was very insular and very Catholic. Having come from a public high school rather than a parochial school, this professor found "the Catholic life at the school very closed. When an ambulance went by, everyone stopped to say a Hail Mary."

As the boundary between the Catholic world and the larger society became more porous and as Catholics became identified with mainstream American culture, ideas about the institution's responsibility for religious education changed in certain respects. For much of the school's history, the faculty and administrators not only viewed the spiritual formation of students as their primary commitment but also perceived this formation as something that would insulate Catholic souls from corruption by the larger society. A policy statement from the nineteenth century declared that although profession of faith was not a prerequisite for admission, "the chief aim of the College is to educate the pupils in the principles and practices of the Catholic faith." The program of religious training administered by the school involved mandatory attendance at daily mass and catechism, a weekly lecture on church doctrine, monthly confession, and an annual religious retreat. Most faculty members and administrators were Jesuit priests who wore clerical garb and served as spiritual counselors to students. When residence halls were built to house students who did not commute, Jesuits staffed these buildings and watched over the students almost constantly. The school calendar revolved around sacred events and holy days, and student activities were often religious. Even extracurricular activities centered on the cultivation of devotional piety. Younger students were encouraged to develop greater piety by joining the Sodality of the Immaculate Conception, which was devoted to the Virgin Mary. Older students were invited to join the Society of St. Cecilia, which provided sacred music at the required daily mass and various other celebrations. According to one history of the early days of the school, both the material and intellectual culture of the institution revolved around "a network of symbols which created a sacred space-time canopy over the whole of the educational process and fostered student identification with an array of heroic and saintly figures from the Christian and Jesuit past."

Especially among conservatives, I found considerable sadness—even grief—over the loss of this insular, sacred world. For many on campus, memories, images, and stories about this sacred, coherent, and protected world of the past functioned as a kind of mythic ideal against which the current state of affairs was measured and found to come up short. One professor of theology conveyed an almost desperate anguish about this erosion of piety and implored me to draw attention to what was happening to the school. "This used to be a Catholic university saturated with Catholic culture," Professor Roger Martin told me one afternoon when we happened to cross paths outside the day after I had visited one of his classes. "Now it's an American Catholic university saturated with American values and culture." As we talked, his head and shoulders slumped and his soft voice conveyed disappointment and dismay. "We don't ask how many faculty are Catholic. Some are, and some of those aren't such good Catholics," he said. "We opt for the best people, period." This commitment to secular standards of academic excellence, he went on to explain, went hand in hand with a decline in piety. "We used to be very activist here. We were a religious training program. We expected students to make a religious retreat every year." He told me that a turning point had occurred in the mid-1960s. Suddenly, "we didn't push or strengthen student religious activism as we did before. It became a matter of one of the things that was available to you if you were interested. Now a lot of people ignore the Catholic aspects of the university." Being Catholic used to mean being part of a religiously intact and separate culture. But at the university today, "religion is an individual thing, not a cultural thing."

In the previous few years, a few things had happened that gave Professor Martin some hope that the slide to secularization might be slowed, but he was dubious about the long term: "The new president seems to take a stronger stand. He said we want to be open to people of any religious constituency, race, or gender, but we're also a Catholic university and there's a list of special things to fulfill. We expect you won't be drunk, and we expect you not to have premarital sex. And he followed up on this statement in various ways." Another good sign, according to Martin, was the addition of new priests who "show that faith is credible, that it's not a vacuum or a dodge." But he wondered whether it was really possible to reverse the secularizing trend. "The president may hold things off for another ten to fifteen years. What then?"

Professor Stephen McCarthy also expressed deep concern about the inadequacy of the school's religious culture. In a long meeting in his office, McCarthy described himself as "deeply cynical" about the institution. Because of his friendly manner and the jaunty appearance of his boyish face and colorful bow tie, it took me a while to realize how distressed he really was. Although he was much less conservative than Martin, McCarthy was highly critical of the superficiality of religious life on campus and made it clear that he thought the institution was not living up to its professed goal of being a university grounded in religious principles. He expressed profound suspicion of the religious rhetoric put out by the administration and was eager for me to understand what was really going on. Being religious at EU, or being active in social service, he explained, "is like intramural sports, or study abroad, or music club. It's something you can sign up for and do, but the university doesn't do well in conveying its importance for undergrad life or for the identity of the university." He observed: "The school cuts too many corners compared to my own undergraduate education. It's a play school. The kids are adorable. They are good little dubbers. The social service programs help them feel good about themselves and good about the school."

McCarthy explained that when he joined the faculty in the late 1970s, "it was still 50 percent commuter school and had essentially a provincial identity. Then we caught the bug of greatness and expanded on all fronts. There was nothing we couldn't do. It was during the Reagan administration, not coincidentally, and also a time when one of our alums was running Congress. There was a push toward research and, at the same time, a push to big-time sports. In the mid-80s, the new stadium and sports arena were erected. At the same time, there was a push to become residential and national rather than provincial. A so-called Wall Street Council, comprised of alumni in New York, was deeply involved."

Although he was disdainful of what he called "the narcissistic notion that we could be everything at once," what really troubled McCarthy was what he considered a precipitous drop in the quality of undergraduate education. Coinciding with the push toward greatness, he explained, "the quality of undergraduate instruction declined, and that went hand in hand with the decline in the quality of undergraduate life, and that went hand in hand with the decline in the emphasis on spiritual formation. All three suffered drastically." In response to my expectant look, he provided some specifics. "Classes became larger, faculty became less accessible. There is no serious advisement in arts and sciences—it's just too big. Faculty in arts and sciences are too driven by research. The Catholic elements are too optional and just window dressing. Residential life is just zany. Students are just left on their own."

McCarthy was bothered by what he saw as the hypocrisy of the whole situation and, more specifically, the university's unwillingness to provide resources that the attention to undergraduates implied in its rhetoric would require. "There need to be smaller sections in courses where the formative mission of the school is at stake," he said with exasperation. "The school is getting away with clichés." He expressed particular distress about the religious implications of the situation. "We are all set for total secularization," he asserted. "The university cannot maintain its religious identity the way it's going about hiring faculty. Nobody wants to deal with this issue. The places that survive as Catholic schools will be places where there's a 'flat-footed Catholicism' "—he switched to an exaggerated nasal twang as he said that phrase—"that really is part of school identity. But in this school's path toward empire, the Catholic piece is going to be lost."

Although McCarthy did not want to simply restore the piety of past, as did some of the conservatives on campus, he was convinced that undergraduates had received a better education in the context of that piety than they had more recently at EU. And he agreed with many conservatives on campus that the university had entered a pact with the devil of secularization from which it had neither the will nor the grace to free itself.

This concern about the inevitability of secularization was expressed in many places on campus and commanded the attention of administrators, faculty leaders, and chaplains. Many of the key figures on campus whom I interviewed gave me the clear impression that they were working hard to build a university that would stand as a religious model of higher education and would contribute to an eventual triumph over the forces of secularization. The integration of academic excellence and religious expression these leaders hoped to achieve would exceed anything achieved in the past. The university's place in the larger culture would be on the leading edge of a large-scale revitalization of Catholic intellectual thought and American religious life.

The Progressive Faith

I missed my first appointment with Father Francis Fahey, dean of academic affairs, because of my own father's death. In preparing to meet with him on a later visit, I felt uncomfortable. He had never met me, but he knew my father had died. Everyone I knew on campus called him "Father." But not being Catholic myself, I felt that the situation was awkward. Father Fahey put me quickly at ease. After he flashed a solicitous eye and greeted me by saying, "Hello, friend," in a way that was disarming but not unnerving, we launched into a congenial and efficient conversation. A large man with heavy jowls and an agile wit, he sat comfortably in the wing chair in the living room of the frame house that served as his headquarters. His comments were punctuated with metaphors from baseball—the chair of the philosophy department, he informed me at one point, was "a great second baseman." He couldn't recall the exact date he had assumed his present office, but he could tell me who was playing in the World Series that year. With regard to my question about the role of religion in academic life, he pressed his fingertips together like a cathedral and said: "God can be present anywhere. Even in this conversation."

Like other progressive leaders on campus, Father Fahey argued that the revitalization of Catholic piety now occurring on campus was a more profound phenomenon than the unself-conscious piety of the past. "Between 1950 and 1970, the university was very Catholic," he explained, "but the Catholicism was taken for granted and not really reflected on. There were a few Jews, but the vast majority of students were unexamined Catholics." Those who attended EU before 1970, like most Catholics across the United States at that time, "grew up with the rosary and the stations of the cross, surrounded by a thick religious piety." As a young priest, he remembered getting instructions about "what to say to Protestants and atheists on trains." But as a result of the Second Vatican Council and the upheavals associated with the war in Vietnam, "anticlericalism erupted." In elementary education, "we got into a touchy-feely era . . . when youngsters read the *Velveteen Rabbit* instead of Matthew." Here at EU, "a great failure of will ensued with regard to the Catholic dimension of the university," and for a time, the university "was headed toward being only residually Catholic." But the situation changed dramatically during the 1980s and 1990s. "Today," he stated matter-of-factly, "the university is more Catholic than it was in 1950 or 1980, and more self-consciously so."

The progressives who regarded EU as a center for the development of a revitalized Catholic intellectual tradition conveyed a grand vision of Catholicism's role in the world. In this vision, God was to be found everywhere, including within each of the specialties and disciplines of a major university. The rediscovery of God's presence in these areas of life would bring greater moral and spiritual integrity to all forms of human endeavor. As one university motto put it, "Nothing that can be held intellectually cannot also be held faithfully." Father Fahey explained: "One of the things being part of a university means is following a discipline wherever it goes." This open enthusiasm for truth, wherever it leads, was braced by the confidence that there was no place that faith could not go.

The progressive subculture dominated campus life and supported a variety of programs intended to advance its multifaceted agenda. The force of this subculture was centered among key administrators, who encouraged faculty and student participation. The administrators who presided over hiring, tenure, promotion, and salary decisions took a favorable view of research and writing on religious and ethical issues and extended support to faculty willing to pursue the religious or ethical aspects of various issues and developments in their fields of study. A religious institute on campus sponsored conferences, retreats, and seminars to which faculty were invited. And faculty were eagerly recruited for introductory and capstone courses that led students to reflect on the religious, ethical, and personal dimensions of their academic work.

With regard to campus opinion about efforts to integrate the pursuit of academic excellence with values rooted in a Catholic worldview, some, like Professor McCarthy, pointed to the gap between the image-building rhetoric of these efforts and their limited effect on both student learning and faculty research. Others indicated that they were nervous about being asked to make good on the rhetoric and did not know, or in some cases did not want to know, where to begin. But although considerable hesitation, nervousness, and confusion existed about the school's Catholic identity, the administration was able to generate faculty support for a strategic-planning document, completed in 1997, that linked the academic mission of the school to its religious identity. This document stated that the university sought to establish itself "as a preeminent center for Catholic thought." As such, the university would advance "understanding of the Catholic tradition" and contribute "an informed understanding of this tradition and its values to the social, political and cultural development of society."

This sense of the school's Catholic identity was a good deal more ambitious than the sense of Catholic identity conveyed in the founding statement of the nineteenth century, which simply stated that the school aimed to educate students "in the principles and practices of the Catholic faith." Although it involved many unresolved tensions and unclarified areas, the new consensus that existed about the school's Catholic identity was sufficient to provide a basis for strategic planning that linked the educational mission of the school with commitments to the personal development of students and discussion of ethical and religious values. As one biology professor said, "One of the powerful advantages of attending [this] university is that no one apologizes for exploring ethical dimensions of any subject. Discussion of ethics doesn't take a backseat here." As a theology professor who taught Buddhism said, "There's a feeling of relief that you can talk about religion without doing what the dominant culture does—either address religion from a distance or press and proselytize people." The same professor went on to say, "There's a sense of sacramentality here, a sense that God's presence is possible in all areas of interaction and study."

Personhood and Hierarchy

The progressive religious vision of the university and its role in the world was grand, but it was exemplified by individuals known for their sobriety, moderation, and intellectual rigor. The self-discipline of these individuals made the vision respectable and reasonable. Even someone as fearful of the future as Professor Martin had to admit: "It's a wonderful place. I really think that. It's thanks to a group of people who live celibate lives. They're not just professional administrators—great personal sacrifice is involved." Taking Father Fahey as an example, Martin said earnestly: "I've seldom seen anyone more balanced. You see him at night. Out walking the neighborhoods by himself."

Others also commented on the self-discipline and self-sacrifice that characterized the key administrators at EU. According to Matthew Galloway, the chair of the theology department, when the new president, Father John Fitzsimmons, arrived at the university in 1995, he set out to buy a Chevy for getting around town. He was informed that this was unacceptable—as president, he had to drive something at least in the Oldsmobile-Buick category. Professor Martin also mentioned the congenial atmosphere of the university and attributed it to the tone set by the previous president, Father Stephen O'Connell. "The most striking thing about the university is what a decent place it is," said Martin. "There's a culture of civility that pervades the place and carries over to students. I give a lot of credit for the good atmosphere to the last president. He was just a very decent guy, and what he did flowed down. He didn't pull in a $300,000 salary—everything he made went right back into the school. Everyone knew he lived in a little room like the other priests."

Several people told me that President O'Connell was an excellent financial manager and that he saved the university from potential bankruptcy when he came on board in the 1970s. His stature as a spokesperson for reform in Catholic higher education was also widely admired, as was his success in building the school's academic reputation. As a leading representative of American Catholic higher education, he defended academic freedom before church authorities in Rome. O'Connell argued that no university in the United States would be taken seriously without it. He was also one of the leading proponents of strengthening Catholicism's influence in American society by drawing Catholic students into the educational elite.

With regard to his demeanor, Matthew Crosby, an associate dean in arts and sciences, told me that "O'Connell's conservative by nature and tough as nails. But he wouldn't let his feelings be converted into policy. He would consider that a sin." As president, according to Crosby, O'Connell was "distant and didn't interfere with academic life. Most students would not have recognized him if he walked through campus. He's a quiet person, not the type to dominate a room. Making small conversation with him was painful. But if someone wasn't doing a good job he could fire them and do it quickly." Because of his tough-mindedness, self-discipline, and commitment to Catholic education, Crosby assured me, "you won't find anyone who didn't respect him." And this phenomenon of personal admiration for the president and other key figures was fundamental to the religious ethos of the school. Crosby explained: "The religious or Catholic identity of the school is summed up by the fact that priests model, or personify, values here."

The most politically powerful people on campus served as role models of religious life. This did not mean, however, that they stood out from others or generated exceptional amounts of personal charisma. Instead, the university seemed to move forward through the personal strength and cooperation of a critical mass of like-minded and like-behaving individuals. Although something like this might be said of any successful institution, in this case, reliance on personalities had a definite religious aspect. Many of the people responsible for the running of the university viewed their work—especially their work with or on behalf of students—as a religious vocation and form of ministry. The level and quality of these people's commitment to the university seemed to be remarkable, as did their capacity for self-discipline and cooperative endeavor. To an unusual degree for a high-powered university, quite a few influential people seemed to be "on the same page" and working toward the same goal.

This reliance on personalities and their cooperative relationships with one another was rooted in Catholic structures of authority and hierarchy. Like the Catholic Church, the university was administered from the top down by politically astute individuals whose self-discipline and pastoral concerns were intertwined with the authority of their office. The interpersonal attitudes and behaviors of these individuals, along with the respect they received from others, set the tone for campus life. Courtesy toward others was an important element of university culture—everyone opened doors for others, and janitors and dining hall staff knew students, faculty, and administrators by name and conversed with them easily. But at the same time, there was a very definite chain of command. Faculty played a much smaller role in governance than at many other universities, and the university was ahead of the curve with respect to the current trend toward corporatization in American higher education. According to Professor Leonard Campbell, a longtime member of the faculty, "The institution is neither democratic or egalitarian. It functions as an aristocracy and sometimes as a monarchy. The bigger the decision to be made, the smaller the number of people involved." Corporate structure was not a new development at this institution, however, but an old tradition rooted in the ecclesiastical structure of the Roman Catholic Church.

At least a few faculty members took the view that the top-down approach to decision making was an old-fashioned form of Catholic defensiveness that undermined efforts to create a sense of community. Campbell argued that this was true especially for faculty, whose participation in the overall workings of the university was carefully controlled and strictly limited by the administration. He wanted the administration to become more democratic, especially with regard to faculty participation in planning and policy making. "While the middle and upper administration feel it is dangerous to open things up, I believe that everything is to be gained by open discussion. The priests in authority here," he went on to explain, "tend to have a 'mount the battlements' mentality. If you can just maintain administrative authority, then everything will be OK. Important discussions occur in the waning minutes of meetings here because the rest of the meeting is so well structured."

Susan Light, another professor highly regarded by her colleagues, described the implications of this emphasis on authority for university governance. "The recently retired president had an ad hoc style of management, creating task forces to address issues." In this system, she explained, "there is no faculty senate. With more than 300 members, the faculty of arts and sciences is too large to meet as one body and never does. There was a faculty senate of approximately twenty-five members when I first came in the late 70s, but that was a holdover from the 60s and soon disappeared." In response to my question of why faculty accepted this situation, Light explained that "there have been no crises that have led to a cry for more faculty control of the university, and we know what's happening to colleagues at other universities in difficult straits. Faculty are quite aware of the university's success and financial stability compared with other institutions. If it's not broken. . . ." She added after a pause: "The move to increased concern for research leaves people with little time for university service." But "faculty and administrators are not simply arrayed against each other on this issue," Light went on to clarify. "Faculty have considerable areas of freedom, which we enjoy, and we're not challenged by the economic pressures that face faculty at many other universities." In addition, she explained further, "our president of twenty-two years was diplomatic and well-respected. Although his policy-making committees were largely handpicked, issues were widely discussed, or at least he believed that they were. Changes have been slow, incremental, and handled with skill. Our administrators have been extraordinarily diplomatic and astute and run the university with much acumen, financial and otherwise."

Both Campbell and Light thought the patriarchal character of university life had a chilling effect on both diversity and community. "The university is a corporation, and corporations are patriarchal," Light explained, and "this one is especially so because only a man can run it." With regard to the question of how the top administrators view women faculty and students, she replied: "They embrace and smile on everyone, especially those who feel grateful for being here. They do not understand those who feel oppressed by the structure and rhetoric."

When I asked Father Fahey how the corporate, authoritarian, patriarchal governance structure of the university fit with the magnanimous, democratic, and egalitarian spirit of so many faculty and students, he replied, in his inimitable way: "The bumble bee was not supposed to fly, either." After a pause, he added: "It's the personalities involved. That's what makes this university work."

RELIGIOUS PRACTICE

In addition to the existence of a considerable range of religious opinion among Catholics on campus, a large minority of people—approximately 35 percent of undergraduates and 40 percent of faculty—were not Catholics. Protestants, Jews, Muslims, Hindus, Buddhists, secular humanists, agnostics, and atheists joined the university because of the high quality of its educational programs, institutional services, and opportunities for research, teaching, and learning. Non-Catholic faculty were drawn to the university by its academic reputation, high salaries, and geographical location. Non-Catholic students were drawn by the strong liberal arts core based in a great-books tradition, the excellent reputation of the faculty, the university's location in the pleasant outskirts of a major city, and the general advantages of the institution's commitment to its Catholic identity. These general advantages included, among other things, widespread agreement about the importance of discussing ethical issues across the spectrum of undergraduate instruction and respect for the practice of religion and the dignity of the human person. This agreement and respect fostered a general climate of civility as well as enviable statistics on campus safety.

Commitment to religious life was paramount for a significant number of people I interviewed, and these people often participated in discussions about what it meant for the university to have a Catholic identity. With regard to undergraduate religious opinion, a significant minority of students were dedicated practitioners of religion. According to a survey administered to students taking required courses in theology during the academic year 1996–97, 32 percent of all students prayed at least once a day and 42 percent attended religious services at least two or three times a month.

As these statistics indicate, more than half the undergraduates on campus were something less than constantly dedicated practitioners of religion. Nevertheless, it was my impression that a vast majority would have said that religion was important to them. A small minority of students and faculty were actively resentful of the Catholic Church's efforts to impose its authority on others and ready to challenge any sign of the university administration acting as an arm of the church. Overlapping with this group, a much larger number of students, both Catholic and non-Catholic, were turned off or simply bored by organized religion, especially organized Christianity, defined in terms of allegiance to an institution and its formal traditions and requirements. But these students tended to be open to insight from a variety of alternative traditions and seriously invested in spirituality, defined in terms of ethical concern and personal awakening and development. Both the chaplaincy and the theology department made special efforts to reach these students.

Historically, attendance at mass was strongly identified with Irish Catholics and often functioned as a means of affirming social cohesion and ethnic identity. The popularity of numerous masses held regularly at EU reflected this history. For many students, attendance at mass was part of a weekly routine, along with drinking and studying. Many of the people who attended mass also liked to party, and many of the people who liked to party also liked to earn good grades and cultivate networks of friends and acquaintances. With reference to their concern for personal advancement, alleged hedonism, and lack of interest in finding God through service to others, one of the priests on campus referred to these undergraduates as the "baptized pagans."

Some of the Catholic undergraduates at EU might be described, at least partially, as social Catholics who viewed attendance at mass as an occasion to be with friends and potential friends as well as an occasion to be with God. As one student observed disapprovingly, "I find here that many people go to church because it's a social scene." Another student asserted in a paragraph written for me about student religious life: "I am very critical that many of the people I know that do go to church are *not* good Catholics." But although I heard comments like these frequently expressed, I discovered that the students who went to mass with their friends or went to mass and also partied a lot were not as casual about either the practice or the content of religion as their detractors assumed. I began to wonder if the belief that many students were casual or hypocritical about church functioned for some people on campus as a means of supporting their belief in their own purity and more advanced religious status.

Although priests and other religious leaders encouraged students to do more than attend mass or some other form of religious service, the celebration of mass did figure centrally in religious life on campus. Large masses at graduation and the inauguration of a new president were spectacular events held on the grand plaza in front of the sweeping modern facade of the main library. A splendid white altar was set up for these events, shining, in sunny weather, with sacramental objects and presided over by priests dressed in stunning gowns facing a large and appreciative audience. On a smaller scale, several daily and weekly masses were held during the school year, each with a different ambience. Daily masses were celebrated in the diocesan church on one corner of the sprawling campus and in the Jesuit chapel on campus. Weekly masses were held in several residence halls and in other buildings on campus. During my visits to campus, an informal mass was held on Wednesday nights at 10:00 P.M. in a room filled with comfortable couches. And a mass in Spanish was celebrated for Hispanic students in the Jesuit chapel on Sunday mornings. One of the most popular of these services was the Wednesday noon mass celebrated by Father Patrick Kenney, whose classes in the theology department were also filled to capacity.

At 11:45 one Wednesday morning, I was among the first to arrive for Father Kenney's regular mass. A rotund, short, and bespectacled fellow, he was puttering around the front of the chapel when I arrived, apparently checking to make sure that the material aspects of the service were in order. Seated about three-quarters of the way back in a tranquil and beautifully proportioned Gothic interior that could probably accommodate 250 people, I watched as the pews filled. The vast majority of those in attendance appeared to be students, many of whom knelt with heads bowed and hands tightly clasped in preparation for the service to come. When Father Kenney appeared at the stroke of noon through a side door near the front, he looked angelic in a white gown and a cape of green and gold. Walking out before us and stretching up his arms as if to draw down God's love and encircle us with it, he welcomed us in an intimate, serious, fatherly way.

After the service got under way, people moved back and forth between sitting and standing and between sitting and kneeling. When the kneeling came around for the second and third times and I remained sitting, I was bumped several times from behind, perhaps not inadvertently. A feeling of intensity built up during a long prayer in which Father Kenney and the congregation took turns praying aloud. When he called for special prayers, a young woman spoke up: "Pray for all the people who are suffering with cancer." Behind me on the other side of the chapel, a young man called out loudly: "Pray for people who have had abortions." Another young man behind me shouted, even louder: "Pray to *stop* all abortions." Shortly thereafter, Father Kenney brought this part of the service to a close, and the intense collective feeling that had been mounting subsided. Later on in his homily, he spoke about the importance of not passing judgment on others.

Father Kenney seemed to be in the thick of things with respect to the campus struggle over the nature of Catholic piety. Professor Martin apparently had Kenney in mind when he commended the administration for hiring new priests who showed the students that a life of faith was viable. But Father Salatino shook his head over Kenney, complaining that he was "too liberal and too latitudinarian." After hearing that comment, I was surprised to discover that Kenney attracted a large number of religiously conservative students to his worship services and to his classes. When I called for an interview with the young woman who headed the prolife coalition on campus, she asked if we could meet outside the Jesuit chapel after Father Kenney's Wednesday mass. I waited for her for twenty minutes while she spoke with Kenney personally. She later told me that "he really makes me think about my faith. If I can, I go to every mass he celebrates and sign up for every course he teaches."

Nurturing Student Piety

In the chaplaincy and other parts of the university, strenuous efforts were made to help students organize their lives in terms of religious and moral values. But these efforts, everyone admitted, had not been wholly successful. Indeed, some faculty I spoke to on campus regarded student behavior as completely out of control. According to Professor Stone, "Freshmen routinely go into a tailspin. They come in with an intact worldview, for good or bad, and then it all disintegrates. The twister takes them up, and when it sets them down and they wake up weeks later, they're in a different place and who knows how they got there. They are frantic for friendship and lovers. Women students sometimes complain that there's no dating culture. It's just random hooking up and coupling."

In the fall of 1997, the new president made it clear in his inaugural address that excessive drinking and premarital sex conflicted with the religious values of the institution. Students and faculty concerned about the chaotic aspects of undergraduate life praised the inaugural address. Diocesan officials embarrassed by the rowdiness associated with the school and eager to see the administration take a firmer hand in controlling undergraduate behavior also expressed approval of the president's remarks. But others on campus who feared that a stronger emphasis on obedience to Catholic morality would have a chilling effect on diversity and academic freedom greeted these remarks with nervousness. Still others were skeptical that the president's comments would have any effect and dismissed them as nothing more than administrative window dressing.

Similar concerns greeted other efforts to bring undergraduate life into conformity with Catholic values. For example, in the course of planning residence hall programs for Alcohol Awareness Week, a controversy erupted when some student leaders planned to place crosses in residence hall windows in memory of students who had died in alcohol-related accidents. But other student leaders felt that such a display of crosses was inappropriate because it would exclude or even offend people who were not Catholic and conflict with the university's commitment to diversity. The dispute was resolved by the agreement to commemorate half the deaths with crosses and the other half with red ribbons.

Despite this ambivalence about the school's Catholic identity and the lack of clarity about how far people could go in affirming that identity without jeopardizing diversity, the progressives on campus maintained that many aspects of the university could be influenced by principles and values drawn from a Catholic worldview in a way that affirmed the inclusiveness of the Catholic tradition and alienated only the most adamant opponents of religion. Deliberate efforts to nurture the school's Catholic identity were visible in almost every area of campus life, including the residence halls. The seniors and graduate students selected for residential assistantships were taught to see their work as a kind of ministry and to think about residence hall life and the decisions students make in religious terms. Seated around a big table in the director of housing's suite at a meeting arranged for me, several students working as residence hall supervisors referred to the concept of Christian self-sacrifice to discuss the difficulty but also the essential importance of their own willingness to take the time to sit down and talk with the individuals who lived in their halls.

In answer to my questions about what life in the residence halls was really like and whether religion played any part it in, a thin, intense young woman replied that "everyone knows that the campus rule against cohabitation is associated with Catholic standards of morality. We don't listen at doors or have parietal hours as they do in some Catholic colleges, but students don't argue with you about it." She explained: "They know that it's not just a matter of courtesy to a roommate but that moral judgment is involved." Another person mentioned "the walk of shame" back to their rooms that undergraduate women endure after spending the night with their boyfriends. And with regard to their own lives as student supervisors, celibacy was a requirement. The administrator present at our roundtable meeting, a large, gregarious man with a big voice, broke into the conversation when we began to discuss the celibacy requirement for RAs. "Every year I make the same speech about sex as part of RA training," he said grandly. The students around the table nodded and laughed. "I tell them that RAs do not have sex. I tell them that RAs do not even *want* to have sex. I also talk to them," he said after a pause, "and some people are offended by it, but I tell them anyway, that I have a very definite commitment to the Holy Spirit that is relevant to this work."

The Jesuits and Their Influence on Campus

Since non-Jesuit faculty lived off campus, the Jesuits were the only permanent residents on campus. Their community constituted the core of campus community life and was its dominant symbol. Although the number of Jesuits active on campus had declined significantly, the university's commitment to encouraging the development of Jesuit spirituality across campus had not declined, at least not over the previous decade. But since the Jesuit identity of the school was no longer taken for granted, efforts to cultivate Jesuit spirituality on campus had become more deliberate, more experimental, and more far-reaching.

Some people I spoke to were more involved in Ignatian spirituality than others. Some students were confused about exactly what it was, and some faculty were unclear about its relevance to their work. But the presence of this spirituality and the impact of its role in creating a religious ethos that permeated the school were undeniable. When asked to reflect on how their religious lives had changed during their time at the university, many students mentioned the transformative effect of Jesuits and Jesuit spirituality on their religious lives.

Thanks to the cooperation of faculty members teaching sections of the one-credit elective capstone course that offered seniors an opportunity to reflect on their own spiritual development during their four years at EU, I received dozens of brief self-descriptive essays from students. More than half the essays referred to the impact that Ignatian spirituality or certain Jesuits on campus had made on the students' lives. "I attribute the surge in my

Catholic faith to being in a Jesuit institution," one student wrote. "The Jesuits are the greatest group of people that I have ever met. I now consider myself to be a true Catholic. And I owe the Jesuits for this." Another senior wrote that although the university was "a Catholic institution it does not overpower its students with the Catholic religion. Instead the Jesuits instill in the students their idea of liberal arts and community service." A non-Catholic wrote, as part of the same assignment, "Although I cannot be pegged as a Catholic or a Jew, I do believe that my spiritual life has been enriched and that I will continue to live in the Jesuit tradition of good and service."

Since the time of Ignatius, the Jesuits have been learned men involved in education. Although their primary mission has always been *cura personalis*, "to help souls," and education has never been the only way of accomplishing this mission, they were the first religious order to make formal education part of their ministry. In 1773, when it was temporarily suppressed by the Vatican, the Jesuit order administered more than 800 schools—the largest international network of schools administered by any organization before or since. In the United States at the end of the twentieth century, the Society of Jesus administered more schools than any other religious group.

According to the foundational principles of the Jesuit order, intellectual life and academic work were meant to be pursued in the context of religious practice. The proponents of Ignatian spirituality at EU were strongly committed to this form of integration. Of course, their success in integrating academic and religious life was hotly disputed on campus. But the existence of this commitment to the integration of religious and academic life, its direct connection to various flagship programs on campus, and its prevalence in campus rhetoric were undeniable. As a result, the division between religious practice and the teaching of religion, which is used uniformly in the organization of all of the chapters of this study, is somewhat misfitting. Thus, Jesuit education would be just as appropriate a topic in the section on the teaching of religion as it is here, in the section on religious practice.

Jesuit schools in the United States have been widely respected for delivering outstanding instruction at the secondary, baccalaureate, and graduate levels, especially in the humanities and particularly in philosophy, which has long been a central part of the extensive training program for Jesuits themselves. But their reputation has not always been positive. In the nineteenth and twentieth centuries, Protestant stereotypes of Catholics often featured Jesuits brainwashing less sophisticated Catholics into obeying the pope and performing the rituals of what many Protestants perceived to be an authoritarian and anti-American church. The quality of Jesuit education came under attack from within the order itself in the 1930s, when doctoral education for Jesuit teachers was not yet the norm, and again in the 1970s, when Jesuits questioned the integrity and relevance of their own intellectual and educational systems and struggled to reformulate their identity as a teaching order in relation to the larger world around them.

In the 1970s, the intellectual center of the Jesuit curriculum shifted away from the medieval philosophy of Thomas Aquinas and its emphasis on mastery of the various aspects of a rationally comprehensible world. Although admiration for Thomas by no means disappeared, the philosophical center of Jesuit thinking shifted toward existentialism and its emphasis on the subjective nature of all human experience. This turn toward existentialism enabled Jesuits to catch up with modern philosophical questions about the human mind's ability to know anything outside itself and to address those questions from the perspective of Catholic sensibilities. The influential Jesuit philosopher Karl Rahner interpreted Thomas in existential terms, arguing that the self's capacity to recognize its own finitude involved an experience of self-transcendence that implied the existence, mystery, and power of God.

This turn toward existentialism dovetailed with the long-standing Jesuit mission of helping souls and prompted new interpretations of how that mission might be understood and actualized. Phrased now in terms of attention to the individual person and friendship and mentoring in the course of a person's journey through life, *cura personalis* became relevant in new ways to the cultural situation in which American Jesuits found themselves. Increasing numbers of non-Catholics in the United States began to seek Jesuit educations, and Catholic populations were no longer outsiders to American culture living mostly in ethnic, urban communities. As part of the mainstream of American culture, Catholics were increasingly shaped by the individualism and preoccupation with personal journeying that so strongly characterized American middle-class culture.

At the same time, the world of Catholicism underwent a series of seismic shifts as a result of the deliberations and proceedings of the Second Vatican Council in the early 1960s. These shifts had profound implications for American Catholic education generally and for Jesuits in particular, who perceived themselves and were widely perceived by others as providers of the very best in Catholic education. The documents issuing from the Second Vatican Council urged Catholic leaders to relinquish their intellectual isolation from the modern world and rejuvenate the great doctrines of Catholic thought in response to current intellectual trends and social ills. In the years leading up to the council, the work of a number of influential Jesuit scholars paved the way for the council's reversal of the church's intellectual stand in relation to modern thought. In the years following the council,

Jesuit educators were often at the forefront of this modernization process as well as being stimulated by it.

Also as a result of Vatican II, the Catholic Church recognized the validity of other religions, although it reserved for itself the claim to the fullest expression of truth. This recognition shifted the implicit ground rules that governed non-Catholics' admission to and instruction in Catholic schools. A new spirit of Catholic ecumenism worked to restrain Catholic faculty from attempting to evangelize non-Catholics in ways that might imply disrespect for other religions and opened the way for non-Catholics to become more active in their support of and involvement in Catholic schools. This new ecumenism fit with important aspects of the Jesuits' own history and culture, reinforcing the humanistic aspects of Jesuit learning and the openness to cultural pluralism for which the society was famous and sometimes criticized.

The Vatican Council also addressed the problems of alienation and passivity among Catholic laypeople that had come about as a result of the church's domination by clerics. The council inspired efforts to identify the church with the whole people of God and diminish the religious gulf that separated clergy from other Catholics. The importance of the laity to the church also came to the fore in the council's emphasis on the church's pastoral role, especially with respect to its pastoral responsibilities to the world. The new understanding of the church as the people of God with a pastoral mission to the world stimulated the development of the Jesuits' own self-understanding as educators and helpers of souls. It also prompted Jesuits at EU to explore new forms of cooperation with lay faculty and administrators, experiment with new ways of introducing students to Ignatian spirituality, and help students develop this spirituality in their own lives as laypeople and even non-Catholics.

No less important, the convener of the Second Vatican Council, Pope John XXIII, articulated a social justice mission for the church that drew attention to the gap between rich and poor in modern societies and committed the church to work for more just and humane conditions. This emphasis on social justice was partly an expression of the church's longstanding criticism of modern society, particularly as articulated in Leo XIII's encyclical letter *Rerum novarum* (1891), which attacked industrial capitalism by insisting that wages take account of workers' needs and not be determined simply by economic calculation.

The encyclicals concerning social justice issued by John XXIII in the early 1960s grew out of these earlier protests against the victories of modern nationalism and capitalism but also departed from them in that they committed the church to facing the realities of the modern world more openly than before. The impact of this intensified focus on the poor was intellectually explosive. In 1968, the bishops of Latin America met in Medellín, Colombia, to implement the council's teachings on social justice in terms of "liberation theology." Advocates of this theology interpreted the prophetic texts and social teachings of the Bible as a call to economic liberation for the poor and political liberation for the oppressed. The ideas aired at Medellín played an important role in the international synod of bishops held in 1971 in Puebla, Mexico, which recognized social transformation on behalf of justice as an inherent and important part of Christianity. A subsequent meeting of the Latin American bishops in 1979 summed up this dramatic shift to the left in Catholic social teaching as the church's responsibility to exercise a "preferential option for the poor."

The Society of Jesus was in the vanguard of these efforts to define the responsibilities of the church in terms of exercising a preferential option for the poor. The election of the liberationist Pedro Arrupe as general of the society in 1965 marked a decided shift in focus to social justice issues among many Jesuits and a new emphasis on revisioning traditional Christian teachings in liberationist terms. These alterations in focus and theological interpretation did not gain universal approval, however, and traditionalists within the order were vehement in denouncing them. Arrupe convened the Thirty-second General Congregation of the Society of Jesus in 1974–75 in the hope of unifying the society. Although this hope went unrealized, the congregation nonetheless advanced the society's commitment to conceptualizing faith in terms of justice. The congregation decreed that Jesuits were to be "men for others," later expanded to "men and women for others," phrases implying both pastoral concern for helping souls and activism to promote social justice.

Jesuits became leading activists and spokespersons in promoting the exercise of this preferential option for the poor as an essential part of Christian life and in linking it to the mission of a Christian university. As Ignacio Ellacuria, one of the Jesuits persecuted by government agents for his activism in El Salvador in 1989, explained in a commencement address at the Jesuit-run University of Santa Clara in California in 1982, "The poor embody Christ in a special way; they mirror for us his message of revelation, salvation, and conversion." Ellacuria argued that embodying a preferential option for the poor "does not mean that [a Christian] university should abdicate its mission of academic excellence—excellence needed to solve complex social problems." But the Christian university "should be present intellectually where it is needed: to provide science for those who have no science; to provide skills for the unskilled; to be a voice for those who have no voice; to give intellectual support for those who do not possess the academic qualifications to promote and legitimate their rights." As another Jesuit martyr, Jon Sobrino, said in his address at the centenary celebration of the University of Deusto in Bilbao, Spain, in 1987, "What the option for the poor demands and makes possible at a university is a place of incarnation insofar as the university is a social force, and a specific light for its own learning." As he explained, exercising the option for the poor means "that the world of the poor has entered the university, that its real problems are being taken into account as something central, that social reality is being dealt with by the university and that the legitimate interests of the poor are being defended *because* they are those of the poor."[1]

Although the political implications of these ideas were numerous, significant, and subject to debate, at EU an existential interpretation had gradually become primary. The chaplains, priests, professors, and administrators who promoted this interpretation encouraged students to experience a form of self-transcendence that enabled them to see that they shared a common humanity with others who were less fortunate and that their own good fortune was, in some respects, arbitrary. One student explained this process with reference to a course she took that combined volunteer service with academic reflection: "You get into this course thinking you're going to help others, but you barely touch their lives. Meanwhile," she said, "your life has been changed. At the shelter for battered women where I worked, the women are stuck. They keep coming back and have so many problems. You realize how much you have." After a pause, she went on: "Before taking this course, you believe that people could change and improve their lives if they really wanted to. You think about yourself as on an equal plane with others. But then you realize that you happen to have been born at a different level, and the shoe could be on the other foot. It makes you ask, why am I really here?"

Students were encouraged to undergo this kind of spiritual questioning and development in several courses offered by the theology and philosophy departments and in a variety of extracurricular programs sponsored by the chaplaincy. And it was this experience of self-transcendence, coupled with commitment to helping others, that seemed to lie at the core of what students, faculty, and administrators meant when they referred to Ignatian spirituality. As Father Fahey acknowledged, "To some extent this Jesuit thing is a mantra that everyone can agree with because it is very popular but not pinned down. It can be like 'bullah bullah' at Yale." Although it was freely and frequently invoked, however, the concept of Ignatian spirituality that was bandied about on campus was hardly without shape or meaning. It had definite roots in the *Spiritual Exercises* of Ignatius, in the commitment to integrating academic learning and personal formation, and in the reforms in

Jesuit thinking associated with Vatican II, especially those associated with the liberationist emphasis on social justice and the existentialist emphasis on religious experience as self-transcendence.

The founding document of the Jesuit order, the *Spiritual Exercises* is a manual that guided people through the spiritual implications of their thought patterns and life choices. Focusing on feelings of consolation or desolation associated with particular thoughts and choices, the *Exercises* provided rules and guidelines for a sustained course of introspection. Ignatius developed these rules and guidelines during his recovery from a cannonball wound in the 1520s. After his recovery and decision to become a scholar and friend to the poor, he led others through the process of transformation that he had undergone. The *Exercises* charted the course of his conversion in a way that enabled others to follow the same process.

Since their inception, the Jesuits have been criticized for relying too much on their own introspection and, at least by implication, not enough on the authority of the church or even on authority in their own order. As Father Fahey quipped, "The Jesuits have been described as an autocracy tempered only by the rampant insubordination of inferiors." In part to counter criticism of their lack of obedience and emphasize their devotion to the church, the Jesuits assumed a fourth vow (in addition to poverty, chastity, and obedience) of loyalty to the pope and willingness to travel anywhere at his behest. But in the context of efforts to infuse campus life with Ignatian spirituality, the emphasis on introspection and corresponding freedom from the doctrines and teachings of the Catholic Church was extremely useful, as was the fact that use of the *Exercises* has never been confined to Jesuits.

The Chaplaincy's Role in Shaping Religious Practice

The university chaplain, Father Thomas Cahill, reported directly to the president of the university and was one of the most visible and respected Jesuits on campus. He supervised more than half a dozen other chaplains and a wide variety of extracurricular programs designed to help students develop their spiritual and religious lives. When I met with him in his office in the Student Union on a Monday afternoon, he was tired from having led a retreat the previous weekend with ninety students. But he was full of talk about the weekend, and since it was 4:00 P.M. and he was, as he explained, "an afternoon person," his tiredness seemed to disappear as we talked. A large man about sixty years old, he wore a priest's collar and wanted to know right away what my own religious background was. I told him that I tried to understand what it was like to live within a variety of different religious traditions. I said that I had learned a lot, personally, from many of these traditions but explained that I wasn't committed to any one of these over the others, partly because I believed that commitment to one would undercut my capacity to understand the others. From the expression on his face, I gathered that he found this position unsatisfactory. But he accepted my forthrightness and seemed to resign himself to helping me in any way he could. We had a good interview, and later, he went out of his way to introduce me to students involved in chaplaincy programs.

From Father Cahill and others, I learned that, in addition to the daily, weekly, and special masses it helped organize and advertise, the chaplaincy sponsored an array of programs that might be described as a series of concentric circles with varying diameters of outreach. The programs with the broadest outreach were popular weekend retreats designed to help students understand and improve their own college experience. These retreats, like a number of other programs run by the chaplaincy, made constant use of student leaders. "Why not hire a teenager," Father Cahill asked rhetorically, "while they still know everything?" Several other chaplains explained that student leaders were also effective because they spoke the same language as other students and thus did not have to face the shyness, indifference, or rebellion against authority that adult leaders could generate.

"Catholicism comes across as being about rules and regulations," Cahill explained. "But undergraduates are at a time in life when they're not really interested in rules and regulations." The Jesuit emphasis on introspection and service to others appealed to students, he told me. "Jesuits stress contemplation in and through action, which then leads you back to contemplation," he explained. Moreover, "Jesuits are very tolerant of diversity. They believe in the intellectual life and find ways to link it with faith. Jesuits work with people to find meaning and values in life. For Jesuits, meaning and values come through God and particularly through Jesus." But the meaning and value of life, even Jesus's life, Cahill assured me, were not presented in a way that excluded non-Catholics or even non-Christians. "The only thing sponsored by the chaplaincy that is restricted to Catholics is the liturgy. Jesuits have an incarnational view of the world. They believe you can find God in all things."

Designed to reflect the Ignatian emphasis on personal experience and its role as a basis for moral judgment, retreats for both first-year and upperclass students focused on academic work, social pressures, friendships, sexual relationships, and opportunities for community involvement. In the weekend retreats held for first-year students called "48 Hours," 80–90 students attended each retreat for a total of about 800 students in 1996–97. As Cahill informed me, this was about 30 percent of the total number of first-year students at the university and over 40 percent of those available on weekends. The chaplaincy scheduled these retreats so that they would not coincide with home football weekends or big party weekends. Students interested in attending were required to submit an $85 fee and an application. There was always a waiting list.

The student leaders at these retreats were trained to focus on their own experiences and to help others in the group do the same. Cahill explained: "Stories and storytelling are really important. We use the 'I' language. When we train peer leaders, we tell them to use the 'I' language and to be concrete." In other words, he went on, "What happened on Saturday night? Be specific. But protect confidentiality. The story is important, but don't give the name of a person involved in a way that would violate confidentiality. Students get a high from these retreats. And this high will last a little longer than some others."

As a kind of conclusion at many of these retreats, Cahill told students the story of his own conversion. He described the incident to me as "a St. Paul on the road to Damascus event. I contemplated suicide as an undergraduate. I had a strong academic aptitude and was studying science, but I became depressed and stopped going to classes." At the time, Cahill lived at home, which, he explained, "denied me some opportunities for privacy that would have made suicide easier. One night I literally fell out of bed and landed on my knees. I found Jesus, or more precisely, Jesus found me. My life was saved in that moment. I also knew in that moment that I would become a priest."

The format of "48 Hours" was based on a model of "ritual process" adapted from the writings of cultural anthropologist Victor Turner, who studied the relationship between ritual and social structure in African tribes and other religious societies. The retreat was designed to help students step out of their ordinary lives, attain some distance on what they were doing, and recombine and reconceptualize the elements of their lives. Father Tofanelli, another chaplain involved in these retreats, explained that the weekends were based on "the idea of taking the Indian brave into the forest away from the tribe. Then they come back to the tribe having internalized its mythology in an invigorated way." The "mythology" that students came to understand in a new way was Ignatian spirituality. At the retreats, this spirituality was taught by means of concentration on "I" language and by the sharing of stories about the crises, difficulties, and implications of personal experience.

In addition to the broad outreach of "48 Hours" and a similar series of retreats for upper-class students, the chaplaincy sponsored a somewhat more focused set of programs aimed at students who strongly identified with the Jesuit motto of "men and women for others." These programs involved 300 to 500 students each year, many of whom had attended "48

Hours" as first-year students or participated in the popular service-learning course sponsored by the philosophy and theology departments.

Mary Baer was one of the chaplains responsible for these programs focusing on spiritual development through identification with the poor. A very serious woman in her thirties with dark eyes, Baer was raised a Catholic but left the church because of its policy against women's ordination. Seated on the edge of a chair in her office, Baer discussed a retreat the preceding weekend in which she and her student leaders squeezed 240 students into a center made for 90. "One of the most wonderful parts" of this intense retreat, according to Baer, "was a silent prayer service on Friday night. A very simple service with a few readings, instrumental music, and lighted tapers for the students to hold. We used the image of darkness and light to describe the darkness of oppression and poverty and the light of righteous anger and concern." Baer described this ritual in some detail. "Student leaders came up front, one at a time, saying, with reference to some of the people they worked with, 'I am hungry for space. I live in an apartment with ten people.' Or 'I am hungry for bread. I am standing in line to eat.' They used a passage from Judges." Baer went on to explain how the ritual she supervised aroused anger at the injustices of capitalism and then encouraged students to channel that anger in nonviolent ways. "Israel defeating the Midianites with jars and trumpets and voices. No weapons but the outnumbered Israelites made the Midianites fear that *they* were outnumbered." Baer said that she talked about the importance of nonviolent revolt, which she depicted as "smashing our jars of righteous anger." After this part of the service, people were invited to stay, in silence, if they wanted to. "The students stayed there for an hour," she told me proudly.

Later on in the retreat, the founder of the first women's shelter in the United States delivered what Baer described as "a drop-dead keynote based on the prophetic tradition and its awareness of how the poor are ground underfoot. Today this occurs through corporate greed and the ways things are structured economically." Afterward, Baer said, "there was lots and lots of conversation. The student leaders are excellent facilitators. The conversations focused on feelings about students' own undeserved privilege and about the poverty and oppression of the people they worked with through community service."

Like Father Cahill and the other chaplains I interviewed, Baer stressed the need to reach students where they were, which often meant dispensing with religion initially and focusing instead on spirituality. "Religion means, literally, to bind," she explained. "Although those of us in the professional religious business see this binding as ultimately freeing, binding of any kind is antithetical to the late-adolescent project. It's a time of questioning and stepping back. And this is good," she said after a pause. "I'm grateful when people inspect their religious heritage and wonder about it. This process of questioning often involves spiritual deepening, a newly awakened sense of commitment to the common good. The questioning process of late adolescence involves new interest in diversity, in other 'tribes,'" she said, holding her fingers up like quotation marks, "and a hunger for commitment to another person, a yearning for connection and self-transcendence. Also," she went on, "a realization about the power of one's own mind, and its capacity for self-transcendence. The chaplains hope that the spiritual aspects of this developmental process will eventually meet with religion and that the two will become mutually informing."

At yet another level of its concentric circles of programming, smaller in its breadth of outreach but no less intense or highly valued, the chaplaincy focused on more traditional forms of spiritual formation. In a variety of ways, including weekly and twice-weekly prayer meetings, individual counseling, and special retreats, these programs engaged students who were intensely committed to religious life and not turned off by the structure or authority of traditional forms of religion. Drawing an even smaller number of students, a final and culminating circle of programs was designed for students going through the process of becoming accepted as members of the Catholic Church or preparing for the Jesuit priesthood. Although large numbers were not expected in either of these programs, they represented the core of chaplaincy responsibility. These core endeavors anchored and ultimately justified the chaplaincy's more broad-reaching and less distinctly Catholic programs.

Women's Prominence among Student Exemplars of Ignatian Spirituality

Situated near the center of campus, the School of Nursing was not a peripheral unit but a place where the Jesuit emphasis on integrating humanistic education and spiritual formation was particularly successful. The program of nursing education stressed the importance of philosophy, theology, history, languages, and the arts as well as the belief that knowledge was not an end in itself. According to one faculty member in nursing, "the Jesuit-educated person" used knowledge to serve others and "insists on seeing others as persons in their entirety, as ends in themselves."

A conversation with nursing students around a big table in the dean's conference room revealed some of the ways in which their religious experiences exemplified the Ignatian emphasis on pursuing knowledge for the purpose of helping souls. Margaret McDowell, a tall, blond, curly-haired young woman, described herself "one of seven kids from a typical Irish family. The whole family attended mass every week." In response to my question about how her religious life had changed or developed during her time at EU, she said that she had stopped going to church when she first got to EU but had started going again. "Now it's for me," she explained. "My spirituality has developed as a result of nursing and having to face death. I have a greater appreciation of all religion, not just my own. Belief in the afterlife helps people prepare for death and cope with it. Religion helps people accept death and find closure. Part of the nurse's job is to help people find closure."

Anita Sorell, an outgoing young African American woman, had also gone through a process of distancing herself from religion and then drawing closer to it as a result of her nursing experience. "I gave up religion my junior year in high school and transferred out of a private Catholic school to go to a public school. I became confused," she said. "Why do you need to be religious or go to church or fast? But as a result of studying nursing and doing clinical nursing work here, I've gotten back into religion, at least in a partial way. Now I believe in a higher power—although I'm still unsure about God—and I believe in prayers." Nursing made her think differently about religion. She explained: "One important moment for me was a clinical experience with a patient who was dying. I wished I could have helped him feel that death was going to be OK, and I wanted to assure him of an afterlife. He asked me to pray for him because he didn't know how to pray. I didn't know either, but we did the best we could."

Patricia Thomas spoke quietly when she described her experience working in a children's pulmonary care unit. "It was part of a volunteer program that simply involved giving body warmth to the children. We were not allowed to get more involved," she said. "We found out that one of the boys was brain-dead and that there was just no life there. This fact really had a major impact on one of the other volunteers I was working with. She was not Catholic or religious, but it became really important to her to hold that boy's hand." All of us around the table leaned forward together, listening to this story. "It was the first thing she would do when she came onto the unit, before she went to any of the other children. This had something to do with experience of a higher power, although I can't explain how. It showed me that faith didn't require Catholicism—here was someone who had no involvement in Catholicism but was deeply engaged in a relationship to or an experience of God or something Godlike."

Denise Johnson, another soft-spoken young woman, commented after a pause: "In nursing you need to have some kind of grasp of faith. You wouldn't be a good nurse if you couldn't deal with the religious and spiritual issues your patients have." Margaret McDowell spoke up again, adding another piece to the picture of the religious dimension of nursing that these students seemed to agree on. "When I was put into the hospital for the beginning of my clinical work sophomore year," she said, "it pierced the college bubble for me. It made me more mature, and made me realize that I was lucky to be healthy. The experience made me want to better myself so that I could deliver the best care."

Many other students besides nursing students described to me their investment in Jesuit idealism and its commitment to helping others. Far more often than not, these students were female. Although the percentage of females among Jesuit-identified students across campus was not as overwhelming as it was in nursing, males were definitely a minority among those who identified with Ignatian spirituality. According to one of the chaplains, about 70–80 percent of students involved in chaplaincy activities were female, and the chaplaincy had a hard time persuading an adequate number of males to become involved.

From Father Salatino's aggressively conservative viewpoint, the pollution of liberalism explained the chaplaincy's inability to attract equal numbers of men to its programs. "I had to deliver something to the chaplaincy office one day," he told me during our interview, "and I was struck by the posters outside—one about transgendered something, one about AIDS, and one about eating disorders. It sends the message that they're not interested in you unless you are a cross-dresser, you have AIDS, or an eating disorder. It's hard for guys to be religious," he said, adopting a more serious tone, "partly because of the feminine emotion associated with religion. There's a lot of confusion about gender and a lot of confusion about sex. Guys are turned off to the chaplaincy because a lot of the guys who hang around it are gay. I've never condemned anyone for homosexual tendencies, and a lot of guys have come to me to talk about this issue. But the chaplaincy makes religion seem kooky and queer—in both senses of the term—and feminine."

According to Salatino, "There *is* a feminine dimension to religion, but the product presented by the chapel is off-putting. The chaplaincy has classes to get in touch with your feelings and to get men to cry, based on the sensitivity model. There's something in all this that's not bad," he admitted, "but it's mixed up with all these sixties types trying to keep that time alive. The chaplaincy doesn't sufficiently respect the masks that men wear. God will strip us of our masks at a certain point, but it's important to recognize how important those masks are to people. The chaplaincy needs to have more respect for ordinary people."

The preponderance of women among students who strongly identified with Ignatian spirituality and its commitment to the poor was somewhat ironic in light of the fact that the Jesuit order was exclusively male. For some of the students who were the most serious about their religious vocations, the exclusion of women from the priesthood presented a real problem.

Bridget Olson was one example of an undergraduate deeply inspired by Ignatian spirituality and deeply frustrated by the fact that her sex prohibited her from being a candidate for admission to the Jesuit order. She was a philosophy major and an outstanding student well known to faculty and administrators on campus, as well as to many of her fellow undergraduates, who elected her to high office in the student government. An extremely capable and busy young woman with a part-time secretary, she seemed to be destined for a national or international career in public service. Already, she had amassed a number of significant political accomplishments as a representative of the student body and spokesperson for student concerns to the administration and board of trustees.

Olson's success and popularity were partly due to her unpretentious and disarming demeanor. For all her bold ideas and impressive skills as a speaker and organizer, her appearance and interpersonal behavior were quite down-to-earth. She grew up in an urban environment, spoke with an ethnic accent, and bought her clothes at thrift shops. One of the building custodians whom I interviewed counted her as a good friend.

Olson made it clear to me that her primary concern and passion in life was service to the poor. She said she had first volunteered at a homeless shelter as part of her church confirmation as a child. The Catholic schools she attended while growing up strengthened her desire to live a Christian life and her habits of volunteer service, but it was not until she became a university student that she attained an intellectual understanding of the importance of serving the poor as an essential aspect of Christian life. As a sophomore, she enrolled in a yearlong course that combined volunteer service with academic reading and seminar discussion. For the service component of the course, she went back to the same homeless shelter where she had worked as a child. As a result of the readings and class discussions that contextualized her service, a whole new dimension opened up and she became aware, as she put it, of "the deeper meaning of putting soup in a bowl." The contrast between the university's "Gap and J Crew environment" and the homeless shelter "really hit" her. It was a transformative experience and, as she stressed, an intellectual one. Readings in Plato, Aristotle, the New Testament, and present-day commentaries on American society helped her see that she had an ethical responsibility to help people less fortunate than she and that her own development as a person would be stymied without this outreach to others. As a result of this course, Olson came to understand the importance of community activism and community leadership in her life as a Christian and as a woman.

As a person raised in a Catholic family, in Catholic schools, and in a city with a large Irish-Catholic population, Olson had a strong self-identification as a Catholic. Unlike many of her classmates from more affluent, suburban backgrounds whose identification with Catholicism or any other religious tradition was weaker or complicated by greater exposure to a variety of religious traditions, Olson took her identity as a Catholic for granted. At the same time, however, she had concerns that placed her at odds with some of the official teachings of the Catholic Church.

She expressed frustration over the question of what she would do after graduation. "I know that I am a child of God," she told me one afternoon in her office in the Student Union. "And I know that I have been called by God to a religious vocation. I want to do and be all the things Jesuits do and be." In response to my question about whether she was interested in WomanChurch or any of the alternative Catholic movements that ignored the church's official ban against women's ordination, she was quick to reply. "I don't want to go underground," she said. "I want to be out in the open. I want the real thing. I have a calling from God, and I'm not going to let men stop me. We can't let the people who deny religious office to women win. It's our church too. I would rather fight and fight out in the open. When the people see that women are called and committed, then the administrators will have to listen." Then she paused and sighed. "I would love to be a Jesuit," she said. After another pause, she summed up her dispute with the church. "I feel that the church leads women on, giving them a taste of spiritual responsibility but not allowing them to have the main responsibility. I have felt led on and religiously teased."

Tellingly, Olson's anger at being excluded from consideration for ordination was directed more at the Catholic Church than at the Society of Jesus. As she was well aware, several Jesuits on campus were advocates of women's ordination, and the Jesuit order had gone further in officially committing itself to women's equality than any other male religious order in the Catholic Church. Jesuits on campus cosponsored with the Women's Resource Center a "Take Back the Night" event and were responsive when Olson and others pressed for more women at the altar at masses, especially at the annual baccalaureate mass. In the fall of 1995, a campus forum entitled "Jesuit Solidarity with Women" discussed the document "Jesuits and the Situation of the Women in Church and Civil Society," issued by the Thirty-fourth General Congregation of the Society of Jesus in 1994–95. Although it stopped short of affirming women's ordination and noted "the need for a real delicacy in our response," the document stressed "the essential equality of women and men in Jesuit ministries." It advocated "support for liberation movements for women which oppose their exploitation and encourage their entry into political and social life" and recommended that special attention be paid to the feminization of poverty and the problem of violence against women. "Above all," the document asserted, "we want to commit the Society in a more formal and explicit way to regard this solidarity with women as integral to our mission." The document went on to emphasize that "this work for reconciliation between women and men in all its forms" could "flow only from our God of love and justice who reconciles all and promises a world in which 'there is neither Jew nor Greek, there is neither slave nor free, there is neither male nor female, for you are all one in Christ Jesus' (Gal 3:28)."

Olson found a lot of support on campus for women's ordination. Posted on the door to the office of one of the most influential and highly respected lay theologians on campus during my visits was a picture, with no caption, of a vivacious woman wearing a nun's wimple and clerical collar.

Course Work in Jesuit Spirituality

Every undergraduate at the university was required to take courses in both theology and philosophy. Both departments offered some options in this core curriculum while adhering to the general principle that students should be educated in classic texts in the Western, Christian tradition. Students were able to fulfill their core requirements in both theology and philosophy, as Olson did, by taking a yearlong course that combined academic reflection on classic texts with social service. Although it was not labeled as an introduction to Jesuit spirituality, it functioned in that capacity as effectively as any program on campus.

Admission to the course was not automatic, and more than a few first-year students eager to take the course were forced to wait until their sophomore year before they could gain admission. Out of approximately 2,000 students fulfilling core requirements in theology and philosophy, between 300 and 400 enrolled in the course each year and well over 100 were on the waiting list. Although student leaders responsible for monitoring the volunteer segment of the course worried that further expansion might jeopardize the communal aspect of the course, the philosophy department, which administered the course, was planning an expansion. Other community service programs sponsored by the chaplaincy had grown up around the course. These chaplaincy programs did not involve academic course work, but they did attract students who had already taken the course or wanted some of the experience associated with it.

I interviewed the founder of the course, a somber, dark-haired man about fifty years old, one afternoon in his small office. Many people on campus had mentioned his name to me and pointed proudly to the successful course he had developed as an example of the integration of intellectual and religious life that was characteristic of Ignatian spirituality. But despite being celebrated in this way, Richard Fox seemed sorrowful. I wondered if he was weighed down with the images and stories of people who suffered in poverty and the sheer effort of trying to get mostly affluent and healthy undergraduates to identify with them.

In our conversation, Fox emphasized that the purpose of the course he supervised was to transform students' worldviews by enabling them to discover, through personal encounters with "the losers" in society, the limitations of typical American beliefs about poverty. These typical beliefs included liberal notions that economic justice could be achieved simply by improving the social system as well as conservative notions that economic justice could be achieved by removing obstacles to self-determination. The course was developed, he explained, to help students realize that poverty and suffering were not simply the result of lack of self-determination and that belief in the equality of people who suffer and respect for their dignity required more than a supply of economic entitlements. Such limited and finally negative conceptions of justice were inadequate to explain the feelings that students came to experience as a result of the combination of service work and guided reflection. More specifically, the course was designed to lead students to the idea that agape, the love exemplified by Jesus Christ, was the most appropriate response to the people they met and tried to serve and the most appropriate basis for conceptualizing justice.

I gathered from a number of interviews and a stack of reading material that this innovative course combining social service, academic reflection, and spiritual transformation was not, at its outset, so clearly focused on the personal development of students. Its evolution over thirty years of trial and error reflected an increasingly close identification with the concepts and strategies associated with the existential interpretation of Ignatian spirituality popular among religious progressives on campus. The ethos of the Jesuit order had also evolved during this time along some of the same trajectories, and those who developed the course drew inspiration from larger trends sweeping through the Jesuit order at the same time that they helped shape the meaning of Ignatian spirituality on campus. For example, the order's leadership in breaking down barriers between priests and laity was reflected in the fact that the founder and chief developer of the course, like several other influential interpreters of Ignatian spirituality on campus, was not a Jesuit. Although Fox was strongly supported from the beginning by a Jesuit who chaired the philosophy department, his intellectual influence on the development of the course was evidence that Jesuits were not the sole owners of Ignatian spirituality on campus. Another non-Jesuit spokesperson explained that the university "is not about Jesuits as a particular group of men but about the vision of Ignatius, which Jesus shared, along with many other people, not only Catholics, but Protestants, Jews, and probably others outside the Judeo-Christian tradition."

According to a history of the course written in 1995, its origins can be traced to the 1960s and student protests against the war in Vietnam, which was strongly supported on campus. A small group of pacifists organized the Catholic Peace Fellowship (CPF) in opposition to the war. As one of the first student movements on campus, if not *the* first, the CPF took out an ad in the campus newspaper in the spring of 1966 calling for an end to the war. The CPF also sponsored a series of antiwar activities—countered by activities planned by the anticommunist group, Young Americans for Freedom—during Vietnam Week the following spring.

A campus chapter of Students for a Democratic Society formed out of the ranks of the CPF and called itself the Leftist Collective. Although most of the activities sponsored by the Leftist Collective were linked to a commitment to nonviolence, some of the members of the collective participated in the destruction of the ROTC office on campus. As calls to violence emerged within the Leftist Collective, the pacifist CPF contingent withdrew and joined a religious group formed in the early 1960s to promote spiritual renewal and Ignatian spirituality. This group had evolved out of the Sodality of St. Stanislas, which promoted devotional piety and figured prominently in the extracurricular life of students in earlier years. But the religious group founded in the 1960s focused on helping others rather than on devotional rites, and its members were active as tutors in public schools and other community-service programs. Energized by an influx of students from the Leftist Collective, members of this group formed a Revitalization Corps for community service and received formal recognition and financial support from the student government.

As this student group developed, the Jesuit who chaired the philosophy department became interested in the concept of service learning and in establishing a formal relationship between the group and his department. Engaged in debates within the Jesuit order about social justice and its relationship to the Christian gospel and Ignatian spirituality, he worked to establish the community service program run by students in the Revitalization Corps as part of the core curriculum in philosophy. A proposed course in service learning met with considerable opposition from faculty who resisted the idea of giving academic credit for community service. The program also experienced a variety of internal problems, such as difficulties finding appropriate community service sites and developing guidelines for student work in these community placements. Most important, people had difficulty coming to terms with the gap between the original purpose of the program as an agent of social change and what students were actually doing and learning through community service work. In 1971, the founding undergraduate, Richard Fox, returned to the university to direct the program as a graduate student. During the 1970s, he led the way in creating an important intellectual shift in the program away from its original emphasis on effecting social change to what seemed at the time to be a more realistic emphasis on social action and classroom readings in leftist social criticism. Then he initiated a second important change in the late 1970s after he returned again to the university as a professor. Increasingly convinced that the New Left texts read in the classroom component of the course were dated, irrelevant to students, and not particularly effective in helping them make intellectual sense of what they were experiencing in their community service placements, he and other faculty began to incorporate religious readings from Genesis, Exodus, Job, Matthew, Luke, and Romans. They also included readings in ethics from Plato, Aristotle, Augustine, and Thomas Aquinas as well as essays by twentieth-century writers concerned with problems in contemporary American society and committed to greater development of social responsibility among individuals.

According to Fox and several of his associates whom I interviewed, the course was still not taken seriously by all faculty on campus. And some faculty members teaching sections of the course were dissatisfied with what they perceived as low levels of student interest in social analysis and many students' inability to conceptualize their placement experiences in intellectual terms. But despite these reservations and flaws, the course had grown to maximum capacity and was supported and publicized by the administration as a flagship course representing the university's investment in Ignatian spirituality. Many students I spoke to who had taken the course raved about it and were quite articulate about its methods and goals. The course had given them the opportunity to undergo a process of personal transformation and spiritual growth through direct experience of society's ills and participation in a community of students, professors, and supervisors committed to compassion and justice.

In a series of small group interviews, more than twenty students offered accounts of the personal transformations they underwent as a result of taking the course. One student claimed that his "whole attitude toward life changed." He said he went into the course "as a business major with a goal of making money and came out with a dual major in secondary education and English." Another student commented: "Examination and challenge, that's what the course is about. It's a way of life. Once you're in it, you're in it for life."

This student emphasized that "the element of community in discussion groups" was essential to the transformation that individuals underwent. When his group met again after Christmas break, the first class was spent "hugging each other and finding out how we were." Another student claimed that the course "educates your heart, not just your mind." She went into the course as "a pre-med biology major who wanted to save the world by being a great doctor. Now I've found another way to do that, through interpersonal relationships, just talking to people and respecting them." She added, emphasizing the benefits she derived in her personal development and attitude toward life: "Volunteering is not just doing something for others, it's for me. It's, like, my religion." She still planned to be a doctor but saw medicine as her spiritual vocation: "It's not just my career aim, it's what I'm going to *be*."

A dialogue among some of the students who had taken the course shed further light on the experience of personal transformation and its effect in causing a questioning of received beliefs that led to deeper religious commitment. In a basement classroom with metal tables, a big chalkboard, and chairs with arm-desks drawn together in a circle, I explained the purpose of my study to eight students and asked them to describe how the course had contributed to their spiritual development. Three students started to speak at once. They laughed, and Meg Li, an enthusiastic young woman with Asian features, won out. "Everyone should take this course," she said. "For those who have taken it, it becomes the core of their college experience. It is just an amazing experience. I would take it every year if I could. Taking the course definitely involves a spiritual transformation in terms of your inner being." Everyone nodded. "It's hard to put into words what happens to you. Last year, the year I took the course, I actually experienced a decrease in religion, in the religious beliefs I had. We focused more on societal issues than on theology. But my whole view of God changed." Everyone listened closely. "I don't know what I believe about God any more. I used to believe that God was a person. Now I think of God as more like something inside each person, as agape. But this was hard and confusing because the course coincided with the death of my grandmother, and I didn't know what to believe."

Cindy Moran, a thin young woman with long dark hair and straight bangs, said that her grandmother died too just after the course started. "It was devastating," she said. "She died just after I was reading existentialism and thinking about the possibility that no God existed."

Felicia Stanislov, a pretty brunette in a cable sweater and jeans, confirmed that "the course gives you experiences that cause you to question your beliefs." Her service placement was at a home for sexually and physically abused girls, and her experience there caused her to see her own life in a different way. "I came from a middle-class, traditional Catholic background with three sisters the ages of some of the girls I got to know. I couldn't bear to think of anything like that happening to my sisters," Stanislov said with some feeling. "Where did these girls fit in relation to my notion of God? There is a strong possibility that these girls will never recover from what they've been through. They don't deserve to have had this happen to them, so why are they going through it? They didn't even have faith to rely on." After a pause, she went on: "I thought about talking to them about my belief that their entry into heaven would be easier because of their suffering, but it wasn't appropriate to preach to them. I came to respect these girls, and to learn a lot from them. I respected them a lot the first time they respected me because they were strong enough to be able to trust someone, even after what they had gone through. It made me happy and proud to help."

Recalling how she had been moved by the children she worked with in her placement, Moran said that when she returned to them after her grandmother's death, "the children ran up and hugged me and said they were sorry, even though I hadn't been there very long. One girl wrote me a note saying, 'May you have the love of God,' and it really touched me." Like Li and Stanislov, Moran found that the course made her question her religious beliefs. She was baptized a Catholic but took her life and her religious upbringing for granted until the course led her to reflect more deeply on her own situation. "The course made me realize how lucky I was," she said. "One day I wanted to do an art project with the kids and went to the supply cabinet and found a box of crayons and some really thin paper. We did our project, but I had something else in mind, involving better materials, and I remembered all the things I had to work with in art as a kid." She found herself asking, "Why was it like this? It was so unfair. The course made me more socially aware and changed my ideas about what to do in the future. I don't care about how much money I make."

Sue Ellen Tracey, a curly-haired redhead with freckles who was wearing a big sweatshirt, had been waiting to get into the conversation. Her placement was at a home for battered women. At first, she wondered if the home was doing any good, if it was really helping women deal with their problems. "One of my friends died and we were reading Job in the course," she said. "I learned that suffering is not always paying for a sin. The philosophy and theology texts put me in a different frame of mind. It changes everyone. I really became a different person." The motto of the home where she had her service placement was "A solution, not a shelter," but by Christmas, she confessed, "I didn't think it was providing any solutions because the women kept coming back. I mean I was glad to see them, but I wanted them not to have to come to the home. Then we read Robert Cole's book, *There Are No Children Here*, and I saw the importance of providing stability and consistency." She also saw the importance of her own religious faith. "The course reconfirmed a lot of my religious beliefs. I come from a fairly pious family. Now I see the importance of really believing in what you're doing, not just saying Hail Marys."

Mark O'Cheskey, a sturdy young man with a very earnest expression, confessed that he found the course "really hard and challenging. It was hard for me to leave the after-school program where I worked. It would get dark and I was afraid for the kids. A lot of teenagers got shot, and there were a lot of drugs and prostitution. The kids didn't deserve that," he said with emotion, "having to stay there while I got to go home. We talked a lot about this in the discussion groups," he added. "I became conscious of the way society was set up, the probability of what would become of us as graduates of this university and the probability of what would become of those kids in the projects. They were just like other kids in many ways, full of energy and fun to be with. I identified with them and it was painful." He went on to explain that his class had a speaker who talked about redlining and how the banks had contributed to the deterioration of the part of the city where he had his placement. "In the 1960s during urban renewal, nothing was redeveloped in the area. There is no small economy there. None of the money stays in the neighborhood. The books the kids had were ridiculous," he said with exasperation. "They were so out-of-date and full of typos you couldn't even read them. No one can get ahead like that. They thought of themselves as stupid and not supposed to be able to read. The message sent to young blacks in poverty is to give up."

Li said: "They know they're not going to college. What they have ahead of them is drugs, gangs, and death." Tracey agreed. "The bus ride to the women's shelter alone is enough to stir you," she said. Stanislov saw it differently. "The media portrays the inner city as unsafe, unapproachable, a horrible place you shouldn't enter," she said. "But we went there and got to know people. It affects your political outlook."

Li said she grew up with the American Dream. "My dad really believes in it. He worked his way up from a horrible family. But now I think there is no such thing as an American Dream. How can you get above the books," she asked, referring to O'Cheskey's comment, "which are so bad?" As a result of the course, Li said she "came out with a very different view of welfare than the idea I had, that people are on welfare because they're lazy. That might apply only to a fraction of 1 percent of people. Most people on welfare really need it." The course also led Tracey to question the political beliefs she had grown up with. "My parents are Republican conservatives," she said. "I didn't question that until I took the course. Everyone at the home for women where I had my placement is against the Republicans."

Turning back to the internal change produced by the course, Moran emphasized that "other courses don't change you as a person. This course is about personal and social responsibility, about having a duty to others in the community, not just your family. Like Hillary Clinton's idea that it takes a village to make a child." Stanislov chimed in: "*The Ethics of Authenticity*, by Charles Taylor, argues that you can't really call yourself religious if you haven't challenged what you believe through experience, if you haven't fleshed out what your beliefs mean in real life." Moran agreed: "My first year at East I said, where's the Catholic influence here? I didn't see it until I took this course."

Tracey observed that her commitment to the Catholic faith deepened as a result of taking the course: "I would still call myself a conservative Catholic. I still go to church every Sunday. But now I'm a spiritual person too." Stanislov agreed: "I am definitely a conservative Catholic and strongly pro-life. But I have used what I experienced in this course to challenge my beliefs. When you see the situations of some people, you have a better sense of the idea that it's not even worth it to be born. It challenges my prolife belief. I am not an unquestioning conservative. I believe that life does fulfill God's will and that we all have a responsibility to serve each other."

O'Cheskey summed things up. "The course brings everyone together— liberal, conservative, and not religious. It gives us a common bond even though we're very different. A lot of us are religious," he explained, "and a lot of us have become more religious because of the program. It brought me closer to God and to realizing the importance of God in my life. It also changed my understanding of God. I used to think God was a person up there. Now I think of God as a presence within myself and others. I think of God as agape."

Conservative Aspects of Campus Religious Life

Although support for women's ordination was high and commitment to the church's ban on contraceptives low, most people on campus seemed to agree with the church's position on abortion. A few committed Catholics were prochoice, but the middle of the Catholic road on campus tended to be occupied by opponents of abortion who supported women's ordination. Some who identified themselves as feminists complained about being stigmatized as a result of the perceived linkage between feminism and prochoice. They pointed out that "feminism is the 'F' word" on campus and that even moderate feminists were considered radicals. Stacey Vann, an articulate and savvy senior, explained to me one afternoon in the Women's Resource Center that the university's resistance to anything associated with women's control over their own bodies was the prime example of its oppressive patriarchal character. "The dean of students puts restrictions on us that do not obtain for more conservative groups," she complained. "Any campus discussion of prochoice sponsored by the Women's Resource Center must be balanced by equal time granted to prolife debaters, but the prolifers are not placed under such restriction." At a recent debate on abortion sponsored by the school's Partnership for Life Issues, "the whole thing was moderated by a conservative priest who cast the debate as abortion pro or con. The prolife speaker was brilliant," she acknowledged. In contrast, "the prochoice speaker is a bisexual and an atheist who was extremely emotional and beside the point, dwelling at length on his wife's abortion. At the end, when I asked him what would make him change his position on abortion, he said he would change when conservatives stopped harassing gays."

The previous year, the Women's Resource Center had a big turnout for a bus trip to a Stop the Violence against Women rally supported by the National Organization of Women (NOW). According to Vann, the dean's office "balked when WRC accepted NOW's offer to supply buses for overflow. NOW does a lot of things, and prochoice is just one small part. But the university won't condone anything associated with prochoice."

Vann admitted that, on the whole, the school had become "more laid back" in the course of her four years. "But at the same time, the conservative element has become more strident and well defined. The conservative student newspaper picks on feminists and on the Women's Resource Center and distorts facts about them," she maintained. For example, when her English class analyzed *Playboy* magazine from a feminist perspective, "the newspaper criticized us for reading pornography."

Because the religious culture of campus life had consolidated to focus on spirituality and personal transformation in the course of its development in the 1980s and 1990s, many conservative Catholic students had come to feel at home in academic courses and chaplaincy programs that had initially been developed in accord with liberal and radical ideas about social justice. Because of their involvement in these programs, conservative students often became less rigid in their beliefs. Likewise, the Ignatian emphasis on fidelity to personal experience helped create a culture of interpersonal respect that tended to undercut ideological warfare on campus, foster understanding between individuals, and thaw self-perceptions and perceptions of others that might otherwise be frozen within ideological camps. As a result, many bridges between social justice concerns and deep-seated and, to some extent at least, conservative religious principles had been strengthened or newly constructed.

Nevertheless, a vocal group of students and faculty resisted this trend toward cultural and religious unification. This group perceived such efforts as hopelessly tainted by liberal ideology. In opposition, it focused on obedience to the magisterium of the church as a means of preventing the liberal watering down of true Catholic religious principles.

While I was on campus, the focal point of the controversy over liberalism provoked by this group was the conservative student newspaper. The paper started in the early 1980s as a political paper with a strong anticommunist emphasis. It had a tenuous existence and disappeared in the mid-1980s. When it came back in the late 1980s, it still had a political edge, but the focus shifted from communism to defense of the Vatican and its official teachings, especially with regard to issues of sexuality and gender. Students who worked for the paper went into the health services clinic on campus and asked for birth control prescriptions and abortion referrals. After receiving the prescriptions and referrals, they wrote a story exposing and condemning the easy availability of these things at a Catholic institution. Although they complained about the methods the writers had used to obtain information and defended the clinic, university administrators brought the offending practices to an end.

The paper collapsed in the early 1990s and then sprang to life again after the Women's Resource Center, which was funded by the university, publicized a prochoice rally in Washington, D.C., and urged university students to attend. Conservatives expressed their disapproval, and debate over the event dominated the opinion page of the regular student newspaper for two or three months. Soon after, Mike Leahy, a conservative student who worked for the paper, prepared a reaction piece on *Evangelia vitae*, Pope John Paul XXIII's encyclical on the sacrality of human life. Leahy was keen on drawing out the implications of the document for both academic and social life on campus, but the piece was heavily edited and the editors discouraged him from doing further writing for the paper. He then turned to the conservative paper and led the way in its revitalization.

The paper's faculty sponsor was Father Salatino. Much of the hostility directed toward him was linked to his support of the paper and its aggressive condemnation of religious liberalism on campus. One of the most controversial issues associated with the paper and Father Salatino while I was on campus concerned the posting of offensive signs on office doors. According to Father Salatino, "Last year, a student scrawled 'Prohate Anti-Christian' on my door. I suggested to Joe, an editor at the student newspaper, that they do a satirical piece with me overreacting to this 'hate crime.' When it came out, I thought it was hysterical. Sophomoric perhaps, but Joe is a sophomore." Salatino went on to say that no one associated with the alternative paper had any inkling that a swastika had been scrawled on a history professor's door some weeks before. "It was widely believed that I was satirizing the swastika incident. But I had not even *heard* about it," Salatino insisted. The local media got hold of the story and published articles about anti-Semitism at the university. "One of the articles was really vicious. The whole thing was so ridiculous, so absurd," Salatino said, shaking his head in disbelief. "In the midst of all this, my chairman actually hugged me and said he was so sorry that I had to go through all this. I told him that my conscience was clear and that I just had to go on."

Partly as a result of stories like these, the conservative paper became a serious rival to the regular student paper. Because of the lively debates it aired, almost everyone I talked to seemed to be reading the conservative paper and to have something to say about it. At the same time, the stylistic quality of the paper improved and this attracted an increasing number of student reporters, not all of whom shared the conservative philosophy expressed on the editorial pages. Indeed, some of the students who strongly identified with Ignatian spirituality felt they had a responsibility to get to know and learn to work with the conservative students who had revitalized the paper. This effort to promote better religious understanding on campus had the effect of making the paper more mainstream and less aggressively conservative.

Conservative students also participated in the St. Thomas More Society, which hosted lectures and forums organized from a conservative perspective. During my visits to campus, the society sponsored a debate on abortion, a critique of feminism by a conservative Catholic woman, and a lecture by an Orthodox rabbi who argued that secularization was the common enemy of both Jews and Christians. A panel on women's ordination featured a conservative priest who emphasized women's importance in the church but outlined the reasons why their ordination to the priesthood was inappropriate. The society also sponsored a weekly hour of prayer—called the Hour of Power—centering on the rosary and contemplation of Christ in the Eucharist.

Several of the students who worked on the alternative newspaper or participated in the St. Thomas More Society rejected the term "conservative."

"It's a limiting term," Leahy explained. "I prefer the term 'religious.' Being philosophically respectful of tradition is being religious." This appropriation of the word "religious" irritated some on campus. As one theology professor fumed, "They're arrogant and nasty. The biggest problem with Catholicism at this university and elsewhere is those types. They are extremely visible and vocal, and the Catholicism they represent is repugnant. If I thought that was what Catholicism was, I wouldn't want to have anything to do with it."

The students most closely associated with the conservative newspaper told me that they simply wanted the university to live up to its mission statement, which affirmed the school's Catholic identity. They also said that for the school to become truly Catholic, it must wean itself from its reliance on inclusive, transdenominational interpretations of Ignatian spirituality. As Leahy put it, "That kind of spirituality is a retreat from Catholic identity. If the school continues to embrace it, it will no longer be Catholic."

The preferable form of spirituality, according to Leahy, was rooted in strict obedience to the teachings of the church and devotion to its sacraments. And it was only in the context of that obedience and devotion, he explained to me over pizza in the Student Union cafeteria, not simply in warm feelings of community, that social justice made sense. "There's a large group of religious students on campus who find God through social justice and helping their neighbor," he said matter-of-factly. "They are very people-oriented and community-oriented. They find the Christian spirit in their relationships with other people. There's another group," he went on carefully, "which is not entirely separate from the first group, that puts more emphasis on personal spirituality, internal reality, and the sacraments. The sort of mass these people prefer is more solemn, more focused on prayer within themselves versus a community gathering. They are very directed to Christ and to the sacrifice re-created for us during the mass and believe that community is created through that."

Although he made it clear that he identified with the second group, he was eager to have me know that he, too, wanted to serve the poor and was concerned about social justice. "As a member of the University Leadership Program, I'm helping to start the first Habitat for Humanity chapter on campus. Each side has something to learn from the other," he said fairly. "What *we* have to offer," he said, not so fairly, "is the idea that Christ is revealed through his church." Leahy was a self-confident young man with a sense of his own importance on campus. On the masthead of the conservative paper, his name appeared on a separate line and was the only name preceded by the courtesy title "Mr."

The predominant tendency on campus to interpret faith in terms of concern for social justice troubled Leahy. He came from a conservative

Republican family in the Midwest, and the talk he heard at EU about social justice sounded to him a lot like the liberalism his family staunchly opposed. Even more important, he saw the emphasis on social justice as a kind of wedge issue that loosened loyalty to the hierarchy and official teachings of the church and allowed Catholics to define their faith in an alternative way. He complained that at EU "economic issues are dealt with in light of socialism, Marxism, or capitalism but not in terms of the church's social teachings on justice." He interpreted the campus emphasis on social justice as an extension of "the philosophy of the Democratic Party, which champions government assistance and big federal government." He saw a conflict between this philosophy and the church's teachings that people are subjects rather than objects. And he saw the church's principle of subsidiarity, which emphasized the need for local administration and community gathering in parish life, as advocating local administration of welfare. "So," he reasoned, "there's no reason to criticize the Republican opposition to federal welfare as an opposition to social justice."

Another conservative student active in the St. Thomas More Society agreed. "The Jesuits focus on social justice and on building a just community," explained Tom Fogarty, an intense, worried young man. "Everything is centered around justice and service," he complained. "I would like to see that emphasis more fully integrated with Catholic dogma and specifically with the Catholic doctrines of salvation, sin, heaven, and hell. Students are leading unvirtuous lives," he declared, getting to what was for him the real moral issue. "A lot of fornication and heavy drinking goes on, and the Jesuits do little to intervene or counter with programs for virtuous living. Here it is countercultural not to drink to excess, not to have premarital sex."

In the past, Fogarty believed, respect for the church and Catholic morality was stronger. Jesuits were once leaders in this regard, but they now led the way in religion's decline. "The school used to have a lot more Jesuits, required chapel three times a week, and a lot more required theology and philosophy. Then the Jesuit order went through a period of reform and secularization around Vatican II," and as a result, he asserted, "a lot of the supernatural was taken out. A lot of meditation and prayer was taken out. A liberationist tendency took over, to the extent that Jesuits have become barely distinguishable from the world. The emphasis on finding God in all things is too general and all-encompassing," he complained. "There's a lot of moral subjectivism among the Jesuits here. There's a lot of anti-authority and liberal ideas. The Jesuits are set in opposition to the church. They are more open-minded than the church, more respectful of ideologies like feminism. They try to penetrate current issues of feminism and homosexuality and get justice and love in there. But," he assured me, nodding in some approval, "there is opposition to these trends within the order, and the order is deeply divided."

"Students don't see much Catholicism here," Fogarty maintained. "The Catholic presence is not really noticeable. At least one of the chaplains would like to do more with Catholicism. He leads a prayer group that is good and a retreat based on the spiritual exercises of Ignatius. But there are too many other chaplains who are secularly oriented. There would be a huge scream if he moved the chaplaincy more in the Catholic direction. No one has found a way around this problem."

Although most of the students involved in explicitly conservative activities came from staunchly conservative families and saw their activism at the university as a way of being true to their heritage, some discovered the conservative subculture on campus after an odyssey of confusion and anxiety. Ted Kozack outlined his passage from doubt and despair: "I went through a transformation, you could call it a conversion, in my junior year in high school. Before that I was a hippie punk." Having grown up with "only a vague notion of the Catholic faith because of the general catechesis problem rampant in Catholic religious education, I had little guidance through a very emotional phase in my life," this brooding, handsome young man told me over pasta. "I fell into the hands of Jesuits at a Jesuit high school. Although I didn't know it at the time, these were Reform Jesuits. Their emphasis on love and justice just didn't seem adequate to me. It didn't explain why Christ came down." The first Jesuits he encountered at EU made things even worse. "They questioned whether you can really know or really have any answers. Scripture was approached through historical criticism, which led to doubting the validity of Scripture and focusing on inconsistencies, which were not presented as only apparent." But things turned around for Kozack the summer after his first year when he read a book by one of the conservative professors in philosophy. In that book, he said, "I found intelligent answers to my doubts and a ladder to climb out of the dark hole I had fallen in. I took a course with him the next year and became a philosophy major," Ted said gratefully. "He showed me that reason can be applied to show the possibility of religious truths. He also helped me see that reason was like a car that takes you to the lake. Once you're there, you have to get out of the car and jump in. But I had been stuck in the middle of nowhere with no car to take me to the lake."

Another conservative philosophy major, Brad Williams, came to the university for a Catholic education. He saw the emphasis on social justice as an intellectual cop-out and a way to dodge obedience to the official teachings of the church. "There's absolutely no hostility to practicing the faith here," Brad told me over coffee at Dunkin' Donuts. "Just great indifference. The social service emphasis is a kind of retaliation against the way the church was before Vatican II," he explained. "People are resistant to intellectual discussions of faith because they lead you to get into what's right and what's wrong and people here back away from that. They're into individual subjectivism. Whatever feels good for you is OK with me. Social justice is an attempt to make up for what this approach lacks. I can't use my intelligence—that leads to right versus wrong—so I'll use my emotions and physical labor to help others." From Williams's perspective, this emphasis on social justice left out the doctrines of faith. "There's a plethora of masses, but do people understand the theological implications of the mass or its supernatural effect? People don't understand what it is to be Catholic."

According to Williams, the problem with EU and with American culture more generally was that "many people believe there is no truth to pursue." Although most students came to the university for materialistic reasons, he believed they wanted something more. "Students crave for more faith, for more of the supernatural," he told me earnestly. "They know that natural life is futile. Students are hungry for Catholic spirituality, and they are just given scraps. At the same time, they are scared of more commitment. They know they would have to change their life-style. Getting rid of bad habits is the hardest thing to do, and the support for it just doesn't exist here."

These conservative students saw themselves as countercultural with respect to the hedonism and indifference to religion that they felt characterized the vast majority of their peers. In this respect, they were similar to the most committed advocates of social justice on campus, who also viewed themselves as awash in a sea of materialism and spiritual indifference. But the conservatives were often critical of what they considered the prevailing tendency to define faith in terms of justice and wanted to contrast this tendency with their own commitment to defining faith in terms of the sacred authority of the institutional church. They were quite adamant on this point and regarded it as essential to their countercultural, Catholic identity. The positions taken by these students came partly from received ideas from their families and partly from the positions taken by aggressively conservative faculty. At the same time, their ideological fervor was also tempered by their exposure to professors and chaplains who encouraged them to be more open-minded and less judgmental.

Religious Life on the Margins and Outskirts of Catholic Inclusiveness

Some non-Catholic students seemed to feel like fish out of water at this Catholic university. A new professor in the theology department, Sarah

Friedman, who was also a rabbi, commented that Jewish students felt "a bit overwhelmed. And they have a hard time finding other Jewish students." Moreover, she continued, "I've noticed Jewish students being apologetic about their religion as a way to fit in." She encouraged them to be more confident and public about their religion. " 'They will respect you more,' I tell them. 'We're here and proud of being here.' " She also emphasized to Jewish students that Judaism had a strong tradition of social service, and she encouraged them to participate in the social service projects that the school offered.

Some Protestant students also felt overwhelmed, left out, or even angry. In one of the paragraphs that seniors in the capstone course wrote about their religious life during their four years at EU, one student complained: "This is a Jesuit school, and I am not of the Catholic faith. I, therefore, did not participate in church services at college. My roommates go to church weekly, and I am somewhat envious that they were able to find a religious community at school." Although one nonreligious student reported that the university "has been good about not excluding those who are not Catholic," another Protestant student was vehement about the painfulness of not fitting in. "I've often felt like a religious outcast. I felt like the Catholics looked down on me for not attending mass weekly or for eating meat on Fridays during Lent. Being a Protestant, I did not attend mass nor did I go to a Presbyterian church off campus since I had no way of getting there. On two occasions I did attend mass at the Catholic church near campus, but I felt I did not belong there. I often say prayers and talk to God even though privacy is difficult to find at college."

The Center for African, Hispanic, Asian, and Native American Students (AHANA) served a diverse population. AHANA students who were not Catholics seemed especially appreciative of the communal environment of the AHANA center, which enabled them to draw together as ethnic and religious outsiders. Ladonna Morales, a Hispanic Pentecostal who served as assistant director of AHANA, explained to me that many of the students who came to AHANA had different behavior patterns and expectations from those of other students on campus. As a result, Morales explained, "it can be difficult to support them. They are unlikely to go to the counseling centers on campus." Among the various services AHANA provided, a "Gospel Caravan" was available to take students to Protestant churches on Sunday mornings. "Church environments are places where AHANA students are accustomed to finding support, and we try to build on that," Morales explained. "We have a lot of closet Christians—students who go home every weekend to go to church. They're very open about their beliefs back at home, but here they're different. They don't let anyone know that they're Christian."

One of the difficulties, Morales explained, was that AHANA students often came from strong Protestant backgrounds and their understanding of what it meant to be Christian differed from the dominant understanding on campus. "Catholic students are drawn to serve others," she said. "They're always trying to be of service, it's part of what being Catholic is, and it's what the Jesuit aspects of the university encourage." Morales also pointed to the strong emphasis on maintaining moral purity in Catholic culture. For example, student gambling "is seen by many as a betrayal of Catholic and Jesuit values, even though people who expressed this idea didn't use explicitly Christian language to explain it. Parents send their children here because they think they will be safe, that this is a protected environment, and that their children will be morally uplifted or at least be able to maintain their morality." For Hispanic and African American Protestants on campus, "these are not the things that are at the forefront." In addition to engaging in quite different forms of worship, "they have financial issues. They want to give back to the people and the communities who helped them get here. They feel an obligation to reach back and bring others along with them."

A conversation with nine AHANA students confirmed that belief in God played an important role in their personal identities but that the Protestant students had conceptions of what it meant to serve God and live a life of faith that alienated them at times from others on campus and made them feel like strangers. As we sat in a cozy attic room in the AHANA center around several old wooden tables, one young African American woman drew a clear distinction between what she understood to be a Christian life and the culture of service on campus. "I associate the emphasis here on service with humanism," Tamara Pence said. "Students involved in the service movements here are often trying to find spirituality in righteous works and not through Christ," she asserted. Lesa Palmer, an African American woman heavily involved in the gospel choir, agreed. "It's good to help the needy, but you can help the needy and still go to hell. It's not going to get you into heaven. There are a lot of people here who believe in God, but do they know God? I don't think so. You can give a million dollars to the poor and not have faith." Robert Martinez, a Hispanic Protestant, summarized the point. "The service-learning course in philosophy represents the emphasis on service in the Jesuit tradition. The Jesuits and their interpretation of Christianity won the Counter Reformation. At least at this university, they've won."

Barry Rodriguez, a Hispanic Catholic, disagreed. "A good act is a good act," he said, "whatever you believe. If you help someone, you help someone. It's still good whether or not you believe in God or know God. I was raised a Catholic and grew up in a Dominican community, a community that was mostly Dominican but not Catholic. The community was in a black neighborhood, and the Catholic church we went to was in a white neighborhood. I know what it's like to stick out as someone who is different." Here at EU, he said, "it's really easy to feel lost and alone. All these social groups form so quickly, and it's easy to get left out. Things are very balkanized here. You feel isolated and can feel that people are lining up against you. I like coming to AHANA because everyone says 'Hi.' AHANA is one place you can be genuine."

Although he disagreed with the Protestant students on the issue of good deeds, he identified with their feeling of being different and alone. And he praised their kind of church. "Going to Catholic church can be really tedious," he complained. "In the black Protestant churches, everyone dresses up, it's a special occasion, there's a big meal afterwards, a real sense of community, and a real connection with the older people. In Catholic church, you just show up wearing whatever."

Part of the alienation these students expressed derived from the disparity between their financial situation and that of many other students on campus. In many cases, AHANA students received financial aid from the university as part of its program to increase and support diversity in the student body. But as one of the priests on campus told me, most of the undergraduates came from affluent backgrounds and took their own culture of wealth for granted. In his view, the socioeconomic disparity between AHANA students and the vast majority of other undergraduates was the biggest factor in the isolation of minorities. Several of the African American and Hispanic students I spoke with described this alienation in terms of the cold shoulder they got from some of their classmates. One African American staff member at AHANA confirmed that "there are insidious forms of racism at the university that students have to face."

TEACHING RELIGION

Philosophy's Role in Intellectual Debate

The philosophy department was home to the popular service-learning course and its focus on what proponents described as the kind of faith that seeks justice. Important aspects of this core course in service learning were carried forward in the philosophy curriculum, and many students who took the course went on to take more courses in philosophy. As one student said, the course "makes a lot of philosophy majors." Although both the philosophy and theology departments were responsible for staffing most of the sections and students fulfilled both their philosophy and theology core requirements by taking the course, the course had always been administered by the philosophy department and instructors from that department played central roles in shaping its design.

The curriculum in philosophy followed up on the existentialist dimension of the service-learning course with a strong program in classical philosophy that traced fundamental questions about the meaning of life from ancient Greek philosophy through modern existentialism to current developments that have grown out of this European tradition. Although service learning was not incorporated in more advanced courses, the content of those courses often justified the concern for personal and social responsibility on which the social service component of the introductory course was based.

The philosophy department was more unself-consciously and thoroughly Catholic than the theology department, where dialogues between Catholicism and other religions played a central role. The philosophy department was a place where questions about the intersection of reason and the Catholic religion took center stage. Moreover, the department was tied to the Jesuit tradition more closely than any other in its great-books tradition, investment in graduate education, and commitment to bringing Ignatian spirituality to bear on philosophical issues. At both the undergraduate and graduate levels, the curriculum in philosophy followed the basic curriculum of traditional Jesuit education. Some students complained that such a traditional approach made it difficult to pay sufficient attention to women philosophers and anything outside of the Western, Christian tradition, but the department was firmly committed to its approach. Teaching in the introductory survey course that covered the major philosophical and theological texts of the Western tradition was a condition of employment in the philosophy department and, as the chair of the department put it, "a means of rounding out the education of recent Ph.D.'s from other universities whose training may not have been sufficiently comprehensive."

The consensus that existed within the department with regard to the curriculum helped the faculty "avoid the ideological fragmentation that besets academic departments elsewhere," the chair noted. "We've all got to be able to discuss Descartes." This consensus helped explain why philosophy drew both strongly conservative and strongly liberal students. The two most prominent, activist students on campus during 1996–97, the conservative leader Mike Leahy and the progressive student body president Bridget Olson, were both philosophy majors. The philosophic tradition of Western Christianity was important in shaping the self-understanding of both progressives and conservatives on campus and an important context for debate.

Several religiously conservative faculty members in philosophy attracted many students and encouraged them to conceptualize religious issues in black-and-white terms. At one level, this ultraconservative cadre stood against the dominant campus tendency to soften ideological differences through personal language and sympathy. At another level, they were simply following the same rules their more progressive colleagues followed and being good philosophers by staking out a clear intellectual position, defining the opposition, and employing skills of logic and debate to promote and defend their position.

A recent planning report issued by the department took note of philosophy's appeal to students who were serious about the intellectual aspects of their own religious development: "Philosophy is always by its essence an open and rational inquiry. This attitude is attractive to students, and meets a deeply felt need. They therefore are comfortable discussing questions about moral problems and religious faith with philosophers." Moreover, the document went on, "We take it that one of the principal contributions we can make to their intellectual, moral, and spiritual development is to provide a forum where they can express their deepest questions and be taken seriously, and where they can enter into dialogue with one another, with the works of great philosophers, and with a sympathetic and responsible instructor."

Philosophy has played a central role in Jesuit higher education for centuries and continues to function as a means of integrating the curriculum in many Jesuit colleges and universities. As at other Jesuit institutions, the philosophy department at EU performed this integrative function by focusing on Catholic responses to issues and questions that emerged across the academic curriculum.

How Religion Was Taught in the Theology Department

The theology department did not have the long-standing tradition of centrality to Jesuit higher education that the philosophy department had. Historically, philosophy formed the core of Jesuit education at both the undergraduate and graduate levels, whereas theology, narrowly defined as catechesis and apologetics, played a relatively minor role in the academic curriculum, especially at advanced levels. At EU, a weekly lecture hour on "Christian doctrine" was originally part of the students' religious training program, but it was not considered part of the academic curriculum. At the end of the nineteenth century, the weekly lecture became an appendage of the curriculum, and students were granted academic credit for demonstrating their mastery of its contents. Until the 1960s, this course and its successors functioned as a defense of orthodox Catholicism that inoculated students against the heresy of modernism. This inoculation was deemed essential to the spiritual formation of students, which was in turn deemed fundamental to the mission of the institution as a Catholic college. Although not a prominent part of the academic curriculum, the courses that prepared students to withstand modernism were essential to the school's ethos, its community spirit, and its smooth operation and control over student opinion and behavior.

Unlike the philosophy department, whose strength derived from its long-standing adherence to a classical curriculum, the theology department had struggled against its origins as an appendage to the academic curriculum and undergone radical transformations in its mission, size, and curriculum. Not surprisingly, the consensus about the curriculum that enabled liberal and conservative faculty in philosophy to disagree without calling the commonality of their enterprise into question simply did not exist in theology. But at the same time, the experimentation and innovation that characterized the theology department since the 1960s played a crucial role in the university's overall commitment to the difficult mission of combining open-ended intellectual inquiry with fidelity to Catholic tradition.

In the late 1950s, the theology department offered only eight or ten courses a year, each one of which was essentially catechetical. In the wake of Vatican II, the number of theology courses increased dramatically, and the department expanded the range of its offerings to include courses that compared Catholicism and Christianity with other world religions and acquainted students with a variety of scholarly approaches to the study of religion. In the 1970s, the department offered more than 100 courses a year. During that time, according to Matthew Galloway, the chair of the department in 1996–97, "the department debated whether to call itself religious studies or theology, decided on theology, and then proceeded to make religious studies hires, first in Bible, then in history and ethics." As I later learned, others in the department disputed the idea that any of the new people could be accurately described as "religious studies hires." But as Galloway told the story, new hires and the approaches to the study of religion they introduced created dissension, and "in the eighties, the department broke out in civil war, with the Jesuit-based systematic theologians pitted against newcomers. Everything ground to a halt, and the department was ready to go outside for a chair." Galloway went on to say that those who wanted the department to base its teaching on the official teachings of the church were the losers in the war over the department's identity. "They have retreated—or been relegated—to the sidelines," he said. As the department moved away from its original mission of providing religious training for students to studying Catholicism in relation to other religions of the world, the role of the theology curriculum in promoting Ignatian spirituality became less straightforward and clearly defined. As Galloway reported, "The theology department does not play a key role in conveying Ignatian spirituality. In fact, a few years ago, grad students even complained that the department was too academic and that there wasn't enough spirituality and community."

Galloway acknowledged that not everyone agreed with his view of the department. He even gave me a list of people who disagreed with him in order to make it easier for me to hear, as he called it, "the other side." But as I became more acquainted with faculty members in theology and their writings, I began to see that the division Galloway referred to was not nearly as significant as the consensus that existed about the importance of the department's role on campus. Moreover, I mistook Galloway's somewhat flippant comment about the department's retaining the designation as a theology department and then proceeding to make religious studies hires to mean that the department had shifted in the direction of being a religious studies department. I discovered the inaccuracy of this impression after basing an early draft of this chapter on it and then inviting departmental faculty to a meeting to discuss their reactions. Several faculty members in the department, one of whom seemed angry that I thought anything different, told me in no uncertain terms at that meeting that the whole department was firmly committed to its mission not only as a department of theology but also as a department of theology at a Catholic university. Everyone around the table seemed to agree. And no one at the meeting was on Galloway's list of people on "the other side."

The issue at stake in my mistaken interpretation was the way in which Catholicism was presented in relation to other religions. In religious studies, religion is usually presumed to be a universal aspect of human culture, with a great variety of manifestations but also underlying universal dimensions. The operative assumption in religious studies is that any one religion should be approached, as least initially, as being on a par with every other religion. Once one began to study a particular religion in a particular time and place, it might become apparent that it fostered violence, slavery, and discrimination against women. On those evidentiary grounds, it might be compared with another religion at another time and place that fostered nonviolence, equality, and women's rights. But in religious studies, one would never go into a study, at least not consciously, with the presumption that one religion was better than another or, God forbid, that one religion was superior to all others.

During my meeting with the theology faculty, it became increasingly clear that it was departmental policy always "to extend the presumption of truth to Catholicism." Although it had been obvious to me earlier that some faculty did just that, I had not realized the degree of consensus on the issue.

My misperception in this regard had a lot to do with my own background in religious studies. It was simply hard for me to believe that a fine department dedicated to the study of religion would offer courses on a variety of religious traditions while agreeing, officially and completely, on the inferiority of all but one. During the meeting, I remember looking into the beautiful eyes of the professor who taught Hinduism, silently imploring him to speak up for the great religious tradition he taught. He met my gaze with equal intensity and silently stood his ground with the others.

According to one theology professor, courses in theology not only granted the Roman tradition the presumption of truth but also represented that tradition in its most engaging intellectual form. "Catholicism at this university is at its best in classes and in service work. Students get turned on to religion in theology classes." Students who chose theology as a major were "interested in a vital, living approach to religion." They wanted to know things like "What is true friendship? What is Christ's nature as a friend? What does it mean to be a member of the church? What is the relationship between conscience and Catholicism? Where does evil come from? What is the Christian response to the poor? What is true love, and how is it related to sexual ethics?"

This is not to say that the theology faculty always approached theological issues subjectively or relied on "I" language as a means of instruction. According to Galloway, the "bias" of theology faculty was "toward texts rather than experience. The department stresses that religion is a cognitive activity and not just a warm fuzzy feeling." Several faculty did, in fact, take a personal and experiential approach, but by and large, the theology faculty were perceived as quite objective. Of the 258 undergraduates surveyed in theology courses during the spring of 1997, 66 percent reported that their professor did not advocate any particular religious perspective. Whereas 37 percent reported that their course focused on personal spirituality, 63 percent reported that their course focused on the objective study of religion. Although 93.4 percent described their professor as knowledgeable and 79.8 percent as fair, only 4.3 percent described their professor as biased, 6.6 percent as skeptical, 9.7 percent as secular, 12.8 percent as conservative, and 19.5 percent as liberal. In the survey, 44 percent of the students reported that the professor was spiritual, 44 percent reported that the professor was religious, and 34 percent reported that the professor was inspiring. Although most of the students surveyed were in the second semester of a two-semester course, 46 percent reported that they did not know enough about their professor's beliefs to say whether those beliefs were similar to or different from their own. Among students who interacted with their professors outside of class, 71 percent reported that the professor never discussed his or her religious beliefs outside of class, 76 percent reported that the professor never offered spiritual guidance, and 62 percent reported that the professor emphasized the importance of scholarly objectivity outside of class.

Despite the relatively high degree of restraint from religious advocacy that characterized faculty in theology, students tended not to feel restrained from discussion of their own religious views in class. In the survey, 83.4 percent of the students said they felt at least somewhat free to bring their own religious beliefs into class discussions, and 39 percent said they felt very free to do so. Whereas 48 percent said the course strengthened their religious faith, only 5.1 percent said it weakened their faith. The vast majority of students found the course at least somewhat helpful for thinking about the meaning of life, understanding other religions, and especially providing a historical context for understanding Christianity. Whereas 76 percent said the theology course they were taking led them to question their own religious beliefs and values and 73 percent said it led them to change the way they thought about God, 73 percent said the course led them to grow spiritually and 72 percent said they had learned to be more tolerant of other religions as a result of taking the course.

Christian Theology

Although the theology department extended the presumption of truth to the Catholic religion, it had shifted away from appeals to the sacred authority of the church as a means of conceptualizing its mission and curriculum. Courses that explained this authority and helped students develop a firmer relationship to it had not disappeared, however. To fulfill their requirement in theology, students could select a yearlong course focusing on texts in Christian theology. Although one of the courses in this category offered a wide-ranging survey of the history of Christian thought, the other focused solely on Catholic doctrine. The latter was designed to help Catholic students attain a deeper and more comprehensive understanding of the sacred authority of their church.

In one session of this course that I attended at the beginning of Holy Week, Professor Anthony Marcelli, a small, serious, soft-spoken man with gray hair clipped like a monk's, began class by announcing the schedule of masses at the parish church at the north end of campus. Then he handed out a sheet containing a fourth-century text describing the Christian Easter Vigil, remarking in a reverential way that "it is appropriate for us to meditate on this document on Tuesday of Holy Week as we move toward Triduum" (Holy Thursday, Good Friday, and Easter Sunday). Then he turned his attention to a recent assignment to write short essays on the Eucharist and read excerpts from the best of these.

In the first essay he read, the student confessed that "I was mystified when I was younger about the change of bread and wine and understood it as magic. Then I outgrew the magic and fell back on a purely symbolic interpretation, which I now see is not enough. Jesus is truly present, and this is a mystery. I had missed out on the Spirit." The second insight consisted of a single sentence: "I had always known Jesus Christ was present in the Eucharist, but not in so many ways—in the celebrating community, in his word, in the person of the priest, and, most of all, in the prayer of blessing over the Eucharist." Marcelli told the class: "There's some really good theology here." And the last essay identified the Eucharist as "a testimony to the eloquence of the church's confession of faith—as food nourishes the body, the Eucharist nourishes the spirit. The believer must receive the Eucharist in order to live a life of faith."

Turning to questions about the Eucharist that students had also been asked to write, Marcelli again chose three to read to the class. The first concerned the connection between Christ's sacrifice and the mass. "On the one hand, I know the mass is more than a symbol of Christ's sacrifice," Marcelli read. "On the other hand, I know Christ isn't sacrificed again in the mass. What exactly is the connection?" The second question focused on the form of the connection established in the Eucharist. "Is it Jesus with the recipient? The recipient with the Catholic community? The Catholic community with Jesus? Or all three?" Marcelli answered this one. "All three," he said. The third question concerned the exact point at which transubstantiation occurred. "Is there an exact point? Or is it in all the aspects of prayer and belief?"

Professor Marcelli incorporated responses to all of these questions in the lecture that followed entitled "The Eight Principles of Eucharistic Theology." The lecture was clear, straightforward, and objective in the sense that he presented the truth and meaning of the principles discussed as being independent of his own opinion. He explained each of the eight principles before moving on to the next. For example, after stating the first principle, "Every sacrament is an encounter with the living Christ," he explained that "the Eucharist is the high point of that encounter. According to some theologians, it is the sacrament of sacraments because of the intimacy of the encounter—we actually receive the Lord, take in the Lord like food—and because of the intensity of transformation that the Eucharist promotes." Quoting St. Augustine, he explained further that "while food is transformed into us when we eat it, we are transformed into Christ when we receive the Eucharist. Augustine pointed out that when the priest says, 'The body of Christ,' you say, 'Amen,' meaning, 'Let it be so.' Now you have become Christ." When Marcelli moved on to the second principle, "The Eucharist is inseparably both a meal and a sacrifice," he explored its meaning in a similar way.

This class represented the kind of teaching that once dominated the department and now persisted in the curriculum as one aspect of the department's mission. Although everyone agreed that the department had a responsibility to offer courses that instructed students in Catholic theology, the issue of the relationship between open-ended inquiry and the magisterium, or official teachings, of the church was more controversial. The division within the department described by Professor Galloway centered on this issue. Several faculty were devoted to the magisterium and resisted any departure from it, whereas the most well known and widely published faculty in the department, according to Galloway, were "especially articulate in their commitment to open-ended intellectual inquiry." As evidence of this fact, he added that "the department's Jesuit expert on the magisterium continued to press, as an emeritus professor, for the ordination of women." Those who approached the task of undergraduate theological education by means of open-ended intellectual inquiry were clearly in the ascendance. "Department policy is not directed toward proselytizing," another professor explained, "but toward helping students develop tools to think through religious and moral issues for the rest of their life."

A second course in the Introduction to Christian Theology category illustrated this broader approach to teaching theology. In the section of this course I attended, students were exposed to non-Catholic as well as Catholic thinkers and to modes of critical analysis that ultimately shifted responsibility for determining the truth and relevance of any theological position onto themselves. This course was less systematic and catechetical than Marcelli's course on Catholic doctrine. It was really a course in intellectual history. In contrast to Marcelli's course, it tended to undercut any assumptions students might have had that theology was above and beyond history and historical change. The course also exposed students to opponents of Christianity whose views have impacted Christian thought. Perhaps most important, the course encouraged students to think critically about Christianity's role in Western culture.

Professor Emily Hansen, a tall, open-faced woman who spoke with a European accent, taught the class I attended. In response to my request to the faculty of the theology department that they write brief descriptions of how each instructor approached the study of religion, Hansen wrote that she wanted "to introduce students to the complexity of theology as an academic discipline, which can also be used as an effective tool in dealing with humanity's perennial questions about the deeper meaning of life. Thus," she went on, "I strive to avoid the extremes of making the class an arid intellectual exercise on the one hand, or turning it into an outlet for undigested religious emotions on the other. While giving considerable time to students' personal religious questions, I want to teach students especially how to frame their questions theologically."

The class I attended focused on Friedrich Nietzsche, the nineteenth-century father of existentialism. Hansen opened the hour by saying, "Nietzsche is the most troubling thinker we're dealing with because he launches the most frontal assault on Christianity, or to be more specific, on the Christianity of the Enlightenment." Then she asked, "Should we read him in a class in Christian theology?" The class was silent, so she answered the question herself: "Christianity says love your enemies. Perhaps it's also good to know your enemies."

Before getting into Nietzsche's thought, Hansen recapitulated the Enlightenment thought of Kant and Schleiermacher. "Kant moved theology out of the realm of metaphysics and knowledge, where Aquinas located it, and made religion a subset of the realm of morals. For Kant, you live by the categorical imperative as if it were divine commands," she explained. "Schleiermacher gave religion more of an independent place, locating it not in knowing or acting but in feeling, which he defined as immediate intuitive awareness. The essence of religion was intuitive awareness of and experience of dependence on the infinite." For Schleiermacher, she said, "you can't have proof for the existence of God any more than you can have proof for the existence of love."

The students became more engaged as Hansen went on to compare feelings of God with feelings of love. After developing the comparison, she talked about how Kierkegaard, Nietzsche, and Newman responded to these Enlightenment thinkers. "They view Christianity as much more troubling and disturbing than Kant and Schleiermacher did," she said. They were less systematic than Kant and Schleiermacher, more interested in history, and critical of the easy optimism of the Enlightenment. Kierkegaard and Nietzsche attacked the very idea of progress. "Kierkegaard wanted to retrieve the uniqueness of Christianity, which he situated in paradox and which required a leap of faith. Christianity puts a call out to people that may even be unethical, as in the call to Abraham to sacrifice his son. Kierkegaard distinguished Christendom from Christianity, the latter what we should be as followers of Christ, the former an easygoing religion comprised of Pharisees."

Hansen asked if anyone had read Nietzsche in other classes and, if so, what they remembered about his ideas. One student recalled that "he praises artists." Another said that "he was big into competition and that his idea of the superman eliminates God, so there is no one above the human race."

Hansen nodded approvingly but paused over the term "competition," saying she would agree "if we mean competition among values, not competition in a commercial sense." Then she resumed: "Nietzsche had an insight. He was prophetic. But his thinking borders on a breakdown, and indeed, he had a mental breakdown. He was born in 1844, the son of a minister. I can relate to that because I'm the daughter of a minister. He didn't attack Christianity out of ignorance."

Later on, in discussing Nietzsche's "first period" at Basil, when he wrote *The Birth of Tragedy* and developed the idea of Dionysian and Apollonian types, she asked the students if they were familiar with Dionysus. Two people raised their hands and said they had read Euripides's *The Bacchae*. She went on: "Nietzsche thought modern culture was too subdued by Apollian culture. He was opposed to democracy and socialism as ideals of a false equality. In this first period, Nietzsche adored Wagner and celebrated artistic genius and aristocratic individualism. He understood equality to mean mediocrity." In his second period, when he wrote *Human All Too Human*, she told the class, Nietzsche "gives up the artistic genius idea. He wants a saner and less Dionysian view of reality and criticizes a morality that is against life." It was during this period, she explained, that "he proclaims 'God is dead,' meaning that our yearning for a bigger-than-life being is a superstitious way of sanctioning our own ideas about how we would like things to be. Postulating a world as it really is—as Kant did—is not right because the postulation is always an ideal world, and not reality, which is jumbled and full of tensions and paradoxes."

"In the third period," Hansen observed, "Nietzsche moves to the idea of the superman and the transvaluation of values. We should live through and face up to the competition of values, and we ourselves can supersede the values on which we once depended. Rather than being dependent on God, we can be better and more noble, almost like God. But," and she paused, looking around at the students, Nietzsche believed that if we "repress or sanitize our will to power, we create violence. Here Nietzsche is prophetic—no one in civilized Enlightenment Europe expected World War I to break out, but his ideas can be said to have anticipated it."

She explained that in this third period, Nietzsche contrasted the natural morality of good versus bad with the slave morality of good versus evil. "In natural morality, strength is good and the strong protect the weak because it is in their best interest to do so," she said. "Beginning with Judaism, there was a rebellion of slaves against this natural morality, and the strong and self-affirming is now seen as evil, while the weak and victimized is seen as good. Christ on the cross is naturally bad because a human life is broken but now becomes the norm of goodness." Then she asked the students, "Do you think he has a point, or is he promoting a cruel, rugged culture that can't be called civilized?

One student agreed that in today's culture "weakness is now seen as good." But, he said, he was "irritated by Nietzsche's style." Another student said that Nietzsche came up in her history class and that "his ideas were contextualized in terms of the realities of war and the rise of socialism in late-nineteenth-century Europe." Running out of time, the professor wrapped things up by saying, "If you repress the will to power too much, which has been done in Christianity, it can lead to a drive to power that cannot be contained." And she pointed again to Nietzsche's prophetic voice with respect to the eruption of violence in World War I.

This class illustrated some of the innovation in the teaching of theology introduced during recent decades. The subject of the class—Friedrich Nietzsche, a critic of the whole enterprise of Christian theology—would never even be mentioned in a curriculum focused on the sacred authority and official teachings of the Catholic Church. But it would be a mistake to simply categorize the class as a deconstructive exercise. Although she encouraged students to use critical analysis in thinking about Christianity and relied on methods of interpretation that did not appeal to supernatural reality or rest on sacred authority, the instructor spoke to the students as persons with a stake in Christian civilization and responsible for understanding it, passing judgment on it, and contributing to its development. From the outset of the lecture, she located herself and her students as insiders within Christian culture whose understanding of this culture might benefit from a dialogue with Nietzsche's analysis.

Another professor who offered a written description of his approach to teaching Christian theology was more strenuous in emphasizing his orientation as a Christian. "I understand theology to be 'faith seeking understanding,' " he wrote. "My usual approach to teaching undergrads is to present major classical texts in the history of theology, especially the Bible, Augustine, Aquinas, and Luther, and to show their inspiration, depth, insight, and importance for us today." He went on to explain: "It's clear to my students that I think the material is of central importance for life, especially for the life of the Christian. I appreciate this university as catholic, Christian, and Roman Catholic, and frankly I wouldn't want to teach in a university that wasn't committed to all three." He added: "I consider my job as a college professor, like my marriage and family, to be a 'vocation' rather than simply a professional career." Drawing a contrast between himself and "scholars of religious studies at secular universities," he said that his sense of vocation "influences the way I regard students and particularly the way in which I feel bound to them in service and respect. I take my interchanges with students both inside and outside the classroom with great seriousness. My hope is," he concluded, "that the college students whom I can serve will in turn serve others, particularly by exhibiting and inspiring faith, hope, and charity."

Biblical Studies

The biblical studies branch of the curriculum was grounded in introductory courses on "the biblical heritage" that fulfilled the undergraduate requirement in theology. These courses introduced students to a variety of literary critical and social scientific methodologies that did not presuppose or require any particular religious orientation. But at the same time, the purpose of these courses was to deepen students' understanding and appreciation of the sacred texts of Christianity.

In a lecture I attended on the Book of Acts, I discovered that the biblical heritage courses not only worked to deepen students' understanding of the sacred texts of Christianity but also could complicate students' understanding of the nature of the church and its claims to religious authority. The lecture was delivered by a competent and well-prepared graduate student, Paul Schmidt, who explored a depth of detail that seemed to overwhelm some of the students seated around me, even though every one of them pressed on diligently through the hour, taking notes. A diffident man in his late thirties wearing a tweed jacket and tie, Schmidt argued that the early church in Rome was one of numerous Christian churches established in the first century and that the canonical books in the New Testament represented a biased and only partial picture of the vitality and pluralism of Christian life in the decades following the death of Jesus.

Handouts of biblical quotations from Acts, Galatians, and Luke provided textual documentation for Schmidt's argument that "the traditional interpretation of Paul's preeminent authority may not be entirely accurate." Using the handouts, he showed that Acts was a sequel to Luke and that Luke foretold, in a Jewish context, everything said to happen in the Gentile context of Acts. Focusing on Luke 24:47, Schmidt said that "the essence of Jesus's message is his looking ahead and laying the groundwork for the message reaching beyond the narrow confines of Judaism." Although Luke and Acts were really two parts of the same story, "what the author of Acts says about Paul doesn't correspond that closely to how Paul sets out the gospel in Galatians. In Galatians, Paul attaches tremendous meaning to the death of Jesus. And the distinction he develops between faith and law is really played down in Acts." In other words, Schmidt explained, "the Book of Acts poses real problems for biblical scholars and scholars of the early church. The author of Acts seems to be telling a different version of Paul's story and seems not to have complete or accurate information about Paul. This raises the question of the extent to which we can base our understanding of what happened in the early church on Acts. We have to examine each statement with critical acumen."

"In the eighth chapter of Acts," Schmidt said after wiping his glasses, "the apostles are forced underground in Jerusalem, and many of their followers fled persecution and ended up in a variety of different places. We'd love to know more about those followers and the communities they started," Schmidt told the students. "But in chapter 9, Acts focuses on Paul to the exclusion of Christian leaders in other parts of the world. We have no information," Schmidt said with some dismay, "on Christian communities in Alexandria, the second largest city in the Empire and the seat of the biggest and most important church independent of Paul. In Rome itself, there is clearly a big church before Paul gets there, but we don't know anything about it before his arrival. And Acts tells us nothing about ordinary garden-variety Christians."

"Another thing scholars wonder about," Schmidt told the class, "is that as much as he was an admirer of Paul, the author of Acts does not seem to see him as being on the same level as one of the original apostles. It may be important that the author uses one of the original apostles, Peter, to justify Paul's authority," he said after a pause. "It may be that the author of Acts was responding to concerns and misgivings about Paul among some contemporary Christians. When Paul begins to convert large numbers of people, this creates problems for the church over questions of circumcision and observance of the Torah."

Biblical studies constituted an important part of the curriculum and identity of the theology department. But as this lecture illustrated, the work in this area was so specialized that the kind of integration between it and other areas of departmental work that some faculty in the department had once hoped for had not materialized. I discussed this problem with Philip Lazlo, one of the leading professors in biblical studies in the department. In the course of the interview, I learned that Lazlo had trained for the Jesuit priesthood but left the society when things "got crazy" during the 1960s. A photo of his handsome sons was prominently displayed in his well-organized office. He was helpful in response to my questions about the influence of the Jesuit philosopher-theologian Bernard Lonergan in the historical development of the department, particularly with regard to its overall sense of mission. Lazlo explained that several members of the department had hoped that the integration of methods and areas of specialization outlined by Lonergan would provide a model on which the department could construct itself and "do Catholic theology seriously in an ecumenical context."

Some of the first dissertations on Lonergan were written by faculty at this university and their graduate students, Lazlo told me. But the promise of integrating biblical studies with other areas of theology never panned out. "The hope was, at least it was my hope, that Lonergan would be used methodologically. Lonergan was interested in how you know what you know and in how you go about knowing things," he said, summing up Lonergan's *Method in Theology*. "We hoped that Lonergan's methods would become means of solving problems. But, instead, people have written about Lonergan rather than using his thought as a means of problem solving. He has become frozen in time."

In Lonergan's vision, ethics, history, and the Bible were to become handmaidens to systematic theology, and systematic theology was to become more public and powerfully active. "In the mid-seventies and eighties, systematics were still central," Lazlo explained. "As we moved toward theology in a larger sense—away from theology as the systematic study of God, Christology, salvation, etc.—to stuff *about* God—including Bible, history, and doctrine—history became separated from theology, and the Bible people became a separate group. There's a lot of goodwill and dialogue, but we're not working as consultants on the same project," Lazlo said matter-of-factly. "We've trained ourselves to be solo practitioners. Of course, no one can do it all. This is the problem of our age—this specialization and independency."

With regard to a proposal to make the theology department the center of Catholic theological studies in the United States, Lazlo had reservations that reflected his sense of the danger of assigning the department a mission of theological leadership and innovation as well as discipleship. "One problem with expanding theology and giving it an even more prominent place in the university," he explained, "is the delicate and quirky relationship with the church at large. The church has a strong conservative trend at the top and a strong pastoral trend underneath," he explained. "How can a theology department best contribute without getting controlled or without getting involved in a public fight with an authoritative structure?"

Lazlo suggested that there were also difficulties involved in integrating the empirical skills of biblical criticism with the more abstract conceptual skills associated with theological reflection. I recognized at least one of these difficulties as a result of having attended Paul Schmidt's lecture. Although the lecture enmeshed students in literary and historical details that raised important questions about the diversity of the early church and the shifting nature of religious authority, it left them without any help in thinking through comparisons with the diversity of Christianity today or possible implications for the authority of the Catholic Church. Adroit handling of these open-ended comparisons and their theological implications was a lot to expect of professors who were geared by training and temperament to making close studies of historical texts. It was a sufficiently important and sufficiently big task "to engage students with the text understood in its historical and social context," Lazlo wrote in his statement on approaching religion in the classroom. Through this kind of engagement, students could come to "understand what is really being said, why the authors thought it important to say what they said, why they said it as they did and what effect they wanted to have on their audience and society."

But despite this clarity about his primary focus and relatively narrow pedagogical obligation, Lazlo had not abandoned the effort to integrate the study of biblical texts with current theological and spiritual concerns. Although engagement with the text in its historical and social context was first and foremost, Lazlo wrote, "I link the historically understood texts with analogous contemporary situations and experiences and with the students' personal experiences orally in class." A lecture of his I attended on the sixth chapter of the Gospel of John demonstrated this effort. Focusing on the use of symbolic language in the text and its implications for how the students in his class thought about the Eucharist, he pointed to passages from John projected onto a large screen from his computer and said: "There are a lot of verbal patterns in John 6, and this patterning is connected to John's drive to get behind the face value of things. The story of the feeding of the 5,000 and walking on water is a *symbolic* story. You should be asking," he told the class, "what is John saying, what is the meaning of being fed, what is it a sign of? John speaks at length about the symbolic meaning of things. We're not just talking about food. Most of my salary goes for food, since I have two teenage sons," he said parenthetically. "John is speaking to members of an ancient agricultural community and telling them they should rather work for eternal food. In verse 35, Jesus says *I* am the bread of life. John makes an explicit comparison with the Exodus manna and takes a clear step beyond that," he went on. "You eat and you don't die; my flesh is bread from heaven. The language is cannibalistic, but you've probably never thought of it as cannibalistic because John has done such a good job of persuading you that the language of food is symbolic. It's metaphoric."

A student asked a question about the historical context in which the narrative was composed. "In John's narrative," Lazlo responded, "Jesus is challenging his fellow Jews to a new identity, and there's a split among the disciples. When the author or authors of John wrote in the mid-to-late first century, the Johannite community had broken from the Jews." In response to another student who returned to the issue of symbolism and wondered just how much symbolic meaning an uneducated community could absorb, Lazlo replied: "People then were much more symbolically oriented than we are today. We're scientifically and empirically oriented. Theology and English teachers have difficulty teaching symbolism, and students have difficulty thinking symbolically. For example, my son is a concrete-minded kid—a true American—and he has trouble with poetry." Lazlo concluded the class with a reference to the symbolism of the upcoming holiday. "Have a nice break," he told the class. "Experience your eternal life this Easter as well as your biological life."

World Religions in an Ecumenical Context

One of the most controversial, innovative, and popular branches of the theology curriculum focused on dialogue between Catholicism and other religions. Department chair Matthew Galloway explained that, as part of its decision to call itself a theology department rather than a religious studies department, "the department took the tack of focusing on theology and of bringing different theological traditions into dialogue with Christian theology. We adopted the view that God's truth existed in an array of different traditions."

To some members of the university community, this dimension of the theology curriculum was controversial because it exposed students to religions other than Catholicism and raised difficult questions about how Catholicism should be compared with them. But this dimension of the curriculum was important to the institution's religiously progressive and academically respectable identity because it placed Catholicism in an ecumenical context and affirmed the institution's openness to religious diversity. At the same time, this openness was limited by firm intent to support and not jeopardize the ultimacy of Catholicism. Although the resources committed to this agenda were not extensive and the steps taken to fulfill it were still rather preliminary, it did represent a significant departure from the defensiveness of the antimodernist agenda that once defined the study of theology at this school.

The decision to incorporate an ecumenical approach to religion within the department had evolved over time. An important figure in this process was described by Galloway as "virtually a Hindu as well as a Jesuit and whose work is studied by Jesuits all over the world and by the Vatican." A pioneer in this process of establishing an ecumenical dialogue between Catholicism and Hinduism, "he showed how Hinduism offers resources for Christians who seek to understand theodicy and sin." This innovator "met with considerable resistance from the old guard in the department," according to Galloway, "not just because he was a comparativist but because he was intent on opening up Hinduism for Christians."

The most recent hire among faculty offering courses in ecumenical dialogue was Rabbi Sarah Friedman, a friendly, brown-haired woman with pictures drawn by her children on her office door. She offered an introductory course designed to promote a dialogue between Catholicism and traditional Judaism through units on liturgy, the Holy Land, and comparative study of Exodus and Matthew. She admitted that "there are important issues in the traditions that don't get addressed because you can't bring them into dialogue. For example, a lot of the ritualism of Judaism doesn't get discussed, especially ritualism involving food and the Sabbath, because food and the Sabbath are not really important in Catholicism." But on the other hand, "sin and atonement get good discussion, and important differences between the two traditions emerge through that discussion."

Friedman had focused her recent doctoral work on the anthropological study of ritual. Although she acknowledged that this approach "enhanced her understanding of religion," she remarked that "it also problematized it because the social scientific approaches understand religion as a humanly created phenomenon, with the Divine emerging as a product of human culture." Having also been trained as a rabbi with "a commitment to teach Jews to know more and care more about their own religious traditions and heritage," she had been accustomed to a division between her religious learning as a rabbi and her academic learning as a scholar of religion. In her short time at EU, she found the erasure of this division at the university personally and positively challenging. The questions were "deeper and different," she explained. "As a representative and spokesperson for Judaism, whatever I do or say becomes a dialogue."

This ecumenical approach to the study of theology was further developed by the hiring of a Buddhist scholar and practicing Buddhist, John Tanquary, a quiet man with glasses and a round, open face. As he explained to me in his office, "I was brought on board as a Buddhist voice, not just as a scholar of Buddhism." His investment in the spiritual practice and theological implications of Buddhism constantly found its way into his teaching. "I am less interested in looking at religion from afar with distancing detachment and more interested in finding how these religions raise fundamental questions in us," he told me. "You can't get a sense of how a religion worked for others without a sense of how it works on you. While anthropological and sociological methods are useful and important, they are not themselves part of religious life, and excessive reliance on them prevents us from understanding what religions are about and why they challenge us."

Tanquary coedited a book on Buddhist theology in which he wrote as a Buddhist theologian as well as a scholar of Buddhist religion. He attributed his ability to do this to being at a university where being theological was not taboo. He thought there were generational differences with respect to the relationship between theology and the objective study of religion. Regarding future trends, he mentioned "the theory that soon theology will reemerge as predominant, and religious studies will be incorporated into theology as a useful critical method."

According to Galloway, Tanquary "has had good success in the course, although he had to be educated in Christian theology in order to teach it. He starts his course with Buddhism and then gets to Christian theology. Students are effectively sucked into Christian theology by means of Buddhism." Through Buddhism, students learned to look differently at the Christian issues they thought they knew about. As Tanquary explained, Buddhism helped students take a fresh look at "sinfulness, Christ as the means of salvation for humankind, and the redemption of all creation."

Focusing on Zen Buddhism and Roman Catholic Christianity, Tanquary's introductory course compared Buddhist and Catholic attitudes toward social action, human nature, the environment, and transcendence. In response to my question concerning how he dealt with confusion between a student's own feelings about a religion and what that religion might have meant for people who lived it in another time and place, Tanquary said he felt this was not a major problem. "You permit that historical confusion to occur, then enter into it and deal with it. For example, a lot of college students want Zen to affirm college student ideas. But you can't contextualize the meaning of religion if you don't allow meaning to come up. I usually deal with a different problem, that of student repulsion for religious material because it comes from an ancient worldview."

Students who signed up for his course, Tanquary went on, "are looking for exposure to diversity. Many students think they know Catholicism and are tired of it, although a significant number, maybe half the students I encounter, are quite devoted to their Catholicism." He observed that although "some students here are really tired of religion and find the required courses oppressive, for the most part, there is a distinct religious flavor here. There's a feeling of relief that you can talk about religion without doing what the dominant culture does, either address religion from a distance or press and proselytize people."

Interestingly, Protestantism tended not to be one of Catholicism's partners in ecumenical dialogue in the theology department partly because students and faculty often equated Catholicism with Christianity. For example, in response to an observation I made that there was a tendency in the theology department to speak of Catholicism as the core and centerpiece of Christianity, Professor Lazlo said, "Well, isn't it?"

Faculty members in theology disagreed on how well Protestantism was represented by the department. Whereas one professor emphasized that Luther and Tillich were important figures in his teaching of Christian theology, another complained, "Protestantism is completely ignored. But how can you teach Catholicism in this country without somehow paying attention to the hugeness of Protestantism, which Catholicism has had to go around?"

Protestantism was sometimes overlooked, but at other times, it was stigmatized and equated with the heresy of modernism. Even some who identified with the progressive side of Catholicism portrayed Protestantism as representing the dark side of the modern world. An instructor in a theology class blamed Protestantism for the problems women have had in gaining recognition for religious leadership. "There was no place for women in the modern movement. Following the Protestant attack on regular life—ordered life, especially cloistered life—there was no longer any widely recognized place for women to pursue holiness, even in places where regular life still existed." Then he asked the class: "How can we today, or how can the Christian tradition today, renew itself? What should we think, looking back and seeing that things were good for women in the early church, good for women in the Middle Ages, and then terrible for women in modernity? Just throw out Christianity?"

CONCLUSIONS

During my visits to EU, I heard a number of people complain that the school was not as religious as it should be. But I was increasingly impressed with the degree and extent to which people on campus were involved in and concerned about religion. Each time I visited, I discovered that religious life on campus was both more complex and more deeply entrenched that I thought it was before. Many aspects of campus life that initially seemed not to be particularly religious turned out to be part of a vast tapestry of Catholic religious life. At first, I only saw the most obvious bits and pieces of this tapestry, but gradually I began to be aware of their relationship to a larger and more implicit pattern.

Undoubtedly, many elements of this pattern still eluded my grasp, but in the religious culture I did discover, several interlocking elements emerged as especially important. First, an inclination to sacramentalism was pervasive. This inclination was manifest not only in the many liturgies that took place on campus, where God was present in the Eucharist and its celebrants, but also more diffusely in the expectation of finding God anywhere. Of course, some people relied on this expectation more intently than others, but across campus, people were on the lookout for manifestations of the Divine and sensitive to its presence.

The inclination to sacramentalism was linked to a deep-seated investment in personal purity. The self-discipline of the most highly placed individuals on campus exemplified this investment, as did the enormous respect they commanded on campus. Although commitment to personal purity and the self-discipline associated with it was expected to involve all areas of life, sexuality was the essential area in which this commitment was presumed to manifest itself. Celibacy was essential to the lives of the priests who served as models of humanity on campus and, in an important way, the highest expression of the consecration of their humanity to God. Celibacy was also essential to the student leaders in residence halls who felt responsible for modeling Christian values for other students. Expectations of celibacy outside of marriage found darker echoes in "the walk of shame" that undergraduate women endured after spending the night with their boyfriends.

Married faculty and staff were obviously exempt from the religious ideal of celibacy. But they were not exempt from expectations of chastity outside of marriage and commitment to the divine purpose of sex within marriage and the sanctity of the marital bond. Several men I interviewed mentioned their religious commitment to marriage and family life. The widespread disapproval of abortion, even among many progressives on campus, also involved issues of personal purity. Abortion was repugnant not only because it was believed to involve the destruction of another human life and potential vessel of divine life but also because it defiled the parents', and especially the mother's, moral purity.

Both the inclination to sacramentalism and the investment in personal purity were connected to religious respect for the poor and a religious desire to serve them. In the theology and philosophy departments, the chaplaincy, and service programs administered through the residence halls, identification with the poor was understood as a means of identification with the suffering of Christ and his love for the poor. It was also understood as one of the most effective means of becoming aware of the common humanity in which each individual life participated. This awareness of the oneness of humanity was an important dimension of the mystical union with Christ available to believers in the Eucharist. Through identification with the poor, students and faculty fed their experience of participating in the eternal life of Christ and his universal power of redemption.

The progressive effort to combine this religious respect for the poor with an emphasis on "faith that does justice" made a number of people nervous or resistant. Although progressives viewed concern for social justice as a powerful and highly appropriate extension of the long-standing traditional Catholic commitment to serving the poor, others suspected it was an attempt to politicize, and thereby diminish, a profound mystical reality. In fact, however, the progressives committed to social justice had not lost hold of the mysticism associated with poverty. Indeed, in concerted efforts to encourage students to understand and empathize with the suffering of poverty, progressives made love for the poor a principal means of experiencing the mystical presence of Christ.

The theology department helped carry forward the underlying commitments to sacramentalism, personal purity, and poverty that characterized campus culture. Through traditional courses in Catholic theology, basic courses in biblical studies, and innovative courses in Buddhism, students learned that awareness of sacred reality was essential to full human life. In courses in ethics and Christian thought, students learned how to reflect thoughtfully on issues associated with sexuality and personal behavior. And in a wide variety of courses across the departmental curriculum, students learned to analyze theological issues in historical contexts characterized by various forms of social structure, violence, and poverty.

Although in these important ways, the theology department contributed to the strength and coherence of the religious ethos at EU, it also carried much of the burden for managing the tension between open-ended academic inquiry and loyalty to Catholic life and teaching. In its ultimate rejection of religious studies and commitment to enhancing Catholic theology, the department had chosen a path that reflected the religious loyalty of most faculty members in theology and assured the department of continuing administrative support. In its appropriation of the methods of religious studies and commitment to critical inquiry, the department had chosen a path similar to that of secular universities and nondenominational colleges. As at least two members of the theology faculty were painfully aware, these two paths were not entirely compatible even though tension between the two was often glossed over and declared to be resolved.

Of all the people I interviewed, the two most deeply troubled about the integrity of the university were both faculty members in theology. Professors Martin and McCarthy were both distressed by what seemed to them to be the university's duplicity with regard to the compatibility between religious life and academic status. Although they differed on how university life should be conducted, both men felt the strain of shouldering a fundamental conflict at the heart of their institution. They also agonized over the responsibility placed on them by the optimistic force of administration rhetoric, which to them rang hollow. To their ears, the proclamation by top adminstrators that "nothing could be held intellectually that could not also be held faithfully" sounded overbold, excessively sanguine, and ultimately hypocritical.

But if faculty in the theology department carried much of the burden of resolving the conflict between religious loyalty and academic freedom, they did so with remarkable strength and competence. Along with the philosophy department, the theology department played a major role in sustaining widespread campus hope that critical inquiry was compatible with religious piety and loyalty to the church. The theology and philosophy departments also played major roles in legitimating the widespread commitment to maintaining a religious culture on campus. The common ground of this religious culture, defined by sacramentalism, purity, and attention to poverty, was often obscured by disagreement over how to interpret Catholic faith and its implications for campus life. Progressives were often accused of selling out the faith, and they, in turn, sometimes accused their detractors of inflexible self-righteousness. Although important issues of political affiliation and personal temperament were often at stake in these disagreements, they also made it hard to see how much Catholics on campus really had in common.

One of the important clues to the existence of a common religious ground was the widespread use of the term "secularization." With the exception of Professor Arthur Stone, who regarded secularization as a wholesome process, everyone else who used the term (and there were many) used it negatively. It was the demon at the door for a lot of people, regardless of their disagreements with one another. But although none of the progressive Catholics I interviewed had anything good to say about secularization, they were perceived by others as opening the door to it and to the assimilation to American social values that went with it. If progressives were somewhat less fearful of secularization, it was not because they approved of it but because they were more optimistic that a revitalization of Catholic life in the United States would overcome it. And they were more hopeful that this revitalization would reorient American society in accordance with religious values.

Interlocking Catholic attitudes toward sacramentality, personal purity, poverty, and secularization permeated campus life despite the fact that a significant minority of students and faculty were not Catholic. Respectfulness toward these attitudes was so deeply embedded in the culture of EU that many non-Catholics participated in this respectfulness and were shaped by it without necessarily identifying it as specifically Catholic. Thus, several non-Catholic students I interviewed participated in many religious activities on campus, including liturgies, and acknowledged that these activities enhanced their religious lives. Of course, some students felt alienated by the Catholic culture of the university, but they consigned themselves to the margins of campus culture and accepted the fact, although not very cheerfully, that they had little ability to change things.

A somewhat similar situation obtained for non-Catholic faculty. As busy employees of the university rather than active participants in its government, most faculty on campus seemed happy to pursue their research and teaching without attempting to change the religious culture in which they worked. Faculty who wanted to participate in the development of that culture were warmly encouraged and were offered various opportunities to do so. But most faculty members chose not to avail themselves of these opportunities and seemed content with the excellent resources, good pay, and pleasant environment that the university provided. To be sure, a minority of faculty, most of them Catholic, actively resisted the openness and ambitiousness of the progressive agenda. Their concerns received considerable attention and were taken quite seriously. Indeed, at the most fundamental level, these spokespersons for traditional piety were significant contributors to the religious culture of campus life. They added considerable weight and authenticity to the university's commitment to sacramentalism, purity, poverty, and resistance to secularization.

Finally, many of the most religiously intense students and faculty I interviewed expressed the opinion that the campus was overrun by hedonistic students who didn't care a fig for religion. I looked for students without religion and repeatedly asked where I might find them. But I never found a single student who failed to express respect for religion. And I never found a student who was not involved, in some way, in religious life. Of course, not everyone was *equally* involved or equally intent on trying to live up to the high standards of spiritual life set by the Catholic faith and by other people on campus. But everyone I talked with was aware of the nature, existence, and power of religion.

NOTE

1. Ignacio Ellacuria, "The Task of a Christian University" (1982), in *Companions of Jesus: The Jesuit Martyrs of El Salvador* (Maryknoll, N.Y.: Orbis Books, 1990), 149–50; Jon Sobrino, "The University's Christian Inspiration" (1987), in ibid., 162.

NORTH COLLEGE

ETHOS

Composed of 3,000 undergraduate students and over 250 faculty, North College (NC) is located in a small town in the northern sector of the United States and is an easy commute by automobile from a large city. Affiliated with the Lutheran Church throughout its history, the school was founded by Scandinavian immigrants as an academy in the late nineteenth century, became a college toward the end of that century, and has always offered an education to students of both sexes.

The 30 buildings on campus, the oldest constructed in 1878, are situated on 345 acres and are built mostly of stone in a version of Gothic or Scandinavian modern architecture. Memorial Chapel, of modified Gothic design, sits in the geographical center of the campus. Its sanctuary is used for daily chapel services and for services of the campus Lutheran congregation, and it houses the offices of the campus pastors and the religion faculty as well as a number of classrooms. There are ample green spaces outside the dormitories and classroom buildings where students congregate, especially in fair weather, but the principal gathering place of the campus is the Student Commons, a modern glass and stone structure that adjoins the administration building of similar design and is only a few steps away from the chapel. Streams of students and faculty flow to the Commons between classes to use the cafeteria, the large snack bar, private meeting and dining rooms, the bookstore, the post office, or the lounge with overstuffed furniture. The Commons also contains the offices of the student government and student affairs and numerous bulletin boards that are always crammed with announcements, banners, petitions, invitations, and personal communiques.

Over half of the students in 1997–98 came to NC from the school's native state, with two neighboring states providing another 8 percent. The largest group of foreign students (just under 1%) hailed from Japan. About half of the students identified themselves as Lutheran (more than three-fourths of them affiliated with the school's denomination, the Evangelical Lutheran Church in America), 15 percent as Roman Catholic, and 11 percent as having no religious affiliation. Over 95 percent of the students were white, 2.5 percent were Asian/Asian American, and .5 percent were African American. Surveys of entering freshmen in 1996 indicated that over half of those students rated themselves "above average" in the area of "spirituality," and nearly 60 percent felt that "the development of a meaningful philosophy of life" was an important goal in their education. Surveys of seniors in 1997 revealed that only 3 percent of the students worked for pay 20 or more hours a week (the largest group, 33%, worked 6 to 10 hours) and 42 percent attended at least one religious service or meeting per week. Among the seniors, 74 percent believed that "helping others in difficulty" was an essential or very important goal in life, whereas only 33.5 percent believed that "being well off financially" was essential or important. The most popular careers projected by the seniors were elementary and secondary teacher (13.5%) and physician (8.5%), with fully 12 percent undecided. The most popular majors were the social sciences (19%), biological science (14%), and fine arts (12.5%).

The mission statement of NC read in part: "North College, a four-year college of the Evangelical Lutheran Church in America, provides an education committed to the liberal arts, rooted in the Christian gospel, and incorporating a global perspective. In the conviction that life is more than a livelihood, it focuses on what is ultimately worthwhile and fosters the development of the whole person in mind, body, and spirit." The president of the college and others who articulated the institutional mission to the college community and the larger public insisted that there was no inherent contradiction between NC as a college of the church rooted in the Christian message and its global perspective, inclusivity, and encouragement of critical, free thinking. As we shall see, NC encompassed a strong Lutheran presence as well as the existence of other religious persuasions, encouraged critical reflection on religion, and was open to religious—and nonreligious— diversity. It officially attempted to preserve an important feature of its Lutheran heritage by refusing to be narrowly religious or denominational. In the words of its president, "From a Lutheran theological perspective, human reason is . . . a divine creation and, though it has its clear limits, it is our principal guide in the secular realm. . . . We run the risk of confusing the two realms [the spiritual and the secular] if we allow the church to dictate what the college does within the college's proper sphere." This appeal to the historic Lutheran doctrine of the Two Kingdoms, which relates but holds separate the heavenly realm of salvation and the earthly realm of the created orders, was not one that most NC undergraduates would have used to define the school, but it accurately reflected the spirit that informed the ethos of the campus and governed much of the practice and teaching of religion at NC.

Sanctity, Tomfoolery, and Combined Messages

The Christmas Festival has been a tradition at North College since 1912, but by the 1990s, it had grown in dimension and popularity to such an extent that it had to be held in four sessions on campus and taped versions were broadcast on television and radio throughout the Christmas season. The festival was a celebration of Christmas through sacred music, and it featured the college orchestra and five of the seven student choral groups, one of which, the college choir, performed around the world. Music not only occupied the heart of the festival; it lay at the center of NC life. More than a third of NC students participated in ensembles or applied music lessons. When a choir or instrumental ensemble returned to campus from a tour, their members stepped off the buses to applauding and cheering students. According to the director of student activities, "The musical groups here are treated the way the Pacers [a professional basketball team] are treated by Indianapolis." Or in the words of a religion professor, "Music is to NC what football is to Penn State. It creates much of the ethos of this place. It serves as a point of pride for the entire community."

The pride on the part of the performers and the capacity crowd was apparent at the Christmas Festival concert, "Dawn of Redeeming Grace," on the evening of 5 December 1997. With the orchestra placed at the front and downstage and the choirs arranged onstage and along the sides of the large gymnasium auditorium, sacred music surrounded those of us who occupied the folding chairs in the center of the gym floor. Lullabies and Christmas carols, psalms and spirituals, hymns and cantatas were executed sometimes by the individual choirs and sometimes as a mass ensemble. Particularly striking were the calypso spiritual "Here's a Pretty Little Baby," sung by the college choir, and "Night of Silence/Silent Night," arranged by one of the choir directors, executed by the combined choirs, and joined by the audience in the last stanza. The applause at the end of the festival was thunderous and prolonged.

But the applause *was* reserved for the end. The concert was a worship service as well as a musical performance, and the printed program reminded the audience that the festival was a celebration of the Advent-Christmas-Epiphany season, and accordingly cameras were forbidden and applause should be held until the conclusion of the service. There was congregational singing of several of the carols, and most members of the audience followed the texts of the sacred music printed in the program. The theme of this year's festival was a version of "Silent Night" lifted from a poem written by the college chaplain, Pastor Ben Plater, and printed on the first page of the program:

When winter's tilt of planet Earth
adds hours to the dark of night,
then we who stretch our days with artificial light
learn once again to wait and welcome dawn.

. . . .

The early blush of rose on such a ripening day
is reason for the soul to sing.
For then the darkness is no longer night.
But we who walk in darkness see a great and gladdening light:
    The Dawn of Redeeming Grace.

Pastor Plater, clad in white vestments, offered several prayers during the concert and, taking a position in the midst of the audience and accompanied by students bearing an elevated cross and an Advent candle, read the Christmas narrative from a large Bible. The ceremony combined Christian liturgy and musical performance, observance of a sacred religious event, and celebration of human skills—a combination that, I would discover, characterized much of the music at NC.

Two months prior to the Christmas Festival, NC celebrated its homecoming with a (badly attended) football game, a parade, a band concert, and other events. At the conclusion of the game (won by NC), the announcer told the departing crowd to be sure to attend the Jello wrestling match on the other side of the stadium between the college pastor and the dean of students. "This may be your only opportunity to see an ordained minister wrestle in Jello," the announcer exclaimed. This was clearly a different role for Plater than that of liturgist.

A crowd of about seventy-five people had gathered on the far side of the football field near a minivan and several blue wrestling mats. Jane, a girl not more than ten years of age, sat quietly in a wheelchair. The daughter of two NC faculty members, Jane had been stricken with an undiagnosed neurological disease. The president of the college, James Thompson, crouched down to talk with her, and she smiled. The Jello match was a fund-raiser for her medical bills, one of several fund-raisers for her in the small town. A male student with a bullhorn told the crowd that the main event, the Jello wrestling contest between the chaplain and the dean of students, would be held in about fifteen minutes. President Thompson left, presumably to attend homecoming receptions and reunions. Another student with long bushy sideburns took the bullhorn and introduced himself as the president of the NC Sideburn Society, which, he explained, was open to both men and women and even to those who did not have facial hair. "We all have the 'inner burn,'" he pointed out. He told a number of jokes in an effort to entertain the crowd before the contestants arrived.

The first student on the bullhorn then read the rules of the Jello wrestling contest. They were cast in the form of commandments and included "Thou shalt not bite thy opponent," "Thou shalt not stuff green Jello down thy opponent's pants," and "Thou shalt not covet thy opponent's beard." The final commandment, "Thou shalt help Jane," announced the purpose of the match. Four large plastic tubs of green Jello were carted from the van and emptied onto the blue mats. Two male students wrestled to warm up the crowd. One wore a mask. Both wore long capes, spandex body suits, and jogging shorts. Before starting the match, each contestant knelt before Jane's wheelchair, telling her, "I fight in your honor." Green Jello flew everywhere as the wrestlers dumped each other onto the mats. By the end of the match, Jello was smeared on the face, hair, and clothes of the contestants.

As the students finished the warm-up match, two bearded middle-aged men, the pastor and the dean, appeared at the top of the hill overlooking the football field. Both wore the red-and-white colors of NC. The pastor sported a Viking helmet with two horns. They ran down the hill toward the Jello mats, knelt before Jane, and pledged their loyalty. Jane laughed as the dean fed green Jello to her golden retriever. The pastor and the dean broke all of the "Thou shalt not" rules of the match, pulling each other's beards and stuffing Jello down each other's pants. The dean taunted the pastor with references to the "Good Book." Plater yelled, "Am I my brother's keeper?," and answered his own question with a resounding "No!" before throwing the dean to the mat. After wrestling for a few minutes, the contestants turned on the director of the college choir who was standing nearby. After inquiring, "Where is that wimpy choir director?," they pulled him onto the mat and covered him in green Jello. The choir director allowed himself to be vanquished despite the fact that he was clearly in better physical condition than either the chaplain or the dean. The students passed around large plastic buckets to collect donations for Jane's medical bills, and the crowd (mostly students) responded generously with bills and coins.

Another combination had emerged in this homecoming event, one as typical of NC as the mixture of worship and performance. Rowdy college fun had been joined with earnest altruism. The school would prove to be as serious about its community service as it was about its music, and its students would enjoy diverse extracurricular events as much as the feats of accomplished musicians.

When asked in an interview what the NC board of regents believed to be distinctive about the college, board chair Marvin Sanders did not hesitate as he ticked off four items: the music program, the global perspective, the stated mission of the college, and the students. A member of the board since 1988 and chair for the previous three years, Sanders had sent two sons to NC and, along with most other board members, frequently dined with the students and stayed in their dormitories when he was on campus. "It's simply amazing," Sanders said, "that a school without a conservatory or a separate school of music could attain the level of excellence in music that NC has reached. The college choir, especially, is world-famous and virtually invented a cappella singing and four-part harmony." He believed that study abroad and service abroad gave many of the students a global perspective. "There are limits to bringing diversity into the college, given the region, but students are sent out into diversity. If we can't get the world to the students, we can get them into the world." Sanders was convinced that the stated mission of the school—a liberal arts college of the Lutheran Church rooted in the Christian gospel—was a clear one that defined the distinctiveness of the institution "and doesn't turn off the non-Lutherans who serve on the board." Sanders remarked that the students struck the members of the board as serious about their education while thoroughly enjoying the opportunities afforded them on campus.

Student Backgrounds, Activities, and Perspectives

Surveys of 1996 freshmen indicated that over 80 percent of them came from families in which both parents lived together, with 47 percent of those families earning annual incomes in the range of $30,000 to $75,000 and 29 percent earning over $100,000. The parents of those freshmen were highly educated. Over 75 percent of the fathers and 73 percent of the mothers held at least a bachelor's degree, and 43 percent of the fathers and 26 percent of the mothers had earned graduate degrees. The business field was the most common vocational area for the fathers (26%), with educators in second place (10%), whereas the mothers were most often educators (25%) or homemakers (13%). A large majority of the entering students viewed themselves as middle of the road or liberal politically, and they were committed to—and brought to college a strong record in—community volunteer service.

Board chair Sanders's observations about the school's emphasis on a global perspective and student attitudes toward curricular and extracurricular activities were borne out by the data. More than half of each graduating class over the last several years had spent some time studying abroad in one of NC's forty programs, with opportunities available from Australia to Zimbabwe. For two years in a row—1995 and 1996—NC was recognized as the top source of Peace Corps volunteers among colleges with enrollments of 5,000 or fewer students. In 1996, 21 graduates worked in 20 different countries, and in 1995, 20 graduates and 15 alumni joined the Peace Corps. In the 1997 senior class, 63 percent of the students performed volunteer activities as part of a college-sponsored program, and 53 percent volunteered through a noncollege group. There were no Greek fraternities or sororities at NC—much to the delight of the director of student activities, who preferred "not to have to deal with that competition"—but over 90 student organizations were available for the 3,000 students, and it was easy to form new student groups simply by petitioning the Office of Student Activities.

Both the director of that office and the university president admitted that although alcohol was forbidden on campus, drinking on and off campus did occur. And, in fact, approximately half of the incidents reported by campus security to the student newspaper in any given week involved the possession and imbibing of alcohol. Nearly a thousand members of the student body made a public pledge of total abstinence, however, and nonalcoholic events like the movie and theater series, rock concerts, winter sports, and performances by the campus musical groups attracted good crowds of students. Lectures, including lectures on religious topics, also drew good student attendance. Over 500 students attended a lecture in October 1997 on religion and Darwinian science delivered by a professor from the University of California at Berkeley, and 150 students were present at a lecture in April 1998 on Buddhism and Christianity given by a professor from the University of Chicago.

The convergence of a global perspective, extracurricular activities, volunteerism, religion, and academic interests was apparent in the student careers of Stanley Fisk, Anita Noll, and Jack Malloy when I interviewed them in 1997. Fisk was serving as president of the Student Government Association. A friendly, energetic, fast-talking senior from Iowa, he planned eventually to attend law school (his father and older brother were attorneys) but thought he would probably go into "some line of business first, after I graduate from NC." A political science major, he noted that his first passion was politics and that someday he hoped to pursue a political career. In addition to his work as student government president, Fisk sang in the chapel choir, served as the public relations representative of the coordinating group for all campus volunteer groups, and participated in intramural sports "here and there." He said that he came from "a strong Christian family background"—American Baptist—and he regularly attended Sunday services on campus, with an occasional visit to a local Baptist church. He also sometimes went to meetings of the campus Fellowship of Christian Athletes (FCA). "Students here are not necessarily brilliant," Fisk remarked, "but they work very hard and they get good grades. There is no big party scene on campus, though some drinking goes on." He observed that students were attracted to music concerts, intramural sports, and lectures like the one the following week to be given by Maya Angelou. "NC students are physically active and healthy," he said, "but they are not big on varsity sports." Fisk liked the size of the school. He found it small enough to create a good feeling of community but "not so small that you can't maintain some distance from people if you want to." And he believed that although the college was clearly affiliated with the Lutheran Church, it honored cultural and religious diversity. Through a couple of courses in religion that he had taken, but above all through his Global Semester in India the previous semester, he had come to believe that "a Christian needs to understand why groups, even groups within Christianity, differ, and how different cultures see things differently."

Anita Noll, an ebullient and thoughtful senior from NC's home state, was majoring in studio arts and art education. An honor student who lived in one of the twelve honors houses on campus, Noll pursued a long list of activities during her four years of college, including participation in the freshman choir and chapel choir, Feminists for Change, Amnesty International, the NC theater, the student senate, campus public radio, career fairs and arts programs in the local public schools, and intramural sports. A Lutheran in background, she attended campus Sunday services regularly but only occasionally went to daily chapel (when she "needed a nice break in the day"). She believed that she reached a crucial turning point in her life during her junior year when her Global Semester allowed her to visit and study in nine countries. The experience gave her an appreciation of diversity, especially religious diversity, that changed her entire outlook on life. "In a way, I was at a low point in my life before I took that Global Semester," she said. "I had just broken up with my boyfriend who was a Roman Catholic, and he proved to me how small my religious commitments were." During her semester abroad, she kept asking: "Why do I call myself a Christian? What if I were not born a Christian? How would I view things if I were born a Muslim and if I had not been born an American?" By virtue of her firsthand exposure to other cultures, she thought she was "now more tolerant of human beings as human beings and their religious differences. My generation is more open to diversity than my parents'. We can't separate gender, ethnicity, culture, and religion. But still all that's pretty abstract until you have encountered a Muslim as a person." After graduation, Noll planned to do a half year of student teaching in India, undertake some volunteer work abroad, and then perhaps go to graduate school to earn a master of fine arts degree.

Jack Malloy, a soft-spoken junior from Kansas who was reared as a Methodist, was a pre-med student pursuing a double major in biology and Spanish. He attended daily chapel regularly, as well as Sunday Lutheran services, where he was "trying to understand the liturgical calendar for the first time"—something his Methodist background did not provide. He sang in the chapel choir and was heavily involved in volunteer work. Malloy interpreted and translated Spanish for patients at a nearby clinic, answered the phone and helped develop medical histories of Hispanic patients in an emergency room, and recently assisted with cleanup and medical relief in a neighboring town that had been devastated by a tornado. He also was involved in a "care ministry" on campus in which he talked with fellow students about death, dying, pain, and eating disorders, although he said "there haven't been a lot of takers" for the program. Malloy mentioned two experiences as a student that had shaped his outlook on his future. During a January term, he went to Costa Rica, where he studied the country's health care, interviewed patients, and assisted local health care professionals. No religious motive lay behind this trip; he "took it simply for the clinical experience and the course credit." But he made an important religious discovery, regardless of his motives. "I saw the importance of folk Catholicism in the lives of the people—the way religion pervades their way of talking and their everyday existence. You can't deal with their health without understanding their religion." That perception, he was convinced, would be carried into his career as a physician. Another experience the previous year, however, persuaded him that limits should be placed on career. During a visit to the home of one of his biology teachers at Christmas, he was impressed by the children of the family reciting the Christmas story from memory and the devotion of husband and wife to each other. The example of the professor and his family convinced Malloy that "God and family are more important than career, that those things are beyond any career."

Fisk, Noll, and Malloy were examples of the manner in which a global perspective, extracurricular activities (especially music), academic interests, and volunteerism intersected in the lives of students at NC. In different ways, religion was also a factor in all three cases. As pervasive as religion was on the NC campus during my visits there, however, and as predominantly Christian as the student body was, the NC religious scene was by no means homogeneous. The variety of religious outlooks on the part of the students was acknowledged by the college pastor.

Religion and the Campus Milieu: The Chaplain's View

Ben Plater was about fifty years old, tall, and thin and sported a full gray beard. When I first talked with him in the fall of 1997, he had been serving as the pastor of the NC Lutheran congregation and the college chaplain for sixteen years. Appointed and paid by the college with the approval of the Lutheran Church, he was chiefly responsible for presiding over the liturgy on Sunday and other Lutheran services, arranging daily chapel services, and counseling students. He also directed the worship at events like baccalaureate and the Christmas Festival, led prayers at other public events such as orientation and the awarding of honorary degrees, and served on the college policy committee along with the president, the dean, and selected faculty members.

Plater told me that although a large majority of students were Lutheran, with Roman Catholics composing the second largest religious group, he believed that "NC students are all over the religious map. There are students who have had it with church and blame Christianity for the ills of the world. There are others who are quite devout. Others come to NC for strictly academic reasons—some don't even know about our affiliation with the Lutheran Church—and they discover that all this religion stuff is pretty interesting." In Plater's judgment, much of the widespread volunteerism on campus was inspired by religious faith, although some was prompted by strictly humanistic concerns. "What seems to be the common denominator here is that everything religious is fair game for discussion." And because of Christianity's undeniable presence on campus, it had to be dealt with in some way. "Not all students attend daily chapel, but it occurs, it is there, you cannot ignore it, you must deal with it pro or con." Furthermore, sacred music was constitutive of the ambience of the place. "Music is the primary literature of the college," Plater remarked, "and sacred music is the primary religious literature of the school." Plater's metaphor was similar to one that Noll used when she spoke of her participation in the chapel choir. The choir directors, she said, "are the storytellers. They bring in the spiritual aspects of music that our society ignores."

Clearly, music, along with global awareness and volunteerism, was a part of the text or story that defined NC. And it was a literature that figured heavily in the practice and teaching of religion at the college.

RELIGIOUS PRACTICE

Worship Services

Most worship at NC took place in Memorial Chapel under the direction of the office of the college pastor. The following services were typical of the range of worship I observed at the school.

At 10:30 on Sunday morning, 12 October 1997, the weather was blustery, rainy, and cold, and the large Memorial Chapel was about half full. Most of the 700 people in attendance at the service of the college Lutheran congregation were students, but 20 or 30 adults were present as well. The men were attired mostly in slacks and sports shirts, with a few wearing jackets and ties, and the women were dressed mostly in skirts or slacks and blouses. About the same number of women and men were present. A sign-language interpreter sat on a tall stool in front of the congregation. The chancel was divided between a pulpit and a lectern, and a large, elevated altar stood at the rear of the chancel under a floor-to-ceiling stained glass window portraying the Resurrection. The order of worship for the service was a formal liturgy for Holy Communion marking the twenty-first Sunday after Pentecost:

Organ Prelude, Psalm Prelude, No. 1, Herbert Howells
Welcome and Announcements
Entrance Hymn, #834, "Sing Praise to the Lord," Laudate Dominum
Greeting, p. 2
Kyrie, p. 3
Hymn of Praise, p. 4, "Now the feast . . ."
Prayer of the Day
First Lesson, Amos 5:6–7, 10–15
    L: The Word of the Lord
    C: Thanks be to God

Psalm 90:12–17, sung by all, tone #1

    Choir: So teach us to number our days,

      that we may apply our hearts to wisdom.

    All: Return, O Lord; how long will you tarry?

      Be gracious to your servants.

      Satisfy us by your loving-kindness in the morning;

      so shall we rejoice and be glad all the days of our life.

      Make us glad by the measure of the days that you afflicted us

      and the years in which we suffered adversity.

      Show your servants your works

      and your splendor to their children.

      May the graciousness of the Lord our God be upon us;

      prosper the work of our hands; prosper our handiwork.

Second Lesson, Hebrews 4:12–16

    L: The Word of the Lord

    C: Thanks be to God

Gospel Verse, p. 8 (sung twice)

Gospel, Mark 10:17–31

    L: The Gospel of the Lord

    C: Thanks be to God

Sermon

Hymn of the Day, #406, "Take My Life, that I May Be," Patmos

The Apostles' Creed, p. 85

Prayers, p. 85

Sign of Peace, p. 86

At the Offering, "Hail Gladdening Light," Charles Wood

Offertory, p. 12, "As the Grains of Wheat . . ."

Prayer, p. 13, "Merciful God . . ."

The Great Thanksgiving, p. 14

Holy, Holy, Holy, p. 15

Eucharistic Acclamation, #2, p. 16

The Lord's Prayer, p. 18

    p. 18, "Lamb of God . . ."

Hymn, #809, "Surely it is God Who Saves Me," Raquel

Hymn, #803, "Jesu, Jesu," Chereponi

Choir, "Nunc Dimitis," Charles Villiers Stanford

Post-Communion Blessing, p. 19

Post-Communion Hymn, p. 20, "Thanks be to you . . ."

Prayer, A: . . . Jesus Christ our Lord. Amen

Blessing and Dismissal, p. 21

Postlude, "Toccata from *Gothique Suite*," Leon Boellmann

A male and a female student assisted with the administration of communion and read two of the Scripture lessons. Associate Pastor Virginia Kosner presided at the service, and Plater read the gospel and preached the sermon. In her opening announcements, Kosner said that special prayers for the day would be offered for those suffering from AIDS (the AIDS quilt was on campus for the month) and for a student whose grandmother recently entered the hospital. The chapel choir performed professionally in its parts of the service, especially in its rendering of "Hail Gladdening Light" for the offering. The organ boomed, on occasion so loudly that the congregational signing was drowned out. When the choir sang, many in the congregation turned around to face it in the rear balcony.

In his ten-minute sermon, Plater took the story of Jesus and the rich man who was trying to enter the Kingdom of Heaven as the occasion for his remarks. Plater discussed the dilemma that faces those who have wealth. What are we to do? Condemn the wealthy and say we don't want their money for the new building under construction on campus? Get an expensive education and then say to our parents, "I think I will give away all the riches I earn?" Take the wealth and criticize those who give it to us? The answer lies in cultivating an attitude toward wealth that takes Jesus' advice to the disciples seriously: the rich cannot enter the Kingdom on their own initiative, but with God, all things are possible. Caution must be exercised with wealth; we must think of negotiating our life's car down the street of wealth, which is filled with potholes—especially the potholes of greed, finding our worth in wealth, and entrusting our lives to riches. We must trust God and use wealth with love and compassion.

The sermon was a relatively minor part of the service. The music, responsive readings, and prayers led to the climax of worship, communion. Everyone in the congregation went forward to kneel at the altar, where they received bread and small cups of wine. The printed program explained: "If medical/health concerns give you reason to avoid the wine or bread, please remember that since ancient times the Christian Church has taught that Christ is fully present in either element alone, bread or wine."

On the same Sunday, Memorial Chapel was the scene of another service, an evening vespers from 7:30 to 8:30 featuring the 130-voice chapel choir and 80-member College Philharmonic Orchestra. The service was entitled on the printed program "A Prayer for Peace: Music of 20th Century England." The weather was still stormy, but the service drew a large crowd of about 1,300, doubtless due in part to the musical program. Again, most in attendance were students, but a good number of adults were present as well. The congregation was more informally attired than the congregation at the morning worship service, the students mostly wearing jeans, sweat suits, or overalls.

By contrast, the members of the orchestra were clad in tuxedos and black dresses, the choir in red robes, and the pastor and cantor in white vestments.

The vespers followed a formal order of worship, complete with congregational singing and responsive readings, Scripture lessons, and prayers. Following an orchestral prelude, Plater carried a large white candle down the center aisle to the front of the chancel, where the orchestra was already assembled, with the congregation singing during the procession:

> Jesus Christ is the light of the world,
> the light no darkness can overcome.
> Stay with us, Lord, for it is evening,
> and the day is almost over.
> Let your light scatter the darkness,
> and illumine your church.

Later, during the singing of a psalm, the members of the chapel choir moved in procession down the center and side aisles to take their places on the steps of the chancel behind the orchestra. The theme of the Scripture passages, psalms, and litany was peace. The congregational responses and singing were strong, and it was apparent that those in attendance were accustomed to following the parts of a liturgy and joining a cantor in singing a cappella. The choral and orchestral pieces included a particularly complex and difficult Magnificat (Finzi) and a mournful hymn, "Go My Children," set to a Welsh melody. Following a Bach postlude, the congregation broke into loud, prolonged applause. As in the case of the Christmas Festival, this vespers for peace was both worship service and musical performance.

Attendance at chapel services was entirely voluntary at NC, and the twenty-minute chapel services held on weekday mornings could attract student and faculty congregations ranging from 200 to over 1,000 people. The period designated for chapel was used for guest speakers from outside the college, student speakers, and special events such as the awarding of honorary degrees, but most often it was a time devoted to brief lectures or meditations by NC faculty. The service surrounding the lectures was usually informal and abbreviated.

At the chapel service on 23 September 1997, the lectern in Memorial Chapel had been moved further forward and to one side of the altar. Both lectern and altar were draped with green and orange cloths. The sanctuary was about half full. At least 500 of the 600 or so in attendance were students, clad in sweat suits and jeans. The students talked noisily until an organ prelude was struck, then they were silent. The service started promptly at the scheduled time of 11:10 A.M. and ended promptly at 11:30. A brief prayer of thanksgiving was offered from behind the lectern by Associate Pastor Virginia Kosner. The congregation sang the first two verses of "How Great Thou Art" (the Billy Graham Campaign theme hymn) with very loud organ accompaniment. The speaker, who had been seated in a pew at the front, rose and walked without introduction to the lectern. He was Frank Potter, a popular biology teacher whom everyone in the congregation knew. Potter offered a brief homily on "Why I am a Christian biologist," drawing some laughter when he admitted that he could not say he was a "Christian scientist" since that term carried a special meaning. He explained that he grew up on a farm and admired the God of the heavens. "How Great Thou Art" was his grandmother's favorite hymn, and he also grew to love it as an expression of the greatness of the God of the heavens. He got his first microscope at the age of twelve and was awestruck by the microbiotic life he observed. He continued to marvel at the wonders of nature throughout his life—both the patterns of things and the things that human knowledge cannot fathom. He pointed to the birth of his first child, the body's ability to recover from injury and disease, and DNA patterns as things that can be explained only by a Creator. "How could I not be a believer and a scientist?," he concluded. The congregation paid close attention to his remarks. The closing hymn, "Lord of the Dance," was sung in its entirety. Kosner offered a brief benediction, and the congregation filed out quickly. Classes awaited.

Some religious services at NC occurred outside Memorial Chapel and beyond the control of the campus pastors. Student-run prayer groups, weekly meetings of the InterVarsity Fellowship (IVF), impromptu dormitory devotional groups, and the meetings of the FCA were examples of these other services. Most were kindled by the fires of informal evangelical Protestantism rather than by the liturgies of formal Lutheranism. And the music of these student-led groups was quite different: it was more akin to the favorite hymn of Frank Potter's grandmother than to the sung psalms of the vespers. Of all the student-led groups, the FCA was the most popular on the NC campus, and its meetings were the best attended.

On a late September evening, 200 students, about equally divided between males and females, gathered in a large octagonal lounge in a dormitory for the weekly meeting of the FCA. Two large signs on a wall announced the time and place (in various dorms) of Bible study and prayer groups—twelve of them—for volleyball players, runners, football players, and so on. Without any announcement, at 9:00 the students began singing songs, their words projected on a large screen, with electric guitar accompaniment. "I am a wounded soldier. / I will not give up the fight, / for the Great Physician is healing me" were the words of one song; "O God, you are my God," the words of another. Still another, a praise song, was sung with even more gusto than the others:

Seek ye first the Kingdom of God
and his righteousness,
And all these things shall be added unto you,
Allelu, Alleluia.

This was music that could be found at church youth camps and meetings of such parachurch groups as the IVF, Campus Crusade, and the FCA around the country. The students literally swung to it. They clapped, some danced with each other, some waved their arms in the air. At some point in most of the songs, the musician stopped playing the guitar and the students sang the a cappella sections in perfect harmony. The room resonated with voices singing in sync with one another.

Following the singing, everyone sat on the floor at the direction of a male student in front of the crowd. He offered a prayer, thanking God for gathering so many together and asking the Lord to pour forth his grace on the group that night. He then asked for reports. A student stood to describe a successful dinner of the organization, another to report on a membership drive, another to say the capture-the-flag game on Friday was a success, another to announce that a flag game was scheduled for the following Friday, another to point to the Bible and prayer groups. The director of the group introduced the speaker for the evening, Shirley Mott, an English instructor at NC. A middle-aged African American wearing an African-style jacket and sunglasses, she made her way through the students seated on the floor to the front of the group.

She may have been an English instructor, but she was a preacher as well. In a forty-five-minute, rambling, humorous, extemporaneous presentation, she talked about "running the race" as a metaphor for the kind of discipline needed to improve one's intimacy with God. She swept from Genesis to Acts and the letters of Paul to point to how the spirit of God seeks us out. She quoted Scripture from memory, giving chapter and verse. She emphasized that discipline is required to sense God's intimate presence and hence open up our own full potential. She gave an example from her own life: she kept a spiritual journal, which was her form of meditation and personal creativity. Then she asked for testimony from the audience about how they attempted to improve their intimate relations with God. For about fifteen minutes, students volunteered examples from their own lives: reading Scripture regularly, being thankful for opportunities in life, praying and worshiping. The speaker expanded on each student comment and often cited Scripture to illustrate it. At 10:15, she concluded her address, which was followed by loud, long applause.

A male student at the back of the crowd gave a closing prayer, thanking

God that he attended a school where professors were willing to share their faith. He also thanked God for the gift of Jesus on the cross, a gift he said he did not understand but for which he was grateful. The meeting concluded with the singing of a song in perfect harmony. The session officially ended at 10:20, but most students stayed to talk, the guitarist struck up some more tunes, and many people hugged each other.

Other Religious Meetings

At 9:00 P.M. on 16 March 1998, one of the dozen FCA prayer groups convened for its weekly meeting, this group made up of the organization's leaders. The meeting place was a small conference room on the second floor of one of the dormitories. The room was furnished with a small table surrounded by chairs set before a board bearing science equations written in magic marker. Two undergraduate women arrived and erased the science equations, speculating on whether or not they were from organic chemistry. The male president of the FCA and four women students arrived. The seven undergraduates greeted each other and spoke about mutual acquaintances. "I just ran into Tom, and he said you were the coolest person," one woman told another. This was clearly a tight-knit group of people who knew each other well.

The meeting began with the president reading prayer requests from FCA members and one of the women writing the requests on the board. Some of the requests came to the group through e-mail. Others were written on small pieces of paper that had been collected from a prayer request box at the large weekly FCA meeting. Requests soon filled the board, including petitions for safe travel during the upcoming spring break, help during mid-term examinations, success in finding a summer job, and more serious matters. One male student had sent an e-mail requesting prayer for a sixteen-year-old boy who had been one of his charges at a Bible camp the previous summer and whom he had helped "commit his life to the Lord." The youth had attempted suicide by hanging himself with a necktie. "The necktie broke, praise God," the petitioner wrote. According to the e-mail message, the student planned to telephone the boy that evening and would let the FCA know of further developments. He did not know why the boy had tried to take his own life.

Many of the requests were from seniors concerned about career aspirations, possible graduate school plans, and employment following graduation. One asked the group to pray for a student who was "trying to find God." Several of the prayer requests had to do with the FCA itself, including an anonymous note from a student who wanted to "feel comfortable at FCA." That message was greeted with knowing sighs of disappointment from the group; later in the meeting, they discussed how to make people feel more at home at the FCA by sponsoring social events and dinners at the cafeteria and attempting to be friendlier to newcomers at large group meetings. One request simply asked that the "Holy Spirit sweep through FCA." Another requested prayer for the following evening's large group meeting. The prayer group was asked to pray for the FCA spring break missions trip, a student who was nervous about giving his testimony at an FCA meeting because it included unsavory details from his past, and a student who planned to give a presentation on the Crucifixion at an FCA meeting. One of the women asked the group to pray for an upcoming public appearance on campus by an "antigay speaker," who, she said, had the potential for being divisive. She wanted the group to pray that the "Christians on campus, regardless of their views on homosexuality, show Christian love toward each other and engage in honest dialogue." "The Christians on campus are going to be at the core of this" on both sides of the issue, she noted, adding that "this is a real opportunity for Christians to witness." Very few of the prayer requests concerned athletics, although many of them came from varsity athletes. One of the few that did mention sports was a request for a thanksgiving prayer on behalf of a woman skier who "went all-American after taking third place in a slalom race," despite the fact that she had broken her wrist earlier that day.

After all of the prayer requests were written on the board, members of the group joined hands and bowed their heads to pray. The president explained that each person around the table should take a turn. He began by thanking God for the opportunity to come together. "Father, thank you for all you have given us," another student prayed. Most began their prayers with praise or thanksgiving followed by a specific petition on behalf of one of the students listed on the board. The student praying would look up at the board as the group moved through the prayer requests in the order in which they had been written down. Although many of the requests were for secular matters like jobs, graduate school, and exams, those praying relativized the importance of the requests even as they prayed for success in these areas. "God help us to remember that you are more important than exams," one entreated. "Give Janine a peace about her decision," another intoned, asking God to signal the appropriate course of action by giving the petitioner a special sense of peacefulness when she made the right choice. The human element of the group's leadership was also downplayed. "Let the leadership of this group not be human leaders but you Lord," the president of the group petitioned. Many of the prayers emphasized that the FCA and its leaders were merely tools of God's work on campus. There were also moments of levity. One student prayed for another student present at the table, thanking God that "most of her requests for prayer are unnecessary." Everyone laughed.

The prayer portion of the meeting lasted about thirty minutes, and at the end, people were smiling across the table at one another.

During the final portion of the meeting, the students used colorful magic markers to make postcards for half of the students they had prayed for; they would make postcards for the others the following week. Some of the markers had patterns on their tips, including shamrocks (for St. Patrick's Day, coming up the next day), snowflakes, and footprints. "This is a great stress reliever," one student exclaimed, adding that she loved being able to put off studying for exams because she had to color cards at the FCA. The students wrote notes wishing "Happy St. Patrick's Day" to their recipients and letting them know they had been prayed for by the FCA leadership prayer group. The cards would go into the student post office boxes the next day.

Interviews at the end of the session revealed that two of the students were Lutherans. The president said he was a Presbyterian who attended a Lutheran church camp and now worshiped in a Baptist church. The woman sitting next to him advised that he should consider opening himself up to "charismatic experiences." He laughed and said that the Southern Baptists in his home city of Omaha really did know how to worship (seemingly equating charismatics with Southern Baptists). One student indicated that she was Catholic, which evoked surprise from the rest of the group. The students voiced considerable respect for Associate Pastor Virginia Kosner, noting the ways she had reached out to the non-Lutheran groups on campus like the FCA and IVF. "She's great," one of the female students commented, adding that Kosner had "found a way to include everyone in the student [Lutheran] congregation."

One sign of Kosner's attempt to reach the evangelical parachurch groups on campus was her willingness to speak to their meetings and advise their members. On the wall of one of the stairways connecting the first and second floors of the Commons, a large banner announced that on 22 September, "Pastor Kosner will speak on 'The Body of Christ' in the Commons Faculty Lounge. InterVarsity Fellowship. 8:30 P.M." On that evening, about forty students, two-thirds of them female, gathered in the lounge as two male students playing guitars and a female playing a violin performed folk music. Chairs had been moved to the walls, and a lectern and overhead projector had been set up at the front of the small room.

The meeting started at 8:40 P.M. with the singing of several songs accompanied by the musicians, the words projected on one wall. One of the songs, "O God, You Are My God," was the same piece that would be sung in the FCA gathering, but the IVF group did not swing and clap to the music. One of the guitar players offered a brief prayer, with special words for a recently deceased fellow student, and he asked everyone to sit on the floor. The guitar player announced that the theme of the meeting would be "The Body of Christ" and that a game illustrating the theme would now be played. Five volunteers were given slips of paper indicating their "identities" as parts of the body—legs, hands, eyes, mouth, and so on. All were blindfolded except "eyes." Two blindfolded girls straddled and rode two blindfolded boys; "eyes" led them to a table laid out with bread, peanut butter, jelly, and a knife. She coached "hands" to spread peanut butter and jelly on the bread and feed the sandwich to "mouth." There were many misses, and peanut butter and jelly ended up in the hair of "mouth"—all accompanied by lots of laughter and barked instructions from the audience. The food finally arrived at its proper destination, and the student in charge ended the game.

A female student introduced Kosner, who delivered an extemporaneous twenty-minute lecture, constantly moving from behind the lectern. She remarked that she was a dancer as a student at NC, and thus she had a special appreciation for the glories and limitations of the body. She discussed four meanings of the phrase "Body of Christ." First, God favored us by taking up in Jesus a body like ours so he could know feelings like love and agony. Second, Christ's body is a healing body; we become full and glorious people by participating in him. Third, all branches or denominations of Christians are different parts of the Body of Christ that need each other, the message of the game just played. And fourth, Christ is embodied in us as we have faith. She then invited the students to continue to think of how these meanings of the Body of Christ could be strengthened in their own lives. There was warm applause for the speaker, more songs were sung, the guitarist offered a benediction, and most students, who seemed to be friends, stayed to talk with one another. The session ended at 9:45.

The type of music was the same as that at the large FCA meeting, but the IVF response to the music was much more restrained. There was the same camaraderie and sense of fun as at the large session and the prayer group of FCA, but the IVF group was more focused on doctrinal content. The IVF meeting conformed to the image of the group that prevailed among faculty and students at NC: IVF members tended to be a bit more intellectual and sedate in their evangelicalism than their FCA counterparts.

Other student-led religious meetings were held on campus, some organized under the auspices of the Lutheran congregation. Sandra Krall, a senior majoring in philosophy with a minor in women's studies, participated in the large FCA meetings as well as a small FCA Bible study group. When I interviewed her, she was heavily involved in a small group that Pastor Ben Plater had helped her organize. She and three other women students met once a week to read aloud and discuss short selections from the Bible and devotional materials. The members of the group also kept "spiritual journals, which is a way we try to be accountable for our own and each other's spiritual development." They discussed their journal entries and helped each other "with personal problems we are having and what we are doing about them." Krall described herself and two other members as liberal. "We are open to religious diversity and have social justice concerns. The other person is very traditional and has a literal interpretation of the Bible. You have to be very careful what you say to a person like that. She could think you are a bad person because you don't hold her conservative views." Krall indicated with apparent relief that the literalist member of the group would be leaving NC next year to attend a more conservative Christian college.

Ernest Harbach, a sophomore with a dual major in religion and music, was the coleader of another group that had received the support and assistance of the college pastors: the Musicians' Devotions and Discussion Group. According to Harbach, the fifteen to twenty members of the group "happen to be musicians, and we don't really deal with music when we meet." He said that instead they focused on scriptural passages, social needs, and their doubts and questions about Christian theology. They sometimes invited a faculty member or pastor to speak to them and sometimes prayed. "But the meetings are not really devotional," he insisted. "They are more intellectual." At one time, Harbach had been fairly heavily involved in the FCA, and many of his friends continued to be active in that organization, but he had recently cut back on his FCA activity. "I find [the FCA participants] too charismatic and conservative, and I have been shifting away from all of that in my outlook. I find the musicians' group much more enjoyable."

Over lunch one spring day, I talked with Mae Jones, a junior majoring in math, education, and Scandinavian studies who was director of the Christian Activities Network, a group of students who coordinated activities of the Christian groups on campus by arranging shared advertising and shared outside speakers for the different programs. Although the network had a faculty adviser, it reported neither to the Office of the Chaplain nor to the Office of Student Affairs. Jones was very active in the FCA, playing guitar for its large weekly meetings and helping plan its smaller meetings and retreats. The group she was most enthusiastic about, however, was one she organized on her own initiative without the sponsorship of any organization: a Bible study group of fifteen freshmen women in her dormitory. The women met once a week for one and a half hours to read and discuss selections from the Bible. Before discussing the selections, Jones would typically point out the main themes in the Bible verses and use a Bible concordance to place the verses in context and connect them to other verses. They ended their study sessions with prayer, praying both for the campus as a whole and for special requests made by members of the group. Participants in the study group had become close friends and met once a week for lunch. Jones was reared by a very devout Lutheran mother, but she did not attend Lutheran services on campus. On Sundays, she and about sixty other NC students went into town to attend a Baptist church. She liked "the family setting of the downtown church and the challenging sermons of the pastor." None of her other religious activities was as important to her as her Bible study group. "It's where the most intimate contact takes place. It's where you can see peoples' hearts and souls and where they are hurting. And it's where I can give the most support. FCA is fun and nonthreatening, but I see more growth in myself and others in my Bible study group."

Thus there was a discernible range of Christian worship and other religious meetings on the NC campus, some of it overlapping in membership and style, some of it quite distinctive. The responses to and interpretations of the different forms of religious practice at NC were by no means uniform.

"Christians," "Pagans," and Others

Virginia Kosner was appointed associate pastor of the college in the academic year 1997–98, the year of my visits to the campus. Previously, there had been a part-time associate pastor, but the money for that position had run out. The position was now endowed by a local family and by other gifts, mostly from churches. Kosner graduated from NC in 1987 and went on to obtain a ministerial degree at a Lutheran seminary in the same state. In addition to sharing with Pastor Plater the duties at daily chapel and Sunday services, her activities included counseling students, helping students with their Bible study groups, and speaking to groups like the FCA and IVF. She also was responsible for serving as a liaison between the Lutheran congregation and other religious groups on campus. She understood the last task to entail "being a pastor to the students in those groups rather than trying to control them."

Kosner told me that "the way religious life is worked out today is similar to my student days. There are quite a few Christians on campus who don't conform to the more intellectual approach of the Lutheran campus ministry." She noted that these students wanted a religious practice that was "more upbeat and emotional." Many of these students went to Sunday services downtown rather than on campus and engaged in Bible study and prayer groups in the dorms. She and Plater did not feel they should intrude on this student-led piety, although they often gave advice or accepted speaking engagements at the request of these students. She found that some of these students were literal in their interpretation of the Bible and even criticized Lutherans for their liberalism. She said of this group of students, "I don't want to dampen student enthusiasm, but I fear some of the students are learning a 'We are the winners, and you others are the losers in religion' attitude." She also noted that many religious students—probably the majority—attended chapel and the campus church infrequently and others—about 700 to 800 in a typical Sunday congregation—were regulars at Sunday campus services. She pointed out, however, that there was a great deal of overlap between the evangelical Christians and those who attended Lutheran services. Many students from the FCA and IVF, as well as those who discovered Christianity in summer camps, came to Sunday services of the campus Lutheran congregation. This crossing over between evangelical Christian practice and Lutheran practice was what Kosner herself did as a student, so she was very sympathetic with students who followed such a pattern. She continued to be impressed by the number of student-initiated and student-led groups that arose on campus. "There are Bible study and prayer groups everywhere. I learn about a new one from a student every day."

Not everyone was as sympathetic to the student-led, parachurch, evangelical groups as Kosner. Paul Shawn, a junior majoring in history and the president of the campus Lutheran congregation who planned to become a Lutheran minister, had little use for the evangelical students. Shawn sneeringly referred to such students as "sweet, happy, superficial little Christians. They have been shaped by the youth camps, and they seem to be looking for an extended youth experience instead of an adult church." As president of the campus congregation, he was supposed to serve as student liaison with the different Christian groups on campus, but he was not comfortable with that role. "It has been difficult to work with IVF, FCA, and the Bible studies. When I attend their meetings, I can hardly keep from throwing up." He also objected to the influence of the evangelicals on the Lutheran services on campus, believing that pastors Plater and Kosner were so eager to accommodate the evangelical interests that many of the Lutheran worship services had become too informal, too lacking in Lutheran liturgy.

Unlike Shawn, Gerald Small did not find the evangelicals repulsive, but like Shawn, he believed they were superficial. A professor of religion on the NC faculty for twenty-two years and an alumnus of the college, Small said he had seen the religious climate of the school change since the 1960s. When he was a student in the late 1960s, he said, "there were a few charismatic and some non-Christian religious types around, but they were considered weird and outcasts." Small was convinced that a massive rebirth of both religious indifference and religious enthusiasm had occurred over the previous thirty years, movements that he considered two sides of the same coin. "We have two student bodies here," Small claimed. "Most, perhaps 80 percent, stand somewhere along the indifference spectrum." The others, those the indifferent students referred to as "the Christians," were the students who considered themselves "spiritual," by which they seemed to mean an "ill-defined, nonorganized ultimacy of self-orientation." These spiritual ones were "the Bible camp Christians" who tended to gravitate to the FCA and IVF. Since they found many NC faculty who supported and encouraged them in their religion, Small said he had formed a "countergroup to these Christians." A group of about twenty students had been joining him at his home on Wednesday nights, the same night many of the "Christian" groups met, to "bring up whatever issues they have, and we discuss them." This countergroup understood that the discussion did not need to result in any conclusions or consensus on the part of the group. The sessions were simply designed to let the students think aloud about religious themes. The students, in Small's language, tended to be "the bookish, the seekers, the thoughtful. Some of them are old-fashioned scientific types who have trouble fitting religion into their scientific perspective. Some come from Indonesia and have trouble understanding Christianity. Some are just real pagans." Professor Small periodically offered a section of the required introductory religion course for these skeptical students entitled The Bible for Pagans.

Some students did fall into the categories that Small proposed, and they had less than positive attitudes toward students in the other category. On the one hand, in addition to Paul Shawn, Mary Delillo had little use for the evangelical Christians on campus. A triple major in religion, economics, and French, Delillo said she grew up in a very secular family. Her father was of Catholic background and her mother was a Chinese Buddhist, but she had no religious training either at home or in a church. "Unlike my classmates, I knew something was missing. I didn't know anything about religion. I hadn't even gone to Sunday school." To correct her deficiency, she started taking courses in religion, including Small's Bible for Pagans class. Her course work at NC and a six-month study abroad in Indonesia convinced her of the importance of religion in culture, and she had begun to concentrate her study on politics, Christianity, and Islam. She credited Small's Bible for Pagans class for "really opening up the importance of religion for me," and she regularly attended the informal Wednesday evening sessions at Small's house. She believed she had discovered that her classmates on campus who seemed to know so much about Christianity really did not know much more than she did. And she considered the evangelical Christians on campus to be basically anti-intellectual, even childlike, about religion, in that they simply accepted without reflection certain beliefs that were handed to them.

On the other hand, Mae Jones thought the NC campus reeked of paganism. Despite the good attendance at the services of the Lutheran congregation and the apparent dominance of Christianity on campus, Jones believed that real Christians were hard to find and it was not easy for them to network. "NC is not overwhelmingly Christian," she observed. "You can go along just fine academically without being influenced by Christianity. The atmosphere here is very tolerant, which is not always good. It's just, 'Believe what you want.' There is no push to stand up for your beliefs. People don't want to offend. If you have no religious beliefs, then that seems to be OK too." She was convinced that many NC students are too intellectual, too rationalistic to be good Christians. "They think that everything has to be proven, they want to figure out everything with their heads, try to rationalize everything. Of course, that's why we are here—to figure things out—but there needs to be a balance between what can be proven and what should be taken on faith."

Other students did not have polarized views of campus religious life. Like Kosner, they saw no necessary conflict between groups—if for reasons somewhat different from hers. Student government president Stanley Fisk, for example, attended Sunday services at the chapel and at the Baptist church downtown, and he occasionally showed up for the large weekly meetings of the FCA "as much for fun and fellowship as for religion. And it's a good place to meet respectable people of the opposite sex." Anita Noll, whose Global Semester in several countries opened her up to the value of religious diversity, believed that she had become more accepting of everyone, including "the nonquestioners" or those the "pagans" called the "Christians." "Maybe those nonquestioners have already gone through the questioning stage or are about to," Noll remarked. "We can't assume that everyone has to be at the same point on the spectrum." She still found it "hard to be tolerant of intolerance, but I am more at peace with myself," and as a result, she had been surrounding herself with different types of people, "some who are questioning and some who are firm in their faith."

Although students like Stanley Fisk and some of the members of the FCA leadership prayer group participated in both the Lutheran congregation and the evangelical meetings—constituting the overlap observed by Kosner—others had been drifting away from the evangelical groups. As we have seen, that was true of Ernest Harbach, for whom the members of the FCA began to seem "too charismatic and conservative." It was also true of Kevin Solomon. A senior from Iowa majoring in religion and music, Solomon was a Lutheran who served as student chaplain for the college choir. During his first two years at NC, he was heavily involved in the IVF, but he said "there got to be a belief clash. They had a more fundamental mind-set than I did, and I was beginning to ask big questions about Christianity and taking religion classes, and I was all over the map spiritually. They [the IVF] wanted me to stay in one place spiritually." One of his religion classes in particular, Jesus and the New Testament, moved him beyond IVF. "The course got me to thinking about the historical Jesus and the different agendas in the New Testament. It added to my confusion but forced me to open my perspective wider."

Religious practice on the NC campus was thus entirely Christian. But as the two college pastors recognized, the Christian practice was more diverse than one might have suspected at first. It included Lutheran liturgy, daily chapel, weekly evangelical meetings, student-led Bible study and prayer groups, the merging of musical performance and worship service, life-changing exposure to different cultures and religions, and open-ended religious discussion groups. And the interpretations of campus Christianity by members of the community were equally diverse, comprising disparate senses of how the religious practices coalesced and conflicted. Although there is no denying that tensions existed between groups, especially tension between evangelicals and others, the discord did not seriously divide the campus. In Pastor Plater's language, a commonality could be found in the certainty that "everything religious is fair game for discussion." Perhaps Solomon captured the spirit of the place best when he said: "Everyone who comes here eventually knows the school is rooted in Christianity. Because that is taken for granted, much personal religious searching can be permitted. Going abroad and discovering that not everyone is a Lutheran and engaging in Buddhist meditation are allowed as experiments, but not many students jump too far away from their [Christian] tradition." Solomon felt that because the college, in keeping with its Lutheranism, promoted a "liberal, tolerant, an almost passive attitude, extremes can play out and balance. We don't try to run each other out of town."

TEACHING RELIGION

The teaching of religion occurred in several parts of the NC curriculum—in philosophy, music, the sciences, history, and many other courses available to undergraduates—but instruction in religion was clearly concentrated in the school's religion department.

The Religion Department

The NC Department of Religion consisted of 20 full-time faculty who in an average semester taught 1,000 students in 40 course sections. Over 70 students majored in religion, many of them choosing to "double major" in another discipline as well. The major required eight religion courses distributed over the three areas of sacred texts, religion in history and culture, and religious thought. One of those courses had to be the capstone seminar, a class devoted to a topic chosen by the professor and designed to integrate the learning of seniors. The department described its overall purpose as follows: "as an integral part of the liberal arts curriculum, to attend to the religious elements of culture—scriptures, rituals, symbols, traditions, beliefs, worship practices, values, and theologies. At North College the study of religion emphasizes study of the Christian tradition, its history, practice and contemporary expression."

The study of religion was required of all NC students. Until a few years before my visit, all students were required to take three courses in religion chosen from a wide spectrum of offerings, with the only proviso being that no more than one of the courses dealt with religions other than Christianity. After that time, all students were required to take a specific course during their freshman year, Bible in Culture and Community, as well as one other course in Christian theology at some point in their college careers. In 1987, the college adopted a mission statement that included the goal of exposing students to "opportunities for encounter with the Christian gospel" and the intention "that its graduates combine academic excellence and theological literacy with a commitment to lifelong learning." In 1994, the faculty committee in charge of general education instituted the two religion requirements as a way of living up to the mission of assuring that NC graduates would be biblically and theologically literate.

The new general education requirements created considerable consternation and some discord among the faculty members of the religion department. In order to cover the multiple sections of the Bible in Culture and Community course, faculty untrained in biblical studies were forced to teach that course rather than courses in their areas of expertise. Teachers in areas such as religious history, religion and literature, and biblical studies believed that enrollment in their courses was siphoned off by the requirement that all students take a class in theology. And the meaning of "theology" in the theological requirement resulted in disagreement, the historians in the department claiming that the theologians among their colleagues defined the term too narrowly and ahistorically as systematic theology and the theologians avowing that some of the historians and other faculty began to "fake" theology in their course descriptions in order to attract students. Still other religion faculty were persuaded that the focus on the Bible and theology was an unfortunate abandonment of the global perspective of the college, with insufficient attention being given to the religious traditions of the world.

In fact, a large majority of the religion faculty taught and did research in the Bible and the Christian tradition. As religion department chair Niels Larsen put it, the department was "underrepresented in the religious traditions." Judaism and Islam were taught on an occasional basis by adjunct faculty, but "because of the prospects of downsizing in the college, it is unlikely that the department will make appointments in those areas anytime soon." Hinduism and Buddhism were represented on the faculty, however. Hinduism, in Larsen's words, "is taught from the inside by a prominent Hindu; Buddhism is taught from the inside by a non-Buddhist."

Just as there was considerable variety in Christian practice at NC, however, there was abundant variety in the department's course offerings on the Bible and the Christian heritage. Classes in the fall semester of 1997 included Christian Theology and Human Existence, Introduction to Feminist Theology, The Lutheran Heritage, Religion in America, Hebrew Bible, Christian Ethics, Political Theology, as well as courses in Hinduism and Buddhism. Furthermore, the different sections of the required course that caused so much agitation, Religion 121, Bible in Culture and Community, covered a wide array of approaches to the study of the Bible.

The Required Bible Course

After much discussion and debate, the members of the religion faculty agreed that all sections of the required course in the Bible would share a common core but would allow teachers to pursue their distinctive interests and approaches. The core consisted of the use of the Christian Bible as a textbook, explication of "the basic story line of the Bible" on the part of the instructors, and study of "the dialogue between the biblical tradition and the cultures and communities related to it" by all students. Beyond those common features, the instructors were at liberty to assign other readings, select from the Bible what they deemed most significant for the purpose of fostering biblical literacy, and focus on the cultures and communities they thought the students should observe in dialogue with the biblical tradition. And, indeed, liberty was taken. The topics for the sections of the course in the fall semester of 1997 had a wide range: American Experiences, Religious Experiences; Values, Institutions, and Conflicts; Methods, Models, and Meanings: Understanding the Bible; Suffering and Hope: The Bible and the Problem of Suffering; Laws and Prophets in Judaism, Christianity, and Islam; Male and Female, God Created; The Bible and Christian Ethics in American Life; The Book and Community of the Gospel; and Bringing the Bible to Life: The Bible as a Love Story. Two of these sections illustrate the diversity that prevailed in the teaching of the required Bible course at NC.

Scott Laughner typically taught a section of the required Bible course three times a year. A Harvard-trained specialist in the New Testament, Laughner was a wiry, bearded man in his early fifties who had been on the NC faculty for over twenty years. Despite his training in biblical criticism, the topic for his section of the required Bible course in 1997 was American Experiences, Religious Experiences, a title that summarized the way in which his course section moved back and forth between American settings and biblical text. He explained to me that "in the near future I would like to offer a special section of the course for NC international students—those who have recently moved to [the nearby city] and are unfamiliar with American culture. But for now, I want to show students how biblical and American stories have influenced each other. It's also a way of getting the students to examine some of their unexamined assumptions about what it means to be an American." Laughner felt that most of his students were unaccustomed to thinking about religion in context—any context—since their own religion had been so privatized. "When they do get the point that religion shapes and is shaped by American communities and contexts, it's fun to see the 'lights come on.'"

In addition to reading passages from the Bible, Laughner's students during the fall semester of 1997 were assigned James Baldwin's novel *Go Tell It on the Mountain* for a perspective on African American experience and religion and Chaim Potok's novel *The Chosen* for a portrait of modern Judaism, as well as short readings in biblical interpretation and American religious history. Written assignments included brief research papers and critical reviews of reading assignments and three "personal essays" in which students reflected comparatively on their own religious experiences and the stories they read. In the first personal essay, written early in the semester, students wrote about key persons or events that had shaped them, as well as answering the question, "What thoughts do you have about studying religion in college?" The second personal essay asked the students to compare and contrast their own experiences with those of characters in Baldwin's *Go Tell It on the Mountain*, and the third essay assignment encouraged them to reflect on what could be learned from *The Chosen* "about your self and life in American culture." It was apparent from the essay assignments that Laughner expected his students to attain self-understanding as well as an understanding of others, that he wanted the students' own experiences, as well as the Bible and the American experience, to enter into his section of the basic Bible course. That expectation was apparent in his class sessions as well.

Laughner divided the students in his Religion 121 sections into work groups of three or four people, which convened as study groups outside of class and as discussion groups during class periods. Considerable class time was usually devoted to the meetings of the students in their work groups. That was true of his fifty-five-minute class on a late October morning in 1997. Chairs were arranged in a jagged circle facing a table and blackboard at the front of the room. Twenty students, fifteen of them females, most dressed in jeans and sweaters and toting backpacks, had taken their seats before the beginning of the class. Laughner entered the classroom exactly at the starting time of 10:45, attired in slacks, dress shirt, and tie, leaned against the table in front, and asked, "OK, how is the reading of the novel [Potok's *Chosen*] going?" A few students responded, "Fine" or "Good." "We want to get the plot and characters of the novel straight and then talk about where you are headed with your papers," Laughner continued. He told them to break up into their small groups and "get clear on plot, characters, how Potok and the authors of the other assigned readings go together, and all that stuff."

For the next fifteen minutes, the students worked together in their groups. The group nearest me in the back of the room did not appear to accomplish much. A woman in that group remarked to the only other member of her group, another woman, "I just don't get it. I read the novel twice, and I still just don't get it." The two spent their time poring over the underlining in their copies of the novel. The other four groups were engaged in doing what the professor asked, with one student in each group carrying most of the conversation. While the students met in their groups, Laughner wrote a long list of terms on the blackboard, including "Sephardic," "Hasidim," "Ortho-dox," "Zionist," and a list of the Jewish Holy Days. Then he moved from group to group, crouching down to their seated level, entering into the conversation, and answering questions. He spent no time with the group in the back since its members indicated they had no questions for him.

Laughner then returned to the front of the class and asked each group to share questions or observations about Judaism and Potok. He used the questions and comments as occasions to deliver minilectures on a number of topics. One female student observed that there might be similarities between Jews returning to Israel as a homeland and her returning to her home in New York City. Laughner replied "Yes and no" to her observation and gave a brief lecture on Zionism, why a homeland has been so important to some Jews, and the deep divisions between Jewish groups within the contemporary state of Israel. Another female student said she could not understand why a nation-state was so important to Jews. Her remark led Laughner to discuss how the Jewish Enlightenment in France freed Jews for the professions, the Enlightenment ideas at the base of the American found-ing documents, and Jews' belief in the need for the protection of a free and enlightened state. He asked why some Jews, like the Hasidim, would oppose

Zionism. The student who spoke first volunteered that man, not God, had established the state and the Hasidim could not accept that. Laughner indicated his agreement and added that the state had been established "by secular, or to the Hasidim, by nonreligious men at that." Then Laughner picked up the biblical theme of the Chosen People and said that for ancient Israel, revelation was in history, time, and presupposed action by the people, not just reaction, but most Jews in the modern world had only had the chance to react because of their subordinate position in different cultures. During these short lectures, Laughner never appealed to notes. He sometimes sat briefly in a chair near the front table and sometimes walked around in front of the table, but more often he squatted in front of the table and in the middle of the circle of chairs. He was a study in constant motion and strong knees.

With about fifteen minutes remaining in the class period, Laughner sent the students back to their groups, this time to discuss what they would write about in their papers. They spent seven or eight minutes on this task, with all but the two-person group in the back talking fairly animatedly about their paper topics. When Laughner called the full class back together, he asked if they had questions. One student wanted to know if she could work on the topic of the covenant as a "special relationship with God," and Laughner approved. Another wanted to know how to pursue one option given in the syllabus, that of portraying himself as a character in the novel. Laughner said the student could do that by making a visit to the past from the point of view of the present or perhaps by placing himself in the past. Another student asked what it meant, as stated in the course syllabus, to "gain self-understanding through the novel." Laughner answered that it could mean understanding the American context of Judaism and other religions better or "discovering something about yourself you didn't already know." Laughner then took the last two or three minutes of the class to point out some passages in *The Chosen* that he hoped the students would "let drop into their heads"—one having to do with things not always being what they seem, another with the difference between friendship and merely liking someone. Several students gathered around the professor after class to discuss the writing assignment.

It is not surprising that a survey of students in one of Laughner's sections of the basic Bible course revealed that over 90 percent believed that "the objective study of religion" best described the course and that a large majority considered their professor a knowledgeable, objective, fair-minded source of information. But a sizable majority of the students also said they felt quite free to express their own beliefs in class and thought they grew spiritually as a result of the course. It would appear that Laughner's dual purpose of expanding student knowledge—of the Bible and its relation to American contexts—and advancing self-knowledge through the study of religion was realized to a large extent.

An altogether different approach to the required Bible course was taken by Professor John Wolf. Whereas Laughner's approach had been influenced most by his wide reading in American literature and history, anthropology, and the history of religions, Wolf's approach had been shaped by his extensive work in systematic theology, the history of Christian doctrine, and biblical interpretation.

The Christian Bible was the only required book for Wolf's section of Religion 121. Wolf stated on the first page of the syllabus: "There is of course a certain amount of historical and other information to be communicated along the way. I have decided not to assign a textbook for this purpose; for the most part, I will do it myself in class." In addition to exposing the students to a reading of the passages of the Bible in historical context, Wolf's aim was, as stated in the syllabus, "to show how the Bible—like any other important work—is always read within and for the life of some community. In this section, the referenced community will be the one that made this book in the first place, the Christian church. Thus the course will be to some degree also a course in Christian theology. I will function as the resident representative of the church and its theology."

Wolf was a short, stocky, bearded man in his sixties who had been teaching at NC for eight years. A widely published and well-known Lutheran theologian and ordained clergyman, Wolf had no reservations about wearing his clerical collar to class. "I want my students to know who I am," he explained in an interview in his office—"an advocate of Christianity." He said that he did much the same sort of thing in his Bible course section that was done in a good church catechesis class, dealing as he did with key doctrines and ideas that spring from biblical texts. The difference was that many of today's NC students had less exposure to these doctrines and their biblical sources than students in a catechesis class. Many years earlier when he taught at another Lutheran college, the students had been so heavily catechized that he had "tried to loosen them up by getting them to question most everything they had been taught. Now just the reverse is true. They have to be taught things for the first time." He related a story about a very bright and hardworking NC student who asked him midway through one of his recent courses, "Who came first, Moses or Jesus?" Although he assumed the role of advocate of Christianity, a role that entailed speaking as a theologian for the Christian church as the community of the Bible, Wolf asserted, "I always try to put an 'if' in my teaching, to get the students to thinking on their own about Christian doctrines. What follows 'if' we do not believe

Jesus rose from the dead?" He also insisted that he was more descriptive in the classroom than some of his colleagues gave him credit for. "The students know so little about their own Christianity, it would be unfair of me to argue against them constantly. They need some basic information about their own faith." He also remarked that much of his teaching could be described as walking a tightrope between exploring the truth of Christianity and allowing nonbelievers to study Christianity from the outside. "In any case, I tell all my students, believers and unbelievers alike, that they need to know Christianity in order to understand their culture."

On a Tuesday in October 1997, Wolf met his section of Bible in Culture and Community to focus on the prophet Amos. Seventeen students were present at the beginning of the class; another three arrived a few minutes late. Female students outnumbered males three to one. The course was meeting in the same classroom used by Laughner, with the same furniture arrangement: chairs in a circle facing the table and blackboard at the front. Wolf, wearing a dark plaid jacket over a black shirt with a clerical collar, started the class on time. Because the section met on a Tuesday–Thursday sequence, the time allotted for the class was almost an hour and a half—from 11:45 A.M. to 1:10 P.M.—and during the lunch hour at that. A couple of the students seemed tired and hungry and one woman must have been sleepless the previous night because she could hardly keep her eyes open from the time she entered the room, but most of the students seemed attentive and alert. It was apparent from the outset of the class that unlike Laughner's section of the course, Wolf's section would have a clearly theological emphasis.

After passing out a sheet with questions for the next assigned reading in Isaiah and Ezekiel, Wolf began a series of short lectures punctuated by his questions to the class and their questions to him. He had placed two hand-written pages of notes on the lectern, but he referred to them only twice, and then briefly, during the entire class period. He sometimes jumped up to sit on the table to read from the Bible, but mostly he walked among the students and talked to them—sometimes loudly and enthusiastically and sometimes quietly, often removing and replacing his glasses as he spoke. Most of the student discussion was conducted by two students—a man who wore a knit hat and a woman who sat next to him—but a good third of the class participated in the discussion. Wolf warmed to the subject of the prophet Amos by sketching the history of prophecy, describing the prophet as someone who was seized by God and used to make the divine presence manifest. Later, Wolf discussed Amos not writing his own words as evidence that his prophecy occurred over several years, the division of the land of Israel into two kingdoms, and the threats from Assyria. He read from the Bible frequently, but more often, he quoted it—especially the various prophets—from memory.

Much of Wolf's class was carried out in a question-and-answer format. He asked if anyone was reminded of anything in the New Testament by the "word of the Lord" language in Amos. A woman said she was reminded of the Gospel of John. Wolf agreed and gave a short theological lecture on the word of God, observing that God's speaking through the prophets was a creative word rather than mere information. Another female student wanted to know how one could tell whether a person was really a prophet. Wolf answered that this was a constant problem in religion, not just in ancient Israel, and said that one must sort through prophecies. In his opinion, there were two crucial questions: Does the prophet himself obey Torah, and is the prophecy consistent with what God has already done for his people? Two student questions—one asking why God chose one prophet and not another and the other inquiring how there could be false prophets and true ones—set Wolf off on a theological disquisition in which he argued that God chooses in mysterious ways, that not all religions can be true because they are so different, that God chooses peoples and individuals somewhat arbitrarily to reveal his truth, and that unlike Hinduism and Buddhism— and probably most religions—Judaism and Christianity believe in a God who relates to us personally, not impersonally, and is a "talkative God." He mentioned his recent visit to a museum in New York City where images and statues of the Buddha conveyed distance and impersonality, imparting a much different sense of what is "holy" than one encounters in the personal Holy One of Israel and the church.

When a female student asked about the condemnation of wealth in Amos and whether it applied to today's Christians, Wolf confessed that "the jaws of hell open before me when I read that passage" because Judaism and Christianity offer no good solutions to the problem of how the wealthy can deal with the poor short of pursuing the monastic life. "The Bible gives little comfort to those of us in the middle class." Wolf admitted that he himself liked nice things and could not possibly be monastic, and then he briefly alluded to the defense of the poor and the condemnation of capitalist wealth on the part of current Christian liberation theologians. The student seemed puzzled that she had not received a more direct, and perhaps different, answer to her question. The class period ended, and Wolf sent his students on their way by reminding them of their reading assignment in Isaiah and Ezekiel for Thursday.

Wolf had assumed his advertised role as theologian for the Christian community by elaborating on the ideas and contexts in a book of the Christian Bible, spelling out that book's Christian theological implications, holding forth on the incompatibility of biblical religions and other religious traditions (and implying the superiority of the former), and candidly admitting a conundrum respecting poverty and wealth for which he had no easy answer. Wolf encouraged student questions. For the most part, however, he used those questions as occasions for his own elaborations rather than opportunities for the expression of student opinions. In class, he lived up to his self-description as a purveyor of information (in the absence of any textbook but the Bible) and as an advocate of Christian theology.[1]

Approximately a third of the NC students who took religion in any given semester were enrolled in the multiple sections of the required Bible course, with the remaining enrollees distributed in twenty other courses offered during the semester. Courses that met the general education theology requirement tended to have larger enrollments than courses that did not meet the requirement. But there were important exceptions to that pattern.

Theology

Theologian John Wolf, of course, taught upper-level classes in Christian theology—courses like Political Theology and Essentials of Christian Theology—but his courses were not the only ones designed to meet the theology requirement. Such classes were also taught by other theologians, ethicists, and historians who had given their courses a theological cast. Ethicist Ted Christian and historian and department chairman Niels Larsen were examples.

Ted Christian joined the NC religion department in 1979 immediately after receiving a doctorate in Christian ethics. His course, Christian Theology and Human Existence, offered in two sections in the fall semester of 1997, met the general education theology requirement. The course focused on the themes of human corruption and redemption, "with an emphasis on corruption," according to Christian. The students read Christian theologians like St. Augustine and Reinhold Niebuhr, but they also read writers and philosophers like Albert Camus, C. S. Lewis, Flannery O'Connor, and Blaise Pascal. Christian said he liked to start the course with Camus's *The Fall* because Camus "shares the Augustinian view of [fallen, corrupt] human nature, but in an empty universe." Both sections of the course were well enrolled: thirty-five students were in one class, thirty in the other. Christian believed that it was "one of the more popular courses in general education" because it addressed a student concern about human nature and because it drew students from his "great conversation" courses, a kind of "great books" course of study taught by faculty from various disciplines that introduced students to major ideas, epochs, and writings of Western civilization. Christian admitted that many of his students found the course a bit dour and pessimistic, but he insisted that the aims of the course were legitimate: "to get the students to arrive at some sense of the overlap of Christian and non-

Christian views of human corruption and to gain a deeper appreciation of the Christian accounting of human behavior." He also wanted to set that accounting—its dark side, especially—against the "superficial optimism of contemporary culture which most of the students seem to share."

Christian was chair of the religion department at the time theology was made a general education requirement, a requirement he said he "fought tooth and nail." In and of itself, requiring theology was not a bad idea in his judgment, but he thought the department had insufficient staff to teach it adequately. Nonetheless, he held that "there is a sort of normative edge to what most of us [in the department] do, but without indoctrination of any sort." He said he and his colleagues respected atheists as well as believers, non-Christians as well as Christians. "We are exposing students to normative Christian content, and they can do with that content what they like," he noted. To be sure, however, some faculty and students tended to be more interested in that task than others. "Conservative students around here think we are not advocating Christianity enough" and were mistrustful of faculty who brought critical reflection to bear on Christianity or who pointed to a variety of perspectives within the religion. "These students congregate in a sort of core and have a grapevine. They tend to gravitate to courses offered by John Wolf, who is certainly no fundamentalist but with whom the conservative students feel more comfortable." Christian suggested that the non-believers on campus were attracted to courses by Gerald Small, the teacher of The Bible for Pagans class, but he also thought that many, perhaps most, NC students were in some sense Christian believers who were open both to critical reflection on their religious tradition and to the "normative edge" of most of the religion faculty.

Niels Larsen, another religion professor who joined the NC faculty immediately after graduate school, had no reservations about the theology requirement or normative reflection as long as they were not narrowly defined. Larsen said that as a historian of Christianity, he was "comfortable doing Christian theology, but not in the abstract." He felt that one legitimate approach to theology was to deal with values and normative judgments in historical context. He used this approach in his Christian Theology in Historical Context class, a course that counted toward the theology requirement. He had previously offered a similar course entitled The Christian Tradition, which he revised to meet the current theology requirement, but it took him several revisions before the general education curriculum committee would accept the course. The committee kept insisting that normative theological issues be made more explicit in his course.

The course was finally redesigned to study more intellectual and theological issues and more creeds and theologians from history. Divided into four periods of history beginning with early Christianity and ending with the present period, the course was obviously the construct of a historian. But the syllabus revealed the manner in which Larsen exposed his students to theological issues as well and the ways he invited them to make value judgments. In two short essays and one long paper, the students were required to reach their own conclusions about theological and other intellectual issues. For example, in an essay on the meaning of Christ, students were asked to elaborate on whether the modern Christian theologians they were reading offered "explanations that retain traditional belief in the uniqueness of Jesus." In another essay, the students were asked to assess John Calvin's doctrine of predestination: "Evaluate what you see as the strengths and weaknesses of his viewpoint. Is it possible to defend the view of salvation 'by grace alone' without reaching Calvin's conclusion about predestination?" In the description of the long paper, the syllabus stated that "the paper should be more than a collection of facts. Historical or theological writing involves interpretation or evaluation as well as description. The paper should defend a thesis, or answer a specific question, or critique an argument you have encountered." But the course outline also clearly indicated that the students would not be judged on the positions they took; instead, they would be judged by the clarity of their arguments, the extent of their research, and the quality of their writing.

Not all of Niels Larsen's colleagues in the religion department were as eager to give their courses a theological bent, and in some of these courses, enrollment had suffered as a result. Dorothy Allen, who had joined the NC faculty ten years earlier after teaching at another Lutheran college, specialized in Lutheranism in America, church history, and women in Judaism and Christianity. She regularly taught a section of the basic Bible course (entitled Male and Female, God Created), but she said in an interview that she felt her other courses had been constrained by the narrow way in which theology had been defined at NC. She had to abandon her church history survey course because of falling enrollments, and her course in American Lutheranism had low enrollments, both suffering the consequences, she believed, of not meeting the theology requirement. Although she said she had "no problem dealing with normative, theological questions" and that "the wide distinction sometimes made between subjective and objective approaches to religion simply does not apply to me," she thought that, especially among the theologians on the religion faculty, the theology requirement had fostered "a kind of mind-body dualism. Theology is the 'mind'; everything else—history, biblical studies, literary studies—is the 'body' which [the theologians think] anybody can attend to."

Allen's colleague James Cutter had a similar criticism of the theology requirement and the prevailing definition of theology at NC. An expert in religion, literature, and ethics, Cutter felt some of his central teaching interests had been "squeezed from the curriculum" by the theology requirement. He had not been able to offer his three favorite courses in religious autobiography—on virtue and autobiography, women's religious autobiography, and multicultural autobiography—because they did not meet the theology requirement and hence were underenrolled. "The morale of the religion faculty is at stake," according to Cutter. "More importantly, the learning of the students is at stake. To be sure, theology needs to be a part of a religious studies curriculum at a place like NC, but it is only one piece of the field."

Despite the disagreement about the theology requirement among the religion faculty and the different ways they had responded to the requirement in their teaching, most of the religion professors were united in their aim of elevating the understanding of religion on the part of NC students. In fact, Small and Allen used identical language to describe that aim. "The overall purpose of our faculty as a whole," according to Small, "has remained pretty constant for a long time. Students should get smart about religion. That is one of the chief goals of a Christian college like NC." Allen commented: "We all try to get students to be smart about religion as they get to be smart about other things." For Christian students, that entailed "seeing that they can be intellectual about their faith. For nonbelievers, it means realizing that having faith doesn't mean you have to be dumb." The aim of helping students of different stripes "get smart" about religion showed up in many other parts of the religion curriculum, in courses taught by professors with different academic interests and distinctive approaches to their subject matter.

Other Religion Courses, Other Teachers

Karen Cassidy was starting her twenty-second year at NC in 1997, and she was the first female appointment—and the first non-Lutheran appointment—in the religion department. "Things have changed since 1976," she remarked in an interview. "We have hired more women and lots more non-Lutherans." Her area of expertise was religion in America, and she often offered a course in that area as well as a section of the required Bible course. In the fall semester of 1997, she was teaching two sections of The Feminist Perspective and Christian Ethics.

Although two of the courses she sometimes taught had been approved as meeting the theology requirement, History of Christianity and Types of Protestantism, she did not consider herself a theologian. "I am a historian rather than a theologian," she insisted. "I know theology probably more than most historians of American religion, but above all, I would describe myself as a historian whose topic happens to be religion." In any case, she said she was not a theologian in the sense that she constructed theological ideas or doctrines. "I am aware of constructive feminist theology, but my interest is the history of women and religion in America." Cassidy believed that what differentiated her more than anything else from most theologians was that she was "aware of the ambiguities and multitudinousness of issues, and I am willing to live with that ambiguity. And I am an Episcopalian, and that also means I can live with ambiguity!" She thus tried to get her students to see religious phenomena from the inside as well as the outside and make their own judgments about their value. For example, she examined worship in Eastern Orthodoxy and among Quakers, and she did not tell students that one was better than the other. "Theologians are not so inclined to restrain themselves." She said she wanted students to "be respectful observers, gain a better understanding of religion, and not dismiss a religious perspective or practice superficially." She did not care whether or not the students themselves were religious, only that "they take religion seriously, which some do and some don't. But most seem to find it interesting, even those who simply take a course for credit at first." Despite the division among her departmental colleagues over the issue of theology, Cassidy thought most of the religion faculty recognized the difference between "devotions" and "teaching about religion." She mentioned as an example her colleague Sinad Banik, a Hindu involved in Hindu-Christian dialogue who taught *about* his religion as an insider but not as a proselytizer.

Banik confirmed his colleague's perception of his teaching approach when we spoke in his office. A British-educated Hindu from India, Banik had earned an international reputation as a spokesman for his Hindu faith in Christian-Hindu dialogues, but he was also known among his faculty peers and students as a highly committed teacher of undergraduates. He most frequently taught a course in Hinduism, but his other courses included a freshman seminar entitled Sages of the East, a general survey called Understanding the Religious Traditions of the World, a comparative examination of religious truth claims in Religious Pluralism and the Nature of Community, and the advanced course Major Developments in Hinduism. Banik admitted that initially he was apprehensive about teaching as a Hindu in a Christian college. When he first arrived at NC in 1985, he was interviewed by a reporter from the student newspaper, and in that interview, he described religion "as a common human journey, a pilgrimage." Many letters of protest were sent to the president of the college, primarily from alumni and pastors who saw in his statement and in his appointment "signs of syncretism," a compromise of the Lutheran missionary task, and a "wrong influence on the minds of Christian young people." The faculty stood by him, as did the college president at the time, but on what Banik took to be the wrong grounds, namely that Hinduism is nonproselytizing, rather than on the principle that it was important for undergraduates to learn about Hinduism and other non-Christian religions. But that controversy disappeared, and he now felt he had the full support of the school and very much enjoyed teaching at NC. "My own religion is important to me, and this is a school where I can feel comfortable with that because religion is taken seriously. A school with a religious identity takes other religions seriously."

Banik said that in his Hinduism courses, he emphasized to the students that he was a "Hindu scholar rather than simply a scholar of Hinduism." He explained to them that his religion was an expression of who he was and what brought him to the study of religion. The study of Hinduism was therefore less the imposing of a method on a religion than "part of what shapes me. I am existentially committed to Hinduism." He saw it as his task in teaching his own religious tradition to "help my students see how the Hindu traditions, worldview, and the definition of human existence give significance and purpose to peoples' lives. I am very interested in meaning and purpose in my teaching." He claimed, "I cannot put my commitments aside, so I declare my commitments to my students up front." He saw absolutely no problems with this approach since the students were free to ask questions about his religion, even personal ones concerning his religious practices. Such an approach opened up good discussion in the classroom and helped the students understand religion from the inside. At the same time, he led the students in struggling critically with controversial issues in Hinduism, like caste and gender, and with "what is normative and what is contextual in my religion." When he taught courses in world religions, he was less concerned with pointing to his own personal beliefs. "I become in those courses an advocate of the religion we are studying at the time. I want the students to see each religion from the inside, to see what it means to the people and what commitment means in that tradition."

Banik was convinced that most of his students responded well to his insider's approach to the study of religion. An increasing number of students were "not closely connected to and influenced by the Christian tradition. They are searching, but not from a rootedness in the Christian tradition. They come to class with very little knowledge of Christianity." Thus their questions were "more existential than theological." Another group of students in most of his courses, probably the largest, came from Christian families but were "troubled with the religious answers they have received." They brought some background in Christianity to class, but they wanted to gain a better understanding of Christianity and religion through exposure to diverse religions. "They have friends who are non-Christians, and they see those friends finding meaning in their lives through other religious traditions. They want to know how to deal with them, and traditional Christian claims about other religions bother them." Finally, "a fair number of" students were deeply committed Christians and strong defenders of their faith, and they tended to be defensive about their religion. Sometimes they became angry with Banik as a teacher because he seemed to deny the uniqueness of Jesus and did not treat the Bible literally. About half of his freshman seminar seemed to be made up of such students, and they were offended when he treated Jesus alongside other sages. "I take no delight in undermining someone's deep religious commitment. I see too much meaninglessness and uprootedness in the world to want to upset such people. Yet that should not be a reason to misunderstand the religion of others. Hopefully they will move to a richer understanding of their own and others' religions so that the truth claims of others are not dismissed." Banik added that at least the Christians who were passionate and even defensive about their religion could see the importance of truth claims in all religions. And in any case, they took his courses. In fact, his courses were always heavily enrolled.

Judith Lindfoot, who taught Buddhism at NC, shared some of Banik's perceptions of student responses to non-Christian religions. Although she herself was not a Buddhist, she said she tried to get the students to view a religion other than their own from the inside. Appointed to the NC religion faculty in 1982 immediately after receiving her doctorate, Lindfoot taught courses in Buddhism and the religions of China and Japan; Understanding the Religions of the World; Buddhism, Peace, and Justice; and, in the interdisciplinary Asian studies program, Asian Cultures in Comparative Perspective. Most of her courses were cross-listed in the Asian studies program. Lindfoot described her teaching as that of "a sympathetic outsider; that is, I explain from within a tradition." She believed that she was the first NC teacher to have taken such an approach to Asian religions since she replaced missionaries who taught those religions from a Christian theological point of view. In the classroom, she would often become "an advocate temporarily" of the religion being studied so the students would sympathize with a religious practice or idea that might otherwise strike them as stupid. But then she would move to a more critical, analytical, and objective position. "Sympathy and advocacy first," she adopted as her motto. Above all, Lindfoot had three goals as a teacher. First, she wanted to help her students conceive of a construction of reality different from their own, to "leave their own worldviews for a while and see through another's eyes." Second, she wanted the students to gain some basic knowledge about Asia—if nothing else, to become familiar with Asian terms and ideas. And third, she encouraged her students to come to a greater self-understanding under the conviction that "one understands one's own worldview best after understanding another worldview."

Like her Hindu colleague Banik, Lindfoot felt that her approach to religion was altogether appropriate to the contemporary student generation, but unlike him, she had not been pestered by many conservative Christian students. "My students tend to be quite different from those of many of my colleagues," she explained. "My students feel alienated from Christianity and feel they are having Christian theology shoved down their throats" by the Bible and theology requirements. (She wondered, as an aside, whether her department had not "set the clock back by requiring NC undergraduates to take religion.") Most of the students brought with them to her classes "questions of meaning—what the religion can mean to me personally—as well as concerns for justice and social change." Many of her students were "seekers" who had little if any religious background and training and yearned to know what religions had to say about the environment and social justice. She was certain that her "sympathetic outsider" approach to religion spoke to the concerns of these students. Her classes also drew "types [of students] who want something more or other than the academic study of religion. They want to learn the practice of Zen meditation, for example, but I refuse to become their guru. I send them to Zen practitioners in [the nearby city] or to other practitioners."

Although she found the religion department too heavily weighted toward Christian theology and biblical studies, like Banik, Lindfoot wanted me to understand that she enjoyed teaching at a church-related college. In fact, she described her context as liberating. "NC is a place where people think religion is important, where religion is taken seriously. I have friends in state universities who don't seem to be as free to advocate the religion they are teaching." And the heavy emphasis on the Bible and theology in her department had not adversely affected the enrollments in her classes. Her courses in Buddhism were filled before the end of registration.

Student Responses to the Study of Religion

Some NC students, those whom Professors Banik and Small characterized as "conservative" or "church camp evangelicals," did not respond favorably to the academic study of religion offered by the religion department. Mae Jones, the FCA member who was enthusiastic about the freshman Bible study group she had organized, had taken the required Bible course and Types of Protestantism, and she was critical of both. Neither course, she wanted me to know, changed her perspective on religion, and both were disappointing. The section of the Bible course she took involved a literary and feminist approach to Scripture, and she found it "cold" and devoid of "the faith perspective." "All it did," she said, "was point out the contradictions and fallacies in the Bible. And we didn't even get to Paul. It gave a slanted view of Christianity as patriarchal, and the Bible was not taught as God-inspired." The Types of Protestantism class was not what she had expected. She wanted to learn some Christian theology in the course, "but all we got was a historical survey of Protestantism."

Robert Huber, a sophomore majoring in economics and Asian studies who came from a Pentecostal background and was active in the IVF, was more ambivalent about his study of religion than Jones, but he was as surprised as she was by the required Bible course. "I didn't take too well to Religion 121," Huber said. "The professor was in your face. I think he was probably a Christian, but he made you question everything about Christianity—the reality of God, the divinity of Jesus—everything you believed. He made me question everything. That was hard for me. It may make my faith stronger in the long run, but some of us found our faith breaking down in class."

Other NC students, especially those who had taken several courses in religion, were certain they had been challenged and even liberated by the radical questioning of religion that Jones and Huber had found threatening. That was true of Mary Schultz, a senior majoring in classics who was raised a Roman Catholic. Schultz said that when she enrolled in the required Bible course, "I thought, 'This is going to be the worst course and the worst semester in my life.' I expected just another Sunday school class." Instead, the course "challenged everything I had been taught" and "for the first time made me think about religion." She took more courses in religion, seeing their connections with her interest in the classical world, and came to believe that "it is possible to integrate [different] religious philosophies with one's own faith. You don't have to give up one to have the other. You don't have to be paralyzed by ambiguity."

Schultz's experience with the study of religion was similar to that of Heather Christensen, a junior majoring in religion and English. Christensen grew up in a Lutheran home, but she stated that she "frankly didn't learn much about religion—mine or anyone else's" before taking religion courses at NC. "Things are so different from what we learned in church. The contexts of religious belief are so important." She found the religion faculty to be "open about where they are coming from. They don't hide their own religious opinions, but they don't impose their opinions on you. They have no religious agendas." She felt that the faculty simply wanted students to see that religion is nuanced, that it is not just a matter of "this is all right, and this is all wrong." They achieved this, she said, by moving back and forth between their own views and objective descriptions of the views of others. In one of her class meetings, Professor Lindfoot even showed how Buddhists practice meditation, but she also encouraged the students to view Buddhism objectively. Christensen admitted that at one point she had hoped the study of religion "would help me in my own personal development, but then my interest got more academic. At first, I was questing for my own religious view and wanted to borrow from different religions to make my own view. But now I believe that NC can't provide that help. Not many religious traditions are taught here. Things are examined selectively and in depth, and that's OK with me."

Kevin Solomon, the senior majoring in music and religion who left the IVF because that organization wanted him to "be in one place spiritually," claimed that Sinad Banik and John Wolf had been his most influential teachers, but for very different reasons. Solomon had taken two of Banik's courses and had been impressed by the way in which Banik "has taken the burden of religious diversity upon himself" since he was the faculty member most responsible for teaching about diverse religions. Students were sometimes late in discovering that Banik was a world-famous scholar because he was so modest. Above all, Solomon had learned from Banik that "you can stay true to your own religious tradition yet be open to other traditions." In a quite different way, John Wolf had also been important to Solomon's development. Solomon had taken several courses with Wolf and had always found the professor to be intimidating but learned. During the first course, Solomon thought: "Yes, this is the Lutheran Christianity I was reared in. He put the pieces together for me." In the next course, he thought, "I used to believe that, but not anymore," and he wondered why Wolf would discuss one subject in Christianity but avoid another. At an academic conference where Wolf was featured, Solomon found himself thinking: "You don't seem open to dialogue. You are just academic and impersonal, and you have views which you think everyone is supposed to live up to." In a recent course, however, Solomon realized that "Professor Wolf is saying these things not to get stuck in mud but because this is what he believes. And I could now respect that as my own background. But I am the next generation, and how will I sprout from the branch of that background? So Wolf has been a kind of gauge for me."

Solomon mentioned another person on campus who had an enormous impact on his religious and intellectual development: director of the college choir and professor of music Charles Blake. Blake and other faculty outside the religion department also engaged in teaching religion to NC students.

Teaching Religion across the Curriculum

Scores of courses throughout the NC curriculum treated religion, some by including religion as a crucial component among several topics under consideration, others by concentrating on religion as the principal object of study. An English course on the Middle Ages dealt with biblical epics, mystical writings, and sermons as well as secular poetry and romances, whereas another course in the English department examined the roles of faith and doubt in the works of such modern authors as Franz Kafka, Willa Cather, Flannery O'Connor, and Elie Wiesel. Offerings in the history department included an introduction to the "radical tradition" in Islam, a study of Mahatma Gandhi as saint and revolutionary, an examination of the Protestant Reformation in Europe, and a look at religious developments under the Russian czars. The psychology department offered a course in the psychology of religion, and the sociology/anthropology department a course in the sociology of religion as well as a cultural anthropology course with a strong component in religion. In a survey course in the Department of Philosophy, students compared the philosophical traditions of Buddhism, Jainism, Hinduism, Confucianism, and Taoism, and in that department's course in philosophical theology, they took up the study of the Christian doctrines of God, the Trinity, evil, and the Incarnation. The art department attended to religious movements in courses in medieval art and the arts of India and Southeast Asia, and the music department offered a concentration for a bachelor of music in church music. The program in interdisciplinary studies provided opportunities for the comparison of biblical texts with modern literature, as well as a study of the relations between Western Christianity and Eastern Orthodoxy. In many of these courses, the professors aimed to cultivate religious self-understanding on the part of the students as well as understanding of the subject matter. That was certainly true of philosophy professor William Scottsdale.

Scottsdale was an energetic, fast-talking, witty, friendly professor who in 1997 had been teaching at NC for thirteen years. The author of several books on the philosophy of religion, he possessed a divinity school degree as well as a Ph.D. in philosophy. The courses he taught represented his wide-ranging interests: War and Peace, Metaphysics, Philosophy of Art, Philosophy of Agriculture (taught with a biologist), and Philosophical Theology. Although he handed out a syllabus at the beginning of each course, no syllabus was fixed. He explained: "I reinvent each course as I discover topics that interest the students."

In an interview in his office, which was crowded with books and papers, Scottsdale pointed out that in his course on philosophical theology, the students' most burning question had to do with theodicy: How could a good God allow evil to occur? The interest in this question, he believed, correlated with the compassion and concern for justice apparent in the service orientation of the NC students. But the students brought other questions and issues to the class as well, many springing from their never having given much thought to their faith. Scottsdale said that for a very large number of his students, perhaps the majority, there was "a big break between faith and reason. They are not naturally inclined to defend their faith philosophically. They tend to be very good students on the whole, but their faith has been pretty privatized." As a result, he attempted to coax them into thinking about that missing ingredient in their lives by examining the question of what counted as evidence for religious truth, the arguments for and against the existence of God, the nature and extent of evil, the truth or falsity of miracles, and ideas of heaven and hell. The overall goals of the philosophical theology course were to introduce the students to the methods of philosophical and theological reflection, help them "locate themselves and others unlike them in a spread of issues," and equip them "to argue their own positions." Scottsdale insisted that he never hid the fact that he was a Christian. He thought that would be unfair since he asked the students to argue for their own positions of faith or unfaith. He told his students that his views often changed, frequently because of student arguments. And he made clear that "atheists are not disadvantaged in this course." Indeed, he found that most of the students were willing to engage him and their peers in argument. "I want the class discussions and arguments to be fun and good-humored," he said, "and they are that. No one is punished for a position taken in my class."

Chemistry professor James Curtis also encouraged his students to argue positions in his class on science, religion, and ethics. A youthful-looking, soft-spoken man who had been on the NC faculty for fifteen years, Curtis taught chemistry and science courses for nonscience majors, as well as advanced courses for science majors. With support from a major foundation, in the fall of 1997 he offered the Spirit of Science class, which was designed for science majors and other NC students who had substantial exposure to scientific study. The course focused on the relationships among science, theology, and ethics. He got the idea for developing the course while teaching science to nonscience students in the NC interdisciplinary program. Students in that course brought up the topic of religion constantly, especially the issue of God as creator and preserver of the universe when quantum mechanics, evolution, and theories of the origin of the universe were under discussion. He decided to undertake the Spirit of Science course as a way of moving such issues to a higher level of sophistication.

In a detailed syllabus that assigned a large amount of reading in theology and scientific theory that included the topics of quantum mechanics, cosmology, thermodynamics, and evolution, seven weighty sets of questions specified the goals of the course:

1. How does our scientific understanding of the world influence our religious faith? Has science itself become a religion, with its symbolism, mythology, ritual, and authority?

2. How does our scientific understanding of the world influence our morality? How does what we know about how the world "is" shape our understanding of how we "ought" to act in the world?

3. How does our religious faith influence how we do science? How much ought we to allow or encourage our religious perspective to influence our scientific endeavors? Can, or should, the study of ethics influence how we do science?

4. What are the basic values we hold in our personal and professional lives? How have these values been shaped by our religious upbringing? By our scientific understanding? Are we willing and able to change these values in response to new religious experiences and/or new scientific developments?

5. What are the basic values of the scientific enterprise? How have these been shaped by historical, ethical, and theological forces? Ought we to continue to practice science using these same values, or should science be modified to embody differing values in response to historical, ethical, theological, and even scientific developments?

6. What are the myths of science? What religious functions do these serve? Does, or can, science provide meaning and a sense of purpose to our lives? Or must we supplement our understanding of science with some kind of religious understanding?

7. In what ways is science evil? In what ways is science good? In what ways is science ethically neutral? Ought science to aim to be any one of these?

This list was followed by Professor Curtis's explanation in the syllabus that the "we" in the questions meant "the community of scientists at the end of the twentieth century in the United States" and "in the private sense . . . individuals who are struggling to know how to act in our personal and professional lives in our culture." The syllabus clearly stated that in the discussion of these "sensitive, controversial, and contentious" issues, "we

must learn to respect the opinions and feelings of each other while expressing our own opinions and feelings clearly."

Curtis told me that he called special attention to questions concerning the
way in which science has been shaped by metaphysical issues, religion, social
circumstances, and history "because these science students think that now
that they have mastered uses of the scientific method, they know it all." In
other words, he wanted to shake them out of their intellectual complacency.
Curtis felt that he got a good response to his iconoclasm because he was a
scientist himself: "I know the language and can command the respect of
science students." He also believed that many of his students took the course
to try to reconcile their religious beliefs with their scientific work, "and this
is the only course on campus where that is explicit and can happen in a
dialogical atmosphere." He knew that one student in the class professed
atheism but was interested in how her classmates "could see theism and
science working together." Curtis confessed that he was still in the process of
forming his own view of the relation between science and religion, but he
was leaning toward what the theologian Ian Barbour has called the "dialogical" option, a position in which religion and science occupy different
spheres but inform each other. He said his own interests tended to be much
more theoretical than those of the students, but he let his students argue
with each other over such practical ethical questions like when cloning is
moral and when it is not.

The NC music department was saturated with religion and offered students another form of instruction in religion outside the boundaries of the
religion department. Besides the fact that the music department offered a
B.A. in church music along with courses like Music in Christian Worship,
the directors of all seven choirs included sacred music in their concerts,
several directors composed or arranged sacred music, and the directors of all
of the choral groups considered one of their chief roles to be instruction in
religious texts. For Charles Blake, professor of music and director of the
college choir, teaching music meant instruction in the religious meaning of
the music. It also meant providing religious inspiration and counsel.

At the end of the day on 29 October 1997, Blake was rehearsing his choir
for the Christmas Festival in a small rehearsal room in the music building.
He started by having the members of the choir stand on their risers and go
through their relaxation routine, which consisted of massaging each other's
shoulders, after which they did voice warm-up exercises. During the next
hour, the choir rehearsed parts of five numbers they would perform at the
festival, and Blake devoted most of his efforts to working on timing and
tone, cajoling, urging, and using humor ("Come on, give me Big Mama
tones") until the choir members sang the parts to his satisfaction. He moved

quickly back and forth between a piano and a lectern, announced a few breaks during which many of the students drank from water bottles, and snapped his fingers authoritatively to prompt and stop the singers. At one point during the singing of a spiritual, Blake stopped the choir abruptly and said softly: "You can't just sing this cerebrally; you must find its spirit." On the next try, they got it right. Getting it right for Blake often meant finding the spirit, the religious core, of the music.

Blake was a youthful, highly energetic alumnus of NC who had been college choir director for eight years, after having previously taught and directed the choir at another denominational college. During an interview in his small office, it was apparent that he enjoyed talking about the NC music program and its religious dimensions. He spoke with pride about all of the NC choirs and their directors, but he acknowledged that his choral group was the "ambassador choir." He estimated that 80 to 90 percent of the music his choir performed was sacred, and he said he called the choir's performances "sacred concerts" to differentiate them from the worship services that were the responsibility of two of the other choirs on campus. He considered music as such to be "a gift from God. Excellent musical performance is a way of giving back to God." He said he wanted the music for which he was responsible to "convey the power of spirit and message" in such a way that the lives of both the performers and the listeners were shaped by God. "This is not evangelism in the sense of converting," Blake claimed. "It is letting the power of God work to transform lives." When people were so touched by music, they were hearing more than just good music. "It is a form of the proclamation of God." He pointed out that when he had warned a Jewish student in his choir that most of the music was Christian in content and intent, the student had said he could appreciate the music without necessarily accepting it. Blake told a story about the choir's recently working with a famous composer on a recording. The recording was not going well until the choir, at Blake's insistence, got "behind the notes to the spiritual meaning of the piece." Then the composer was moved to tears by the performance.

As director of the choir, Blake thus considered himself a teacher of religion, but that role entailed for him more than helping his students find the spiritual meaning of the music. It also involved the cultivation of the religious lives of the choir members. He said he tried to encourage the students to "keep God and Jesus in the foreground" of their lives. He gave some examples of how that foregrounding could occur. On a tour in New Zealand, the students broke into the singing of Psalm 92, in praise of God's glory and beauty, when they were on a retreat to the foot of a glacier. On the same tour, in Australia the students and the college pastor, who was also on the trip, held a special "sharing" and prayer session for a friend who had recently died back in the States. Holding hands, the group sang "Watch over Thee." "It was the healing balm of Gilead," in Blake's view. A student who was not particularly religious said of the experience: "I understood for the first time what grace means." When he was working with the choir in rehearsals, Blake often would try to relate the sacred texts to the lives of the students. He recently spent some time with the AIDS quilt exhibit on campus and discussed with the choir the "mystery of why God allows suffering." Such discussion helped the choir "put their hearts into the music." He would often talk about the slave songs and point out that the spirituals the students were singing were about "how children, and childlike slaves, are loved by Jesus." He recalled that as a student at NC, his choir teacher had talked about the religious meaning of "The Little Drummer Boy," which the students were treating as a poor piece of music undeserving of serious attention. After the teacher reminded the choir members that "all that little boy had was his drum, that was all he had from God," Blake said, the choir "took the piece seriously."

Blake then rushed to his computer, saying, "Just so you won't think I'm making all this up, let me read you some letters." He began to call up saved e-mail messages. One message, representing what Blake called the "religious right," was from a female prone to depression who wrote that she deeply appreciated Blake's expression of the love of God and believed "God will continue to use you." "From the left," another student, skeptical of religion, wrote that she was comforted after the suicide of a friend by the singing of Psalm 43: "O, my soul, why be sorrowful; hope in the Lord." She concluded: "That hit a chord. I needed that." Blake then went to his desk and pulled from a drawer a card from the grandmother of a student thanking the choir director for the comfort the choir's music had given her grandson after the death of a relative.

In wrapping up his observations, Blake said he regretted that at NC little attention was paid to a question that had been explored constantly at the college where he had previously taught : What is the integration of faith and learning? He felt some faculty feared that such a question would threaten academic integrity. "At times it seems we go to great lengths to break the students' faith," he said, whereas students should be given more opportunities to express their faith. During a search for a new NC president a few years earlier, a couple of faculty members had said to him over lunch: "I hope we don't hire another damn theologian." To Blake, that attitude expressed a fear of raising the issue of faith and learning. He remarked that he thought the current president, who was a historian rather than a theologian, was doing a good job of promoting NC as a "college of the church," but he believed more exploration of NC as a "Christian college" was needed.

In attempting to provide opportunities for the expression of faith through music and devotions and to instruct musical performers in the sacred meaning of notes and text, Blake generated both critics and supporters on campus. On the one hand, Gerald Small, the professor who taught the Bible for Pagans course, indicated in no uncertain terms that he was not impressed by the religious content of NC music. Small doubted that more than 10 percent of those who sang in the choirs took the religious content of the music seriously. He believed that the "music world [at NC] is increasingly marginalized as religious. Music here is aesthetic performance that is integrated with religion by very few, despite Charles Blake's praying and preaching to the choir." Paul Shawn, the student who dismissed the evangelicals on campus as "sweet, happy, superficial little Christians," criticized the allegedly sacred music on campus for a different reason. He thought that commercialism had replaced sacrality in the music at NC. He declared, for example, that "if you scrape away the facade of the Christmas Festival, you will see it is not a sacred event at all. It's a money-making enterprise for the college that uses cheap labor." And Elizabeth Page, who sang in the chapel choir, said she had joined the choir strictly to perform and was uncomfortable with the "somewhat enforced spirituality" of the devotions and prayers conducted by the director. She said she had friends in the college choir who felt the same way about the devotions in that group.

On the other hand, Kevin Solomon and Ernest Harbach—both members of the college choir—appreciated that Blake demanded the best in musical skills, pointed out the religious meaning of music, and showed concern for the spiritual welfare of his students. "Music is very important to me when I am having trouble with things," Harbach revealed. "The organist for the student congregation and the director of the college choir will often talk about the importance of faith as well as musical interpretation, and that makes the music even more helpful to me." According to Solomon, the student chaplain of the college choir, "Blake emphasizes musical discipline, but he also encourages us and is sympathetic to our musical faults." Solomon appreciated that Blake made no attempt to hide his own religious faith and could even be "in your face with his religion." Solomon liked it when Blake talked about his faith and the religious relevance of the music in rehearsals, and especially on tours, "when he is with the students daily." Anita Noll, who described the choir directors as the "storytellers" on campus, reported a similar experience in the chapel choir. By stressing the religious text "almost as much as getting the notes right," she said, the director of that choir tried to "direct our emotions along a spiritual journey."

In different ways, much of the teaching of religion at NC was directed toward the spiritual journeys of students. To be sure, there were diverse approaches to the study of religion at the school, ranging from the "respectful historical observations" of Karen Cassidy to the cultivation of spirituality through music on the part of Charles Blake, from the "insider advocacy" of Hinduism of Sinad Banik to the "sympathetic outsider" perspective on Buddhism of Judith Lindfoot, from the correlation of religion and literature by Scott Laughner and James Cutter to the strict attention to the Bible and Christian doctrine on the part of theologian John Wolf. Yet most of these professors encouraged their students to develop their own religious positions, argue for a given religious point of view, and relate their understanding of religion to their own spiritual journeys. Many of the teachers were forthright in the declaration of their own religious perspectives. There was no evidence of proselytizing in the classroom—"Atheists are not disadvantaged in this course," in the words of philosophy professor William Scottsdale—but many who taught religion at NC were not at all reluctant to urge both objective understanding of religious phenomena and personal self-understanding on the part of their students.

Furthermore, when the courses offered by the religion department are considered in conjunction with the wide array of courses across the curriculum that took up the subject of religion, it is apparent that North College honored the study of religion as much as its practice—and in the case of the choirs, the practice and the teaching of religion could run together. Religious literacy, especially literacy in the Christian Bible and other Christian traditions, had been made a priority in the liberal arts education of NC. In the words of religion professors Small and Allen, NC students had plenty of opportunities to "get smart about religion."

CONCLUSIONS

The mission statement of NC indicated that the school was a college of the Lutheran Church, and certain structural arrangements reflected that statement of mission. The college was a legal corporation of the Evangelical Lutheran Church in America, it received a small amount of financial support from the denomination, its charter required that 75 percent of its governing board be Lutheran, and it supported a Lutheran congregation on campus. The college mandated no confession of faith from students or faculty, however, and it imposed no denominational quotas on membership in the college community.

The denominational identity of NC students has changed over the years, but the majority of the students have always identified themselves as Lutherans. About 65 percent of the students were Lutherans in 1970, compared to 60 percent in 1980, 55 percent in 1990, and just under 50 percent in 1997. Comparable statistics on the religious identity of faculty are unavailable. A survey of NC faculty conducted by the school in 1995, however, did reveal faculty attitudes toward religious and denominational commitment. The overwhelming majority supported the mission statement of the school, most agreed that the church-related character of the school was being maintained, and the majority believed that the Christian identity of the college did not compromise the achievement of academic excellence. A majority of the faculty, however, had serious reservations about requiring any kind of public commitment of faith, and faculty were about equally divided on whether the school's identity depended on having a particular number of Christians on the faculty. And although a majority of the faculty said that their religious convictions were pertinent to their teaching, there was no consensus on how those convictions should show up in their instruction.

Those statistics and the statement of mission suggest that NC possessed a Lutheran Christian identity, but one with porous and flexible boundaries. In fact and in theory, NC attempted to preserve a visible Christian core while permitting, even encouraging, religious and cultural diversity surrounding the core. In the view of President James Thompson, the Lutheran heritage itself honored both the sacred and the secular and refused to confuse the two by making Christianity or the church a controlling influence on institutions of higher education. According to a leading historian of Lutheran higher education in America, respect for the secular order in all of its diversity has been a characteristic of Lutheran attitudes toward college life beginning with Martin Luther himself: "Luther's philosophy of education grew directly out of his concept of the two kingdoms. He placed education squarely within the 'orders of creation' or God's 'secular realm.' . . . Without claiming a unique Lutheran approach to higher education, Lutheran theology would hold all of higher education, including its own, to the highest standards of openness and integrity."[2] None of this is to say that openness to diversity was either all-inclusive or devoid of tensions at a Lutheran college like NC. The practice of religion at the college demonstrated both the limits that can be placed on religious diversity and the tensions that can ensue between practicing Christians.

This study discerned no religious practice at NC other than Christian practice. There can be little doubt that the exclusively Christian practice was largely self-selected since the overwhelming majority of students were Christians (83.4%, with only 1.7% Buddhists, .2% Muslims, and .5% Jews). The school had made very clear in its public relations that it would be a Christian college affiliated with the Lutheran Church, and it underwrote only a Lutheran congregation for its students. The sacred music that was so constitutive of the ethos of the campus was overwhelmingly Christian. As Kevin Solomon observed, it did not take students—or visitors—long to realize, if they did not know it before they came on the scene, that "the school is rooted in Christianity." It is important to note, however, that the exclusive core of Christian practice was not imposed on anyone. Attendance at chapel and worship services was completely voluntary, and 700 people or 23 percent of the student body typically attended services of the Lutheran student congregation. Eleven percent of the students indicated that they had no religious preference. A variation on Professor Scottsdale's disclaimer—"Atheists are not disadvantaged in this course"—was true of the practice of religion at NC. Those who did not practice religion were not penalized at this school. It is also noteworthy that for all of the religious, ethnic, and cultural homogeneity of the campus, the study-abroad and service-abroad programs exposed many students to religious, ethnic, and cultural diversity. In the words of Marvin Sanders, chair of the board of regents, "If we can't get the world to the students, we can get them into the world."

A certain amount of diversity existed within the boundaries of Christian practice, a diversity that created some tensions on campus. The presence of evangelicals accounted for most of this diversity as well as most of the tensions. The office of the college pastor, especially through the efforts of Associate Pastor Virginia Kosner, was willing to work with the evangelical Christians who were attracted to the FCA, the IVF, Baptist church services downtown, and student-run Bible study and prayer groups. Many of those students, who according to Kosner sought a religious practice that was "upbeat and emotional," were also involved in the Lutheran congregation and attended daily chapel. But tensions were apparent in the evangelicals who considered the Lutheran services boring and stodgy, in the "pagans" who found the evangelicals dogmatic and anti-intellectual, and in the faculty and Lutheran students who believed the evangelicals to be superficial and closed-minded. Furthermore, whereas students like Anita Noll thought toleration of religious diversity was the hallmark of religious maturation, others like Mae Jones thought such toleration was "not always good" because it consisted of a refusal to stand up for one's beliefs. It would seem that NC allowed a certain amount of variety within the traditions of Christian practice and created a degree of toleration of the tensions arising from that variety.

A similar situation of unity and diversity emerged in the teaching of religion at the college. The overwhelming majority of courses in the religion department were in biblical and Christian studies, with a scattering of courses in other religions. Courses outside the Christian tradition were honored by the religion faculty as a whole, however, and the elective courses in Buddhism and Hinduism were well enrolled. Furthermore, the faculty in the department had managed to incorporate diverse approaches and contents into their largely Christian and biblical curriculum. The multiple sections of the required Bible course, for example, permitted teachers to approach the Bible from a variety of angles—from the point of view of traditional Christian doctrine or that of feminism, from the perspective of developments in American culture or that of Christian ethics, and from many other perspectives. Most of the professors in the religion department sought to correlate objective understanding of religion with the religious self-understanding and development of the students, but a variety of approaches were used to realize that goal. Although none of those professors did any proselytizing, some were "advocates" of religious perspectives in the sense that they tried to get the students to see the values and truth of those perspectives "from the inside"; others were more concerned with assisting students in gaining a critical, historical, or literary viewpoint on religion; and many wanted to do both. And in view of the courses with religious content in various departments, NC students had the opportunity to examine religion by using the methods of psychology, sociology, anthropology, philosophy, science, literary criticism, and the fine arts. There was a certain coherence in these diverse methods and contents in that they were all directed toward "getting students to be smart about religion." But there were tensions, as well, most arising from the religion requirements in the general education program.

The required Bible course created grumbling among faculty who not been trained in biblical studies but would have to teach sections of that course. The requirement that all students take a course in theology created strains between theologians and others in the department who were disturbed at the narrow definition assigned to the word "theology" and the belief that the required course drained students from their elective courses. Professor John Wolf thought that the old three-course requirement, which gave students considerable latitude in meeting the religion requirement, was certain to be dropped as a general education policy and that there was a real danger that no religion would be required, leading to a massive decline in departmental enrollments. The new two-course requirement thus saved the day in his judgment. Wolf acknowledged, however, that his was "a minority opinion in the religion department," and indeed most of Wolf's colleagues whom I interviewed were opposed to the requirements in the Bible and theology. There was also some negative student sentiment about the requirements, especially among evangelicals who were offended by what Mae Jones called the lack of "God-inspired" teaching of the Bible.

Professor Judith Lindfoot was convinced that any kind of religion requirement "sets the clock back," and in a sense, she was correct. Since the end of World War II, the dominant pattern at colleges and universities, including denominationally affiliated ones, has been the elimination of required religion courses. For the most part, required Bible courses have gone the way of required chapel. The retention of the religion requirement in the new general education program, however, was an attempt to live up to the stated mission of the college of fostering biblical and theological literacy. It might also be seen as a response to the widespread religious illiteracy in the culture at large. Public polls indicate that Americans, even those who hold the Bible to be the inspired word of God, are woefully ignorant of the contents of the Christian Bible.[3] Given that cultural situation, the Bible requirement in particular may be construed as NC's way of "setting the clock forward."

The music department, especially as represented by the pedagogy of Charles Blake, embodied still another approach to teaching religion at the college. In addition to instructing his choir members in the meaning of sacred texts, Blake conveyed to his students an understanding of music as a gift of God that both singers and hearers might offer up to God in return. Religious music in particular was for him and for the students who responded to him and his authority a "balm of Gilead," an inspiration, a holy sacrament. Sacred music defined much of the ethos of NC and was the source of much of its religious identity. It was also the supreme instance on campus of the merging of religious practice and religious teaching.

The teaching and the practice of religion, both of which were mainly Christian in form and content, set a tone on campus that bespoke the self-understanding of NC as a Christian school, a college of the church. The students and faculty who did not share Christian convictions were not coerced into adopting the Christian worldview, but in the words of Pastor Plater and Professor Banik, they were compelled "to take religion seriously."

NOTES

1. We have no survey results from Wolf's class, unlike the section of Laughner's course, in which students responded to questions about the objectivity of the course, their freedom to express their religious views, the effects of the course on their spiritual development, and so on. Although Professor Wolf distributed the surveys to his class, he chose not to return them to the researchers of this study.

2. Richard W. Solberg, "What Can the Lutheran Tradition Contribute to Christian Higher Education?," in *Models for Christian Higher Education: Strategies for Success in the Twenty-first Century*, ed. Richard T. Hughes and William B. Adrian (Grand Rapids, Mich.: William B. Eerdmans, 1997), 76, 78. See also Solberg's *Lutheran Higher Education in North America* (Minneapolis: Augsburg, 1985).

3. See, for example, George Gallup Jr. and Jim Castelli, *The People's Religion: American Faith in the 90s* (New York: Macmillan, 1989), 60.

CHAPTER SIX

CONCLUSION

As we indicated in the introduction to this book, we make no claims to having provided a comprehensive overview of religion in American higher education today. The study of four institutions of higher education, as diverse as those schools may be, does not produce an all-encompassing map. Nonetheless, the four schools do occupy significant points on the educational scene, and some generalizations about the practice and teaching of religion on the four campuses and the role of religion in the campus cultures can begin to sketch the contours of larger patterns of religion on the American campus.

RELIGIOUS PRACTICE

If the definition of religion includes spirituality as well as the more traditional, denominationally based forms of religious expression, we can say with utter confidence that opportunities for undergraduates to practice religion were widely available at all four schools. To be sure, religious practice was undertaken by a higher percentage of students at the three schools with religious denominational connections, and religious practice figured more prominently in the ethos of those schools than at the state university. Yet the so-called secular culture of West University by no means disadvantaged religious practice.

The undergraduates we interviewed, as well as many of the campus professionals who helped us interpret the religion of undergraduates, preferred to use the words "spirituality" and "spiritual" instead of "religion" and "religious" when describing undergraduate attitudes and practices. James Brand, student government president at South University, summed up a typical student attitude when he replied in answer to a question concerning whether students on his campus were very religious: "No, but most of them are very spiritual." Like numerous other students we encountered, Brand understood "religion" to mean institutions or organizations, whereas he took "spirituality" to mean a personal experience of God or ultimate values. Furthermore, more often than not, "spiritual" and "spirituality" connoted a quest, a journey, something not yet completed, whereas "religion" and "religious" signified something completed, fixed, handed down. Chaplain Mary Baer of East University saw the significance of the distinction when she remarked: "Religion means, literally, to bind. Although those of us in the professional religious business see this binding as ultimately freeing, binding of any kind is antithetical to the late-adolescent project. It's a time of questioning and stepping back."

In addition to the age factor, seismic shifts in American culture and society also account for the preference for spirituality as a journey or quest as opposed to religion as a tie to a tradition or organization. Sociologist Robert Wuthnow has observed that massive changes beginning in the 1960s have decisively shaped the religious perspectives and practices of Americans, especially young Americans. Such upheavals include the widespread breakdown of the nuclear family, the growing loss of confidence in such basic institutions as government and churches, the launching of lone individuals into cyberspace by way of their computers, and a galloping consumerist market that offers an astonishingly wide array of goods, including religious products. The situation created by these turbulent changes has resulted in a religious posture characterized more by seeking, nomadic wandering and choosing among diverse options (spirituality) than by the more stable posture of dwelling in or inhabiting safe, sacred places (religion). "For seeker-oriented spirituality," in Wuthnow's words, "the congregation is less aptly characterized as a safe haven; rather, it functions as a supplier of spiritual goods and services." And although the social changes have not led Americans totally to abandon religious institutions, younger Americans especially have "increasingly pursued spirituality in other venues, and even the religiously involved [have] found inspiration from a wider variety of sources."[1]

Tom Beaudoin, himself a member of that younger cohort of Americans known as Generation X, adds that the popular culture of Gen-Xers available through television, computers, and videotapes leads them easily to cross boundaries of time and space, gives them virtually unlimited access to lifestyles and perspectives around the globe, and promotes a kind of "experience grasped in moments." Such experience lends itself to the "bricolating" of spirituality. "*Bricolage* means making do with the materials at hand to solve particular (in this case religious) problems and questions. This term describes the way Gen-X pop culture brings together diverse religious symbols and images, forever recombining and forming new spiritualities. Gen-X pop culture does not respect the boundaries of tradition or religious dogma."[2]

Influenced as they have been by the forces described by Wuthnow and Beaudoin, most of the undergraduates we encountered on the four campuses could be characterized as spiritual seekers rather than religious dwellers, and many of them were constructing their spirituality without much regard to the boundaries dividing religious denominations, traditions, or organizations.

At West University, some of the largest regular religious gatherings were the weekly meetings of Campus Crusade for Christ, an organization not tied to any particular denomination, and the programs of mainline campus ministries like the Newman Center and the Wesley Foundation were directed more toward the cultivation of student spirituality than toward the maintenance of denominational identity. Many North College students who were actively religious were drawn both to the liturgies of the Lutheran congregation and to the songs and pieties of the evangelical parachurch groups, and many more were exposed either as performers or as auditors to the sacred music that often cast a generalized Christian aura over the campus. At South University, although the chaplain was a Presbyterian minister and most students were reared as Baptists, denominational alliances were virtually undetectable, standard orders of worship were blended with contemporary gospel music, and students found their spirituality in rap and hip-hop culture as well as in revivalistic worship. East University was unmistakably Roman Catholic, but a large number of the Catholic students were spiritual seekers open to and affected by a variety of alternative religious traditions, and they often defined their religious postures in terms of ethical concern and spiritual awakening. By no means atypical was Fay Warner at West University, who during her college career moved from Roman Catholicism and the Newman Center to the Wesley Foundation peer ministry staff to membership in the Disciples of Christ Church. And by no means unusual was Kevin Solomon at North College, whose religious quest had taken him from heavy involvement in the InterVarsity Fellowship to movement beyond that organization because "they wanted me to stay in one place spiritually" to the appreciation of religious diversity through the study of Asian religions to a critical appropriation of his own Lutheran heritage.

Despite the general trends of spiritual quest and bricolage on all of the campuses, however, the specific context of each school gave different shades of meaning to the religious practices of the students. West University, a state university committed to the avoidance of giving advantages to any religious group, made various forms of practice available to its students through some thirty religious organizations. As a result, the practice of religion at West University ranged from the masses attended by some 1,200 students at the Newman Center to the gathering of a few undergraduates in the Christian Science group, from the very visible evangelical piety of football players involved in Athletes in Action to the virtually hidden inductive Bible study groups of the InterVarsity Fellowship, from the formal Shabbat services at the Hillel Jewish Student Center to the informal dinner gatherings of the

University Pagan Circle. To many of the ministers on this campus, religious practices and organizations were seen as united in offering undergraduate students alternative life-styles—alternatives to alcohol, sexual promiscuity, materialism, and careerism, which they believed characterized university culture as a whole. But from the point of view of most of the students interviewed, nothing seemed to hold the different practices together except the sheer diversity of religious practice and the wide choices available for the spiritual quest.

At South University, religious practice was comparatively homogeneous. Focused on the worship conducted and created by the campus chaplain, most of the religious practices of the undergraduates drew on the expressive forms of African American Christianity. There was, to be sure, a combination on that campus of mainline Protestant formalities and Baptist, Pentecostal, and contemporary gospel informalities, but student spirituality took place in the context of the historic traditions of African American churches. Although South University students were exposed to the religious practices of other religions—for example, Jewish and Muslim prayers during Religious Emphasis Week—the religious atmosphere they breathed in chapel services, athletic team devotions, and Religious Emphasis Week itself was that of African American Christianity. And unlike the situation at West University, virtually every major public event on campus was a worship service, from the coronation of the homecoming queen to the Founders Day celebration to commencement exercises.

Many of the public events at North College were also instances of spiritual practice, and the only noticeable occasions of worship were Christian. The variety of practice came chiefly from the alternatives to Lutheran worship provided by parachurch groups and student-led Bible study groups, prayer groups, and discussion sessions. And although there was considerable toleration of diverse religious perspectives, and indeed of no religious perspective at all, the presence of the Lutheran congregation and its pastors and the stated definition of the school as a college of the church provided North College with a fairly clear Lutheran Christian identity. As student Kevin Solomon said, "Everyone who comes here eventually knows the school is rooted in Christianity."

It was also apparent to any observer that East University was in no uncertain terms a Roman Catholic school. In addition to the Catholic material culture that enveloped anyone who set foot on the campus and the many masses available to the students, the place was permeated by commitment to Jesuit spirituality. Many East University students, including those who were reared Catholic but were seeking a more existential, personal form of spirituality, believed their Catholicism was deepened by the Jesuit ideal of the integration of academic study, personal formation, and service in the world. Especially among those students influenced by the progressive Catholic faculty and priests on campus and the yearlong service-learning course, "spirituality" took on a quite specific meaning: self-transformation and a life of service to others.

In point of fact, significant connections between personal spirituality and volunteer social service were apparent on all of the campuses we studied. The connections were most evident at East University and North College, with the former offering programs and classes that promoted the Jesuit ideal of "men and women for others" and the latter combining study abroad and service abroad as key ingredients in higher education and religious and personal development. The testimony of East University students provided striking examples of the effects the yearlong service-learning course could have on their lives. One student said: "For those who have taken [the course], it becomes the core of their college experience. . . . Taking the course definitely involves a spiritual transformation in terms of your inner being." Another commented: "The course made me more socially aware and changed my ideas about what to do in the future. I don't care about how much money I make." But the joining of service and religion appeared on the other two campuses as well. South University modeled its service and service-learning programs on the work of the black churches in the area, and many of its service partners were those same black churches. West University student Carey Spoonheim found in the Newman Center a "spiritual high" that inspired her to want to do "good things with my life" through social service.

The influence also often flowed the other way, from service back to religion, with volunteer work deepening and expanding personal spirituality. Margaret McDowell, a nursing student at East University, said her spirituality developed and her appreciation of all religions expanded because of her career in health care. Bridget Olson on the same campus indicated that work in a homeless shelter complemented by study in a service-learning course transformed her view of herself as a Christian and a woman. And then there were Anita Noll and Jack Malloy at North College. Noll said her exposure to cultural and religious diversity during study and service abroad made her "more tolerant of human beings as human beings and their religious differences." Malloy believed his work in a Costa Rican health clinic expanded his view of Christianity and his vision of his future career as a physician. We found more instances of personal spirituality aligning itself with public concerns and responsibilities among the students than occasions of retreat into a privatized, atomistic spirituality. Our study tended to confirm the suggestion of the director of the Peace Corps that it was more appropriate to refer to the current crop of college students as "Generation

Next" than as "Generation X" since they are busy shaping the future of their communities through a flurry of volunteer activities.[3] There is, of course, no evidence that all or even most student volunteerism in the nation is driven by religious motives, but we did find a number of cases in our study of significant junctures between volunteer service and student spirituality, junctures that definitely should be included as part of the larger picture.

We discerned many instances of an informal mode of teaching that sought through edification and inspiration to enhance religious practice. Some of this devotional instruction was promoted at evangelical Bible study groups, many of them student-led. Outside the boundaries of the curriculum and in dormitories and meeting rooms all over campus, clusters of students on their own initiative or with the sponsorship of parachurch groups like Campus Crusade for Christ, the InterVarsity Fellowship, and the Fellowship of Christian Athletes met to pray and read the Bible for the sake of their Christian development. Devotions among evangelical varsity athletes performed a similar function. In many cases, the evangelical students preferred to hold their meetings without the direct control or official sponsorship of campus ministers, and those ministers appeared to be sensitive to the students' need to govern their own gatherings. There was a kind of student religious populism at work here or the attitude that the Bible was directly available to the students and should be studied devotionally according to their own needs. Yet by no means all devotional instruction was so populist. At East University, although devotional meetings utilized many student leaders, most of the meetings operated under the auspices of the university chaplaincy. And at West University, denominational ministers undertook devotional instruction, especially during spiritual retreats.

We were particularly struck by the popularity of the evangelical groups on the West University and North College campuses. In their larger weekly meetings and their retreats, these groups drew good attendance and appealed to the students' sense of fun and fellowship as well as devotion. The singing and swinging, the food, the games and joking, and the chance to bond with friends were as central to the meetings as the faith-sharing, prayers, Scripture reading, and occasional lecture. The informal environments offered by the evangelical groups were important opportunities for the creation of an intimate community at a vast, personally intimidating university like West University, but they were appealing scenes at the much smaller North College as well. An undergraduate woman at West University looked forward to a Campus Crusade retreat where she and others would have "a chance to hang out, focus on God, get to know each other, and have good fellowship." And the president of the student government at North College said he attended the weekly meetings of the Fellowship of Christian

Athletes "as much for fun and fellowship as for religion. And it's a good place to meet respectable people of the opposite sex." The evangelical meetings brought to light what we discovered in many campus contexts: college students often like a good mix of fun and religion.

On all four campuses, there was a commitment to honoring religious diversity and a refusal to coerce students to adopt any particular religious perspective or practice. The atmosphere of freedom of choice was, of course, most evident at West University. As a public, state-supported university, West University naturally did everything in its power to avoid either advantaging or disadvantaging religion. That university's student-fee support of diverse religious organizations and its use of campus ministers for counseling students with "spiritually based concerns" constituted attempts to pay tribute to religious diversity among the student body while preserving religion's right to exist and prosper on campus. But commitment to religious diversity also appeared at the denominationally affiliated schools. Although the majority of the students at North College were Lutheran and the only religious body supported financially by the college was the office of the Lutheran pastor, opportunities for other forms of religious practice were available to the students, and these opportunities, especially those provided through the Fellowship of Christian Athletes and InterVarsity Fellowship, were utilized with enthusiasm by the undergraduates. And there were no requirements for attendance at chapel or other occasions of worship at North College. At East University, Catholicism was privileged and students were strongly encouraged to develop their religious lives, but they also were free to accept or reject the Catholicism of the school, attend or not attend mass, grow into a deeper appreciation of the Catholic tradition or continue a nominal Catholicism, attend Protestant churches downtown or affiliate with other non-Catholics at the AHANA center. For all of the relatively homogeneous character of the African American spirituality at South University, chapel was not required, students were exposed to non-Christian religions through courses and Religious Emphasis Week, and the school was tied very loosely to its Presbyterian heritage.

The honoring of diversity and freedom of choice, however, by no means spelled the absence of religious tensions on campus. The collection of people with diverse views and practices in the same space, whether it be in a town or a college, is as likely to breed what Peter Berger calls "cognitive contamination" as it is to yield tension-free, easygoing toleration. Living with people of different religious worldviews and behaviors creates the potential for conflict as one's own worldviews and behaviors are threatened by those of others.[4]

Indeed, such conflicts did occur on the campuses in our study. At North

College, most of the conflicts centered on the evangelicals. Although a number of the students who participated in the activities of the InterVarsity Fellowship and Fellowship of Christian Athletes also attended the services of the Lutheran congregation, other students active in one group had little use for the other. Some active Lutherans, religious questers, and those attracted strictly to the intellectual dimensions of religion found the evangelical Christians to be superficial, dogmatic, anti-intellectual, or childlike in their faith and practice. And some evangelicals believed the typical Lutherans to be stodgy, coldly rationalistic, and lacking in true Christian spirit and conviction.

The key religious conflict at South University sprang from the different visions of the president and the chaplain respecting the aims of campus worship—and indeed of middle-class African American Christianity as such—with the chaplain offering a form of worship that included the emotionalism and informality of revivalistic Christianity and the president desiring a form of practice that elevated the students' religious taste with formality and decorum. At East University, there were clear tensions between progressive Catholic students who found the core of their faith in social service and acts on behalf of social justice and the conservatives who discovered that core in devotion to the authoritative teachings and the sacramental life of the church. Some non-Catholic students at East University felt overwhelmed and excluded by the Catholic ethos of the place. Most of the tensions at West University were similar to those at North College. West University students involved in InterVarsity and Campus Crusade found the approach to God too indirect, student leadership too limited, and religious convictions too lukewarm among the mainline campus ministries, whereas a mainline campus minister like Wesley Foundation director Cal Huff saw himself offering a "counterrevolutionary ministry that encourages quiet reflection and isn't so superficial."

Judged strictly in terms of numbers, religious practice at the schools in this study exemplified a healthier "supply" than "demand," to use Betty DeBerg's language. Such a situation was most apparent at West University, where fewer than 10 percent of the undergraduates participated in the programs of thirty organizations registered with the university and attendance at Newman Center and Campus Crusade activities seemed large only in comparison to programs sponsored by other religious organizations. But to some extent, the situation was the same at the other schools. A significant minority, but a minority nonetheless, of East University students attended religious services at least two or three times a month. Events like the Christmas Festival and other religious occasions featuring musical groups attracted very large audiences at North College, but that attendance was probably due in part to the popularity of musical performances on campus. The typical service of the Lutheran congregation at North College attracted 700 students out of 3,000, and the large weekly meetings of the Fellowship of Christian Athletes drew about 200. The number of congregants at the worship services of South University, with its 1,300 students and 80 faculty, ranged from 150 to 200, and attendance at weekday religious events was smaller still.

Such figures, however, are not the only measure of religious vitality. Certainly they provide no grounds for judging the campuses to be secularized in the sense that religion has been marginalized. Given the students' proclivity to define themselves as "spiritual" rather than "religious," as seekers rather than dwellers, attendance at traditional worship services and other events of religious organizations does not capture the full meaning of their spiritual quest. Equally important, margins require a center, and it is questionable that any college or university possesses a clear center that serves as a centripetal force that consistently and decidedly draws all of its members together. Even at a sports-minded place like West University, there was no evidence that the "Buccaneer spirit" unified the campus and the diverse student groups. And although music, especially sacred music, created much of the ethos of North College, at that much smaller school, neither music nor religion nor sports served as a unifying center. The absence of a stable, unifying center, however, does not preclude a campus ethos, atmosphere, or set of sentiments that serves as a shaping setting for religious practice. We will take up the importance of ethos on each campus in the last section of this conclusion.

TEACHING RELIGION

We found the academic study of religion to be as vital and appealing to undergraduates as religious practice on all four campuses. The only possible exception was South University, which lacked a religious studies department and a religious studies major. Even there, however, religion courses were offered, they were popular among students, and some fulfilled general education requirements in liberal studies. Furthermore, at South University as well as the other schools, religion was treated in a wide array of courses across the arts and sciences curricula. Yet one of the most apparent findings of our research is that a religious studies department seems essential if colleges and universities want to make the academic study of religion an important part of academic life on campus. And general education require-ments and curricula that include religion provide large numbers of students with exposure to the academic study of religion.

At North College and East University, the two church-related schools in the study, the academic study of religion figured prominently in both the general education and specialized curricula. The mission of both institu-tions called for academic attention to religion. East University students were exposed significantly to Christianity, especially in the philosophy depart-ment's long-standing focus on the Western (and extensively Christian) philosophical tradition and the theology department's courses on Catholic doctrine. Over the previous few decades, however, the theology department had given increasing attention to ecumenical dialogue between Christianity and other religions. In the context of Protestant church-related higher edu-cation, North College's general education curriculum required more reli-gion courses than is probably the case at most similar colleges. Responding anew to the institution's mission statement, the general education commit-tee at North College began deliberately to enforce guidelines mandating that religion courses take up Christian theology, both in content and in method, in significant ways. And although courses that met general education re-quirements tended to attract larger numbers of students, there was an ample supply of religion courses at North College that embodied virtually all sub-disciplines of religious studies and some that taught about religious tradi-tions other than Christianity.

Faculty at church-related institutions have faced an increasing religious pluralism in the student body, a pluralism that reflects U.S. society at large. No longer able to assume that virtually all of their students have been reared in the denominational tradition, faculty have had to rethink the role of religion classes, particularly if they are required of all or most of the stu-dents. How does one teach Christian theology to students who are not Christian or to those who have not been nurtured in a religious congrega-tion? Should one? What religion courses should the school require? At both East University and North College, recent additions to the religion or theol-ogy faculties have been specialists in Asian religious traditions and Judaism. Hiring a more diverse religion faculty and offering a wider range of religion courses have been key ways in which these church-related institutions have responded to the religious diversity of their students. Indeed, the religion department at North College and the theology department at East Univer-sity recently hired religious studies faculty trained in the study of religion rather than simply in Christian theology.

The number and popularity of religious studies courses at the public university we studied may seem even more surprising. The religious studies faculty at West University was large and well respected on campus, and it offered a myriad of courses at all levels of instruction. Seventeen of these courses fulfilled some general education requirement, and these popular general education courses attracted some good students to the religious studies major. A significant number of other academic programs and departments across the university either used courses in religious studies to fulfill their requirements or offered their own courses in which religion was a major theme.

The approach to the teaching of religion varied on a continuum from advocacy at one extreme to distanced objectivity at the other. Not surprisingly, the faculty members who explicitly espoused the truth of one religious tradition over all others—who were advocates of a religious tradition or point of view—taught at the church-related and African American schools. At East University, the philosophy department, which was responsible for key courses in the core curriculum, taught only the Western philosophical tradition. This department was thoroughly Catholic and committed to reflection on the intersection of reason and the Catholic religion and to a common intellectual project that the faculty believed contributed to the religious formation of their students. This common intellectual project, interestingly enough, could also consist of service-learning experiences for students. The theology department at East University was equally dedicated to a Catholic mission, although it lacked the long-standing "great books" curriculum that gave philosophy such a stable role in university life. Not content since the 1970s with a role that had been primarily catechetical or apologetic, some departmental faculty began to define theology more broadly to include courses in biblical studies and the history of Christian thought, for example, taught without the goal of advocating the truth or superiority of Catholicism. A split in the department between professors who held onto the older more catechetical model and those who let it go mirrored a conflict across the campus between those who believed that East University had lost its Catholic identity and needed to regain it and those who believed that the university's Catholic identity was strong enough (or so powerful that it stifled dissent and cultural/religious pluralism). Perhaps Professor Marcelli best represented the advocacy model at East University. He announced the schedule of masses in his classes and presented Catholic eucharistic theology as being true independent of his own opinion. Yet in an ethos in which public religiosity and advocacy were common and expected, even the Jewish rabbi in the theology department found herself functioning as an advocate, "a representative and spokesperson for Judaism" on campus. And the department recently hired someone who was "brought on as a Buddhist voice" to engage in ecumenical dialogue with Catholic voices.

At North College, there were also institution-wide expectations that Christianity, if not ethnic Lutheranism, would be advocated on campus. Although he was a minority voice in the religion department, Professor Wolf believed that an advocacy model was most appropriate for him, and perhaps he represented it best in the department. He self-consciously chose to "function as the resident representative of the church and its theology," and he wore a clerical collar in class to reinforce his role. Yet religious advocacy in his classroom was softened by the presence of unbelieving students or by radically uneducated Christian students. Wolf realized that it would be unfair for him to argue against students' naive understanding of Christianity, and so he sought to "walk a tightrope between explaining the truth of Christianity and allowing nonbelievers to study Christianity from the outside." At South University, Reverend Robertson clearly exemplified the advocacy model. He designed his course on African American spirituality specifically to deepen and enrich the spiritual lives of the students enrolled in it.

The public and private rhetoric of religious studies professors at West University reinforced, and sometimes insisted on, a relatively objective treatment of all religious traditions and views. Yet, as several of the professors said, "there is a fine line between enthusiasm and advocacy." Professor Falk, while adamantly refusing to advocate Judaism, his own religious tradition, did make explicit claims in class about the religious value of the Hebrew Bible. Professor Martin in the philosophy department wanted his students to study Buddhism from the inside, gleaning religious truths from it for their own lives.

On all four campuses, the religious advocacy approach to teaching religion had important limits. We neither saw nor heard of any cases in which students were graded down for expressing religious viewpoints that differed from those of their professors. And although some students (for example, at North College) felt uncomfortable or threatened by the perspectives of their professors, we did not detect any instances in which students were belittled or ostracized for their religious beliefs by the faculty teaching their courses.

At the other extreme of the continuum of approaches to teaching religion was a model we call "distanced objectivity." In this case, professors ruled out-of-bounds any value judgments about the subject matter. This end of the continuum seemed to be more sparsely populated than the opposite extreme. The clearest examples of its proponents were on the religious studies faculty at the state university. West University's Professor Hanson, himself a practicing Christian, insisted that the religious studies classroom was no place for either him or his students to air their own religious beliefs. Rather, the primary goal of religious studies was the objective, dispassionate study of the "other"—those whose religious beliefs and practices differed radically from one's own. The assumption here was that in order to see the other clearly, one must put one's own biases aside. Hanson's dedication to neutrality or objectivity had its limits, however. No instances were observed in which students were chastised or ridiculed for written or oral comments that were too subjective.

Professor Benton, also at West University, advised students in his mysticism class to avoid turning in papers that described their subjective responses to the texts assigned; rather, they were to interpret these religious texts according to objective and scholarly criteria. Professor Shannon, who taught a course in sexual ethics, embodied a modified form of the distanced-objectivity model. Shannon resolutely, in intention and practice, kept her own opinions out of the classroom. She was, on that score, impossible for Betty DeBerg to read. Yet she clearly wanted her students to express their opinions in class on days dedicated to debates as well as throughout the course.

The teaching of the vast majority of professors at these four schools fell somewhere between the advocacy and objectivist extremes. In his chapter on South University, Conrad Cherry named the middle ground the "empathetic/analytical" model. Several faculty in the North College religion department represented this model quite well in that they stressed an attitude of respect for religious people and religious traditions of all kinds without advocating any particular tradition. Professor Cassidy wanted her students to learn to be "respectful observers, gain better understanding of religion, and not dismiss a religious perspective or practice superficially." Professor Banik was "an advocate of the religion we are studying at the time." Professor Lindfoot began by explaining a religious tradition from within, acting as an "advocate temporarily of a religion so that students will sympathize," then she moved to a more critical objective position. According to Professor Christian at North College, he and most of his colleagues "exposed students to normative Christian content, and they can do with that content what they like."

Inherent in this middle-ground model was a commitment on the part of faculty to marshaling acceptable and often diverse scholarly methods to analyze and better understand religious phenomena. Professor Hansen at East University designed an introductory course in Christian theology that was primarily a historical study of Western philosophical theology. Professors of biblical studies often relied on a large number of different scholarly methods such as archaeology, philology, anthropology, history, literary criticism, and geography. Professor Madison, who taught biblical studies at

West University, focused on the New Testament in a "critical and appreciative kind of way." His approach was critical in that it used methods of academic analysis or criticism; it was appreciative in that he spoke of the New Testament as a classic, as a text that holds religious meaning for many. At South University, when he wore the hat of professor, the university chaplain emphasized the scholarly study of religion over either the subjective response to it or the religious development of his students. Across all four campuses and in several different departments, we observed dedicated teachers who found religion to be an important and worthwhile human enterprise and brought the best critical scholarship to bear on it. As much as some religious studies professors at West University dismissed the advocacy model as inappropriate at a state university, they also rejected a doctrinaire secularism that would dismiss the human appeal and importance of religion altogether.

The academic methods and intentions of faculty aside, we discovered that for the students the religious studies classroom was often a site and resource for religious meaning and personal transformation. The line between the practice and teaching of religion thus could become blurred. In some instances, the blurring of the boundaries was invited by the faculty themselves. Choir director Blake at North College, for example, sought both to instruct and to religiously inspire his student musicians, and the core course at East University required students to perform volunteer work, often among the poor, at the same time that they were assigned readings in Christian classics. Students often described religion courses as the most important religious experiences of their university careers, experiences that changed their perspectives on the world. Even at the public university, where the transformation of students' lives was a goal infrequently expressed by those who taught religion, students who were interviewed spoke of the important life issues raised in these courses, the all-night discussions they had about them, and the religious studies major as something undertaken for personal development rather than preparation for a specific career. At West University, a student in the sexual ethics class remarked about the course, for example: "I have to face issues with which I disagree with my tradition and wrestle with them. . . . It has made me grow as a person both spiritually and ethically." And a religious studies major at West University who spent days and days trying to decide what she believed completed the major because she had finally found an academic field about which she was passionate. "This major is for me," she said. "I'm so used to being career oriented, and this didn't have anything to do with a career but with my *life*." In short, many students took religious studies courses because the courses forced them "to think" and spoke to their search for meaning.

From the outset of our study, we wanted to attend to the ethos of each of our campuses and were especially interested in how ethos affects and is affected by religion. Admittedly, the ethos of any culture is an ever-shifting and somewhat amorphous thing, and we had no illusions that the ethos of campus life would be any less fluid or porous than that of any other culture. Nevertheless, we believed that the general atmosphere on each campus would make a difference in the practice and study of religion among undergraduates.

At the Catholic university, East University, many people described the current religious atmosphere on campus with reference to the insular religious environment of the past. In the almost mythical time before Vatican II and the 1960s, the university had been a provincial commuter school where, in the language of some of the current natives, most students "grew up with the rosary and the stations of the cross, surrounded by a thick religious piety." Jesuits exerted a ubiquitous pastoral presence, "every student was expected to make a religious retreat once a year," and "everyone stopped to say a Hail Mary when an ambulance went by." But as time went on, the number of Jesuits active in student life diminished. Meanwhile, academic standards for student admission were raised, faculty became more driven by research, and the nature of Catholic theology expanded to include ecumenical interest in Hinduism, Buddhism, and Judaism.

Although more than a few people grieved over the current state of piety on campus and believed that a tragic and perhaps irreversible decline had occurred, the progressive Catholics whose leadership dominated the school took the view that the Catholicism of the past, however sweet and comforting, had been unself-conscious and "not really reflected on." In their opinion, the cocoonlike world of the past was best left behind as a new generation of intellectually sophisticated and religiously committed activists stepped out into the world to shoulder the responsibility for the betterment of society and, by extension, the redemption of the world. Thus strong disagreement existed among both faculty and students about whether things were getting better or worse. But almost everyone agreed that religion and spirituality were good things and that they should play an important role in campus life. The vast majority of students and faculty held religion in high esteem, including those in the religiously quiet majority who devoted most of their time to academic work and profane play.

A handful of Jesuit administrators represented the religious ethos of the school, along with the more numerous students and faculty engaged in their own, somewhat less visible and less official efforts to embody Jesuit spirituality. Even conservatives who lamented the loss of a more insular, Catholic world acknowledged that the president and other exemplars of Jesuit spirituality were responsible for "the good atmosphere" that existed on campus. "He was just a very decent guy," one conservative faculty member said of the recently retired president, "and what he did flowed down. He didn't pull in a $300,000 salary—everything he made went right back into the school. Everyone knew he lived in a little room like the other priests."

Certain students also embodied the religious ethos of the school. The student body president wielded remarkable clout among students, faculty, administrators, and trustees, in large part because of her passionate and articulate devotion to Jesuit spirituality. Her popularity and political power on campus represented the groundswell of Jesuit spirituality in the student body, especially among women. "I know that I am a child of God," she asserted, "and I know that I have been called by God to a religious vocation. I want to do and be all the things Jesuits do and be." Such heartfelt commitment to the personal expression of Jesuit ideals was fairly widespread on campus, although not always expressed so insistently or with such inescapable reference to touchy issues like women's ordination. Respect for the personification of Jesuit ideals was the common ground of religious culture on campus that progressives and conservatives shared.

In certain respects, the religious ethos of South University and North College was similar to that of East University. Although at South University and North College images of a sacred past did not play such a vivid role, the cultures of the two schools were defined by a religious ethos that tended to generate commitment to school missions and programs. Like the Catholic school, the African American and Lutheran schools focused on the personal embodiment of Christian ideals, which entailed responsibility for and identification with the suffering of others. In all three schools, this personal and social commitment to Christian ideals created a common ground that could unite otherwise disputing factions. And in all three schools, this common ground was broad enough to resonate with very different levels of religious intensity among students, faculty, and administrators, as well as both sides of more clearly defined religious disputes.

At the school affiliated with the Lutheran Church, North College, music played the constructive role in defining campus culture that Jesuit spirituality played at East University. Participation in one of the musical performance groups at the Lutheran school enabled students and faculty to express religious enthusiasm in a way that facilitated identification with the spirit of the campus and funneled its idealism into the larger world. Although not everyone was a religious performer or religious virtuoso directly engaged in the construction and maintenance of campus culture, most students and faculty served as an appreciative audience when not busy with other things.

A somewhat distinctive aspect of the religious ethos at the Lutheran school was its occasional incorporation of various forms of secularity, ribaldry, and even impiety. Certainly a serious sacrality was bound up with the sacred music that pervaded the campus, but boundaries between sacred and secular forms of music could be transgressed, and this iconoclasm could extend to other aspects of campus culture as well. One of the high points of homecoming weekend was the fund-raiser for a sick child that involved a Jello wrestling match between the college pastor and the dean of students. The rules of the match included "Thou shalt not bite thy opponent," "Thou shalt not stuff green Jello down thy opponent's pants," and "Thou shalt not covet thy opponent's beard." In response to the dean's taunts about the "Good Book," the pastor yelled, "Am I my brother's keeper?," then shouted, "No!," as he threw the dean to the mat.

In contrast to this playful assault on religious boundaries and authority at the Lutheran school, the religious ethos of the African American university was not something to be poked fun at or subjected to parody. It certainly involved as much fun, pageantry, theatrical display, and artistic talent as the religious ethos of the predominantly white, middle-class Lutheran school. And it was no less productive of feelings of camaraderie, exuberance, and uplift. But it was usually pressed into the more serious service of enabling students to gain a secure foothold in the middle class and beat the relatively high odds of poverty, ill health, incarceration, and job discrimination that stood against them. Religion at the African American school was about salvation in a very real social sense as well as in a supernatural or spiritual sense. As the president of the student body, an ordained Baptist minister, said to his fellow students at the opening convocation: "You have come [here] to raise yourselves to excellence. You have come to lay to rest the rumors that members of our race are lazy slackers. You have come here to succeed."

Religion played an important, supportive role in this mission. On homecoming weekend at this school, the coronation of the queen ceremony, which celebrated the beauty, talent, and strength of women in African American culture, began with a choir singing the hymn "Holy Spirit." The ensuing "Grand Procession of Fulfilling the Promise" showcased subordinate queens representing various campus organizations, each accompanied by a tuxedoed king, as well as the queen herself, who embodied the promise of success undergirded by gospel values. After the crowning, a dancer performed to "Didn't My Lord Deliver Daniel," her hands continuously rising to the heavens in praise. The queen closed the evening with a gospel/blues piece that employed the language of the Book of Isaiah and Handel's Messiah. Much is apparent here about the manner in which religion saturated the ethos of South University: this public event, like every other public event on the campus, was a worship service.

The state university, West University, differed in important respects from the Christian schools. No pervasive religious ethos existed there. The job of defining campus culture often fell to the athletes and their extensive support and promotion system, which generated almost as much campus-wide attention, school spirit, and personal celebrity as religious enthusiasm did at the Christian schools—although even varsity athletics did not unify the campus. Not that the state school was inhospitable to self-ascribed religiosity. If demand for it was weak, supply was healthy. Students found no shortage of well-designed and well-publicized religious groups and activities from which to choose. And university administrators, especially those in student services, encouraged these organizations, partly because they perceived them to be valuable allies in the war on binge drinking and providers of spiritual counseling.

At this state school, many opportunities existed for religious activists to express their piety openly and enthusiastically. It is true that religious activists, especially Protestant ones, regretted that their piety did not have greater effect on the campus as a whole. Yet it was precisely the absence of both a strong Christian ethos and a de facto religious establishment on campus that provided space for the equal status of other groups. The vitality of this more complete and open religious pluralism came through in the classroom as well as in the Student Union, dormitories, and locker rooms. An instructor in Buddhism encouraged his students to get involved in Buddhist practices, and one of the most popular professors on campus was a Jew who lectured to hundreds of students every semester on the Bible and Judaism. The absence of a pervasive religious ethos on campus created a space in which non-Christian religions and non-Christian religious opinions about such things as the Bible could gain equal footing.

In sum, religious practice was more pervasive at the three schools affiliated with religious denominations, where the ethos of campus life involved religious sensibilities associated with Catholic, Lutheran, or African American Protestant culture. At the state university, the percentage of undergraduates engaged in organized religious activity was smallest, but those who did participate demonstrated considerable commitment and zeal. At all four schools, we found various degrees of religious enthusiasm, including cadres of intensely religious students who defined both their life and learning in terms of religious ideals.

We discovered little resistance or hostility at any school to either the practice or the teaching of religion. Only at the Catholic university, where the most strenuous and concerted efforts were made to bring campus life into conformity with religious ideals, did we hear anyone complain about campus religion being oppressive. On all four campuses, lively differences of opinion on religious matters were aired, and in the vast majority of cases, religion was respected and widely viewed as a salutary dimension of human life.

Placing these observations in the context of the history of religion in American higher education, several points emerge that merit particular attention. Religion appeared to be more optional than in the past, when student behavior was much more closely supervised and students could be reprimanded for deviating from religious norms. Until the second half of the twentieth century, attendance at chapel was obligatory at most church-affiliated schools. Even at state schools, students were required to conform to moral standards that were rooted in religious (especially Protestant) principles. In the four schools we visited, this kind of coerced religious activity had disappeared. And with the exception of some religious conservatives at the Catholic university who might have liked to see religious requirements for student behavior reintroduced, most of the people we interviewed would probably recoil at such an idea and view any such requirements as counterproductive to internally motivated religious commitment.

Students at all four schools were free to choose whether or not to practice religion and, if they chose to practice, how deeply to become invested. Not surprisingly, the freedom *not* to be religious was most widely exercised at the state school. At the state, Lutheran, and Catholic schools, the most intensely religious people on campus could be extremely critical of others who seemed to them to be insufficiently religious.

In addition to being more optional, religion on the four campuses appeared to be more pluralistic than in the past. Throughout much of American history, students at many church-related schools were encouraged to view people who practiced other religions as objects of missionary conversion, and throughout the nineteenth and early twentieth centuries, many of those colleges functioned as nurseries for missionary vocations. But these same institutions also led the way in encouraging respect for other religions and in advancing scholarly understanding of the religions of the world. On many American campuses in the twentieth century, the desire to understand non-Christian religions and the effort to conceptualize religion as a universal human phenomenon rather than something defined by Christianity developed in response to supersessionary, missionary attitudes toward other religions. As our study suggests, this newer commitment to religious understanding could sometimes reshape rather than supplant the older tradition of missionary commitment. In all of the schools we visited, many of the most intensely religious people we interviewed were full of missionary zeal.

But this zeal tended to be tempered by respect for religions other than their own and by the belief that God was worshiped and served in many different ways.

On all four campuses, respect for religious difference was pervasive at both the academic and the practical levels. Courses in theology were required at both the Catholic and Lutheran schools, and in this respect, studying religion was more mandatory than practicing it. But even in the required courses at these church-related schools, students were exposed to diverse religious forms and approaches to religion. Similarly, opportunities to practice a variety of religions were readily available on all four campuses. Even at the Catholic and Lutheran schools, where Catholicism and Lutheranism were in effect the established religions, students had opportunities to observe and participate in different religious traditions.

At the schools in our study, we found little evidence that the strong tendencies toward religious freedom and religious pluralism led to any lack of religious vitality. At the Catholic school, a number of intensely religious people believed that the quality of religious life suffered because it had become optional—like the Glee Club or aerobics. But our interviews with religious people on all four campuses did not confirm that religious practice was taken less seriously because it was voluntary. If anything, the ethos of religious choice seemed to stimulate religious interest and religious enthusiasm. Of course, this connection between religious volunteerism and religious enthusiasm is a very old American trait.

As for the students who opted not to be religious or those who invested less in religious life than some of their peers, it may well be true that in the past many of them would have been swept up in the more totalizing religious cultures surrounding them. Their incorporation into a religious atmosphere probably would have made them think and behave in ways that conformed, at least to some extent, to established religious standards. The religious requirements of the past certainly implied the importance of religious conformity. But they probably also encouraged passivity with respect to inherited traditions and ignorance and intolerance of other religions.

With regard to the theories, discussed in the introduction, that American higher education has undergone a steady process of secularization, on the basis of our empirical study we affirm instead that religion has become more optional and pluralistic. Certainly it is true that church oversight of church-related colleges has declined. The shame involved in not being religious has also declined. But we found both the practice and the study of religion to be vital aspects of the slices of American higher education that we observed. Indeed, we found religion on the four campuses sufficiently vital and inviting to make us wonder if it had ever been more so in the past. It is possible that young people in American culture have never been more enthusi-astically engaged in religious practice or with religious ideas. And it is possi-ble that religious practice and education have never been more connected with personal responsibility for society. More clearly, our study reveals that the ethos of decentered, diverse, religiously tolerant institutions of higher education is a breeding ground for vital religious practice and teaching.

NOTES

1. Robert Wuthnow, *After Heaven: Spirituality in America since the 1950s* (Berkeley: University of California Press, 1998), 15, 72.

2. Tom Beaudoin, *Virtual Faith: The Irreverent Spiritual Quest of Generation X* (San Francisco: Jossey-Bass, 1998), 45, 178.

3. Cited in *U.: The National College Magazine*, May 1997, 7. The same issue of *U.* calls attention to a 1996 survey by the Higher Education Institute that found that in the previous year, 72 percent of college freshmen performed volunteer work.

4. Peter Berger, *A Far Glory: The Quest for Faith in an Age of Credulity* (New York: Doubleday, 1992), 38–39.

As the senior researchers for this project, we chose to study schools that were most unlike the institutions in which we taught. (Betty DeBerg, now at the University of Northern Iowa, was a professor at Valparaiso University when she conducted the research on the state university.) We made that choice on the principle that as ethnographic outsiders to other cultures, we would bring fewer assumptions to our investigations if we examined types of schools with which we were most unfamiliar. On average, we and the research associates who assisted us spent a total of at least thirty days "in the field" at each school, conducting the research over a period of one academic year but concentrating most of our hours in the fall semester. Conrad Cherry and Amanda Porterfield commuted to their campuses of study in blocks of three to six days. Betty DeBerg was able to take up residence at West University during much of the fall semester, which turned out to be a boon given the size and complexity of that school.

We were guided, although not slavishly, in our qualitative studies by the methods of James P. Spradley in his *The Ethnographic Interview* (New York: Harcourt Brace Jovanovich, 1979) and *Participant Observation* (New York: Harcourt Brace Jovanovich, 1980). Above all, we attempted to live up to Spradley's principle, borrowed from anthropologist Bronislaw Malinowski, that the purpose of ethnography is "to grasp the native's point of view, his relation to life, to realize *his* vision of *his* world."[1] That meant that in our interviews, we sought to discover the language of the "natives" when we spoke with them about the teaching and practice of religion on their campuses and to let them speak in that language in the descriptive parts of this book. We also sought out numerous "informants," especially people who by virtue of their positions or length of residence at the schools could bring wide acquaintance with their campuses to bear on their descriptions and interpretations of campus religion. And we returned to key informants to fill in gaps in our notes and to compare their perceptions with those of other people we interviewed. We sometimes used focus groups of students or faculty in our interviewing process, allowing the persons in the groups to trade ideas with one another. We were led to the events we observed by our interviewees and by announcements in student newspapers and on bulletin boards, as well as (for some of the classes we observed) course listings and student scuttlebutt. We always obtained permission to observe the events, and when we thought it would be neither intrusive nor compromising of our observer status, we participated as well as observed. On most occasions, we sought to be inconspicuous if not withdrawn observers, and when we had reason to think that our presence may have materially affected the dynamics of a situation, we recorded that impression.

In both our interviews and our observations, we followed a research cycle that moved from descriptions or the recording of answers to our fundamental questions about the teaching and practice of religion to the analysis and comparison of the descriptions and back again to the descriptions in a quest for the most illuminating concrete event or language. We recorded notes from our interviews and observations soon after the sessions or events, usually in the evening following a day's work. We frequently read back over our notes, indicated any patterns of teaching and practice that seemed to be emerging, and raised further questions that we needed to answer on the next visit. All three of us used askSam software for our field notes, a program with a capacity for word and phrase searches through multiple data files that allowed us to compare events and interviews and lift out sections from our notes appropriate to analysis and the writing of this book. Altogether, our field notes amounted to over 1,500 pages. We read one another's notes in printed or electronic form, met frequently to discuss our discoveries and interpretations, and received periodic commentary on our research from a colleague with advanced expertise in ethnography. When it came time to write the chapters of this book, we combed back over our field notes to select events and languages from the large mass of interviews and observations that seemed to capture most concretely and specifically a larger whole.

At the conclusion of our academic-year visits, we reported summaries of our research to interested parties at each of the schools and received their responses to our interpretations of the teaching and practice of religion on their campuses. These faculty, students, administrators, and other key informants to whom we reported helped us further apply our findings to the cultures of their campuses and, in a number of cases, corrected some errors of fact and impression that had found their way into our research. We also believe that as empathetic outsiders, we may have brought to light some things about the schools that our hosts as insiders had not seen or that resided at the level of their latent consciousness.

We supplemented our observations and interviews with bulging files of materials that helped us understand the milieu and the religion of each place, such as student newspapers, announcements of meetings, memoranda, school and department mission statements, student handbooks, calendars of events, directories of student organizations, and published and unpublished histories of the schools. And although we wanted the focus of our research and writing to be qualitative, we did use sparingly data derived from some survey instruments. The results of the in-class survey (appendix B) of undergraduate students in a number of classes provided some crucial data, but we also drew on summaries of the schools' own quantitative instruments when they were available: freshman and senior surveys, student profiles, retention and graduation rates, and the like. In the provision of these data, as in the opening of the campuses to our visits, the officers of the schools were altogether cooperative.

NOTE

1. James P. Spradley, *The Ethnographic Interview* (New York: Harcourt Brace Jovanovich, 1979), 3.

IN-CLASS QUESTIONNAIRE

INDIANA UNIVERSITY–PURDUE UNIVERSITY, INDIANAPOLIS

The Center for the Study of Religion and American Culture is conducting a study of the teaching of religion at your school. We are very interested in your personal response to this course, taught by Professor X.

This survey is anonymous and voluntary. Your answers will remain completely confidential. Thank you for your help.

BACKGROUND QUESTIONS

1) Gender (Male or Female) _____

2) College Major _____

3) Home City and State (before attending this school) _____

4) Age _____

Class in School (Freshman, Sophomore, Junior, Senior, or Other) _____

5) Race (circle the appropriate category)
   (A) White
   (B) Black
   (C) Latino
   (D) Asian/Pacific Islander
   (E) Native American

6) What is your current religious preference? Is it Roman Catholic, Southern Baptist, Reform Jewish, some other religion, or no religion? Please name the religious group that you most closely identify with. Be as specific as possible (for example, if Baptist, indicate whether it is the Southern Baptist Convention, the American Baptist Churches in the USA, or some other Baptist group).

_____

7) Which religious labels best describe you (circle all that apply)?
   (A) Agnostic (F) Protestant   (K) Spiritual   (P) Buddhist
   (B) Atheist   (G) Catholic   (L) Nation of Islam (Q) Charismatic/Pentecostal
   (C) Muslim   (H) Conservative (M) Evangelical   (R) Progressive
   (D) Christian (I) Liberal   (N) Fundamentalist (S) Traditional
   (E) Jewish   (J) Born-again   (O) Hindu   (T) Other _____

8) Educational background of parent with the highest educational level (circle highest level attained)
   (A) Less than high school degree
   (B) High school degree
   (C) Vocational or trade school

(D) Some college
(E) College degree
(F) Graduate or professional degree

9) What, in your opinion, are the most reliable sources in matters of truth? Choose up to *three* answers, ranking them in order of importance (with "1" being most important):

Your own personal experience _____
What parents and family teach _____
Newspapers/broadcast news _____
What science teaches _____
Your favorite music/movies _____
The teachings of Scripture _____
What religious leaders say _____
What teachers/professors say _____
What friends say _____
Other (specify) _____

10) How often do you attend religious services?
(A) Never
(B) Less than once a year
(C) About once or twice a year
(D) Several times a year
(E) About once a month
(F) 2–3 times a month
(G) Nearly every week
(H) Every week

11) Do you participate in any campus religious groups (for example, campus ministry groups, the college or university chapel, Bible study groups, volunteer organizations, or prayer groups)?

If so, which groups? _____

12) How has your level of participation in religious activities changed since coming to this school?
(A) Increased greatly
(B) Increased somewhat
(C) Decreased somewhat
(D) Decreased greatly
(E) Neither increased nor decreased

13) Would you say that your own religious beliefs are:
(A) Very similar to those of your parents
(B) Somewhat similar to those of your parents
(C) Somewhat different from those of your parents
(D) Very different from those of your parents
(E) Don't know enough about parents' religious beliefs

COURSE QUESTIONS

1) Why did you take this course? Choose up to *three* of the following reasons, ranking them in order of importance (with "1" being most important and "3" being least important):

_____ The professor had a good reputation
_____ To learn more about my own religious tradition
_____ To learn more about other religions
_____ Easy course
_____ Interesting topic
_____ Fit well with my career plans
_____ Friend suggested
_____ Part of my spiritual journey
_____ Parents suggested
_____ To fulfill a requirement
_____ Other reason _____

2) This course has focused on (circle *all* of the answers that apply):
(A) The objective study of religion
(B) Developing empathy for other religions
(C) Political action
(D) Ethics
(E) Personal spirituality
(F) Study of sacred texts
(G) Philosophy/theology/religious thought
(H) Ancient languages
(I) Community service
(J) Social-scientific approaches to religion
(K) Other _____

3) Would you say that your own religious beliefs are:
(A) Very similar to those of the professor
(B) Somewhat similar to those of the professor
(C) Somewhat different from those of the professor
(D) Very different from those of the professor
(E) Don't know enough about professor's religious beliefs

4) Would you say that your own religious beliefs are:
(A) Very similar to those of other students in the course
(B) Somewhat similar to those of other students
(C) Somewhat different from those of other students
(D) Very different from those of other students
(E) Don't know enough about other students' religious beliefs

5) Which labels or phrases best describe the professor for this course? Please circle *all* of the labels which apply.

(A) Fair	(G) Secular
(B) Tolerant	(H) Inspiring
(C) Skeptical	(I) Knowledgeable
(D) Spiritual	(J) Biased
(E) Liberal	(K) Religious
(F) Conservative	(L) Other _____

6) During the *class periods* for this course, how often did the professor:
Talk about his/her personal
religious background (A) Frequently (B) Sometimes (C) Rarely (D) Never
Express his/her own moral and
ethical convictions (A) Frequently (B) Sometimes (C) Rarely (D) Never

Encourage tolerance for non-Western religions	(A) Frequently (B) Sometimes (C) Rarely (D) Never
Pray in class	(A) Frequently (B) Sometimes (C) Rarely (D) Never
Reveal his/her political opinions	(A) Frequently (B) Sometimes (C) Rarely (D) Never
Criticize traditional religious perspectives	(A) Frequently (B) Sometimes (C) Rarely (D) Never
Emphasize the importance of scholarly objectivity	(A) Frequently (B) Sometimes (C) Rarely (D) Never
Bring his/her religious beliefs into the lectures	(A) Frequently (B) Sometimes (C) Rarely (D) Never

(7) How often did you talk with the professor outside of class?
(A) Frequently (B) Occasionally (C) Rarely
(D) Never (if "Never" skip to the next question)

In your interaction with the professor outside of class, to what extent did he/she:

Talk about his/her personal religious background	(A) A great deal (B) Somewhat (C) Not at all
Express his/her own moral and ethical convictions	(A) A great deal (B) Somewhat (C) Not at all
Encourage tolerance for non-Western religions	(A) A great deal (B) Somewhat (C) Not at all
Pray in your presence	(A) A great deal (B) Somewhat (C) Not at all
Reveal his/her political opinions	(A) A great deal (B) Somewhat (C) Not at all
Criticize traditional religious perspectives	(A) A great deal (B) Somewhat (C) Not at all
Emphasize the importance of scholarly objectivity	(A) A great deal (B) Somewhat (C) Not at all
Discuss his/her religious beliefs	(A) A great deal (B) Somewhat (C) Not at all
Offer spiritual guidance	(A) A great deal (B) Somewhat (C) Not at all

8) How free did you feel to bring your own religious beliefs into class discussions?
(A) Very free
(B) Somewhat free
(C) Not very free

9) Did the professor advocate any religious perspective or perspectives in particular?
(A) Yes   (B) No

If "yes," which religious perspective or perspectives did he/she advocate (circle *all* of the answers that apply)?

(A) Christian	(D) Protestant	(G) Evangelical	(J) Liberal	(M) Liberation Theology
(B) Jewish	(E) Afrocentric	(H) Muslim	(K) Buddhist	(N) Conservative
(C) Catholic	(F) Feminist	(I) Secular	(L) Hindu	(O) Other

_____

10) This course gave me a greater understanding of (circle *all* of the answers that apply)

(A) Christianity	(G) Biblical text	(M) Ministry
(B) Judaism	(H) Comparative religion	(N) Spirituality
(C) Catholicism	(I) Protestantism	(O) Other _____
(D) Islam	(J) Theology	
(E) Buddhism	(K) Ethics	
(F) Hinduism	(L) Philosophy	

11) Looking back over your experience this semester, would you say this course:
  (A) Strengthened your personal religious faith
  (B) Weakened your religious faith
  (C) Did not strengthen or weaken your faith

12) After taking this class, do you:
  (A) Have a more positive view of other religions
  (B) Have a less positive view of other religions
  (C) Have the same view of other religions as before
  (D) Course did not focus on other religions

13) How helpful was this course for:

Thinking about the
meaning of life   (A) Very helpful (B) Somewhat helpful (C) Not helpful

Understanding your
  own religious
  tradition   (A) Very helpful (B) Somewhat helpful (C) Not helpful

Understanding other
  religions   (A) Very helpful (B) Somewhat helpful (C) Not helpful

Providing a historical
  context for
  religion   (A) Very helpful (B) Somewhat helpful (C) Not helpful

Encouraging political
  and social
  activism   (A) Very helpful (B) Somewhat helpful (C) Not helpful

14) To what extent has this course led you to:

Be more tolerant of other
  religious traditions   (A) A great deal (B) Somewhat (C) Not at all

Question your own religious
  beliefs and values   (A) A great deal (B) Somewhat (C) Not at all

Grow spiritually   (A) A great deal (B) Somewhat (C) Not at all

Change the way you think
  about God   (A) A great deal (B) Somewhat (C) Not at all

Increase your interest in
  service and volunteer
  activities   (A) A great deal (B) Somewhat (C) Not at all

15) After taking this class, are you (choose one answer only):
  (A) More critical of the teachings of your religious tradition
  (B) More appreciative of the teachings of your religious tradition
  (C) Neither more critical nor more appreciative
  (D) Both more critical and more appreciative

16) Which of the following statements corresponds most closely to the views expressed in the class discussions for this course?

(A) Religious institutions should attempt to encourage individual morality
(B) Religious institutions should attempt to encourage social justice
(C) Neither statement
(D) Both statements

17) Which of the following statements corresponds most closely to the views expressed in the class discussions for this course?
(A) The best way to address social problems is to change the hearts of individuals
(B) The best way to address social problems is to change societal institutions
(C) Neither statement
(D) Both statements

18) The professor for this course was:
(A) Appreciative of your religious tradition
(B) Critical of your religious tradition
(C) Both appreciative and critical of your religious tradition
(D) Indifferent toward your religious tradition

19) How has your experience in this course changed your religious beliefs?

20) How have your religious beliefs changed since you enrolled at this school?

Church of Jesus Christ of Latter-day Saints, 5, 64
Church of the Brethren, 31
Church-state separation, 14–15, 53
City Table (soup kitchen), 39, 51
Clark, Thomas C., 53
Clergy, 8; education of, 1–2, 4; as administrators, 3, 4
Clinton, Hillary, 185
CMA. *See* Campus Ministers Association
CMC. *See* Campus Ministry Center
Codes of conduct: at South University, 87–88, 141
Cole, Nicholas (WU professor), 72
Cole, Robert, 184
Columbia University, 2
Community service, 279–80; at West University, 35, 39, 49, 78; at South University, 96–98, 141, 279; at East University, 180–85, 194, 195–96, 279; at North College, 224, 225, 228, 229, 279
Concerns circle, 39
Cone, James, 131
Congregationalists, 5
Copernicus, 134
Cornerstone (student group), 14
Corporate structure: at East University, 157, 158
Counseling, student: at West University, 33, 281, 292; at South University, 108–9
CPF. *See* Catholic Peace Fellowship
Crime, campus, 87–88
Crosby, Matthew (EU associate dean), 156
Cults, religious, 75
Curriculum, 2, 8; religion as a cross-discipline topic, 71–72, 80, 113, 122, 123, 135–37, 139, 141, 263–70, 273, 283, 285; service-learning programs, 97–98, 180–85, 194, 195–96, 279, 285; religion as an avoided topic, 132–35, 139; theology and philosophy courses, 178–85, 195–211, 216, 253–56, 263–64, 273, 284, 285, 294. *See also* Religious studies; *specific course types*
Curtis, James (NC professor), 264–66
Cutter, James (NC professor), 255–56, 270

Daoism, 51
Davis, Beverly (SU professor), 135
Death penalty, 48
Delillo, Mary (NC student), 242
Disciples of Christ, 31
Discordianism, 51
Distanced-objectivity teaching approach, 285, 286–87
Dress codes, 88
Drinking. *See* Alcohol consumption
Drug use: at West University, 78; at South University, 88
Druidry, 51
Durkheim, Emile, 135

Eastern Orthodox Christianity, 14, 31
East University (Catholic institution) (EU), 6, 7, 143–218; Jesuit influences, 143–44, 149, 163–70, 173, 176–80, 190–91, 194, 196–97, 278–79, 289–90; campus ethos, 143–58, 289–90, 292–93; religion's role on campus, 144–47; values concerns, 145, 150, 154, 161–63; non-Catholics at, 145, 158, 192–95, 217–18, 282; worship services, 145, 159–61, 177; secularization perspectives, 147, 150–52, 217; conservative viewpoints, 147–52, 175, 185–92, 196–97, 218, 282, 289–90; student newspapers, 148, 186, 187–88, 189; international students, 149; athletics, 151; community and social service programs, 151, 176, 178–85, 193, 194, 195–96, 215, 279; progressive viewpoints, 152–55, 162, 215–16, 217, 282, 289; administrators, 154, 155–58; women at, 158, 161, 173–78, 186; religious practice, 158–95, 277–82, 294; drinking concerns, 159, 162; student spirituality, 159, 163–64, 166, 168–69, 171–85, 189, 278–79, 289–90; religious studies, 159, 178–85, 195–214, 284, 285, 287, 288, 294; abortion perspectives, 161, 185–86, 187, 215; student behavior concerns, 161–63; sexuality issues, 162–63, 175, 187, 215; theology and philosophy courses, 178–85, 195–211, 216, 284, 285, 294; student organizations, 180, 188–89; biblical studies, 207–11, 216

Hare Krishnas, 75
Harris, Raymond (WU dean), 75–76
Harvard College, 1, 4
Hasel, Gerhard, 57
Hasidism, 129, 130, 248–49
Haskins, Margie (SU student affairs director), 88–89
Hawkins, Alice (SU student), 111, 140
Hebrew Bible: academic study of, 56–59
Herberg, Will, 14
Higher education: religion's changing role in, 1–5, 8; religion's integration into curricula, 2; sectarian institutions, 2; secularization of, 2–6, 8, 294
Hillel, Rabbi, 119
Hillel Jewish Student Center, 14, 16, 25, 31, 37, 42, 48–50, 76, 277
Hinduism, 211–12, 246, 257–58, 270, 273, 289; at East University, 158
Hirsch, Frank (WU Hillel Center director), 31, 49
Holocaust study, 70
Holsten, Joyce (WU Campus Crusade staffer), 50
Homecoming: at South University, 90–94, 141, 278, 291–92; at North College, 222–24, 291
Homosexuality, 35, 236; evangelical Christians' opposition to, 26–27; as religious studies topic, 67, 68, 69; conservative Catholics and, 175, 190
Huber, Nicole (WU student), 59
Huber, Robert (NC student), 261
Huff, Cal (WU campus minister), 34–38, 39, 40, 41, 51, 282
Hughes, Howard, 19–20
Hunter, Jane (WU InterVarsity minister), 22–24, 26
Hussein, Saddam, 127

Ignatius of Loyola, 143, 164, 168, 169, 180
Indigo Girls, 47
International students: at West University, 25, 50; at East University, 149; at North College, 220, 247
InterVarsity Christian Fellowship (IVF), 234, 280; at West University, 13–14, 16, 20–23, 30, 31, 42, 76, 282; at North College, 233, 237–38, 241–44, 263, 272, 277, 281, 282

Isaiah, 56, 57
Islam: at West University, 14, 50, 75; at South University, 114, 116, 117–18, 121, 122; at East University, 158; at North College, 246, 263, 271
IVF. See InterVarsity Christian Fellowship

Jackson, Jeffrey (SU student), 111, 136, 140
James, Roland (WU professor), 56–58
Jane (NC professors' daughter), 223–24
Japanese Club, 50
Jehovah's Witnesses, 64
Jesuits. See Society of Jesus
Jewish students and studies. See Judaism
John Paul II, Pope, 187
Johnson, Denise (EU student), 174–75
Johnson, James Weldon, 91
John XXIII, Pope, 166
Jones, Kate (WU student), 51–53
Jones, Mae (NC student), 239–40, 243, 260–61, 272, 273
Judaism: at sectarian universities, 2; at West University, 14, 16, 25, 30, 31, 37, 42, 48–50, 58–60, 76, 79, 277, 292; Torah study groups, 49; Hebrew Bible study experience, 56–59; Holocaust course study, 70; at South University, 114, 116, 119–20, 121, 122, 128–31; Cabalism, 129; Hasidism, 129, 130, 248–49; music's role in, 130; rabbis' roles in, 130; at East University, 158, 193, 212, 285, 289; at North College, 246, 248–49, 271

Kafka, Franz, 263
Kant, Immanuel, 133, 204, 205
Kemp, Jane (SU student), 111, 140
Kennedy, Laura (SU professor), 97, 98
Kenney, Patrick (EU professor), 160–61
Kierkegaard, Soren, 204
King, Martin Luther, Jr., 96
King, Rodney, 120
Koran, 117
Kosner, Virginia (NC associate pastor), 231, 232–33, 237, 238, 240–41, 243, 272
Kozack, Ted (EU student), 191
Krall, Sandra (NC student), 238–39

Native American traditions, 51
NC. *See* North College
Nelson, Bill (SU football coach), 113
Nelson, James B., 68
Neopaganism, 14, 16, 51–52
Newman Center, 14, 16, 20, 31, 37, 40, 42, 44–50, 79, 277, 279, 282
New Testament: academic study of, 60–62, 207–11, 288
Newton, Isaac, 134
Niebuhr, Reinhold, 253
Nietzsche, Friedrich, 204–6
Noll, Anita (NC student), 226–27, 228, 229, 243, 269, 272, 279
North College (Lutheran institution) (NC), 6, 7, 219–74; campus ethos, 219–29, 290–91, 293; working students, 220; student spirituality, 220, 242; international students, 220, 247; music's importance at, 221–22, 224, 228–29, 231–32, 266–72, 274, 277, 282–83, 290–91; worship services, 222, 229–35, 241, 272; homecoming, 222–24, 291; importance of community at, 224, 225, 228, 229, 279; student organizations, 225; study- and service-abroad programs, 225, 226–27, 272, 279; religious practice, 229–44, 271–72, 277, 278, 280–83, 294; evangelical Protestantism at, 233–34, 237, 240–44, 272, 273, 277, 280, 281–82; athletics, 236; religious studies, 244–70, 272–74, 284, 286–88, 294; religion course requirements, 245–53, 254, 273–74, 284, 294; biblical studies, 245–53, 260–61, 270, 273
NOW. *See* National Organization of Women

Objectivity: religious studies and, 56–62, 64, 65, 79–80, 285, 286–87
O'Cheskey, Mark (EU student), 184, 185
O'Connell, Stephen (EU former president), 155–56
O'Connor, Flannery, 253, 263
Old Testament studies. *See* Hebrew Bible
Old Testament Theology: Basic Issues in the Current Debate (Hasel), 57
Old Testament Theology in a Canonical Context (Childs), 57

Old Testament Theology in Outline (Zimmerli), 57
Olson, Bridget (EU student), 176–77, 178, 196, 279
Ordination of women, 176, 177–78, 185–86, 290
Orientation programs: at West University, 31–33, 36, 74–75; at South University, 86, 87
Osborne, Joan, 132

Pagan Circle, 16, 51–52, 227
Page, Elizabeth (NC student), 269
Palmer, Lesa (EU student), 194
Pan-Hellenic Council, 89
Parachurch groups, 234, 237; at West University, 30, 76–79, 277, 282; at North College, 237, 241–44, 272, 277, 278, 281. *See also specific groups*
Partnership for Life Issues, 186
Pascal, Blaise, 253
Peace Corps, 225
Peer ministers, 36–37, 40, 41, 42
Peg (WU student), 52
Pence, Tamara (EU student), 194
Pentecostals, 111, 137, 140
Pete (WU student), 17
Peters, Scott (WU student), 29–30
Philosophy: religion versus ethics and, 133, 134; existentialism, 165, 168, 169, 179, 196; East University courses, 195–97, 217, 284, 285; North College courses, 263–64
Pietism, 4
Plater, Ben (NC chaplain), 222, 223–24, 228–29, 231, 232, 238, 240–41, 244, 274
Plato, 176, 181
Pluralism, 8, 80, 166, 284, 293–94
Polotov, Isaac (SU speaker), 128–31
Poor people, Catholic commitment to, 215–16, 217; social justice concerns, 166–69, 186–87, 189–92, 216
Potok, Chaim, 247, 248
Potter, Frank (NC professor), 233
Prayer groups, 280; at North College, 235–37, 241, 272, 278
Presbyterian Church: at South University, 6, 85, 94, 140, 142, 281; West University ministry, 31
Princeton University, 2

Protestantism: university establishment, 2; West University ministries, 14, 16–31, 33–42, 76–79; East University adherents, 158, 193–95, 213–14; anti-Catholicism and, 164. *See also* Christianity; Christian universities; Evangelical Protestantism; *specific sects and denominations*

Psychic phenomena, 52

Purity, personal, 215, 217

Quakers, 31

Rabbis: role of, 130

Rahner, Karl, 165

Rasmussen, Jerry (WU lay minister), 44, 48

Ratzinger, Joseph, 68

Rausch, Hal (WU campus minister), 35

Reagan, Mary (SU professor), 135

Redlinger, Morrie (WU admissions director), 34

Religion: Supreme Court opinion opens the way for academic study of, 53; teaching about versus teaching of, 53; academic study of, 53–62; Tillich's definition of, 54; science and, 71, 133, 134, 136, 137, 264–66; in interdisciplinary curricula, 71–72, 80, 113, 122, 123, 135–37, 139, 141, 263–70, 273, 283, 285; avoidance of as course topic, 132–35, 139; ethics versus, 133, 134; impact of cultural change and, 276. *See also* Religious practice; *specific religions*

Religious advocacy teaching approach, 285–86, 288

Religious Emphasis Week (SU), 114–22, 141, 278, 281

Religious practice, 275–83, 292–95; at West University, 13–53, 275, 277–78, 280–82; Bible study groups, 22–24, 38, 238–41, 272, 277, 278, 280; chapel services, 28, 29, 99, 232–33, 272; academic study of, 53–62; at South University, 94, 99–122, 140–42, 275, 277, 278, 281–83; memorial services, 99–103, 108, 113; meditation services, 116–17; at East University, 158–95, 277–82; 294; at North College, 229–44, 271–

72, 277, 278, 280–83, 294; vespers, 231–32; prayer groups, 235–37, 241, 272, 278, 280. *See also* Worship services

Religious studies, 8, 283–88, 294–95; contemporary view of, 3; Supreme Court rulings on, 53, 79; academic study of religion and, 53–56, 80, 283–84; at West University, 53–76, 79–80, 285–88; objectivity in, 56–62, 64, 65, 79–80, 285, 286–87; student spirituality and, 62–71, 178–85; sexual ethics included in, 67–70, 288; as major, 72–74, 79, 244–45, 285, 288; at South University, 110, 122–42, 283, 286, 288; analytical/empathetic approach to, 135–37, 139, 287–88; absence of as major, 138–39, 283; at East University, 159, 178–85, 195–214, 284, 285, 287, 288, 294; at North College, 244–70, 272–74, 284, 286–88, 294; advocacy teaching approach to, 285–86, 288

Rerum novarum (papal encyclical), 166

Resident assistants, 162–63

Retreats, religious: at West University, 18, 47, 280; at East University, 150, 170–72

Revitalization Corps, 180–81

Ritual, academic study of, 67

Robertson, Gary (SU professor), 110, 128–32, 135, 139, 286

Rodriguez, Barry (EU student), 194–95

Roman Catholicism: at sectarian universities, 2; American immigrants and, 5; West University ministry, 14, 16, 20, 31, 37, 40, 42, 44–50, 78, 79, 277, 279, 282; Second Vatican Council, 153, 165–67, 169, 192, 198; Vatican and, 164, 187; ecumenism, 166, 211, 212, 284, 289; social justice concerns, 166–69, 186–87, 189–92, 216; liberation theology and, 167, 169; homosexuality issues and, 175, 190; position on women's ordination, 176, 177–78, 185–86, 290; feminism and, 186, 190; at North College, 220, 228. *See also* East University; Society of Jesus

Rosenberger, Richard, 15

Rosenberger et al. v. Rector and the Visi-

tors of the University of Virginia et al. (1995), 15

Sacramentalism, 214–15, 217, 282
Sacred music: at North College, 221–22, 224, 228–29, 231–32, 266–72, 274, 277, 282–83, 290–91
St. Thomas More Society, 188
Salaries: of campus ministers, 77
Salatino, Michael (EU professor), 147–48, 161, 175, 187–88
Sanders, Marvin (NC regent), 224, 225, 272
Santeria, 51
Schleiermacher, Friedrich, 204
Schmidt, Paul (EU graduate student lecturer), 207–8, 209
Schultz, Mary (NC student), 261
Schyller, Matthew (WU faculty member), 64–65
Science: secularization theories and, 5; evolution theory study, 71, 133, 136, 137; religion and, 134, 264–66
Scottsdale, William (NC professor), 263–64, 270, 272
SDS. See Students for a Democratic Society
Second Vatican Council, 153, 165–67, 169, 192, 198
Secular humanism, 158
Secularization: of higher education, 2–6, 8, 294; Bible study and, 53; East University perspectives, 147, 150–52, 217
Self-transcendence, 168, 169, 173
Serrano, Andres, 39
Service learning: at South University, 97–98, 279; at East University, 180–85, 194, 195–96, 279, 285
Sexual ethics: as religious studies subject, 67–70, 288
Sexuality: West University students and, 23–24, 33, 78; East University students and, 162–63, 175, 187, 215; celibacy and, 163, 215. See also Homosexuality
Shaki Modeling Troupe, 89, 114
Shamanism, 51
Shannon, Debra (WU professor), 67–69, 287
Shawn, Paul (NC student), 241, 242, 269

Shinto, 51
Shipps, Bill (WU Campus Crusade staffer), 18
Simon, Luke (SU athletic director), 112–13
Sloan, Douglas, 3
Small, Gerald (NC student), 241–42, 254, 256, 260, 269, 270
Smiley, Carla (SU student), 92–94
Sobrino, Jon, 168
Social justice: South University perspectives, 124, 131; Roman Catholicism and, 166–69, 186–87, 189–92, 216
Social service programs, 279–80; at East University, 151, 176, 178–79, 193, 215
Society of Friends, 31
Society of Jesus: at East University, 143–44, 149, 163–70, 173, 176–80, 190–91, 194, 196–97, 278–79, 289–90
Society of St. Cecilia (EU), 150
Sociology courses, 5–6, 136, 137
Sodality of St. Stanislas, 180
Sodality of the Immaculate Conception, 150
Solomon, Kevin (NC student), 243–44, 262–63, 269, 272, 277, 278
Sorell, Anita (EU student), 174
Sororities, 89, 97
Southern Baptist Church, 31
South University (historically African American university) (SU), 6, 7, 83–142; Presbyterian Church at, 6, 85, 94, 140, 142, 281; campus ethos, 83–98, 141, 290, 291–92; concerns about graduation rates, 86; orientation programs, 86, 87; working students, 87, 89, 141; crime on campus, 87–88; code of conduct, 87–88, 141; zero tolerance policy, 88, 89; athletics, 89, 112–13, 140–41; student organizations, 89–90, 92, 114; gospel music, 90, 103–7, 141, 277; homecoming, 90–94, 141, 278, 291–92; worship services, 94, 99, 103–11, 114–16, 120–22, 141, 278, 282; religious practice, 94, 99–122, 140–42, 275, 277, 278, 281–83; Founders Day, 94–96, 140, 141, 278; importance of community service at, 96–98, 141, 279; religious studies, 110, 122–42, 283, 286, 288; student spirituality, 110–14,

121–22, 131–32, 139–42, 278; evangelical Protestantism at, 111, 141, 142; student religious participation, 112, 283; Religious Emphasis Week, 114–22, 141, 278, 281

Spiritual Exercises (Ignatius), 168, 169

Spiritual Growth Group (WU), 40, 41, 42, 55

Spirituality, 275–80, 283; West University students and, 41, 43, 62–71, 75, 79; African American, 110, 121–22, 128–32, 135, 140, 141, 278; South University students and, 110–14, 121–22, 131–32, 139–42, 275, 278; Jewish, 128–30; East University students and, 159, 163–64, 166, 168–69, 171–85, 189, 278–79, 289–90; North College students and, 220, 242

Spiritual journals, 239

Spoonheim, Carey (WU student), 47–48, 279

Sports. *See* Athletics

Stanislov, Felicia (EU student), 183, 184, 185

Stark, Rodney, 5–6

Stein, Richard (SU speaker), 119–20

Stimpson, Ian (WU student), 43–44

Stone, Arthur (EU professor), 147, 161, 217

Stone, Dave (WU Campus Christian Fellowship director), 25–26

Stuba, Jon (WU student), 48–49

Student Christian Association (SU), 89, 104, 108

Student counseling. *See* Counseling, student

Student Counseling Center (WU), 33

Student handbooks, 8; at South University, 88

Student newspapers, 8; at East University, 148, 186, 187–88, 189

Student organizations: at West University, 13; Supreme Court funding ruling, 14–15; at South University, 89–90, 92, 114; at East University, 180, 188–89; at North College, 225. *See also* specific groups

Student religious groups, 3, 8; Supreme Court free speech rulings on, 14–15. *See also* specific groups

Students, 8; as religious activity leaders, 22, 24, 76–77, 120, 170, 171, 280; as peer ministers, 36–37, 40, 41, 42; international, 50, 149, 220, 247; personal responses to religion courses, 64–65; religious studies majors, 72–74, 79, 244–45, 288; celibacy among, 163, 215. *See also* specific students

Student services, religion-related: at West University, 31–50, 76–79. *See also* Campus ministries

Students for a Democratic Society (SDS), 35, 180

SU. *See* South University

Supreme Court, U.S., 14–15, 53, 76, 79

Sweeney, Betty (SU vice president), 85–86, 87, 89, 116, 117

Syed, Ali (SU speaker), 117–18

Tanquary, John (EU professor), 212–13

Taylor, Charles, 185

Teachers. *See* Faculty

Teaching of religion. *See* Religious studies

Ten Commandments, 59

Tennent, William, 1–2

Theology courses: at East University, 178–85, 195, 197–211, 216, 284, 285, 294; at North College, 253–56, 273, 284, 294

Thomas, Patricia (EU student), 174

Thomas Aquinas, 165, 181, 204, 206

Thompson, Corrine (WU Zion Campus Ministry director), 26

Thompson, James (NC president), 223, 271

Thurman, Howard, 131, 132

Tillich, Paul, 40, 54, 214

Tofanelli, Andrew (EU chaplain), 146, 147, 171

Tolerance, 68, 107, 170, 272, 281–82

Tom (WU student), 51–52

Tompkins, Andrew (SU professor), 133–34, 135, 136, 139

Torah study groups, 49

Tracey, Sue Ellen (EU student), 183–84, 185

Tree of Life, 59

Trible, Phyllis, 57

Troeltsch, Ernst, 135